Wireless and Mobile Network Architectures

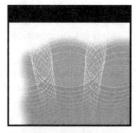

Wireless and Mobile Network Architectures

Yi-Bing Lin
Imrich Chlamtac

Wiley Computer Publishing

JOHN WILEY & SONS, INC.

New York • Chichester • Weinheim • Brisbane • Singapore • Toronto

Publisher: Robert Ipsen
Editor: Carol Long
Associate Editor: Margaret Hendrey
Managing Editor: Micheline Frederick
Text Design & Composition: Integre Technical Publishing Co., Inc.

Library of Congress Cataloging-in-Publication Data:

0471-39492-0

Printed in the United States of America

10 9 8 7 6 5 4 3 2 1

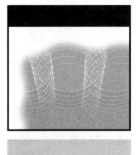

Contents

Preface

The evolution of radio and mobile core network technologies over the last two decades has enabled the development of the ubiquitous *personal communications services* (PCS), which can provide the mobile user with voice, data, and multimedia services at any time, any place, and in any format. To paraphrase the definition of *Encyclopaedia Britannica* "In the broadest sense, PCS includes all forms of radio-telephone communication that are interconnected to the PSTN, including cellular radio and aeronautical public correspondence, but the basic concept includes the following attributes: ubiquitous service to roving users, low subscriber terminal costs and service fees, and compact, lightweight, and unobtrusive personal portable units."

How popular wireless communication has become in less than a decade of accelerated deployment can be attested to by the size of the market, as well as the capitalization and the penetration of cellular technologies worldwide. However, as the Internet matures, and with it the wireless connection to it, existence without a continuous, ubiquitous connectivity is fast becoming more unthinkable.

Not surprisingly, such a wide scope of PCS deployment and services provide the user with a powerful tool that embraces virtually all existing aspects of communication, while offering mobility and ubiquity unavailable before. In this book, we introduce this fascinating world of PCS networks. We describe the fundamental concepts of PCS architecture, the protocols and management software that make it run, the standards that are making it a universal solution, and the mobile services that are changing the face of society as we know it.

A number of books have been dedicated to describing PCS technology; as such, they tend to start from radio aspects and move up to the mobile network aspects. In our view, the factors that make PCS unique, and what has driven the accompanying social and economic revolution, are not primarily technological in nature. No doubt, the recent evolution in transmission and radio aspects of a wireless communications system, with the ever growing appetite for more bandwidth, faster connection, lower cost, and clearer channels, are among the key ingredients in the PCS success story, we believe that it is the mobility aspects of PCS networks and the mobile services that are revolutionizing the communication, and our usage of it, in the twenty-first century.

In this book, therefore, we approach our topic from this important angle of systems, networks, and services. Given the availability of texts on radio technology, we devote only one chapter (Chapter 3) to that topic. We then turn our focus on mobile network protocols based on IS-41 (ANSI 41) and GSM Mobile Application Part (MAP). We follow with in-depth discussions so that the readers understand how these protocols are built on top of SS7, ISDN, and AIN. We pay particular attention to relate IS-41 (U.S. standard) to GSM MAP (European standard), pointing out the common guidelines of these two protocols. We describe the most important mobile services, including mobile database overflow, failure restoration, mobile number portability, mobile prepaid service, international roaming, mobile VoIP, and wireless application protocol (WAP). We also report on advanced industrial developments in PCS.

Consequently, this book could be subdivided into five distinct units.

PCS Network Management.   The first group of chapters consist of Chapters 1 to 4 and provide the basic knowledge of PCS network management. Chapter 1 briefly describes the PCS technologies and their histories. We elaborate on cellular systems, including AMPS, GSM, DAMPS, and IS-95 CDMA, and cordless/low-tier PCS systems, including CT2, DECT, PHS, and PACS. We also introduce the third-generation mobile technologies.

Chapter 2 describes two aspects of mobility in a mobile telephony network: handoff and roaming. We briefly describe inter-BS handoff and intersystem handoff procedures. Then we introduce PCS/PSTN interconnection, and describe the roaming management procedures for location tracking and call delivery.

Chapters 3 and 4 detail the handoff procedure. A handoff is required in mobile system when a mobile phone moves from one base station coverage area to another during the course of a conversation. These two chapters address several issues that need to be considered for handoff management: handoff detection, channel assignment, and radio link transfer.

IS-41 Mobile Systems.   Chapters 5 to 8 emphasize IS-41-based mobile systems. To support interconnection between a PCN and the PSTN, it is essential that the mobile communications protocol interacts with the PSTN signaling system for mobility management and call control. Based on IS-41, Chapter 5 describes the interactions between a mobile network and public-switched telephone network in four aspects: interconnection interfaces, message routing, mobility management, and call control.

Chapter 6 discusses two applications of IS-41: intersystem handoff and authentication. We describe several types of intersystem handoff including handoff-forward, handoff-backward, handoff-to-third, and handoff path minimization. Then we introduce the EIA/TIA TSB-51 authentication schemes and two adaptive algorithms based on these schemes. The purpose of the adaptive algorithms is to reduce the authentication traffic in the network.

Chapter 7 describes network signaling for PACS, a low-tier PCS system that utilizes IS-41-like network management protocols. This chapter covers basic call control, roaming, and handoff management. One of the distinguished features of PACS is that the Advanced Intelligent Network (AIN) protocol is used, and the general AIN switch and the Service Control Point (SCP) provide the flexibility to implement PCS network/ service applications.

Chapter 8 describes the Cellular Digital Packet Data (CDPD) architecture/protocols, as well as the potential service applications. We also abstract some major features of the CDPD medium access control layer, mobile data link protocol layer, and network layer.

GSM Systems.   Chapters 9 to 18 are devoted to GSM systems. Chapter 9 provides an overview to the GSM system, describing the GSM architecture, the location tracking and call setup procedures, security, and data services.

Chapter 10 addresses the software platform for GSM network signaling. We describe the GSM MAP service framework and the MAP protocol machine, and give several examples to show how the MAP service primitives work.

Chapter 11 describes GSM mobility management, beginning with the basic location update, call origination, and call termination procedures. Then we show how these basic procedures can be modified to resolve advanced issues, such as mobility database failure and overflow.

Chapter 12 describes the point-to-point short message service. We show the GSM short message architecture, and discuss the mobile-originated and the mobile-terminated short messaging procedures.

Chapter 13 describes international roaming in GSM. We explain why call delivery to a GSM roamer is so expensive in the current implementation. Then we present solutions that reduce the network cost for GSM calls to international roamers.

Chapter 14 discusses operations, administration, and maintenance (OA&M) aspects of GSM. Based on the concept of TMN, we use call recording and HLR management as examples to illustrate GSM OA&M.

Chapter 15 describes number portability, a network function that allows a mobile subscriber to keep a "unique" telephone number when the person switches the mobile service provider. We show how IS-41 and GSM MAP can be modified to support this feature.

Chapter 16 elaborates on integration of voice over IP (VoIP) and GSM. In the integrated system (which we refer to as iGSM), a GSM user is allowed to access VoIP services when he or she moves to an IP network. iGSM tracks the locations of a subscriber as long as the subscriber turns off or on the terminal (GSM MS or IP terminal) when he or she leaves or arrives at the network. To interwork GSM and IP networks, we propose a protocol translation mechanism between GSM MAP and H.323. Based on this mechanism, we show how iGSM registration, deregistration, and call delivery procedures work.

Chapter 17 discusses mobile prepaid service, a telecommunication service that requires a customer to pay before making calls. This chapter compares four mobile prepaid service solutions. We first identify the requirements for mobile prepaid service. Then we describe mobile prepaid service approaches, including wireless intelligent network, service node, hot billing, and handset-based. These approaches are compared, to provide guidelines for the service providers to select their prepaid service platforms.

Chapter 18 introduces the General Packet Radio Service (GPRS). GPRS reuses the existing GSM infrastructure to provide end-to-end packet-switched services. We briefly describe the air interface and the air interface for enhanced GPRS. We elaborate on individual protocols in the GPRS signaling plane, the industrial solutions of the GPRS network components, GPRS charging, and the development efforts from GSM to GPRS.

The Wireless Internet.   Chapters 19 to 21 describe wireless Internet and how IS-41 and GSM can be integrated and evolved into new generation of mobile systems.

Chapter 19 describes WAP, the tool for the convergence of wireless data and the Internet. We introduce the WAP model, the WAP protocol stack, and WAP mechanisms such as user agent profile and caching. Then we show how WAP can be implemented on various wireless bearer services. Finally, we describe several tools that can be used to develop WAP applications, and the Mobile Station Application Execution Environment that integrates WAP into the third-generation mobile systems.

Chapter 20 describes the various types of PCS system integration, and discusses the implementation issues involved in the integration of PCS systems.

Chapter 21 explores the development of third-generation (3G) mobile networks. We discuss the paradigm shifts in 3G networks, the two major 3G radio proposals, WCDMA and cdma2000, improvement efforts on 3G core network, quality-of-service issues, 3G handset issues, and several 3G trial systems.

Other PCS Technologies.   Chapters 22 to 24 elaborate on other PCS technologies such as paging, wireless local loop, and wireless enterprise systems.

Chapter 22 introduces the paging systems. We focus on one-way, personal selective wireless calling systems, and discuss the paging user access interface, the intersystem interface, and the air interface.

Chapter 23 introduces wireless local loop (WLL) that provides two-way communication services to near-stationary users. We discuss currently deployed WLL systems based on a wide range of radio technologies, including satellite, cellular, and microcellular.

Chapter 24 describes how mobile communication affects enterprise telephony. Although we focus on telephony, our discussion can be easily generalized to accommodate the corporate data aspects of enterprise networking.

Linkage among Chapters

The chapters in this book are tightly linked though each covers a different topic. To illustrate the various PCS concepts we use a consistent example:

location update. In the OA&M, network signaling, mobility, security/ handoff, mobile prepaid, and other chapters, location update is presented in the proper context. We use another example to show how the IS-41 phone number design (in the IS-41 mobility management chapter) affects services such as number portability and prepaid services. Further chapter connection is made via the question sets at the end of each chapter. We ask two types of questions, one to refresh the reader's memory; for example, "What are the main parts of the GSM SMS protocol stack?" This type is suitable when the book is used in an undergraduate course or as an overview of PCS systems for managers, engineers, or anyone who wants a comprehensive view of this area. The second type of question requires active participation; these questions are research-development-oriented. For example, a question in the paging chapter asks how to design the "call after paging" service. The intention of this second type of question is to prompt readers to develop their own solutions. These questions will appeal to:

- Radio experts, who want to understand how mobile core network and services work
- Software experts with no radio background
- College seniors and graduate students

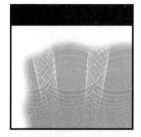

Acknowledgments

We would like to thank Anthony R. Noerpel and Herman C.-H. Rao for providing valuable materials to enrich this book. Many important concepts developed in this book come from discussions with William C.Y. Lee. Many of the views on wireless and mobile services covered in this book have evolved from our activities as editors of the journals *ACM/URSI/Baltzer Wireless Networks (WINET)* and *ACM/Baltzer Mobile Networks and Applications (MONET)*, our involvement with the ACM MobiCom Conference and the ACM Special Group on Mobility, as well as other work on IEEE and ACM journals listed in the reference chapter. We are grateful to these sources and organizations for helping develop the views and vision offered by this book. We extend special thanks to Sajal Das, Stephen Gibbs, Y. R. Huang, Gerald Maguire, Man-Fai Ng, and Michele Zorzi, who proofread the early draft of the book and whose innumerable comments made the book a better product. Lin's work was supported in part by the Lee and MT1 Center, NCTU.

Yi-Bing Lin
Imrich Chlamtac

April 13, 2000

Introduction

The term *personal communications services* (PCS) refers to a wide variety of wireless access and personal mobility services provided through a small terminal, with the goal of enabling communications at any time, at any place, and in any form. Business opportunities for such services are tremendous, since every person (not just every home) could be equipped, as long as the service is fairly inexpensive.

Several PCS systems have been developed to meet rapid growth prompted by heavy market demand. Most of them are connected to the *public switched telephone network* (PSTN) to provide access to wireline telephones. Examples include high-tier digital cellular systems (mobile phone systems) for widespread vehicular and pedestrian services:

- Global System for Mobile Communication (GSM)

- IS-136 TDMA based Digital Advanced Mobile Phone Service (DAMPS)

- Personal Digital Cellular (PDC)

- IS-95 CDMA-based cdmaOne System

and low-tier telecommunication system standards for residential, business, and public cordless access applications:

- Cordless Telephone 2 (CT2)
- Digital Enhanced Cordless Telephone (DECT)
- Personal Access Communications Systems (PACS)
- Personal Handy Phone System (PHS)

Furthermore, wideband wireless systems have been developed to accommodate Internet and multimedia services. Examples include:

- cdma2000, evolved from cdmaOne
- W-CDMA, proposed by Europe
- SCDMA, proposed by China/Europe

The PCS umbrella also includes:

- Special data systems such as Cellular Digital Packet Data, RAM Mobile Data, and Advanced Radio Data Information System (ARDIS)
- Paging systems
- Specialized mobile radio (SMR) access technologies
- Mobile-satellite systems such as the existing American Mobile Satellite Company (AMSC), as well as numerous proposed mobile satellite systems, including S-band, L-band, low-earth orbit (LEO), mid-earth orbit (MEO), geosynchronous orbit, and geostationary earth orbit (GEO), for both data and voice applications
- Unlicensed industrial, scientific, and medical (ISM) band technologies, as well as wireless local area networks (LANs) should also be thrown into the PCS mix

This book describes network management, protocols, and services for PCS systems. Besides the mobile telecommunications issues, we also cover wireless Internet, another important topic. We attack this problem from the telecommunication aspect. An alternative approach is to investigate wireless Internet issues from the data communication aspect, specifically, *mobile IP*, which we do not cover in this book. (Refer to [Per98] for complementary reading.) And because this book is designed for readers without a radio background, we try to avoid the details of the physical radio technologies. (As a complementary reading for physical radio design issues, refer to [Lee98].) In the remainder of this chapter, we briefly describe PCS technologies; we elaborate on them in the subsequent chapters.

1.1   PCS Architecture

PCS technologies have grown rapidly in the telecommunications industry. Two of the most popular are:

- Cellular telephony
- Cordless and low-tier PCS telephony

These technologies have similar architectures, as shown in Figure 1.1. This basic architecture consists of two parts:

Radio Network. PCS users carry *mobile stations* (MSs) to communicate with the *base stations* (BSs) in a PCS network. MS is also referred to as handset, mobile phone, subscriber unit, or portable. Throughout this book, we will use these terms interchangeably, depending on the context. For example, the term *subscriber unit* is used when we describe wireless local loop; the term *portable* is used when we

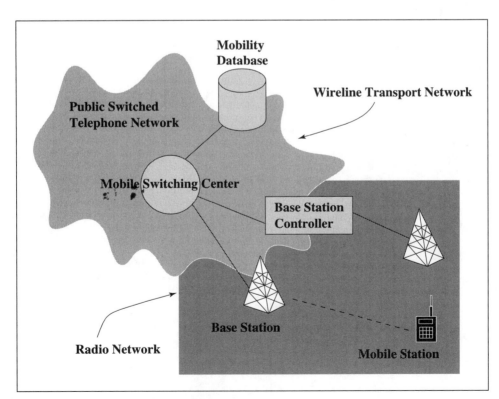

Figure 1.1   The basic PCS network architecture.

describe the low-tier systems such as PACS; and the term *mobile station* is used when we describe the GSM system. Modern MS technology allows the air interface to be updated (e.g., from DECT to GSM) over the air remotely. The MS can also be remotely monitored by the system maintenance and diagnostic capabilities. Different types of MSs have various power ranges and radio coverages. For example, hand-held MSs have a lower output power (where the maximum output power can be as low as 0.8 watts for GSM 900) and shorter range compared with vehicle-installed MSs with roof-mounted antennas (where the maximum output power can be as high as 8 watts in GSM900).

The radio coverage of a base station, or a sector in the base station, is called a *cell*. For systems such as GSM, cdmaOne, and PACS, the base station system is partitioned into a controller (*base station controller* in GSM and *radio port control unit* in PACS) and radio transmitters/receivers (*base transceiver stations* in GSM and *radio ports* in PACS). The base stations usually reach the wireline transport network (core or backbone network) via land links or dedicated microwave links. Figures 1.2 and 1.3 show base transceiver station and base station controller products.

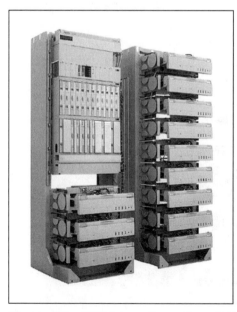

Figure 1.2 CDMA base transceiver station (by courtesy of Nortel).

Figure 1.3 CDMA base station controller (by courtesy of Nortel).

Wireline Transport Network. The *mobile switching center* (MSC) connected to the base station is a special switch tailored to mobile applications. For example, the Lucent 5ESS MSC 2000 is an MSC modified from Lucent Technologies' 5ESS switching system. The Siemens' D900/1800/1900 GSM switch platform is based on its EWSD (Digital

Figure 1.4 Mobile switching center (CDMA MTX MSC by courtesy of Nortel).

Electronic Switching System) platform. The Ericsson MSC is based on its AXE switching platform. The MSC is connected to the PSTN to provide services between the PCS users and the wireline users. The MSC also communicates with mobility databases to track the locations of mobile stations. Figure 1.4 illustrates an MSC product.

Although cellular and cordless/low-tier PCS systems have similar architectures, their design guidelines differ, as elaborated in the following two sections.

1.2 Cellular Telephony

This section gives an overview of four popular cellular telephony networks: AMPS, GSM, DAMPS (IS-136), and CDMA (IS-95).

1.2.1 Advanced Mobile Phone Service (AMPS)

AMPS was the first cellular system. Developed during the 1970s in the Bell Laboratories, this first-generation analog cellular system has been considered a revolutionary accomplishment. The AMPS specification was generated from a laborious process of research, system design, and switching design over a period of 10 years. From 1974 to 1978, a large-scale AMPS trial was conducted in Chicago. Commercial AMPS service has been available since 1983. Based on *frequency division multiple access* (FDMA) technology for radio communications, AMPS was designed as a high-capacity system based on a frequency reuse scheme. Voice channels are assigned to radio frequencies using FDMA. A total of 50 MHz in the 824–849 MHz and 869–894 MHz bands is allocated for AMPS. This spectrum is divided into 832 full-duplex channels using 664 discrete frequencies, that is, 832 *downlinks* and 832 *uplinks*. Downlinks are the transmission paths from base stations to handsets, and uplinks are the transmission paths from handsets to the base stations.

In the frequency reuse scheme, cells are grouped into clusters. Cells within a cluster may interfere with each other and thus must use different frequencies. Frequencies may be reused by cells in different clusters. In AMPS, the typical frequency reuse plan employs either a 12-group frequency cluster using omnidirectional antennas or a 7-group cluster using three sectors per base station. Thus, there are about 50 channels per cell. Motorola uses a 4-cell, 6-sector design in its AMPS system. AMPS follows the EIA/TIA IS-41 standard for roaming management, as described later in Chapter 5.

Compared with the digital alternatives in the United States, AMPS service offers more complete geographical coverage at a cheaper service charge (partly due to the low cost of mass production of handsets). However, digital networks are replacing AMPS because the digital technology can cope with higher user densities, and offer lower costs. In 2000, Taiwan started replacing AMPS with the IS-95 CDMA system. After the replacement, the new system will provide the same service at less than half the bandwidth of the radio spectrum; the extra bandwidth will be released for other usage. Note that after the AMPS voice service is replaced by the digital systems, the AMPS infrastructure can be utilized to support mobile data systems such as Cellular Digital Packet Data (CDPD), described in Chapter 8.

1.2.2 Global System for Mobile Communications (GSM)

GSM is a digital cellular system developed by Groupe Special Mobile of Conference Europeenne des Postes et Telecommunications (CEPT) and its successor European Telecommunications Standard Institute (ETSI). An important goal of the GSM development process was to offer compatibility of cellular services among European countries. GSM is a revolutionary technology that combines both *time division multiple access* (TDMA) and FDMA. With TDMA, the radio hardware in the base station can be shared among multiple users. In GSM, a frequency carrier is divided into eight time slots where the speech coding rate is 13 Kbps. In a GSM base station, every pair of radio transceiver-receiver supports eight voice channels, whereas an AMPS base station needs one such pair for every voice channel. The GSM MSs control their RF output power to maintain interference at low levels. The GSM air interface has been evolved into *Enhanced Data Rate for GSM Evolution* (EDGE) with variable data rate and link adaptation. EDGE utilizes highly spectrum-efficient modulation for bit rates higher than existing GSM technology. EDGE requires upgrade of existing base transceiver station, which supports high-speed data transmission in smaller cells and at short ranges within cells. EDGE does not support ubiquitous coverage; that is, it supports island coverage in indoor, pico, and micro cells.

The GSM development process was similar to that of AMPS, except that no large-scale trial was conducted. The intellectual property rights of the GSM radio system from all vendors were waived, making GSM hugely popular. It took about four years to create the GSM specification. The GSM roaming management protocol is specified by GSM Mobile Application

Part (MAP), which provides similar functionality as IS-41 (the details will be discussed in Chapters 9 through 11). GSM features include most features a digital switch can provide, for example, point-to-point short messaging, group addressing, call waiting, multiparty services, and so on.

1.2.3 EIA/TIA IS-136 Digital Cellular System

Also referred to as digital AMPS (DAMPS), American Digital Cellular (ADC), or North American TDMA (NA-TDMA), IS-136, the successor to IS-54, supports a TDMA air interface similar to that of GSM, and is thus considered an evolutionary technology. It took four months to create the IS-54 specification, and no significant trial was conducted. IS-54 was renamed IS-136 when it reached revision C.

Using TDMA, every IS-136 frequency carrier supports three voice channels, where the speech coding rate is 7.95 Kbps. IS-136 systems operate in the same spectrum with the same frequency spacing (30 KHz) used by the existing AMPS systems. Thus, the IS-136 capacity is around three times that of AMPS. An existing AMPS system can be easily upgraded to IS-136 on a circuit-by-circuit basis. In this way, the evolution from AMPS to DAMPS can be made gracefully. IS-136 is also defined for the new PCS spectrum allocation at 1850 to 1990 MHz. Like GSM, features of IS-136 include point-to-point short messaging, broadcast messaging, group addressing, private user groups, hierarchical cell structures, and slotted paging channels to support a "sleep mode" in the handset, to conserve battery power. Like AMPS, IS-136 uses the IS-41 standard for mobility management.

1.2.4 EIA/TIA IS-95 Digital Cellular System

This digital cellular system was developed by Qualcomm, and has been operating in the United States since 1996. IS-95 is based on *code division multiple access* (CDMA) technology. CDMA allows many users to share a common frequency/time channel for transmission; the user signals are distinguished by spreading them with different codes. In theory, this technology optimizes the utilization of the frequency bandwidth by equalizing *signal-to-noise ratio* (SNR) among all the users, thereby more equitably sharing the system power resources among them. While AMPS users who are near base stations typically enjoy SNRs in excess of 80 dB, users at the edge of cell coverage areas experience SNRs near the lower limit. With CDMA, users who are near base stations transmit less power, maintaining the same SNR as users at the edge of a cell's coverage.

By utilizing the minimum necessary amount of power, systemwide co-channel interference is kept at a minimum.

IS-95 MSs may need to maintain links with two or more base stations continuously during phone calls, so that, as multipath varies, the base station with the best received signal on a burst-by-burst basis will be selected to communicate with the MS. More details on CDMA technology are given in Chapter 4, Section 4.3.

The channel bandwidth used by IS-95 is 1.25 MHz. This bandwidth is relatively narrow for a CDMA system, which makes the service migration from analog to digital within an existing network more difficult than at AMPS and D AMPS. In the third-generation wideband CDMA proposal, the bandwidth has been extended to 5 MHz. The speech coding rate for IS-95 is 13 Kbps or 8 Kbps. IS-95's capacity is estimated to be 10 times that of AMPS.

The IS-95 development has been similar to that of AMPS, but no large-scale trial was conducted; it took two years to generate the specification. Prior to 1997, the most significant IS-95 development effort was taking place in Korea. In 1991, the Korean government decided to implement IS-95 technology. The Korean IS-95 system began commercial operation in April 1996. The maximum capacity consists of 512 BTS (320 traffic channels per BTS) connected to 12 BSCs. These BSCs are then connected to a mobile switching center (called MX) using 768 E1 lines.

Like AMPS, IS-95 uses the IS-41 standard for mobility management. One of the third-generation mobile system standards, cdma2000, is evolved from the narrowband IS-95.

1.3 Cordless Telephony and Low-Tier PCS

This section introduces two cordless telephony technologies, CT2 and DECT, and two low-tier PCS technologies PHS and PACS.

1.3.1 Cordless Telephone, Second Generation (CT2)

CT2 was developed in Europe, and has been available since 1989. The first CT2 products conformed to the final version of the CT2 specifications, CAI (Common Air Interface). CT2 is allocated 40 FDMA channels with a 32-Kbps speech coding rate. For a user, both base-to-handset signals and handset-to-base signals are transmitted in the same frequency. This duplexing mode is referred to as *time division duplexing* (TDD).

The maximum transmit power of a CT2 handset is 10 mW. In the call setup procedure, CT2 moves a call path from one radio channel to another after three seconds of handshake failure. CT2 also supports data transmission rates of up to 2.4 Kbps through the speech codec and up to 4.8 Kbps with an increased error rate. CT2 does not support *handoff* (see Chapter 2 for the definition of handoff), and in a public CT2 system, call delivery is not supported. Incoming calls have been supported in an enhanced version of CT2, but its efficiency has not been proven. The CT2 call-delivery architecture is described in Chapter 2, Section 2.4.

1.3.2   Digital European Cordless Telephone (DECT)

DECT specifications were published in 1992 for definitive adoption as the European cordless standard. The name Digital European Cordless Telephone has been replaced by Digital Enhanced Cordless Telephone to denote global acceptance of DECT. DECT supports high user density with a *picocell* design. Using TDMA, there are 12 voice channels per frequency carrier. Sleep mode is employed in DECT to conserve the power of handsets. DECT may move a conversation from one time slot to another to avoid interference. This procedure is called *time slot transfer*. DECT also supports *seamless* handoff (see Chapter 4, Section 4.2.1 for more details).

Like CT2, DECT uses TDD. Its voice codec uses a 32 Kbps speech coding rate. DECT channel allocation is performed by measuring the field strength; the channel with quality above a prescribed level is autonomously selected. This strategy is referred to as *dynamic channel allocation*. DECT is typically implemented as a wireless-PBX (private branch exchange) connected to the PSTN. An important feature of DECT is that it can interwork with GSM to allow user mobility, where the GSM handsets provide DECT connection capabilities.

1.3.3   Personal Handy Phone System (PHS)

PHS is a standard developed by the Research and Development Center for Radio Systems (RCR), a private standardization organization in Japan. PHS is a low-tier digital PCS system that offers telecommunications services for homes, offices, and outdoor environments, using radio access to the public telephone network or other digital networks. PHS uses TDMA, whereby each frequency carrier supports four multiplexed channels. Sleep mode enables PHS to support five hours of talk-time, or 150 hours of standby-time. PHS operates in the 1895–1918.1 MHz band. This bandwidth is partitioned into 77 channels, each with 300 KHz bandwidth. The band

1906.1–1918.1 MHz (40 channels) is designated for public systems, and the band 1895–1906.1 MHz (37 channels) is used for home/office applications.

Like DECT, PHS supports dynamic channel allocation. PHS utilizes dedicated control channels, that is, a fixed frequency that carries system and signaling information is initially selected. The PHS speech coding rate is 32 Kbps. Like CT2 and DECT, the duplexing mode used by PHS is TDD. Handoff can be included in PHS as an option. PHS supports Group 3 (G3) fax at 4.2 to 7.8 Kbps and a full-duplex modem with transmission speeds up to 9.6 Kbps.

1.3.4 Personal Access Communications System (PACS)

PACS is a low-power PCS system developed at Telcordia (formerly Bellcore). PACS is designed for wireless local loop (see Chapter 23) and for personal communications services. TDMA is used in PACS with eight voice channels per frequency carrier. The speech coding rate is 32 Kbps. Both TDD and *frequency division duplexing* (FDD) are accommodated by the PACS standard. In FDD mode, the PACS uplink and downlink utilize different RF carriers, similar to cellular systems. The highly effective and reliable *mobile-controlled handoff* (MCHO) completes in less than 20 msec. Details of MCHO are given in Chapter 3, Section 3.2. PACS roaming management is supported by an IS-41-like protocol, as described in Chapter 7. Like GSM, PACS supports both circuit-based and packet-based access protocols.

1.3.5 Unlicensed Systems

In addition to these standardized cordless radio technologies, unlicensed communications devices for cordless telephony may make use of the *industrial, scientific, and medical* (ISM) spectrum. A number of commercially available products (wireless PBXs, wireless LANs, cordless telephones) make use of the ISM spectrum to avoid the delays associated with spectrum allocation, licensing, and standardization.

The applicability of the AMPS analog cellular air interface for cordless telephones and office business phones (using the 800 MHz cellular spectrum) has been tested by several cellular service providers. From a customer's perspective, these trials have been an overwhelming success, indicating desire for interoperability between private and public wireless access. From a service provider perspective, the service is difficult to operate and maintain because of hard-to-control interference from the private systems into the public system. The TIA interim standard IS-94 describes the air interface requirements for this application of AMPS. It also describes the protocol and interface between the cordless base station and the network, to control the base station emissions as necessary to limit interference to the public system, and to register and deregister the location of the handsets to and from the private cordless base station at the service provider's mobility databases for the purpose of routing calls. Authentication of the handset is included in this protocol. The networking protocol described by IS-94A is extensible to digital cellular systems, and it affects interoperability between any public systems using licensed spectrum and any private systems using the unlicensed spectrum.

1.4   Third-Generation Wireless Systems

Mobile telecommunication systems have been evolving for three generations. For the mobile systems introduced in Section 1.2, AMPS is the first-generation system; GSM, IS-136, IS-95, and the low-tier systems described in Section 1.3 are second-generation technologies. These systems have been designed primarily for speech with low-bit-rate data services. They are limited by their vertical architectures. Most system aspects have been specified from services to the bearer services. Consequently, any enhancements or new services affect the network from end to end.

Compared with second-generation systems, third-generation systems offer better system capacity; high-speed, wireless Internet access (up to 2 Mbps), and wireless multimedia services, which include audio, video, images, and data. Several technologies, such as General Packet Radio Service (GPRS) and EDGE, bridge second-generation systems into third-generation systems. (Both GPRS and EDGE are discussed in Chapter 18.) In third-generation systems, new network technologies such as ATM (Asynchronous Transfer Mode) backbone, network management, and service creation are integrated into the existing second-generation core networks. Air interfaces such as *Wideband CDMA* (W-CDMA) and cdma2000 are major third-generation radio standards. (Various aspects of the third-generation technologies are elaborated in Chapter 21.)

The increasing number of Internet and multimedia applications is a major factor driving the third-generation wideband wireless technology. Some studies indicate that more than 20 percent of the adult population in the United States are interested in wireless Internet access. By the end of 1999, wireless data services were marketed as modem access for laptop. As the advanced third-generation infrastructure becomes available, and the inexpensive wireless handheld devices (e.g., wireless personal data assistant and wireless smart phones) become popular, subscribers will begin to enjoy instant wireless Internet access. The services include sales force automation, dispatch, instant content access, banking, e-commerce, and so on. (Details of wireless Internet are discussed in Chapter 19.)

1.5 Summary

As the foregoing discussions made clear, cellular and cordless/low-tier PCS systems require different design guidelines. These technologies are typically distinguished by the characteristics listed in Table 1.1. A direct conclusion from the table is that cellular technology supports large, *continuous coverage*, and high-speed users with low-user bandwidths and high delay or latency. On the other hand, low-tier and cordless technologies support low-mobility users but with high bandwidth and low latency or delay.

Surveys on PCS technologies are given in [Cox95, Pad95, Tut97, Chl98b]. Refer to [Luc97, ATT87] for more details about the MSC in cellular systems. Documents and specifications for high-tier cellular systems include [ANS89] for AMPS, [EIA94, EIA92] for IS-136 TDMA, and [EIA93c] for IS-95 CDMA. Several chapters in this book will focus on IS-41 and GSM MAP. Documents and specifications for cordless and low-tier systems

Table 1.1 Characteristics of Cellular and Cordless Low-Tier PCS Technologies

SYSTEM	HIGH-TIER CELLULAR	LOW-TIER PCS	CORDLESS
Cell size	large (0.4–22 mi.)	medium (30–300 ft.)	small (30–60 ft.)
User speed	high ($\leq$ 160 mph)	medium ($\leq$ 60 mph)	low ($\leq$ 30 mph)
Coverage area	large/continuous macrocells	medium micro and picocells	small/zonal picocells
Handset complexity	high	low	low
Handset power consumption	high (100–800 mW)	low (5–10 mW)	low (5–10 mW)
Speech coding rate	low (8–13 Kbps)	high (32 Kbps)	high (32 Kbps)
Delay or latency	high ($\leq$ 600 ms)	low ($\leq$ 10 ms)	low ($\leq$ 20 ms)

include [Ste90, Rad92, ETS91a] for CT2, [ETS91b] for DECT, [Kob94] for PHS, and [JTC95, Noe95, Noe96b] for PACS. Interworking between DECT and GSM is described in [ETS96a].

1.6   Review Questions

1. What are the differences between cellular and low-tier PCS or cordless telephony? Can we effectively deploy public low-tier PCS services as we can cellular services? Use PHS as an example to justify your answer.

2. What are the two major parts of a typical PCS network architecture?

3. What are the benefits of *digital* PCS systems?

4. How do TDMA, FDMA, and CDMA work? Compare the capacities of these three technologies using AMPS, GSM, and cdmaOne (IS-95). Specifically, since GSM utilizes eight time slots per frequency, explain why the capacity of GSM is not eight times that of AMPS. (Hint: In AMPS, the spectrum is divided into frequency carriers of 30 KHz. On the other hand, the carrier spacing of GSM is 200 KHz.)

5. Different GSM configurations have been implemented in Taiwan. For example, in the FarEasTone GSM network, an MSC may connect to one BSC, and the BSC can connect to several hundreds of BTSs. On the other hand, in the Pacific Telecom GSM network, an MSC may connect to four BSCs where every BSC connects to less than one hundred BTSs. Discuss the trade-offs of these two configurations.

6. What do the terms *uplink* and *downlink* stand for?

7. Explain TDD and FDD and compare their advantages and disadvantages.

8. What is the major difference between design for licensed and for unlicenced low-tier PCS systems?

9. What are the differences between the second-generation mobile technology and the third-generation mobile technology?

CHAPTER

2

Mobility Management

This chapter provides an overview of the PCS system architecture, and discusses *mobility management*, one of the most important issues in PCS network. The performance of the PCS network is significantly affected by the way the network manages the movements of the mobile users. To better understand issues in mobility management, we first study the underlying PCS network architecture, which was introduced in Chapter 1, Section 1.1.

In the PCS system architecture (see Figure 2.1), the mobile service area is covered by a set of *base stations* (BSs), which are responsible for relaying the calls to and from the *mobile stations* (MSs) located in their coverage areas (or *cells*). In the figure, the MSs are mounted on vehicles. The BSs are connected to *mobile switching centers* (MSCs) by land links. An MSC is a telephone exchange configured specifically for mobile applications. It interfaces the MSs (via BSs) with the PSTN. Two types of databases, the *home location register* (HLR) and the *visitor location register* (VLR) are used for roaming management. (Details of these databases will be elaborated in Section 2.2.) There are two aspects of mobility in a PCS network:

Handoff. When a mobile user is engaged in conversation, the MS is connected to a BS via a radio link. If the mobile user moves to the

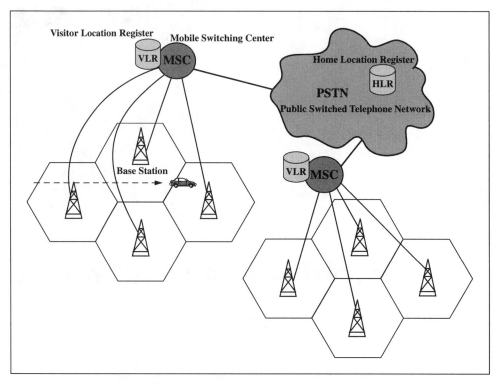

Figure 2.1 A common PCS network architecture.

coverage area of another BS, the radio link to the old BS is eventually disconnected, and a radio link to the new BS should be established to continue the conversation. This process is variously referred to as *automatic link transfer*, *handover*, or *handoff*.

Roaming. When a mobile user moves from one PCS system (e.g., the system in New York City) to another (e.g., the system in Los Angeles), the system should be informed of the current location of the user. Otherwise, it would be impossible to deliver the services to the mobile user.

To support mobility management, protocols such as EIA/TIA Interim Standard 41 (IS-41 or ANSI-41) or Global System for Mobile Communications (GSM) Mobile Application Part (MAP) have been defined for PCS networks. Based on the mobility management protocols, this chapter describes how handoff and roaming are managed in PCS networks.

2.1 Handoff

Three strategies have been proposed to detect the need for handoff:

- In *mobile-controlled handoff* (MCHO), the MS continuously monitors the signals of the surrounding BSs and initiates the handoff process when some handoff criteria are met. MCHO is used in DECT and PACS.

- In *network-controlled handoff* (NCHO), the surrounding BSs measure the signal from the MS, and the network initiates the handoff process when some handoff criteria are met. NCHO is used in CT-2 Plus and AMPS.

- In *mobile-assisted handoff* (MAHO), the network asks the MS to measure the signal from the surrounding BSs. The network makes the handoff decision based on reports from the MS. MAHO is used in GSM and IS-95 CDMA.

Details on the handoff detection issue will be discussed in Chapter 3, Section 3.1. The BSs involved in the handoff may be connected to the same MSC (*inter-cell handoff* or *inter-BS handoff*) or two different MSCs (*inter-system handoff* or *inter-MSC handoff*). We elaborate on these two types of handoff in this section.

2.1.1 Inter-BS Handoff

In inter-BS handoff, the new and the old BSs are connected to the same MSC. Assume that the need for handoff is detected by the MS; the following actions are taken:

1. The MS momentarily suspends conversation and initiates the handoff procedure by signaling on an idle (currently free) channel in the new BS. Then it resumes the conversation on the old BS (see Figure 2.2(a)).

2. Upon receipt of the signal, the MSC transfers the encryption information to the selected idle channel of the new BS and sets up the new conversation path to the MS through that channel. The switch bridges the new path with the old path and informs the MS to transfer from the old channel to the new channel (see Figure 2.2(b)).

3. After the MS has been transferred to the new BS, it signals the network (see Figure 2.2(c)), and resumes conversation using the new channel.

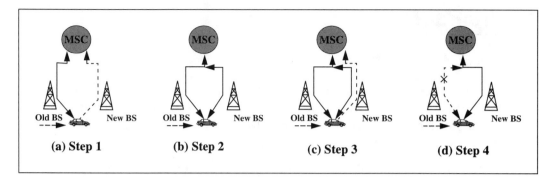

Figure 2.2   Inter-BS link transfer.

4. Upon receipt of the handoff completion signal, the network removes the bridge from the path and releases resources associated with the old channel (see Figure 2.2(d)).

This handoff procedure is used with the mobile-controlled handoff strategy. For the network-controlled handoff strategy, all handoff signaling messages are exchanged between the MS and the old BS though the failing link. The whole process must be completed as quickly as possible, to ensure that the new link is established before the old link fails. Details of the inter-BS link transfer will be discussed in Chapter 4.

If the new BS does not have an idle channel, the handoff call may be dropped (or *forced to terminate*). The forced termination probability is an important criterion in the performance evaluation of a PCS network. Forced termination of an ongoing call is considered less desirable than blocking a new call attempt.

Most PCS networks handle a handoff in the same manner as a new call attempt. That is, if no channel is available, the handoff is blocked and the call is held on the current channel in the old cell until the call is completed or when the failing link is no longer available. This is referred to as the *nonprioritized scheme*. To reduce forced termination and to promote call completion, three channel assignment schemes have been proposed:

Reserved channel scheme. Similar to the nonprioritized scheme, except that some channels in each BS are reserved for handoff calls.

Queueing priority scheme. Based on the fact that adjacent coverage areas of BSs overlap. Thus, there is a considerable area where a call can be handled by either BS. This area is called the *handoff area*. If no channel is available in the new BS during handoff, the new BS buffers the handoff request in a *waiting queue*. The MS continues to use the channel with the old BS until either a channel in the new BS becomes available (and the handoff call is connected) or the MS moves out of the handoff area (and the call is forced to terminate).

Subrating scheme. Creates a new channel for a handoff call by sharing resources with an existing call if no channel is available in the new BS. Subrating means an occupied full-rate channel is temporarily divided into two channels at half the original rate: one to serve the existing call and the other to serve the handoff request. When occupied channels are released, the subrated channels are immediately switched back to full-rate channels.

Studies have indicated that under certain conditions, these handoff schemes can significantly reduce the probability of forced termination as well as the probability of call incompletion (new call blocking plus handoff call forced termination). Details of the channel allocation methods will be elaborated on in Chapter 3, Section 3.3.

2.1.2   Intersystem Handoff

In intersystem handoff, the new and old BSs are connected to two different MSCs. In the description that follows, we trace the intersystem handoff procedure of IS-41, where network-controlled handoff is assumed. Figure 2.3 illustrates the trunk connection before and after the intersystem handoff. In this figure, a communicating mobile user moves out of the BS served by MSC A and enters the area covered by MSC B. Intersystem handoff requires the following steps:

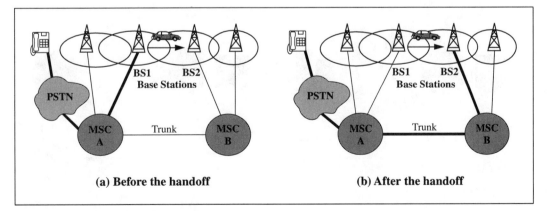

Figure 2.3 Intersystem handoff.

1. MSC A requests MSC B to perform handoff measurements on the call in progress. MSC B then selects a candidate BS, BS2, and interrogates it for signal quality parameters on the call in progress. MSC B returns the signal quality parameter values, along with other relevant information, to MSC A.

2. MSC A checks if the MS has made too many handoffs recently (this is to avoid, for example, numerous handoffs between BS1 and BS2 where the MS is moving within the overlapped area) or if intersystem trunks are not available. If so, MSC A exits the procedure. Otherwise, MSC A asks MSC B to set up a voice channel. Assuming that a voice channel is available in BS2, MSC B instructs MSC A to start the radio link transfer.

3. MSC A sends the MS a handoff order. The MS synchronizes to BS2. After the MS is connected to BS2, MSC B informs MSC A that the handoff is successful. MSC A then connects the call path (trunk) to MSC B and completes the handoff procedure.

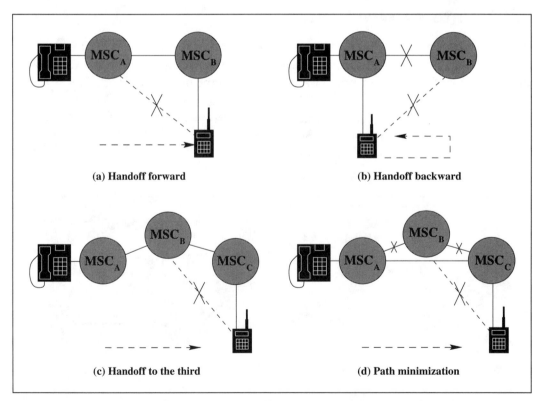

Figure 2.4   Handoff forward, handoff backward, and handoff to the third.

In this intersystem handoff process, MSC A is referred to as the *anchor MSC*, and is always in the call path before and after the handoff, as illustrated in the four cases in Figure 2.4. This anchor approach is used in all existing mobile phone networks because the re-establishment of a new call path (without involving MSC A) between MS and the new MSC would require extra trunk release/setup operations in PSTN, which is not available or is not cost-effective. If the MS moves back to MSC A again, the connection between MSC A and MSC B is removed, as illustrated in Figure 2.4(b). If the MS moves to the third MSC C, then MSC B will be in the call path, as shown in Figure 2.4(c). Note that when the MS moves to the third MSC, the second MSC may be removed from the call path. That is, the link between MSC B and MSC A is disconnected, and MSC C connects to MSC A directly, as shown in Figure 2.4(d). This process is called *path minimization*. Details of intersystem handoff will be discussed in Chapter 6, Section 6.1.

2.2   Roaming Management

Two basic operations in roaming management are *registration* (or location update), the process whereby an MS informs the system of its current location, and *location tracking*, the process during which the system locates the MS. Location tracking is required when the network attempts to deliver a call to the mobile user.

The roaming management strategies proposed in the IS-41 and GSM MAP standards are *two-level* strategies in that they use a two-tier system of home and visited databases. When a user subscribes to the services of a PCS network, a record is created in the system's database, called the home location register (HLR). This is referred to as the *home system* of the mobile user. The HLR is a network database that stores and manages all mobile subscriptions of a specific operator. Specifically, the HLR is the location register to which an MS identity is assigned for record purposes, such as directory number, profile information, current location, and validation period. When the mobile user visits a PCS network other than the home system, a temporary record for the mobile user is created in the visitor location register (VLR) of the *visited system*. The VLR temporarily stores subscription information for the visiting subscribers so that the corresponding MSC can provide service. In other words, the VLR is the "other" location register used to retrieve information for handling calls to or from a visiting mobile user. The registration procedure is illustrated in Figure 2.5 and is described in the following steps:

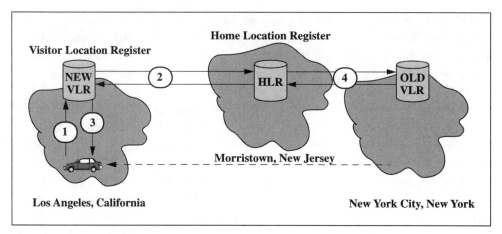

Figure 2.5 MS registration process.

Step 1. Suppose that the home system of a mobile user is in Morristown. When the mobile user moves from one visited system (e.g., New York City) to another (e.g., Los Angeles), it must register in the VLR of the new visited system.

Step 2. The new VLR informs the mobile user's HLR of the person's current location—the address of the new VLR. The HLR sends an acknowledgment, which includes the MS's profile, to the new VLR.

Step 3. The new VLR informs the MS of the successful registration.

Step 4. After step 2, the HLR also sends a deregistration message to cancel the obsolete location record of the MS in the old VLR. The old VLR acknowledges the deregistration.

To originate a call, the MS first contacts the MSC in the visited PCS network. The call request is forwarded to the VLR for approval. If the call is accepted, the MSC sets up the call to the called party following the standard PSTN call setup procedure.

The call delivery (or call termination) procedure to an MS is illustrated in Figure 2.6 and is discussed in the following steps:

Step 1. If a wireline phone attempts to call a mobile subscriber, the call is forwarded to a switch, called the *originating switch* in the PSTN, which queries the HLR to find the current VLR of the MS. The HLR queries the VLR in which the MS resides to get a routable address.

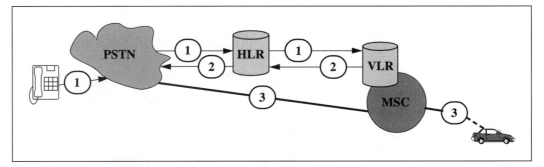

Figure 2.6 Call delivery procedure.

If the originating switch is not capable of querying the HLR (i.e., it is not equipped to support mobility), the call is routed through the PSTN to the subscriber's gateway MSC, which queries the HLR to determine the current VLR serving the MS.

Step 2. The VLR returns the routable address to the originating switch through the HLR.

Step 3. Based on the routable address, a trunk (voice circuit) is set up from the originating switch to the MS through the visited MSC.

2.3 Roaming Management under SS7

The previous section provided an abstract view of roaming management. The missing parts in the picture are the interactions between the PCS network and the PSTN. This section briefly describes how mobile roaming is managed by the PSTN signaling.

Common channel signaling (CCS) is a signaling method that provides control and management functions in the telephone network. CCS consists of supervisory functions, addressing, and call information provisioning. A CCS channel conveys messages to initiate and terminate calls; determines the status of some part of the network; and controls the amount of traffic allowed. CCS uses a separate out-of-band signaling network to carry signaling messages. Signalling System No. 7 (SS7) is a CCS system developed to satisfy the telephone operating companies' requirements for an improvement to the earlier signaling systems, which lacked the sophistication required to deliver much more than plain old telephone service (POTS).

Signaling between a PCS network and the PSTN are typically achieved by the SS7 network. Figure 2.7 shows the network elements that are

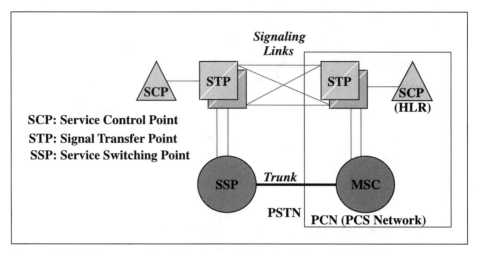

Figure 2.7   Interconnection between a PCS network and the PSTN.

involved in the interconnection between a PCS network and the PSTN. In the figure, the dashed lines represent the signaling links; the solid line represents a trunk. The SS7 network consists of three distinct components:

Service Switching Point (SSP). A telephone switch interconnected by SS7 links. The SSPs perform call processing on calls that originate, tandem, or terminate at that node. A local SSP in the PSTN can be a *central office* or *end office* (EO). An SSP in a PCS network is called a mobile switching center (MSC).

Signal Transfer Point (STP). A switch that relays SS7 messages between network switches and databases. Based on the address fields of the SS7 messages, the STPs route the messages to the correct outgoing signaling links. To meet the stringent reliability requirements, STPs are provisioned in mated pairs, as shown in Figure 2.7.

Service Control Point (SCP). Contains databases for providing enhanced services. An SCP accepts queries from an SSP and returns the requested information to the SSP. In mobile applications, an SCP may contain an HLR or a VLR.

In this network, the *trunks* (voice circuits) connect SSPs to carry user data/voice information. The *signaling links* connect SCPs to STPs, and STPs to SSPs. The SSPs and SCPs are connected indirectly through STPs.

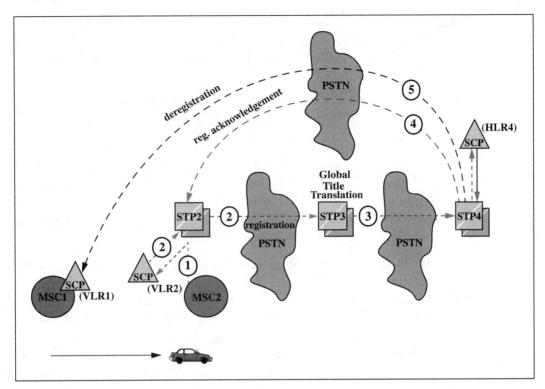

Figure 2.8 Registration through SS7.

2.3.1 Registration

Figure 2.8 illustrates the registration process through the SS7 network. In this example, the MS moves from VLR1 to VLR2.

Step 1. The MS enters the area controlled by MSC2. MSC2 launches a registration query to its VLR through STP2, assuming that VLR2 and MSC2 are not colocated.

Step 2. VLR2 sends a registration message to the MS's HLR (HLR4 in Figure 2.8). VLR2 may not know the actual address of HLR. Instead, VLR2 sends the message containing the MS identity, called the *Mobile Identification Number* (MIN), to an STP (STP3 in our example) that can translate the MIN into the HLR address.

Step 3. The MIN-to-HLR address translation is performed at STP3 by a table-lookup technique called *global title translation* (GTT). STP3 then forwards the registration message to HLR.

Step 4. After the registration, HLR sends an acknowledgment back to VLR2. Since the address of VLR2 is known, the acknowledgment may be sent to VLR2 using a shortcut, without passing through STP3.

Step 5. After step 3, HLR sends a deregistration message to VLR1 to cancel the obsolete record. VLR1 then acknowledges the cancellation (not shown in Figure 2.8).

In steps 2, 3, 4, and 5, the messages may visit several STPs before arriving at their destinations, and the registration process may generate considerable traffic in the SS7 network. Thus, it is desirable to reduce the registration traffic. Two approaches have been proposed to reduce the "cost" of deregistration at step 5 in Figure 2.8:

- In *implicit deregistration*, obsolete VLR records are not deleted until the database is full. If the database is full when an MS arrives, a record is deleted, freeing storage space to accommodate the newly arrived MS. A replacement policy is required to select a record for replacement (it is possible that a valid record is replaced, and the information is lost). The major advantage of this approach is that no deregistration messages are sent among the SS7 network elements.

- In *periodic reregistration*, the MS periodically reregisters to the VLR. If the VLR does not receive the reregistration message within a timeout period, the record is deleted. This approach only creates local message traffic between the MSC and the VLR. Furthermore, no SS7 signaling messages are generated if the VLR is colocated with the MSC.

To reduce the registration traffic at steps 2 and 3 in Figure 2.8, a *pointer forwarding scheme* was proposed, which consists of two operations:

Move operation (registration). When an MS moves from one VLR to another, a pointer is created from the old VLR to the new VLR. No registration to the HLR is required (see Figure 2.9(a)).

Find operation (call delivery). When the HLR attempts to locate the MS for call delivery, the pointer chain is traced. After the find operation, the HLR points directly to the destination VLR (see Figure 2.9(b)).

Depending on the memory capacities of the VLRs, the pointers in the obsolete chain may or may not be deleted. To limit the pointer traversal time in the find operation, the registration procedure in Figure 2.8 may be performed for every k move operations. In other words, the number

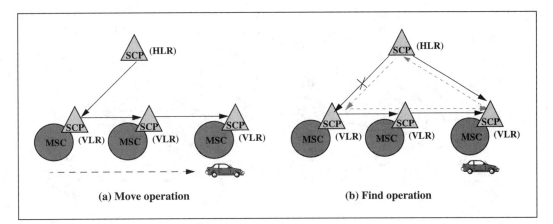

Figure 2.9 Pointer forwarding scheme.

of pointers visited in the find operation will be limited by k. The pointer forwarding scheme should not be considered when the net cost of pointer creation and pointer traversal is higher than the cost of accessing the HLR. As performance studies indicate, the pointer forwarding scheme significantly reduces the network traffic in many cases.

2.3.2 Call Delivery

Similar to the registration process shown in Figure 2.8, visits to several STPs and a GTT may be required to access the HLR in call delivery, as shown in step 1 in Figure 2.10. Several STPs may be visited to obtain the routable address from the VLR, as shown in steps 2 and 3, Figure 2.10.

To reduce the call delivery traffic, a cache scheme was proposed to maintain a cache in the originating SSPs, as shown in Figure 2.11. Another possibility is to maintain the cache in the STP that performs GTTs, that is, STP3 in Figure 2.11. A cache entry consists of two fields: the MIN of an MS and the address of the current visited VLR of the MS. The cache contains entries for MSs recently accessed from the SSP. When the calling party originates a call to an MS, the SSP first checks if the cache entry for the MS exists. There are three possibilities:

Case 1: The cache entry does not exist. The call delivery procedure illustrated in Figure 2.10 is performed.

Case 2: The cache entry exists and is current. The VLR is directly accessed as shown in Figure 2.11.

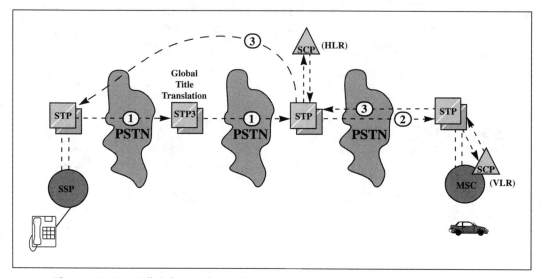

Figure 2.10   Call delivery through SS7.

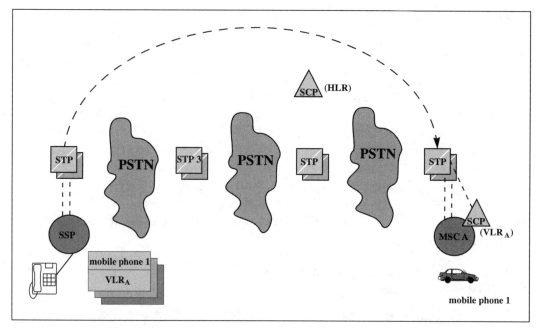

Figure 2.11   Cache scheme.

Case 3: The cache entry exists but is obsolete. The procedure detects that the cache entry is obsolete if the queried VLR's response is negative. The call delivery procedure illustrated in Figure 2.10 is performed.

Note that implicit deregistration and periodic reregistration can be used with the cache scheme, but the obsolete cache information may not be detected until the MS is paged.

Since the cache information may be obsolete, some heuristics are required to determine whether the cached information will be used to locate the MS. One technique is to have the SSP estimate the *cache hit ratio*, or the probability that case 2 is true. If the probability is high, the entry is considered "current" and is enabled; otherwise, the entry is disabled. Another heuristic determines the obsoleteness of an entry based on the period that an MS resides in a VLR as indicated in the cache entry. If the cache entry indicates that the MS has stayed in a VLR for a period longer than a specified threshold, the entry is assumed to be obsolete. The threshold can be adjusted in real time based on cache hit statistics. If case 3 is more likely to occur than case 2, then the cache scheme should not be considered. Performance studies indicate that the cache scheme significantly reduces the call delivery cost in many cases.

2.4   Roaming Management for CT2

In this section, we show how to introduce roaming management to CT2. In a public environment, CT2 is a *one-way calling* PCS system; that is, a CT2 handset can originate outgoing calls, but cannot receive incoming calls. We describe how to construct *two-way calling* mechanism into CT2. As we will demonstrate later, introducing roaming management for CT2 is expensive. Nevertheless, this introduction provides a model so that the reader can understand the design complexity required to implement a total mobility solution for an one-way PCS system.

2.4.1   Basic Public CT2 System (One-Way Calling)

The original public CT2 system was designed as a telepoint service, and did not support call delivery. This architecture is illustrated in Figure 2.12, where a CT2 BS is connected directly to a switch in the PSTN. The CT2 control system is responsible for monitoring and billing, which may be connected indirectly to the BSs through the PSTN. The messages between

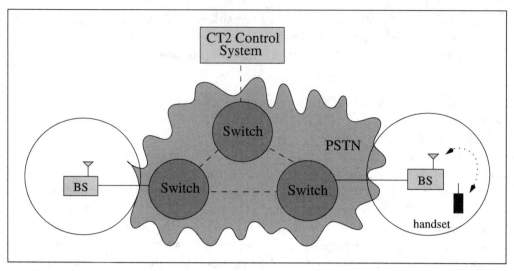

Figure 2.12   Basic public CT2 system.

the CT2 control system and the BSs are delivered through the PSTN. Under this simple architecture, the CT2 system can provide only the call origination service. It is impossible to provide call delivery service as in cellular systems such as DAMPS and GSM. Some CT2 systems (e.g., the systems in Hong Kong) utilized the paging system to provide call delivery; thus, when a wireline user A wanted to call a CT2 user B, A would first page B through the paging system. From the paging message, B identified the telephone number of A, then dialed back to A through the CT2 system. The advantage of this simple approach is that no modifications are made to the CT2 architecture. The disadvantage is the inconvenience caused by the involvement of the paging system, and thus for the reverse charging. Also, if both A and B use CT2 handsets in different CT2 systems, it is impossible to connect the call.

2.4.2   Meet-at-a-Junction CT2 System (Two-Way Calling)

An advanced CT2 system may follow the "meet-at-a-junction" approach to provide the call delivery capability. The CT2 architecture for this approach is illustrated in Figure 2.13. In this approach, the CT2 service area is partitioned into several *location areas*. All BSs in the same location area are connected to an *area controller*. Through the Public Switched Data Network (PSDN) all area controllers are connected to the database, called the *location register*. A handset will register at the location register

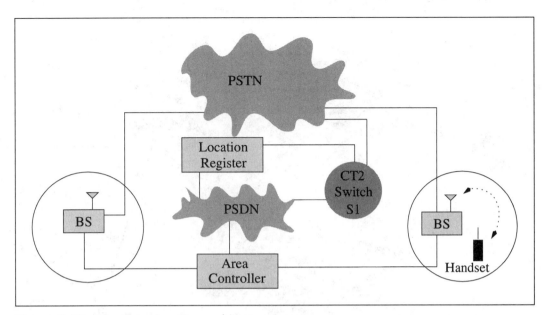

Figure 2.13   Meet-at-a-junction architecture.

after it enters a location area. A location record for the handset is created in the location register, which indicates the location area—the address of the corresponding area controller, where the handset resides. From the registration list of the location register, the BSs poll the handsets periodically. If the polled handset does not reply, the CT2 system assumes that the handset has left the location area and the handset's location record is deleted. If a handset does not receive the polling message for a long time, for example, when the handset moves to a new location area and the movement is not known by the location register, the handset reregisters to reclaim its existence.

The call delivery procedure is illustrated in Figure 2.14 and is described in the following steps:

Step 1. When the calling party dials the number of a CT2 handset, a voice trunk is set up from the originating switch to the CT2 switch S1.

Step 2. S1 queries the location register to identify the area controller of the handset.

Step 3. An alerting message is sent from S1 to the corresponding area controller via the PSDN. The area controller then broadcasts the alerting message to the connected BSs to page the handset.

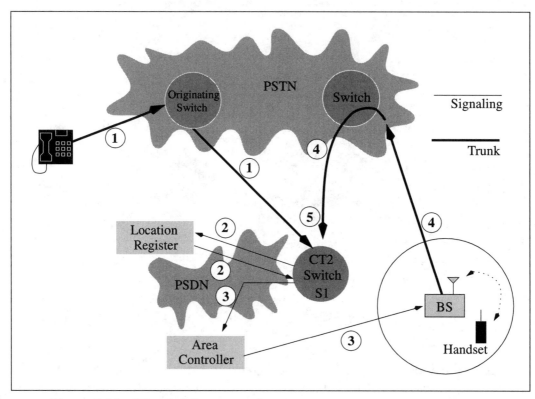

Figure 2.14 CT2 call delivery procedure.

Step 4. If the handset responds, the corresponding base station redials to S1 through the PSTN.

Step 5. S1 bridges the two trunks, and the conversation begins.

Two dials are required in the call delivery procedure, one from the originating switch to S1 and the other from the BS to S1. The CT2 modifications for two-way calling services have been considered expensive. In Taiwan, for example, a CT2 call delivery was considered as two phone calls. The CT2 services in Hong Kong were terminated in 1996. In the same year, many European countries replaced CT2 by DECT as the standard cordless technology. In Taiwan, the bandwidth for CT2 was reclaimed for PACS and PHS in 2000.

2.5   Summary

Based on [Lin96e], this chapter described mobility management (i.e., handoff and roaming) as exercised in most mobile communication networks. Brief descriptions of handoff detection schemes, handoff channel assignment schemes, and intersystem handoff procedures were provided. (Details of these schemes are given in Chapter 3.)

We elaborated on handoff channel assignment schemes, such as the queueing priority schemes and the subrating scheme, to reduce forced termination of handoff calls. These schemes are not implemented in current PCS networks. (The description of the intersystem handoff procedure follows the IS-41, to be elaborated in Chapter 5.)

The description of roaming management is based on IS-41 implemented on top of SS7. (The reader is referred to [Lin97b, Mod90] for a more complete SS7 tutorial.) Compared with IS-41 Revision B, GSM shares the same roaming management concept, but places more emphasis on security provisions. IS-41 Revision C and the newer versions have enhanced the security features [EIA95].

Implicit deregistration and periodic reregistration are described in [Noe96a] to reduce the deregistration traffic. We proposed the pointer forwarding scheme [Jai95, Lin98c] to reduce the registration traffic and the cache scheme [Jai94b, Lin94a] to reduce the call delivery traffic. These two schemes have not yet been implemented into mobile communications networks. Other studies for mobility management can be found in [Fan99a, Liu98, Chl99b, Aky95, Aky96]. Finally, we used CT2 as an example to illustrate how to create the incoming call feature for a one-way calling PCS system by introducing a mobility management mechanism.

2.6   Review Questions

1. What is handoff? What is roaming? How do you perform handoff during roaming?

2. Describe the main steps of inter-BS handoff procedure. Can you design an MS that accommodates both mobile-controlled and network-controlled handoffs?

3. Describe the intersystem handoff procedure. In this procedure, what is an anchor MSC? Should we remove the anchor MSC from the call path after an intersystem handoff? Why or why not?

4. Why is path minimization necessary? Can you find reasons why some cellular service providers do not implement path minimization?

5. Existing cellular systems utilize two-level database structure (i.e., HLR and VLR) to support roaming management. Is it appropriate to implement a cellular system with a single-level database structure?

6. Draw the message flow of an MS originated call procedure. What is the major difference between this procedure and a PSTN call setup procedure?

7. What are the main building blocks of SS7?

8. What does the term GTT refer to? When is GTT needed?

9. Describe the basic PCS location update procedure. Give alternatives to reduce the PSTN signaling traffic due to location update.

10. Design a new algorithm that combines pointer forwarding and the caching scheme. Evaluate the performance of your algorithm. (Hint: You can follow the modeling approaches in [Jai95, Jai94b, Lin94a].)

11. The HLR is a centralized database, which may become bottlenecked during heavy traffic. Design a distributed HLR architecture to resolve this problem. (Hint: See [Lin98c].)

12. Consider a location update strategy called the *two-location algorithm* (TLA). In this algorithm, an MS p has a small built-in memory to store the addresses for the two most recently visited location areas (LAs). The record of p in the HLR also has an extra field to store the corresponding two locations. The first memory location (see Figure 2.15) stores the most recently visited LA. The algorithm guarantees that the portable is in one of the two locations. Figure 2.15 illustrates a sequence of p's movements: $R_0 \rightarrow R_1 \rightarrow R_2 \rightarrow R_1$. When p joins the network, the location is stored in its memory, and a registration operation is required to modify the HLR record as shown in Figure 2.15(a). When p moves to a new location, it checks to determine whether the new location is in the memory. If the new location is not found, the address for the LA p just left is kept; the other address is replaced by the address for the new LA (cf., Figure 2.15(b) and (c)). A registration operation is required to make the same modification in the HLR record. If the address for the new location is already in the memory, no action is taken in the HLR

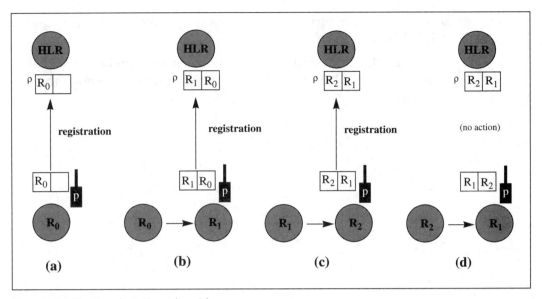

Figure 2.15 Two-location algorithm.

record. In other words, no registration operation is performed (cf., Figure 2.15(d); p moves back to the previously visited LA R_1). Note that in TLA, the MS always has the correct view of the "latest visited LA." On the other hand, the HLR may have an "incorrect view." At steps (a)–(c) in Figure 2.15, both the MS and the HLR have the consistent view of the latest visited LA (which is R_0 in (a), R_1 in (b) and R_2 in (c)). At step (d), the HLR considers R_2 as the latest visited LA, which is incorrect.

When a phone call arrives, the two addresses are used to find the actual location of the MS. The order of the addresses selected to locate the MS affects the performance of the algorithm. If the MS is located in the first try (this is referred to as *location hit*), then the location tracking cost for TLA is the same as the IS-41 algorithm. Otherwise, extra penalty incurs in TLA to locate the MS for the second try (this is referred to as *location miss*; note that the second try is always successful). After the second try, the HLR identifies the LA where the MS is visiting.

There are several alternatives to select the address for the first try. An obvious heuristic is to select the location randomly. Another heuristic is the *latest-LA-first* strategy where the latest visited LA address (in the HLR's view) is selected. Design a heuristic in the

HLR to select the address for the first try. (Hint: See the discussion in [Lin97g].)

13. Why is the CT2 call delivery usually considered to be two calls? Design a CT-2 call termination procedure that can remove this problem.

Handoff Management: Detection and Assignment

PCS handoff was briefly introduced in Chapter 2, Section 2.1. In this and subsequent chapters, we discuss the handoff procedure in detail. Figure 3.1 shows three base stations (BSs) and their coverage areas. Even though cellular base station towers are shown, this discussion is general, which applies to both high-tier cellular systems and low-tier pedestrian systems, in both indoor and outdoor environments. A mobile phone or mobile station (MS) represented by a vehicle in the figure is traversing the coverage areas. The coverage areas are irregular because of the radiation pattern of the base station antennas, buildings, trees, mountains, and other terrain features. Adjacent coverage areas may overlap considerably. Some overlap is desired because handoff is required in mobile communications systems when an MS moves from one BS coverage area to another during the course of a conversation. To continue the conversation, the handoff procedure should be completed while the MS is in the overlap region. As the MS moves toward the edge of the BS coverage, the signal strength and quality begin to deteriorate. At some point, the signal from a neighboring BS (the new BS) becomes stronger than the signal from the serving BS (the old BS). Additionally, the new BS receives a stronger signal from the MS than that received by the old BS. The conversation needs to be handed over to the new BS before the link between the old BS and the MS becomes

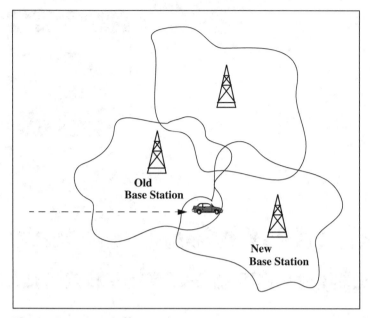

Figure 3.1   Handoff.

unusable. Otherwise, the call is lost. Three issues need to be considered for handoff management:

- Handoff detection
- Channel assignment
- Radio link transfer

This chapter examines handoff detection and channel assignment. Chapter 4 will investigate radio link transfer.

3.1   Handoff Detection

To initiate a handoff, two issues must be considered:

- Who initiates the handoff process?
- How is the need for handoff detected?

Making the decision when to effect the handoff must be based on measurements of the links made at the MS, at the two BSs, or both. While it is obvious that the measurements can be made at either the MS or the BSs, it is not obvious that the decision to effect the handoff can be made either by the network or by the MS. We will describe three strategies for handoff detection in Section 3.2.

Handoffs are expensive to execute, so unnecessary handoffs should be avoided. If the handoff criteria are not chosen appropriately, then in the overlapping region between the two BS coverage area boundaries, the call might be handed back and forth several times between them. If the criteria are too conservative, then the call may be lost before the handoff can take place. The handoff decision-making criteria become even more critical with the evolution to smaller cell sizes, which is happening to increase the capacity of systems and to reduce power requirements of MSs.

Unreliable and inefficient handoff procedures will reduce the quality and reliability of the system. Since the propagation environment is dynamic, even very close to the original BS, the received signal at the MS could temporarily fade due to multipath propagation, so that the signal from another BS might appear stronger for a brief period. During such brief "fades," it is not desirable to effect a handoff as doing so would only be a temporary fix; indeed, the signal might return to normal much faster than the handoff could be implemented. We will discuss several strategies that have been proposed to address these problems.

Handoff detection is based on link measurement. The measurement process determines the need for handoff and the target or new channel for transfer. The propagation between the base station and the MS is made up of the direct line-of-sight path and scattering paths caused by reflections from or diffraction around buildings and terrain. Thus, the signal received by the MS at any point consists of a large number of generally horizontally traveling uniform plane waves. The plane wave amplitudes, phases, and angles of arrival relative to the direction of motion are random. These plane waves interfere and produce a varying field strength pattern with minima and maxima spacing of the order of a quarter-wavelength apart. The MS's received signal fades rapidly and deeply as it moves through this interference pattern. By reciprocity, the BS receiver experiences the same phenomenon as the MS due to the MS motion. The envelope process of this fast-fading phenomenon is Rayleigh-distributed if there is no strong line-of-sight component, and Rician otherwise. As the MS moves, different scatterers and terrain change the plane waves incident on the MS antenna. Therefore, superimposed on the rapid multipath fading are slow variations in the average field strength of the interference pattern due to these new reflection and diffraction paths. This slower fading phenomenon is called *shadow fading*, which has a lognormal distribution. Three measurements are used to determine the quality of a channel:

Word error indicator (WEI). Metric that indicates whether the current burst was demodulated properly in the MS.

Received signal strength indication (RSSI). Measure of received signal strength. The RSSI metric has a large useful dynamic range, typically between 80 to 100 dB.

Quality indicator (QI). Estimate of the "eye opening" of a radio signal, which relates to the signal to interference and noise (S/I) ratio, including the effects of dispersion. QI has a narrow range (relating to the range of S/I ratio from 5 dB to perhaps 25 dB).

Handoff may depend more reliably on WEI (based on a compilation of the measured data for the desired signal over a period of time) of the current channel rather than RSSI. In other words, if WEI is good, then handoff is not performed. However, it is necessary to accumulate WEI measurements over a period of time, whereas RSSI is known instantaneously. To make the handoff decision accurately and quickly, it is desirable to use both WEI and RSSI.

RSSI measurements are affected by distance-dependent fading, *lognormal fading* (i.e., shadow fading), and *Rayleigh fading* (i.e., *multipath fading*). Distance-dependent fading, or *path loss*, occurs when the received signal becomes weaker due to increasing distance between MS and BS. Shadow fading occurs when there are physical obstacles (e.g., hills, towers, and buildings) between the BS and the MS, which can decrease the received signal strength. Multipath fading occurs when two or more transmission paths exist (due to signal being reflected off buildings or mountains) between the MS and BS. There are two types of multipath fading: Rayleigh fading occurs when the obstacles are close to the receiving antenna; in *time dispersion*, the reflected signal comes from an object far away from the receiving antenna.

Ideally, the handoff decision should be based on distance-dependent fading and, to some extent, on shadow fading. The handoff decision is independent of Rayleigh fading. This can be accomplished by averaging the received signal strength for a sufficient time period. The problem is that besides transmitting and receiving the desired signals for the communication link, the MS must also measure or sample all frequencies in the band of interest to find a suitable handoff candidate. Consider a TDMA system. Depending on the radio system's TDMA frame structure and duration, it may take 100 to 500 msec to measure all possible frequency channels. Maintaining a short list of the best candidate channels is a reasonable alternative since the number of measurements of the most likely candidate BSs can be increased. Therefore, the decision will need to be based on a sum of instantaneous power measurements, which can thus average out the Rayleigh fading.

Channel comparisons for handoff are based on RSSI and QI metrics. Since the multipath environment tends to make the RSSI and QI metrics vary widely in the short term, and since it is preferable not to perform handoff to mitigate brief multipath fades because these fades are nonreciprocal, and because such handoffs could cause unnecessary load on the network, the MS should average or filter these measurements before using them to make decisions.

In a TDMA system, the speed of the measurement process depends on the frame structure of the radio system. This capability can be used to visit each frequency channel in turn. The measurements obtained in this process are used to maintain an ordered list of channels as candidates for handoff. The PACS radio system, for example, has a frame duration of 2.5 msec. For a PACS system with 25 frequency channels, this corresponds to visiting each channel every 62.5 msec. A user moving at 1 msec travels around one-third wavelength at 2 GHz in this time interval. If antenna diversity is employed in the radio system at the MS, then the greater of the two values would be selected and the remaining measurements would be discarded.

Filtering should be applied to both RSSI and QI measurements. At least two filtering methods are possible: *window averaging* and *leaky-bucket integration*.

- For window averaging, the MS maintains a number proportional to the average of the current measurements, and the last $w - 1$ measurements, where w is the window size. To implement this method, the MS performs the following procedure for each new measurement:

$$s_k = s_{k-1} + m_k - m_{k-w}$$

  where s_k refers to the sum of the window at time k, and m_k to the measurement made at time period k. Note that the MS must maintain a record of the current sample and the previous w samples.

- For leaky-bucket integration, the MS implements a discrete, digital one-pole low-pass filter:

$$s_k = as_{k-1} + m_k$$

  where $a < 1$ is a constant "forgetting factor."

The window averaging method requires $w + 1$ units of memory (one for the sum and w for the stored measurements) for each channel, whereas the leaky-bucket integration method requires only one unit of memory (the "integral") for each channel. On the other hand, the window average requires only one addition and one subtraction per measurement. For the leaky-bucket integration method, a can be chosen appropriately to minimize the computation cost. For example, if $a = 1 - \frac{1}{4}$, the operation requires only a 2-bit right shift, a subtraction, and an addition. This method must be carefully implemented to avoid problems, due to the limited precision of the variables. Either method is acceptable from a performance perspective.

Note that handoff should be initiated whenever the channel has the best filtered RSSI exceeding that of the current channel by some hysteresis value of the order of 6 dB. A filtering process applied to the RSSI and QI metrics will reduce their usefulness in mitigating sudden "shadow" fades, such as when rounding a corner or closing a door. The downlink WEI can be used to detect and correct these "trouble" situations on an "override" basis. A count C_{down} maintains the number of downlink word errors that is reset every complete measurement cycle. If C_{down} exceeds some threshold, the MS should initiate a handoff when an appropriate channel can be found. Channel selection can follow the same process just given, where the hysteresis value can be lowered.

To reduce the potential tendency of an MS in certain circumstances, to request a large number of handoffs in quick succession, there should be a "dwell" timer. This timer prevents the MS from requesting another handoff until some reasonable period of time after a successful handoff. Adaptive measurement interval for handoffs uses the Doppler frequency to estimate the velocity of the vehicle, and then the averaging measurement interval, so as to average out both multipath and shadow fading. It thus affects handoff only on the basis of path loss.

As the MS moves away from one BS and toward another, the signals received from the first BS become weaker due to increased distance from the BS or path loss; those received from the second BS become stronger. This very slow effect is often masked by the multipath Rayleigh fading and the lognormal shadow fading. Short-term Rayleigh fading is usually handled in mobile system designs by techniques including:

- Diversity techniques such as frequency hopping, multiple receivers, or correlators with variable delay lines and antenna diversity
- Signal processing techniques such as bit interleaving, convolutional coding, and equalizers

Note that Rayleigh fading is frequency-dependent. This means that the *fading dips* (i.e., drops in strength) occur at different places for different frequencies. To reduce the Rayleigh fading effect, the BS and MS may hop from frequency to frequency during a call. Frequency hopping is widely used in GSM networks.

The longer-term shadow fading is usually compensated for in the system link budget margins by increasing the transmitter power and the co-channel reuse distance. *Slow fading* can usually be tracked by *power control* of the MS device.

The path loss component of fading must be handled by handing off the MS to the new BS when the signal from the old BS becomes unusable. Link transfer in response to multipath or shadow fading will usually result in too many handoffs. In addition, since it takes from 20 msec to several seconds to implement a handoff, such a strategy is not an effective remedy for fast fading. However, the detection and measurement of fast fading can play an important role in the handoff detection and decision process. This may be especially true when we consider handing off between high- and low-tier radio systems or between macro and micro cells of the same system. Such is the case when the MS is in a vehicle moving at high speed through micro-cells. In this case, even though the signal quality and strength from the low-tier BS may be momentarily better than that from the serving macro-cell or high-tier BS, a handoff might not be practical because the vehicle's speed will move the communicating MS too rapidly through the coverage area of a low-tier BS. This scenario can cause the network to perform too many handoffs or cause these handoffs to be required so rapidly that they become ineffective due to the delay in setting them up. Thus, it can be seen that if the MS's velocity can be estimated or measured accurately, it would assist handoff detection and the decision-making process significantly.

3.2 Strategies for Handoff Detection

As introduced in Chapter 2, Section 2.1, three handoff detection strategies have been proposed for PCS networks. The schemes whereby the MS controls the handoff are called *mobile-controlled handoff* (MCHO) in literature. Schemes whereby the network exercises control are called *network-controlled handoff* (NCHO). A third class whereby the network controls the handoff but the MS assists with measurements of the links is called *mobile-assisted handoff* (MAHO). The evolution of mobile communications is toward decentralization, implying that both the management and setup of handoff procedures will be partially entrusted to the MS. Thus, advanced mobile systems typically follow MAHO. This section discusses these three strategies and the air interface standards that implement them.

3.2.1 Mobile-Controlled Handoff

MCHO is the most popular technique for low-tier radio systems, and is employed by both the European DECT and the North American PACS air interface protocols. In this method, the MS continuously monitors the signal strength and quality from the accessed BS and several handoff candidate BSs. When some handoff criteria are met, the MS checks the "best" candidate BS for an available traffic channel and launches a handoff request.

The combined control of *automatic link transfer* (ALT, handoff between two BSs) and *time slot transfer* (TST, handoff between channels on the same BS) by the MS is considered desirable, in order to:

- Offload the handoff task from the network

- Ensure robustness of the radio link by allowing reconnection of calls even when radio channels suddenly become poor

- Control both automatic link transfer and time slot transfer, thus preventing unhelpful, simultaneous triggering of the two processes

Automatic link transfer control requires the MS to make quality measurements of the current and candidate channels in the surrounding BSs. The MS's handoff control between channels on the same BS is made possible by passing uplink-quality information, in the form of a word-error indicator, back to the MS on the downlink. Quality maintenance processing, described schematically in Figure 3.2, consists of four components:

- Ongoing measurements and processing of measurement data, which allow the MS to monitor quality

- The trigger decision mechanism, whereby the MS uses the processed measurement data to determine that some action, such as automatic link transfer or time slot transfer, is required

- The choice of the new frequency carrier for automatic link transfer or the new time slot for time slot transfer, which is a process closely allied with the trigger decision

- Execution of the automatic link transfer or the time slot transfer via a signaling protocol between the MS and network equipment

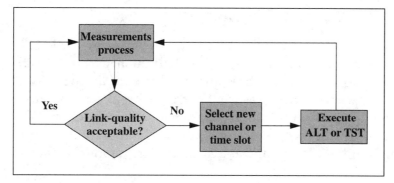

Figure 3.2 MS-quality maintenance processing.

In other words, in an MS, an ongoing measurement process examines radio link-quality information. When certain criteria are reached, the process indicates the need for a handoff and selects a new channel. Finally, the MS, in concert with the network, executes the handoff. The available link-quality information is obtained through various means, and is "data-reduced" to provide a manageable amount of data, while retaining enough information to make good decisions about quality maintenance actions. As part of the demodulation process, the MS receiver generally obtains two pieces of information: RSSI and QI.

QI measurements for the current channel are available to the MS once per frame as a result of the demodulation process. During each TDMA frame period, when the MS is not receiving or transmitting information for the current call, the unit has adequate time to make a diversity measurement (QI and RSSI for each antenna) of at least one additional channel. Downlink WEI also is available to the MS. In addition, the BS can feed back uplink WEI to the MS. This information requires only 1 bit of the downlink stream per burst.

Finally, handoff between channels on the same BS must also be handled in the same context. This is done to ensure that handoff between channels on the same BS, which mitigates only the uplink situation, will not be performed when a handoff could be used to substantially improve both the uplink and downlink. In PACS, because of the use of TDMA on the downlink, the use of the uplink word-error feedback can indicate the need for a handoff between channels on the same BS. On the other hand, DECT uses dynamic channel allocation, and both the uplink and the downlink can be improved by a channel transfer within the same BS. The required handoff time for DECT is 100 msec to 500 msec. For PACS, it is reported to be as low as 20 to 50 msec.

3.2.2   Network-Controlled Handoff

NCHO is employed by the low-tier CT-2 Plus and by high-tier AMPS. In this method, the BS monitors the signal strength and quality from the MS. When these deteriorate below some threshold, the network arranges for a handoff to another BS. The network asks all surrounding BSs to monitor the signal from the MS and report the measurement results back to the network. The network then chooses a new BS for the handoff and informs both the MS (through the old BS) and the new BS. The handoff is then effected.

The BSs supervise the quality of all current connections by making measurements of RSSI. The *mobile switching center* (MSC) will command surrounding BSs to occasionally make measurements of these links. Based on these measurements, the MSC makes the decision when and where to effect the handoff. Because of heavy network signaling traffic needed to collect the information, and the lack of adequate radio resources at BSs to make frequent measurements of neighboring links, the handoff execution time is in the order of seconds. Since measurements cannot be made very often, the accuracy is reduced. To reduce the signaling load in the network, neighboring BSs do not send measurement reports continuously back to the MSC; therefore, comparisons cannot be made before the actual RSSI is below a predetermined threshold. The required handoff time for NCHO can be up to 10 seconds or more.

3.2.3   Mobile-Assisted Handoff

MAHO is a variant of network-controlled handoff whereby the network asks the MS to measure the signals from surrounding BSs and report those measurements back to the old BS so that the network can decide whether a handoff is required, and to which BS. This handoff strategy is employed by the high-tier GSM, IS-95 CDMA, and IS-136 TDMA standards; it is not used by any of the low-tier PCS standards.

In MAHO, the handoff process is more decentralized. Both the MS and the BS supervise the quality of the link, for example, the RSSI and WEI values. RSSI measurements of neighboring BSs are done by the MS. In GSM, the MS transmits the measurement results to the BS twice a second. The decision as to when and where to execute the handoff is still made by the network, that is, the BS and the MSC or BSC. The GSM handoff execution time is approximately 1 second. In both MAHO and NCHO systems, network signaling is required to inform the MS about the handoff decision made by the network—that is, on which new channel to begin communicating is transmitted on the failing link. There is some probability that the link will fail before this information can be transmitted to the MS; in this case, the call will be forced to terminate.

3.2.4 Handoff Failures

In the link transfer procedure, there are several reasons handoff failures can occur, some of which are:

- No channel is available on selected BS.

- Handoff is denied by the network for reasons such as lack of resources—for example, no bridge or no suitable channel card; the MS has exceeded some limit on the number of handoffs that may be attempted in some period of time.

- It takes the network too long to set up the handoff after it has been initiated.

- The target link fails in some way during the execution of handoff.

We have studied the effect of the network response time on the call incompletion probability by an analytic model. Our study indicated that at a small offered load, the network response time has a significant effect on the call incompletion probability. We also observed that the effect of the network response time is more significant if the mobile residence time distribution at a cell has a smaller variance.

3.3   Channel Assignment

Channel assignment schemes attempt to achieve a high degree of spectrum utilization for a given grade of service with the least number of database lookups and the simplest algorithm employed in both the MS and the network. Some trade-offs occur when trying to accomplish the following goals:

- Service quality

- Implementation complexity of the channel assignment algorithm

- Number of database lookups

- Spectrum utilization

Handoff requests and initial access requests compete for radio resources. At a busy BS, call attempts that fail because there are no available channels are called *blocked calls*. Handoff requests for existing calls that must be turned down because there are no available channels are called *forced terminations*. It is generally believed that forced terminations are less desirable than blocked call attempts. Note that the successful handoff access is intimately tied to the radio technology of the channel assignment process, which may be *dynamic channel assignment* (DCA), *fixed channel assignment* (FCA), *quasi-static autonomous frequency assignment* (QSAFA), or some other fixed, flexible, or dynamic process.

Several channel assignment strategies have been developed to reduce forced terminations at the cost of increasing the number of lost or blocked calls. Several handoff-initial-access channel assignment schemes such as the *nonprioritized scheme*, the *reserved channel scheme*, the *queuing priority scheme*, and the *subrating scheme* have been proposed. These schemes were already briefly introduced in Chapter 2, Section 2.1.1. Details of these algorithms are given in this section.

3.3.1 Nonprioritized Scheme and the Reserved Channel Scheme

In the nonprioritized scheme (NPS), the BS handles a handoff call in exactly the same manner as a new call; that is, the handoff call is blocked immediately if no channel is available. The flowchart of NPS is given in Figure 3.3. This scheme is employed by most PCS radio technologies.

The reserved channel scheme (RCS) is similar to NPS except that a number of channels or transceivers in each BS are reserved for handoffs. In other words, the channels are divided into two groups: the normal channels, which serve both new calls and handoff calls, and the reserved

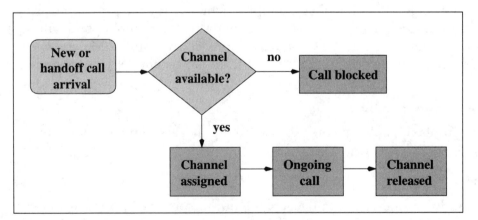

Figure 3.3   Flowchart for nonprioritized scheme.

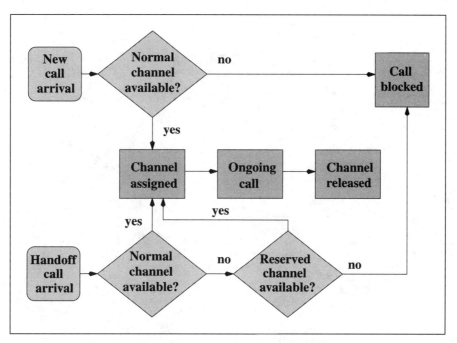

Figure 3.4   Flowchart for reserved channel scheme.

channels, which only serve handoff calls. The flowchart for RCS is shown in Figure 3.4.

3.3.2 Queuing Priority Scheme

The *queuing priority scheme* (QPS) is based on the fact that adjacent cells in a PCS network overlap. Thus, there is a considerable area where a call can be handled by either BS of the adjacent cells, called the *handoff area*. The time that an MS spends in the overlapped area is referred to as the *degradation interval*.

The flowchart for the QPS handoff call channel assignment is shown in Figure 3.5. The channel assignment for a QPS new call is the same as that for NPS. If a channel in the new cell is available for the handoff, the handoff actually occurs. If no channel is available after the MS moves out of the handoff area—the degradation interval expires—the call is forced to terminate. In this scheme, when a channel is released, the BS first checks if the waiting queue is empty. If not, the released channel is assigned to a handoff call in the queue. The next handoff to be served is selected based on the queuing policy. Two scheduling policies for the QPS waiting queue

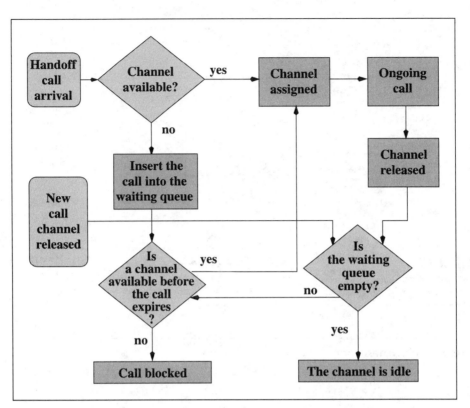

Figure 3.5   Flowchart for queuing priority scheme (handoff call).

have been considered. In the *FIFO scheme*, the next handoff call is selected on a first-in-first-out basis. The *measured-based priority scheme* (MBPS) uses a nonpreemptive dynamic priority policy. The priorities are defined by the power level that the MS receives from the BS of the new cell. The network dynamically monitors the power levels of the handoff calls in the waiting queue. We may view a handoff call as having a higher priority if its degradation interval is closer to expiration. The candidate selected by the network will be the radio link with the lowest received signal strength and the poorest quality, as measured by the MS. This implies the existence of a mechanism for the MS to relay this information to the network over the failing radio link between the MS and the old BS. A released channel is assigned to the handoff call with the highest priority in the waiting queue.

For MCHO, when an MS with an ongoing call enters a handoff area, it checks if there is a channel available in the new BS. If not, this scheme requires a mechanism for the MS to signal to the new BS its desire for a handoff. Then the handoff call is buffered in a waiting queue, and the channel on the old BS is used until a new channel becomes available.

In PACS, a physical channel is provided for MSs to signal a blocked BS of the handoff attempt, although the protocol is not currently specified. For DECT, if a BS is blocked, then no channel exists for the MS to make such a request. For network-controlled handoff systems, like CT-2 Plus, the old BS can always make such a request to the new BS. At this time, a protocol does not exist to inform the MS that it is a handoff candidate but that its handoff is on hold subject to the availability of a transponder or channel.

3.3.3 Subrating Scheme

The *subrating scheme* (SRS) creates a new channel on a blocked BS for a handoff access attempt by subrating an existing call. Subrating is the process of temporarily dividing an occupied full-rate channel into two channels at half the original rate, one to serve the existing call and the other to serve the handoff request. The flowchart for the SRS handoff call channel assignment is shown in Figure 3.6. For a PCS radio system to take advantage of a priority-based scheme for handoff and initial-access channel assignment, there must be a way for the MS to signal to the blocked BS the need for a traffic channel. The radio air interface requires a signaling protocol so that the MS can inform the network through the busy BS of the access request for the handoff. This protocol is described in Chapter 4, Section 4.2.3. Furthermore, a mechanism is required to subrate an existing (e.g., 32 Kbps) call to free up an additional (e.g., 16 Kbps) channel for the handoff access request. There may be some calls for which it is inappropriate to subrate the channel. Our discussion, however, assumes that all calls can be equally subrated.

In general, when a subscriber makes or receives a call, the MS has to acquire an available traffic channel for the connection. For some PCS radio systems using dynamic channel assignment, the MS launches an access request on a *common signaling channel* (CSC), and is then directed to a traffic channel. In these cases, there are a limited number of servers or transceivers in a BS. When a BS is blocked, there is often no transceiver for the CSC since they have all been used for existing calls. In other PCS radio systems, the access attempt can be made directly on an available control channel. The PACS protocol provides for a dedicated time slot at each BS for a *system broadcast channel* (SBC), which is available when all the traffic channels at a BS are in use. The PACS protocol also allows for MSs to indicate to the network the need to make a priority call. This capacity is used for emergency calls and maintenance calls. It can also be used for

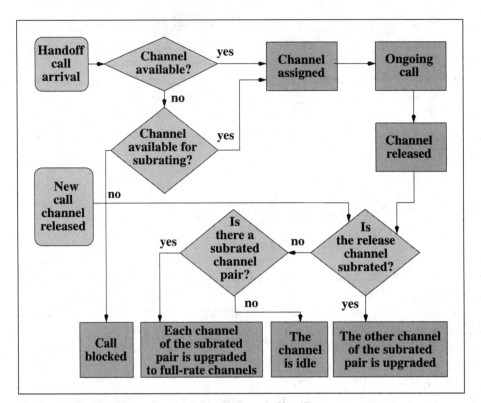

Figure 3.6   Flowchart for SRS scheme (handoff call).

other priority calls, such as handoff call requests when no traffic channels are available at that BS.

With SRS, the cost for temporarily switching the call to a lower bit rate can be absorbed in two ways. The simplest way is to use one adaptive differential pulse code modulation (ADPCM) codec, which can operate in both modes (i.e., 16 Kbps and 32 Kbps) and can be switched between the two. In this case, there is no impact on the channel delay, the current drain, or the cost of the MS. Alternatively, a high-quality 16 Kbps codec could be implemented along with the 32 Kbps ADPCM codec, and the conversation can be switched between the two. While the high quality of the voice can be maintained, the new codec will probably incur higher processing delay, add cost to the MS, and increase the power drained during the time it is in use. There will also be a "hit" associated with the switch between the two codecs because of the different speech processing times. For short durations during a call, if a 16 Kbps voice coder is temporarily substituted, the power consumption might not be impacted significantly or the deteriorated voice quality might be tolerable. Therefore, in addition to studying blocking probabilities, the time interval during which a call might suffer deteriorated quality should also be studied to evaluate SRS.

3.3.4 Implementation Issues

To implement prioritizing handoff schemes, a radio system must have a physical channel, that is, a system signaling channel, for the MS to request the link transfer even when all traffic channels are in use. This channel should always be available, and, therefore, cannot be used as a traffic channel. Some PCS radio systems already reserve a channel for other purposes, such as system broadcast channel, which can be shared by the handoff prioritizing procedure. For systems with conventional handoff procedures, the reserved channel is not necessary because the request is made through the network.

Several analytical and simulation models have been proposed to evaluate the performance of the handoff-channel assignment schemes. The results are summarized here. RCS is easy to implement, and it reduces the forced termination probability more effectively than NPS. The new call-blocking probability for RCS, however, is larger than that of NPS. Thus, RCS is desirable only when reducing forced termination is much more important than reducing new call blocking.

The queuing priority schemes take advantage of the handoff area to buffer the handoff calls. The implementation for the measurement-based priority scheme (MBPS) is more complex than that for the FIFO scheme, but the performance is almost identical. Queuing priority schemes effectively reduce forced terminations, at the expense of increased new call blocking. The probability of incomplete calls for FIFO and MBPS is slightly lower than that for NPS. Queuing priority schemes add hardware/software complexity for both BSs and MSs to manage the waiting queues.

The subrating scheme has the least forced termination probability and the probability of incomplete calls when compared with the other schemes. This benefit is gained at the expense of the extra hardware/software complexity required to subrate a channel. The cost can be shared by other functions of PCS; for example, the idea of channel subrating can be used in emergency service calls (911) when all channels are busy.

To conclude, the selection of a particular handoff and initial channel assignment scheme is a trade-off between implementation complexity and performance. If reducing forced termination is more important than reducing total call incompletions, then RCS, QPS, and SRS are all better than NPS. If implementation cost is a major concern, then RCS and NPS should be considered. To achieve the best performance with a slight voice-quality degradation, SRS should be selected. If BS density is high in a given PCS service area, then a queuing priority scheme may be a good choice, because the overlapping coverage areas between BSs will be large.

3.4   Summary

This chapter described two major issues for PCS handoff management. In the handoff detection issue, we described who initiates the handoff process and how the need for handoff is detected. Details of using Doppler frequency to measure adaptive measurement interval for handoffs are given in [Hol92]. Techniques for preventing unhelpful, simultaneous triggering of both automatic link transfer and time slot transfer are described in [Ber91, Ber89a]. The impact of network handoff response times on call incompletion is given in [Lin97a]. Handoff failure due to *resource blocking* in DECT is described in [Bou93]. Further reading concerning handoff detection issues can be found in [Ber91, Ber89b, Ber88, Gud90, Vij93, Gud91, Gan72, Cla68, Lee95, Kan88, Mur91, Sam94, Sam93, Hat80].

In the channel assignment issue, we described several strategies to handle a handoff call when no channel is available in the new BS. The subrating scheme was proposed and studied in [Lin94e, Lin94d]. The MBPS scheme was investigated in [Tek92]. Further reading for channel assignment issues can be found in [Chl99a, Zen99, Chl96, Hon86, Stu96, Lin96d, Lin94c, Tek91, Yoo93, Fos93].

In the next chapter, we discuss the link transfer procedure for handoff.

3.5   Review Questions

1. What are the three measurements that can be performed to decide on handoff?
2. What is distance-dependent fading? What is Rayleigh fading? What is shadow fading?
3. Describe some filtering methods for link measurements.
4. Describe the three handoff detection strategies: MCHO, NCHO, and MAHO. What are the advantages and disadvantages of the three handoff detection strategies? For example, in terms of load balancing, which strategy is better?
5. Can you implement MCHO or MAHO on FDMA-based systems?

6. Design a model to study the effect of network response time on handoff failure. What are the input parameters and output measures? (Hint: See the model in [Lin97a].)

7. Describe four different channel assignment schemes. Under what circumstances is the reserved channel scheme (RCS) more desirable than the others?

8. How does the degradation interval affects the QPS scheme? Does large cell overlap imply a long degradation interval? Is it practical to have large overlap area (say 50 percent)? Design a model to investigate the impact of degradation interval. (Hint: See the model in [Lin94c].)

9. Design a model to investigate how subrating degrades the link quality. What are the input parameters and output measures? (Hint: See the model in [Lin96d]).

10. In mobile system performance, the term call dropping refers to the connected call that cannot be completed. Describe the relationship between call blocking, call dropping, and call incompletion.

11. GSM call reestablishment service allows a mobile station to resume a call during which the radio link has been temporarily interrupted due to interference or bad signal (which is referred to as an interrupted call). This service increases end-user satisfaction and network-quality perception. Design a model to study call reestablishment service. What are the input parameters and output measures? (Hint: See the model in [Lin99a].)

Handoff Management: Radio Link Transfer

There are several alternatives for classifying link transfer procedures. This chapter identifies a link transfer procedure as either *hard handoff-oriented* or *soft handoff-oriented*. For hard handoff, the mobile station (MS) connects with only one base station (BS) at a time, and there is usually some interruption in the conversation during the link transition. Hard handoff is typically used in TDMA and FDMA systems. Using soft handoff, the MS receives/transmits the same signals from/to multiple BSs simultaneously. The network must combine the signals from the multiple BSs in some way. Thus soft handoff is more complicated than hard handoff.

This chapter describes hard handoff for mobile-controlled handoff (MCHO), network-controlled handoff (NCHO), mobile-assisted handoff (MAHO), subrating (see Chapter 3, Section 3.3.3) under TDMA systems, and soft handoff for MAHO under CDMA systems or some TDMA systems with macro diversity. The link transfer message flows will be illustrated using messages with generic names that have parallels in many air interface protocols.

4.1 Link Transfer Types

Two operations must take place for a successful link transfer:

- The radio link must be transferred from the old BS to the new BS.
- The network must bridge the link to the new BS into the existing call and drop the link to the old BS.

We will discuss both operations. Link transfer can be made from one channel to another channel on the same BS or from one BS to another BS, which subtends the same controller or switch. In these two cases, the network operation is relatively simple. Alternatively, the handoff can take place between BSs whose common point is much higher in the switching hierarchy of the network, in which case, the network operation can be expensive, time-consuming, and difficult. Depending on the network elements involved in handoff, a PCS architecture introduces at least five distinct link transfer cases:

Intracell handoff. The link transfer is performed between two time slots or channels in the same BS. For a TDMA system, intracell handoff is also referred to as time slot transfer (TST).

Intercell handoff or inter-BS handoff. The link transfer is performed between two BSs attached to the same base station controller (BSC); see Figure 4.1(a).

Inter-BSC handoff. The link is transferred between two BSs connected to different BSCs on the same mobile switching center (MSC); see Figure 4.1(b).

Intersystem handoff or inter-MSC handoff. The link transfer takes place at two BSs connected to different BSCs on different MSCs; see Figure 4.1(c).

Intersystem handoff between two PCS networks. The link transfer is between two BSs connected to different MSCs homing to different PCS networks.

Typical holding time of a mobile phone call is around 60 seconds. During this call-holding time, experience indicates that there will be 0.5 inter-BS handoffs, 0.1 inter-BSC handoffs, and 0.05 inter-MSC handoffs. It was reported that the failure rate of inter-MSC handoff is about five times that of inter-BS handoff. These statistics indicate that the frequencies of handoff cannot be ignored and that efficient handoff processing is important. The network implementation of handoffs varies based on the type of link transfer. Each will have a different aspect to its control, and yet must be

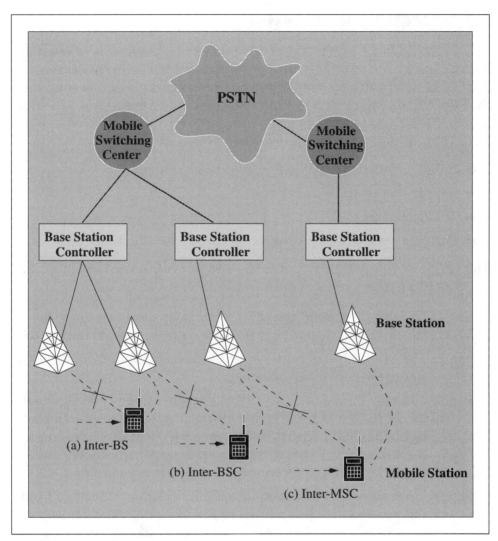

Figure 4.1 Link transfer types.

integrated into a unified control protocol because the MS does not know, a priori, which sort of link transfer will be caused by the selection of its "best" BS. In this chapter, we will focus on inter-BS handoff. Intersystem handoff will be discussed in Chapter 6, Section 6.1.

4.2 Hard Handoff

This section describes the hard handoff link transfer procedures for MCHO, NCHO/MAHO, and the subrating protocol.

4.2.1   MCHO Link Transfer

In MCHO, when a handoff is needed, a new radio channel is selected by the MS, and a handoff request message is transmitted by the MS to the new BS. The handoff can also be initiated by the network. It is, however, still the responsibility of the MS to choose the best BS. In the case of a handoff failure, the MS link-quality maintenance process must decide what to do next. There are several possibilities. The MS may choose to:

- Initiate another handoff to the "next best" channel.
- Simply stay on the old channel.
- Try again later.
- Perform some other action appropriate for the situation.

The MCHO message flow for inter-BS handoff is illustrated in Figure 4.2. The procedure is described in the following steps:

Step 1. To initiate handoff, the MS temporarily suspends the voice conversation by sending a link suspend message to the old BS.

Step 2. The MS sends a handoff request message through an idle time slot of the new BS to the network.

Step 3. The new BS sends a handoff acknowledgment message and marks the slot busy. The network may check other parameters to ensure that it wishes to complete the handoff. For example, there may be a network management check to disallow handoffs from MSs that have been requesting too many of them.

Step 4. Upon receipt of the handoff acknowledgment message from the network, the MS returns to the old assigned channel by sending a link resume message to the old BS.

Step 5. The MS continues voice communication while the network prepares for the handoff.

> **NOTE** If encryption is in use for voice privacy, the handoff request and the handoff acknowledgment are transmitted in the clear since the new BS does not have the cipher key for the session. Also note that handoff request messages may collide with each other or with initial access attempts. That is, while one MS is seizing a channel for a handoff, some other MS may seize the same channel for a handoff, call origination, registration, answer, and so on. The result

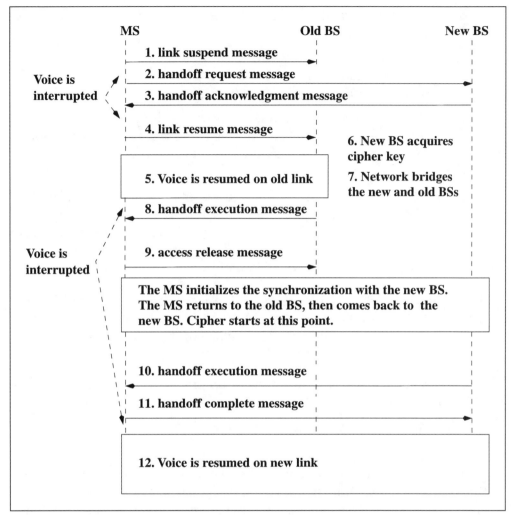

Figure 4.2   MCHO Inter-BS handoff message flow.

could be the capture of one over the other or the loss of both messages.

Step 6. Upon receipt of a handoff request message, the new BS checks if it already controls this call. If so, it is an intra-BS handoff. The BS sends a handoff acknowledgment message and reconfigures itself to effect the handoff. If it is an inter-BS handoff, the new BS acquires the cipher key from the old BS through the MSC. This session privacy key is transferred to the privacy coder associated with the new channel.

Step 7. The MSC inserts a bridge into the conversation path and bridges in the new BS.

Steps 8 and 10. Finally, the network informs the MS to execute the handoff via both the old and new BSs by sending the **handoff execution** messages, 8 and 10, respectively.

Step 9. The MS releases the old channel by sending an **access release** message to the old BS. Note that messages 8 and 9 are not exchanged if the old channel fails before the new channel is established.

Step 11. Once the MS has made the transfer to the new BS, it sends the network a **handoff complete** message through the new channel, and resumes voice communication. The network can then remove the bridge from the path and free up resources associated with the old channel.

By the time the network bridge operation is complete, the new BS has acquired the session key from the old BS. Thus, both messages 10 and 11 are transmitted in the cipher mode. The use of the bridge eliminates the necessity for exact coordination of:

- Switching of the path from the old BS to the new BS (coordinated by the network).

- Transferring of the conversation from the old BS to the new (coordinated by the MS).

Bridges used for handoff should be inserted as quickly as possible. Bridges used in existing switching systems (such as "loudest talker" and "additive" bridges) may be adequate. However, it is possible that specific characteristics will be required in the future, possibly necessitating specialized bridges.

DECT follows a similar MCHO procedure except that the selected new channel and the old channel may use the same carrier frequency. In this case, the MS does not need to switch frequency; this DECT handoff is referred to as *seamless handoff*.

4.2.2 MAHO/NCHO Link Transfer

The network protocol for MAHO/NCHO is different from that for MCHO. Figure 4.3 shows the message flow for handoff in the GSM system using MAHO. The procedure is described in the following steps:

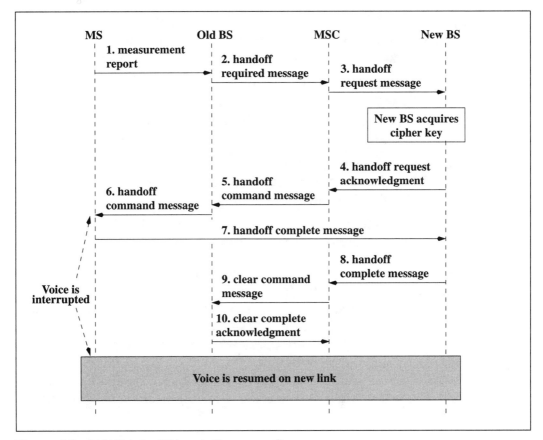

Figure 4.3   MAHO Inter-BS handoff message flow.

Step 1. The MS transmits the radio link **measurement report** to the old BS. In GSM, this information is updated every 0.5 seconds.

Step 2. When the old BS determines that a handoff is required, it sends a **handoff required** message to the MSC. In terms of actions on the network side, the handoff is originated by the old BS in MAHO/NCHO, whereas in MCHO, the handoff is initiated by the new BS.

Step 3. When the MSC receives the **handoff required** message, it examines the list of the candidate BSs supplied by the old BS and selects the highest-ranked BS with an available channel. Then it sends a **handoff request** message to the new BS—the target BS for handoff.

Steps 4 and 5. When the new BS acknowledges the request, the MSC sends the handoff command message with the information regarding the new BS and the RF channel to the old BS.

Step 6. The old BS commands the MS to transfer the link to the new BS.

Step 7. The MS tunes to the new RF channel, establishes the channel to the new BS, and sends the handoff complete message to the new BS.

Steps 8 and 9. The new BS informs the MSC of the handoff completion by the handoff complete message. The MSC then clears the link to the old BS by the clear command message.

Step 10. The handoff procedure is complete when the old BS acknowledges the clear command message.

In MAHO or NCHO, the handoff command to the MS—message 6 in Figure 4.3—is sent over the failing link. The handoff procedure fails if the MS does not receive this message. In MCHO, the handoff request message—message 2 in Figure 4.2—is sent by the MS to the new BS on the new, more reliable, link. As a result, the success of the handoff does not depend on any signaling message over the failing link. Another advantage of MCHO is that it is not necessary to transmit measurement information via the air interface, thus reducing the signaling overhead required to maintain the call.

4.2.3 Subrating MCHO Link Transfer

The procedure of subrating a full-rate channel into subrated channels for a handoff request consists of three parts:

1. Requesting the handoff.
2. Subrating an existing call.
3. Assigning the newly created subrated channel to the MS requesting the handoff.

The message flow for this subrating procedure is given in steps 1–7 in Figure 4.4, as described here:

Step 1. When $MS_{handoff}$ detects the need for a handoff, it attempts to seize an available traffic channel. If an idle channel is found, the link transfer follows the MCHO procedure described in Section 4.2.1. If no traffic channels are available, the MS syn-

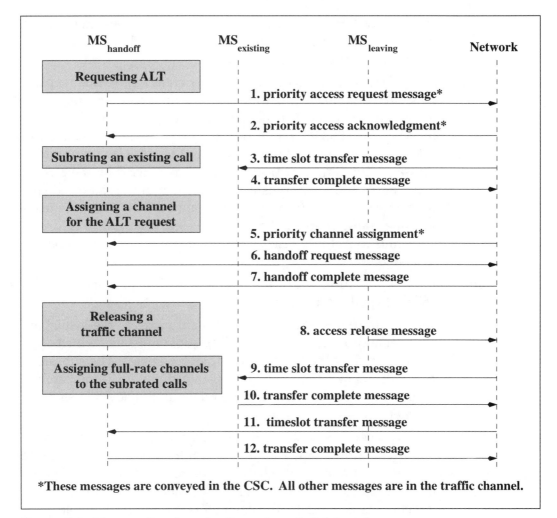

Figure 4.4 Message flow for subrating automatic link transfer.

chronizes to a common signaling channel (CSC) and transmits a priority access request message.

Step 2. The new BS responds with either a priority channel assignment message or a priority access acknowledgment message. In the former case, the BS has a nonbusy channel, which it can immediately make available to the MS. In the latter case, the BS does not have an available channel and is simply acknowledging the receipt of the request message. The MS must continue to monitor the CSC for a **priority channel assignment** message. If no channel is available within a timeout period, the handoff call is forced to terminate.

Steps 3 and 4. An existing caller, $MS_{existing}$, receives a **time slot transfer** message commanding it to perform a time slot transfer to a subrated channel. This action frees up a subrated channel for $MS_{handoff}$, the MS requesting the handoff. This message is acknowledged by the transmission of the **transfer complete** message. The **time slot transfer** message is used by the MS to command an MSC to transfer the time slot in the same BS. The new time slot could be a subrated channel of the currently used full-rate traffic channel. This same message is sent to return both calls to full-rate time slots once a traffic channel becomes available.

Step 5. $MS_{handoff}$ is informed of the newly available subrated traffic channel via the **priority channel assignment** message.

Steps 6 and 7. After receiving it, the MS synchronizes to the available channel and transmits a **handoff request** message, which will be answered by the **handoff complete** message. The subrated channels are switched back to full-rate channels immediately after some occupied channels are released, as shown in steps 8–12 in Figure 4.4.

Step 8. When a user, $MS_{leaving}$, terminates an existing call or performs its own handoff away from the BS, it transmits an **access release** message and releases its channel. The released channel may be either a full-rate channel or a subrated channel. Assuming that the channel is full-rate, the channel is not made available for access this time. Instead, two subrated channels are switched back to full-rate channels, as described in the next steps.

Steps 9–12. The released full-rate channel is assigned to either $MS_{existing}$ or $MS_{handoff}$ through the **timeslot transfer** and **transfer complete** message exchange; both of these users now enjoy full-rate transmission.

It follows that this access protocol should be generalized to also include a means for emergency access. To accomplish this, the message elements of the **priority access request** and the **priority access acknowledgment** messages should include an access random number to resolve collisions and to temporarily identify the MS requesting priority access, the type of priority access (i.e., a handoff or a 911 call) and a requested channel rate. The MS should identify that it does have a subrating capability. The **priority channel assignment** message requires these message elements, in addition to the channel assignment. The channel assignment should include frequency, time slot, and subrated channel code, which identifies the channel used by the MS to request the handoff. For handoff requests, the access random number can be a radio call identifier or some number that identifies the call on the old BS.

4.3 Soft Handoff

Before we discuss soft handoff, we first introduce the code division multiple access (CDMA) *direct sequence spread spectrum* technology. In this approach, the information-bearing signal is multiplied with another faster-rate, wider-bandwidth digital signal that may carry a unique orthogonal code. This second signal is referred to as a *pseudo-noise sequence* (PN sequence). The mixed signal looks very similar to a noise signal, but contains the information signal embedded in its code. The mixing operation is called "spreading." To recover the information-bearing signal, the receiving end must use the same PN sequence to "despread" the mixed signal. Thus, CDMA allows many users to share a common frequency/time channel for transmission, and the user signals are distinguished by spreading them with different PN sequences. Also, an MS can transmit/receive the same information to/from several BSs if they have the same PN sequence. In other words, in a CDMA-based mobile system, an MS may simultaneously receive/send the same information from/to several BSs using multiple radio links. The signaling and voice information from multiple BSs are typically combined (or bridged) at the MSC, and the MSC selects the highest-quality signals from the BSs. Similarly, voice and signaling information must be sent from the MSC to multiple BSs, and the MS must combine the results. Thus, within the overlap area of two cells, an MS can simultaneously connect to both the old and the new BSs, and the link transfer procedure is no longer time-critical.

The following subsections describe the procedures for adding and removing BSs with MAHO soft handoff.

4.3.1 Adding a New BS

CDMA BSs transmit *pilot signals* that assist MSs to track/synchronize the BS downlink signals. The MSs measure the strength of the pilot signals of the serving BSs, that is, the old BS and the surrounding BSs. If the pilot

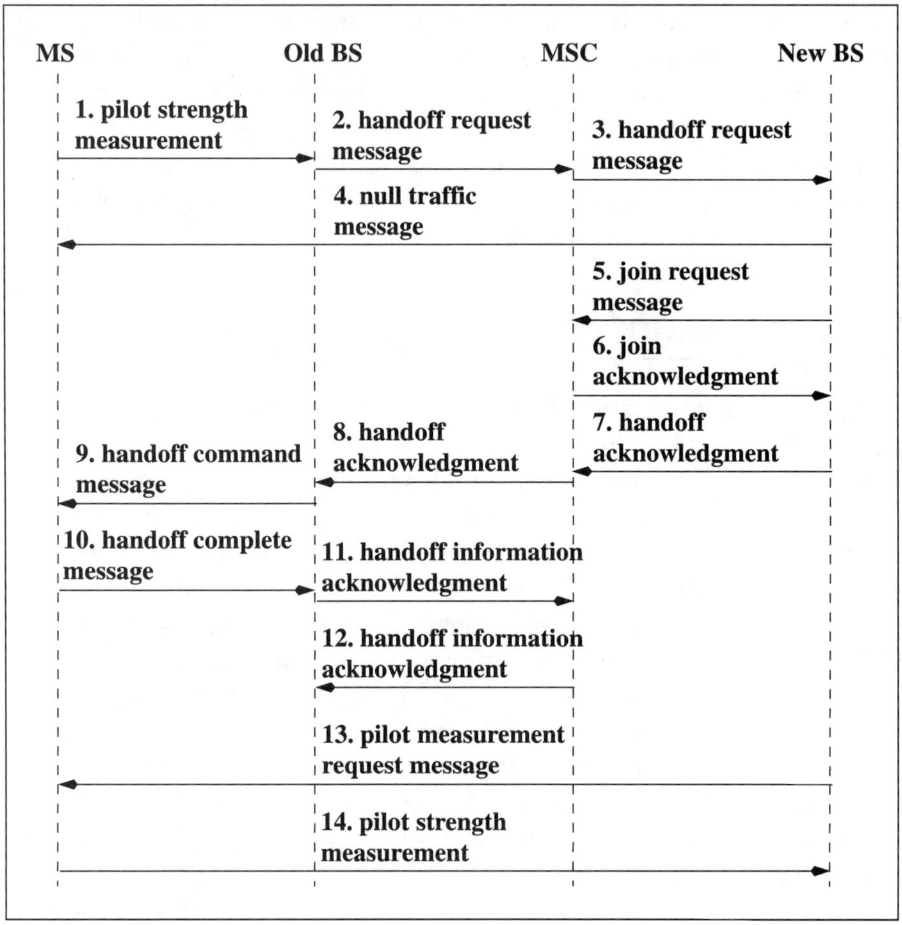

Figure 4.5 Adding a new BS.

signal strength of a surrounding BS—the new BS—exceeds a threshold, then the link between the MS and the new BS is established. The MAHO procedure of adding a new link to an MS is described in the following steps. The message flow is illustrated in Figure 4.5.

Step 1. The MS sends a pilot strength measurement message to the old BS, indicating the new BS to be added.

Steps 2 and 3. The old BS sends a handoff request message to the MSC. If the MSC accepts the handoff request, it sends a handoff request message to the new BS.

Step 4. The new BS sends a null traffic message to the MS to prepare the establishment of the communication link.

Steps 5 and 6. The new BS sends a join request message to the MSC. The MSC bridges the connection for the two BSs, as described in Chapter 4, Section 4.2.2, so that the handoff can be processed without breaking the connection.

Steps 7–10. The new BS sends a handoff acknowledgment message to the old BS via the MSC. The old BS instructs the MS to add a link to the new BS by exchanging handoff command and handoff complete messages.

Steps 11–14. The old BS and the MSC conclude this procedure by exchanging the required handoff information. The quality of the new link is guaranteed by the exchange of the pilot measurement request and the pilot strength measurement message pair between the MS and the new BS.

In soft handoff MAHO, the link between the MS and the old BS may be of good quality. On the other hand, in hard handoff MAHO, the MS and the old BS typically communicate through a failing link.

4.3.2 Dropping a BS

If the signal strength on the link between a BS and the MS falls below a predetermined threshold, the MS requests to remove the BS. Assume that the old BS is to be dropped. The MAHO procedure of dropping an old link from an MS is described in the following steps. The message flow is illustrated in Figure 4.6.

Steps 1–3. The MS sends a pilot strength message to the old BS to remove the BS with the failing link. The old BS and the MS exchange the handoff command message pair to remove the link.

Steps 4 and 5. The old BS sends the relevant call record information to the new BS by exchanging the interface primary transfer message pair.

Steps 6–9. The new BS and the MSC exchange the handoff information message pair to indicate the failing link to be dropped. Then the new BS and the MS exchange the pilot measurement message pair to ensure that the communication between the MS and the network can be continued after dropping the failing link to the old BS.

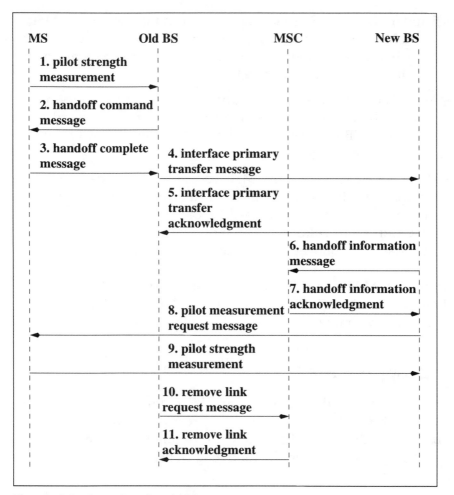

Figure 4.6   Dropping the old BS.

Steps 10 and 11. The MSC and the old BS exchange the remove link
message pair to remove the bridge between the new and the old
BSs and other resources.

In addition to soft handoff, two other types of link transfer are defined
for IS-95 CDMA: softer handoff and hard handoff.

■ In many existing IS-95 cellular systems, a BS is designed with three-
sector directional antenna. Softer handoff occurs when the MS is in
handoff between two different sectors at the same BS.

■ Hard handoff occurs in IS-95 systems when the two BSs connected to an MS are not synchronized or are not on the same frequency band.

4.4 Summary

This chapter described PCS handoff management for inter-BS radio link transfer. We described hard handoff for MCHO, MAHO/NCHO, MCHO with subrating under TDMA systems, and MAHO for soft handoff under CDMA systems. Details of soft handoff implemented in TDMA systems with macro diversity are given in [Yac93]. A typical CDMA network design incorporates an additional switching operation to facilitate soft handoff. Because of the added network elements required to perform soft handoff, CDMA is inherently more expensive to implement than TDMA systems. Tutorials for CDMA systems and soft handoff can be found in [Gar97].

Both fast-power control and soft handoff are difficult to maintain in practice, making practical capacity of CDMA a controversial issue. Hard handoff, the traditional way of handing an active call over from one BS to the next as the user moves through the coverage area, is problematic for CDMA because the handset cannot easily measure signals at different frequencies from candidate BSs. Further reading for handoff link transfer can be found in [Gud90, Nan95, Chu91, Chu92, Bel94b].

4.5 Review Questions

1. Handoff can be performed due to load balancing. What are the advantages and the extra overhead incurred in redistributing calls for load balancing?

2. How does inter-MSC handoff affect the call completion probability? According to the statistics given in Section 4.1, implement a performance model to investigate the impact of inter-MSC handoff. (Hint: See the model in [Lai99b].)

3. Is it possible for an MS to know which type of handoff (intra-BS, inter-BS, inter-BSC, inter-MSC) is performed? If so, can you design a handoff procedure that takes advantages of this knowledge?

4. Why are MCHO and MAHO handled differently in the link transfer procedure? Why can MAHO and NCHO link transfers be handled in similar way?

5. What are the main steps of the MAHO link transfer?

6. Describe seamless handoff in DECT.

7. Compare MCHO, MAHO, and NCHO link transfer procedures. For example, which scheme(s) can balance the workload of BSs during handoff?

8. How can emergency calls be introduced into the MCHO subrating link transfer?

9. How does IS-95 CDMA work? What is soft handoff? What is softer handoff?

10. Compare soft handoff with hard handoff.

11. In IS-95 CDMA, multiple links may be established between the MSC and BSs for a phone call. How does this multiple link consumption affect the performance of the system? (Hint: See the model in [Lin99e]).

12. In an existing AMPS/IS-95 CDMA dual mode system, the handset can hand off from IS-95 CDMA system to AMPS. How does it work? On the other hand, a communicating MS cannot hand off from AMPS to IS-95 CDMA system. Why not?

13. Why are pilot strength measurement messages important in soft handoff?

IS-41 Network Signaling

To support PCS network management, protocols such as EIA/TIA Interim Standard 41 (IS-41; also known as ANSI-41) and Global System for Mobile Communications (GSM), and Mobile Application Part (MAP) have been defined for PCS Network (*PCN*) intersystem operations. Several sections in this book are dedicated to PCS network management; for example, mobility management issues were briefly discussed in Chapter 2, Section 2.2, and detailed record information on the VLR and the HLR are discussed in Chapter 11, Section 11.2. In this chapter, we focus on PCN signaling. To support interconnection between a PCN and the PSTN, it is essential that the mobile communications protocol interact with the PSTN signaling system for mobility management and call control. Interactions between a PCN and the PSTN are addressed in four aspects:

Interconnection interfaces. Enable interaction between a PCN and the PSTN.

Message routing. Exchanges the information among the network elements of the PCN and the PSTN.

Mobility management. Tracks the locations of the mobile users.

Call control. Sets up the call path between a mobile user and the other call party (either a wireless or wireline user).

When a mobile station (MS) moves from the home PCN to a visited PCN, its location is registered at the VLR of the visited PCN. The VLR then informs the MS's HLR of its current location. When a call is delivered to an MS, the HLR is first queried to find its location, that is, the VLR corresponding to the MS's current location. (Details of the registration and location-tracking procedures will be elaborated in Section 5.3 and Chapter 11, Section 11.1. The call setup/release process will be discussed in Section 5.4.) It is likely that two PCNs will be connected through the PSTN, so it is important to understand how the PSTN is involved in PCS mobility management. Our discussion considers IS-41 (ANSI-41) as the mobile communications protocol and Signalling System No. 7 (SS7) as the PSTN signaling protocol.

5.1   Signalling System No. 7

We introduced SS7 architecture in Chapter 2, Section 2.3. Figure 5.1 illustrates an SS7 interconnection between a PCN and the PSTN. There are six types of SS7 signaling links. Two types, the A-link and the D-link are shown in Figure 5.1. Each service switching point (SSP) and service control point (SCP) will have a minimum of one signaling link to each signal transfer point (STP) pair. This signaling link is referred to as the *access link* (A-link). The number of A-links between an SSP and an STP pair can be up to 128, though most switch suppliers have limited the number to 16. Signaling links that connect STPs of different networks (e.g., PCN and PSTN in our example) are called *diagonal links* (D-links). D-links

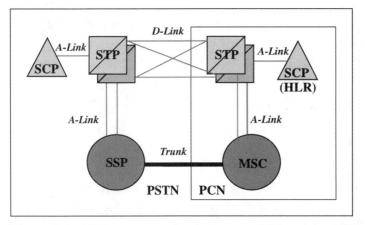

Figure 5.1 SS7 interconnection between a PCN and the PSTN.

are deployed in a quad arrangement with three-way path diversity. The maximum link set size is 64.

The SS7 protocol layers and the corresponding OSI layers are shown in Figure 5.2. These layers are described as follows:

- The *Message Transfer Part* (MTP) consists of three levels corresponding to the OSI physical layer, data link layer, and network layer, respectively. The MTP level 1 defines the physical, electrical, and functional characteristics of the signaling links connecting SS7 components. The MTP level 2 provides reliable transfer of signaling messages between two directly connected signaling points. The MTP level 3 provides the functions and procedures related to message routing and network management.

- The *Signaling Connection Control Part* (SCCP) provides additional functions such as *global title translation* (GTT) to the MTP. The MTP utilizes GTT to transfer noncircuit-related signaling information such as PCS registration and cancelation.

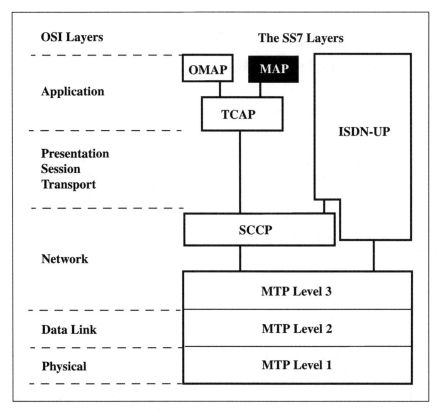

Figure 5.2   The SS7 signaling protocol.

- The *Transaction Capabilities Application Part* (TCAP) provides the capability to exchange information between applications using noncircuit-related signaling.

- The *Integrated Services Digital Network User Part* (ISUP) establishes circuit-switched network connections (e.g., for call setup). Passalong signaling service sends the signaling information to each switching point involved in a call connection.

- The *Operations, Maintenance, and Administration Part* (OMAP) is an application of TCAP. Details of general OMAP are beyond the scope of this book. OMAP for GSM will be discussed in Chapter 14.

- The *Mobile Application Part* (MAP) is an application of TCAP. Both IS-41 and GSM MAP are implemented at this layer. The IS-41-based network management protocol is described in this chapter. The GSM-based MAP protocol is discussed in Chapter 10.

In summary, the IS-41 protocol is implemented in the MAP as an application of the TCAP. The wireless call setup/release is completed by using the ISUP. The MTP and the SCCP provide routing services between a PCN and the PSTN.

5.2   Interconnection and Message Routing

Several types of interconnections between a PCN and the PSTN have been discussed in Telcordia Technical Report TR-NPL-000145. Four types of SS7 interconnection between a PCN and the PSTN using SS7 are elaborated in this section: two for SS7 signaling, and two for trunk (voice circuit) connections. The signaling interface represents the physical signaling link connection between a PCN and the PSTN. The SS7 signaling interconnection methods include:

- *A-link signaling interface*, which involves access links from an MSC to a PSTN STP pair (see Figure 5.3(a) and (c)).

- *D-link signaling interface*, which involves diagonal links from a PCN STP pair to a PSTN STP pair (see Figure 5.3(b) and (d)).

The trunk interface represents a physical SS7-supported trunk connection (for voice/data transmission) between a PCN and the PSTN. The types of the SS7 trunk interconnections are described as follows:

- *Type 2A with SS7 trunk interface* provides connection between a PCN and a PSTN tandem switch. Type 2A with SS7 interfaces is shown in Figure 5.3(a) and (b).

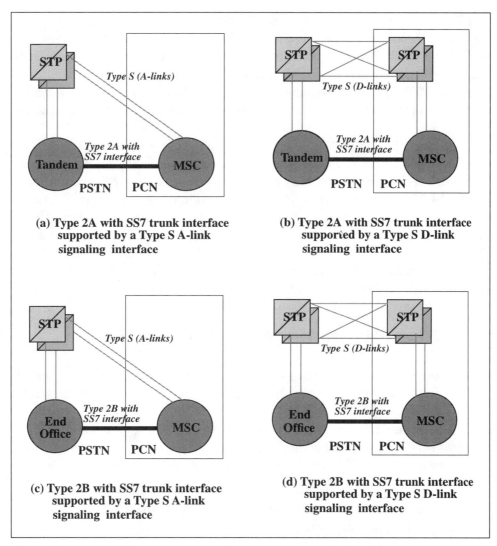

Figure 5.3 Types of interconnection between a PCN and the PSTN.

■ *Type 2B with SS7 trunk interface* provides connection between a PCN and a PSTN end-office switch. Type 2B with SS7 interfaces is shown in Figure 5.3(c) and (d).

Several applications that require calls to be tandemed (e.g., operator services and 800 call setup) are supported by Type 2A with SS7 interface, but are not available to Type 2B with SS7 interface.

We show how signaling messages are delivered with the configuration illustrated in Figure 5.3. Basically, SS7 message routing is performed at the

MTP and the SCCP of a node (SSP, STP, or SCP). At the MTP level, the signaling messages are delivered with the actual destination address. The MTP level receives messages from an adjacent node or from the TCAP, and thus the SCCP layer or the ISUP layer of the same node. The *destination point code* (DPC) of the message uniquely identifies the destination node. Routing to the destination node is determined by the MTP using lookup tables.

In the mobile application, every MS is assigned a *mobile identification number* (MIN). An MS may also be assigned a *universal personal telecommunication* (UPT) number. This chapter assumes that an MS is identified by the MIN. When an MIN is dialed, the originating node may not have enough knowledge to identify the actual address of the destination. In this case, the actual destination address is translated by GTT, performed at the SCCP level of the protocol. GTT is supported in IS-41 Revision B and later versions, but not in IS-41 Revision A. The ISUP messages for wireless call control are not delivered with GTT.

5.3   Mobility Management Using TCAP

More than 50 TCAP operations are defined in IS-41 for three purposes: (1) *inter-MSC handoff*, (2) *automatic roaming*, and (3) *operations, administration, and maintenance*.

A TCAP message consists of two portions: *transaction* and *component*. The transaction portion specifies the *package type*. Five of the seven package types are defined in IS-41. Four of them are discussed here:

- *QueryWithPermission* initiates a TCAP transaction and informs the terminating node that it may end the TCAP transaction.

- Response ends the TCAP transaction.

- *ConversationWithPermission* continues a TCAP transaction and informs the destination node that it may end the TCAP transaction.

- Unidirectional sends information in one direction only, with no reply expected.

The component portion specifies the number and the types of components (operations) to be performed. Four of the six component types are defined in IS-41:

- INVOKE(Last) is used to invoke an operation (such as location registration). Last indicates that the operation is the last component in the component portion.

■ RETURN RESULT(Last) is used to return the results of an invoked operation. If a node receives an INVOKE and the operation is executed successfully, the node will respond with a RETURN RESULT.

■ RETURN ERROR is used to report the unsuccessful completion of an invoked operation. For example, if the MIN in the INVOKE message is not currently serviced by the HLR, the HLR will respond a RETURN ERROR message.

■ REJECT is used to report the receipt and rejection of an incorrect package or component (e.g., ill-formatted). When a node receives a REJECT message, it exits the current task and performs error recovery.

Note that an SS7 transaction always begins with a query message (for example, QueryWithPermission in IS-41) and ends with a response message (Response in IS-41). In IS-41, both the INVOKE and the RETURN RESULT types are Last, which implies that every IS-41 TCAP message performs exactly one operation. In the remainder of this chapter, we omit the notation Last.

Most IS-41 transactions are two-message, query-response transactions. Two exceptions are discussed here:

■ A TCAP message with the operation **FlashRequest** has a package type Unidirectional. This message is sent from the serving MSC to the anchor MSC to convey information for call control. No response is expected from the anchor MSC, and no TCAP transaction is established.

■ A TCAP transaction, including the operation **FacilitiesDirective**, consists of three message exchanges. (We will elaborate on this transaction in Chapter 6, Section 6.1.)

IS-41 TCAP uses SCCP class 0 connectionless service, which provides efficient routing without maintaining message sequencing between two or more messages from the same originating node. Message sequencing is implied in the two-message IS-41 transactions. For the three-message IS-41 transactions described previously, message sequencing is also guaranteed (to be elaborated in Chapter 6, Section 6.1).

Every IS-41 TCAP transaction accompanies a timeout constraint. Typically, recovery procedures defined in IS-41 are executed when a timer expires. For most IS-41 transactions, timer expiration is considered as an error, resulting in a RETURN ERROR TCAP message. The TCAP messages described in this chapter are summarized in Table 5.1. We use location update procedure to describe the message flows of IS-41 TCAP transactions.

Table 5.1   IS-41 TCAP Message Formats

OPERATION	COMPONENT TYPE	PACKAGE TYPE
FacilitiesDirective	INVOKE(Last)	Query WithPermission
FacilitiesDirective	RETURN RESULT(Last)	Conversation WithPermission
FacilitiesDirective	RETURN ERROR	Response
FacilitiesDirective	REJECT	Response
HandoffMeasurementRequest	INVOKE(Last)	Query WithPermission
HandoffMeasurementRequest	RETURN RESULT(Last)	Response
HandoffMeasurementRequest	RETURN ERROR	Response
HandoffMeasurementRequest	REJECT	Response
MobileOnChannel	INVOKE	Response
QualificationRequest	INVOKE(Last)	Query WithPermission
QualificationRequest	RETURN RESULT(Last)	Response
QualificationRequest	RETURN ERROR	Response
QualificationRequest	REJECT	Response
RegistrationCancellation	INVOKE(Last)	Query WithPermission
RegistrationCancellation	RETURN RESULT(Last)	Response
RegistrationCancellation	RETURN ERROR	Response
RegistrationCancellation	REJECT	Response
RegistrationNotification	INVOKE(Last)	Query WithPermission
RegistrationNotification	RETURN RESULT(Last)	Response
RegistrationNotification	RETURN ERROR	Response
RegistrationNotification	REJECT	Response
ServiceProfileRequest	INVOKE(Last)	Query WithPermission
ServiceProfileRequest	RETURN RESULT(Last)	Response
ServiceProfileRequest	RETURN ERROR	Response
ServiceProfileRequest	REJECT	Response

Figure 5.4 illustrates the message flow for the registration and validation process as an MS roams from PCN 1 to PCN 2. This figure assumes that an MSC and the corresponding VLR are connected by an STP. In reality, it is more likely that the VLR is colocated with the MSC. Note that there is extensive information exchanged between MSC and VLR; thus, it is natural to integrate them to a single network element. The registration process consists of six two-message TCAP transactions:

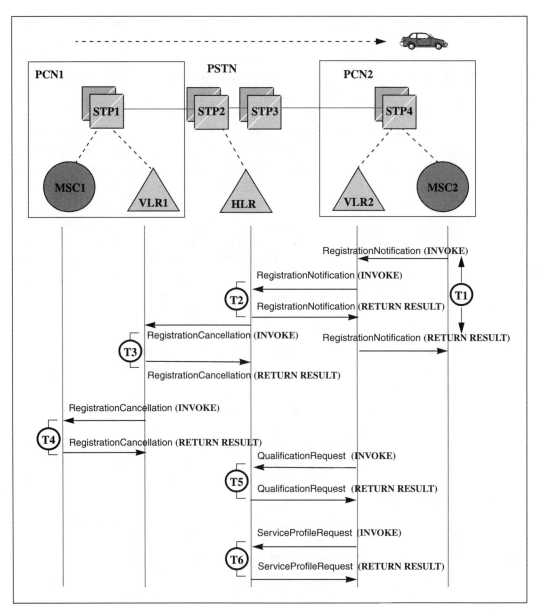

Figure 5.4   IS-41 TCAP message flow for MS registration.

Transaction 1. When MSC2 detects that the MS is in its service area, it sends a **RegistrationNotification**(INVOKE) to its VLR (VLR2).

Transaction 2. If both MSCs, 1 and 2, are served by VLR2, VLR2 finds that the MS had previously registered with an MSC within the domain of VLR2. In this case, VLR2 may take no further action other than to record the identity of MSC1. If MSC1 is not served by VLR2, then VLR2 sends a RegistrationNotification(INVOKE) to the MS's HLR.

NOTE that the RegistrationNotification(INVOKE) message in transaction 2 is likely to be routed by using GTT because VLR2 may not recognize the actual address of the HLR by the MS's MIN. Thus, the MIN is used as the global title address, and the translation type of the message is marked 3, for Cellular Nationwide Roaming Services. Our example assumes that STP 3 will perform GTT; that is, the DPC of the message points to STP 3. After GTT, the actual destination address is found. STP 3 forwards this message to STP 2, and thus the HLR. The HLR confirms the registration by sending a RegistrationNotification(RETURN RESULT) to VLR2. This message is typically delivered without GTT because the actual address of VLR 2 is included as part of the SCCP in the previous RegistrationNotification(INVOKE) message sent from VLR2 to the HLR. Also note that transaction 2 is nested within transaction 1.

Transaction 3. The HLR sends a RegistrationCancellation(INVOKE) to the MS's previously visited VLR (VLR1), which cancels the obsolete registration record.

Transaction 4. The cancellation propagates to MSC1. Since the actual address of VLR1 has been recorded in the HLR in the previous registration operation, the cancellation message may be delivered by using the actual HLR address; that is, no GTT is required. Note that the cancellation process (see transactions 3 and 4) can be performed at any time after transaction 2.

Transaction 5. After transaction 2 is completed, VLR2 creates a registration record for the MS, and sends a QualificationRequest(INVOKE) to the HLR to check the MS's qualification for receiving services.

Transaction 6. VLR2 also sends a ServiceProfileRequest(INVOKE) to the HLR to obtain the service profile for the roaming MS. Transaction 6 is required in call origination/delivery procedures.

5.4   PCN/PSTN Call Control Using ISUP

The ISUP messages are used for call setup/release between the PSTN and a PCN in the interconnection networks using Type 2A or Type 2B with SS7 trunk interfaces (described in Section 5.2). Figure 5.5 illustrates the typical

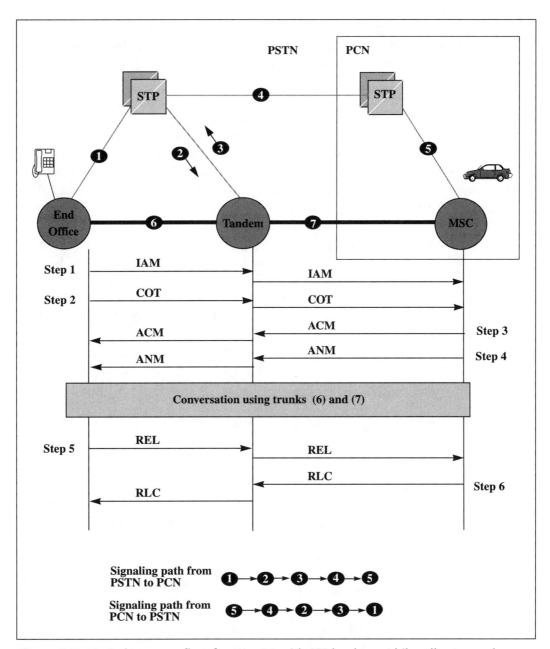

Figure 5.5 Typical message flow for type 2A with SS7 land-to-mobile call setup and release involving a tandem switch.

message flow for Type 2A with SS7 land-to-mobile call setup/release involving a tandem switch (see Figure 5.3(b)). For other interconnection configurations, the message flows between the originating switch and the terminating switch are the same, although the signaling and trunk paths may be different.

The call setup procedure is described in the following steps. The messages exchanged in steps 1–6 are ISUP messages that are delivered by MTP routing. This call setup procedure is general and is not unique to mobile applications. These steps are presented to provide the reader a complete message flow of wireline-to-wireless call setup. When an MIN is dialed, the originating *end office* (EO) notices that the number is for wireless service. Suppose that the EO has HLR query capability. The EO sends a query message to obtain the MS's *temporary local directory number* (TLDN). The messages exchanged among switches, VLR, and HLR are TCAP messages. These messages may be delivered with or without GTT. This example assumes that the EO has the capability to query the HLR. If not, the MIN must be routed from the EO to a specific switch for location query and call setup.

Depending on the implementation, if the mobile called party is busy, the situation may or may not be detected at this stage. If the busy line situation is detected, a busy indication is returned to the calling party. If the mobile user has call-forwarding or call-waiting services, the busy line situation is handled differently. Note that if the called party is a wireline user, the busy line situation is not detected until step 3 is executed.

Step 1. After the MS's TLDN is obtained, the EO sends an Initial Address Message (IAM) to the PCN MSC to initiate signaling for trunk setup. The ISUP messages described in the following steps are delivered by MTP routing. The EO marks the circuit busy, and the information is carried by the IAM. The IAM also indicates whether a *continuity check* is required (to be described in the next step). The IAM progresses switch-to-switch via the STPs to the PCN MSC. The message follows the path $(1) \rightarrow (2) \rightarrow (3) \rightarrow (4) \rightarrow (5)$ in Figure 5.5. When the IAM is sent, an IAM timer is set at the EO. The EO expects to receive a response from the MSC within the timeout period.

Step 2 (if necessary). If the IAM sent from the EO to the tandem specifies a continuity check, the selected trunk from the tandem to the EO is checked to ensure a satisfactory transmission quality. After the continuity check is successfully completed, a Continuity Message (COT) is sent from the EO to the tandem, and the trunk is set up. The same procedure could be performed when the MSC receives the IAM from the tandem.

Step 3. When the IAM arrives at the MSC, the MSC pages the MS. One of the following three events occurs:

- The MS is connected with another call. Even if the system detects that the destination MS is idle at step 0, this MS may be engaged in another call between the end of step 0 and the end of step 2. This situation is referred to as *call collision*. Either the call is processed with call forwarding or call waiting, or the MSC returns a REL message to the EO with a cause indicating the busy line situation. The REL message is described in step 5.

- If the MS is idle, an **Address Complete Message (ACM)** is sent from the MSC to the EO. The message indicates that the routing information required to complete the call has been received by the MSC. The message also informs the EO of the MS information, charge indications, and end-to-end protocol requirements. The MSC provides an audible ring through the setup trunk to the calling party. When the EO receives the ACM, the IAM timer is stopped. The ACM (and other ISUP messages) sent from the MSC to the EO follows the path (5) → (4) → (2) → (3) → (1) in Figure 5.5.

- If the MS does not answer the page, the MSC may redirect the call based on an appropriate procedure or return a REL message to the EO.

Step 4. When the MS answers the call, an **Answer Message (ANM)** is sent from the MSC to the EO to indicate that the call has been answered. At this moment, the call is established through the trunk path (6) → (7), in Figure 5.5, and the conversation begins.

NOTE After the conversation is finished, the call can be disconnected using procedures that depend on who hangs up first. Figure 5.5 assumes that the calling party hangs up first. In the next example, we will illustrate the case when the called party hangs up first. The following steps are executed.

Step 5. The EO sends a **Release Message (REL)** to indicate that the specified trunk is being released from the connection. The specified trunk is released before the **REL** is sent, but the trunk is not set to idle at the EO until a **Release Complete Message (RLC)** message is received, as in the next step.

Step 6. When the MSC receives the **REL**, propagated from the originating EO, it replies with a **Release Complete Message (RLC)** to confirm that the indicated trunk has been placed in an idle state. After the **RLC** is sent, the EO and/or the tandem waits for 0.5 to 1 second before it seizes the released trunk for the next call.

Figure 5.6 illustrates the message flow for a call setup from an MS to a wireline user. The PSTN/PCN interconnection follows the configuration in Figure 5.3(a). In this example, two local telephone companies or *local exchange carriers* LEC1, LEC2, and a long-distance telephone company, or *interexchange carrier*, IXC, are in the call setup path.

The message flow for call setup is very similar to the previous example except that an **Exit Message (EXM)** is sent from Tandem 1 to the MSC. This message indicates that SS7 call setup information has successfully progressed to the IXC. The **EXM** is sent to the MSC when Tandem 1 has received an **ACM**, **ANM**, or **REL** from the IXC, or when an **EXM** timer expires at Tandem 1. We assume that the **EXM** timer expires first. The timer is set after an **IAM** is sent from Tandem 1 to the IXC. The sending of the **EXM** does not affect the completion of any continuity check required on the trunk between the MSC and Tandem 1. On the other hand, if a "continuity check failed" **COT** code is received for this trunk, the **EXM** is not sent to the MSC.

The call release procedure in this example assumes that the called party hangs up first, which is different from the previous example. When the called party (the wireline user in this example) hangs up the phone, a **Suspend Message (SUS)** is sent from the EO at LEC2 to the MSC to indicate that the called party has disconnected. The EO expects one of the following two events to occur within a timeout period of 14–16 seconds:

- A REL from the MSC is received by the EO. The EO disconnects the trunk.

- The called party goes back off-hook. The connection continues, and a **Resume Message (RES)** is sent from the EO to the MSC. The **SUS** timer is stopped. (This scenario is not shown in Figure 5.6.)

If the **SUS** timer expires, the EO disconnects the trunk and a **REL** is sent to the MSC. Upon receipt of the **SUS**, the MSC expects one of the following four events to occur within a timeout period of 10–32 seconds:

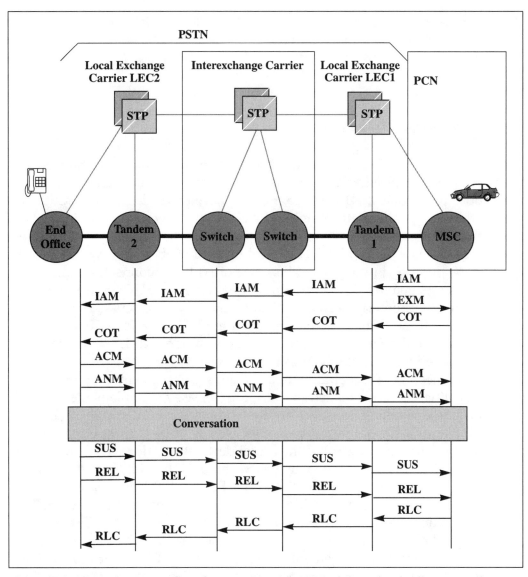

Figure 5.6   Typical message flow for type 2A with SS7 mobile-to-land call setup and release involving local exchange and interexchange carriers.

- The calling party hangs up. The MSC sends a REL to the EO and disconnects the trunk.

- A REL (from the EO) arrives at the MSC. The MSC disconnects the trunk.

■ A **RES** (from the EO) arrives at the MSC. The **SUS** timer is stopped and the connection continues.

■ The MSC **SUS** timer expires; the MSC disconnects the trunk.

5.5   Summary

Based on [Lin95b], this chapter discussed the SS7-supported interactions between PSTN and PCN. We assumed that the mobile communications protocol is IS-41 [EIA91b, EIA95], which includes inter-MSC handoff [EIA91c], automatic roaming [EIA91a], and operations, administration, and maintenance [EIA91d]. Alternatives of handoff and automatic roaming can be found in [Lin94c, Lin94d, Lin94a, Lin94b, Jai94b, Moh94, Tek91].

We described two types of SS7-supported trunk connections and two types of signaling links between a PCN and the PSTN. Other types of interconnections between a PCN and the PSTN are discussed in [EIA93a, Bel93c]. If the trunk is connected from the PCN to a PSTN end office, 911 calls and operator services may not be supported. These services are supported only via the PCN trunk connected to a PSTN access tandem.

All messages for mobility management are implemented by SS7 TCAP. Signaling messages related to call setup/release are implemented by SS7 ISUP. All signaling messages are routed between PCN and PSTN by the MTP and SCCP of the SS7 protocols. Details of IS-41 message routing can be found in [Lin97b]. If the actual destination address is known, the IS-41 TCAP messages are delivered without GTT. All ISUP messages for call control are delivered without GTT. For IS-41 TCAP messages using the MS's MINs, the actual destination addresses may not be known. The destination addresses are translated by the SCCP using GTT. The reader is referred to [Bel91, Bel94c, Bel93d] for further reading.

IS-41 mobility management is implemented by TCAP with connectionless service—that is, out-of-order message delivery. Message sequencing is guaranteed by query-and-response TCAP transactions. The reader is referred to [EIA95, EIA91c, EIA91a] for further reading.

Call setup/release between a PCN and the PSTN follows standard ISUP procedures. The details can be found in Section 5 in [Bel93b] and Section 5 in [Bel94a]. In the PSTN's view, PCN call control is similar to other applications, such as 800 service. The reader is referred to [ANS92a, Bel93b, Bel91] for further reading. Information for SS7 can be found in [ANS92b, ANS92c, ANS92a, ANS92d]. Details of SS7 link types can be found in [Lin97b]; and SS7 OMAP is given in Section 3.4.2 in [Bel93b].

5.6 Review Questions

1. Why is SS7 classified as a common channel signaling protocol? What are the main elements in the SS7 architecture? Describe them.

2. At which level of the SS7 protocol stack does the GTT take place? When do we need GTT in mobility management? Can we modify IS-41 so that GTT is avoided?

3. What are the purposes of the package and the component types in a TCAP message? Reimplement the IS-41 registration procedure using multiple-component TCAP messages.

4. In *timeout deregistration,* an MS is deregistered by default after a certain time period elapses without the MS reregistering. What is the advantage of this scheme compared with the IS-41 deregistration and implicit deregiatration? (Hint: See the discussion in [Por93].)

5. What are the ISUP messages usually used for? Can we implement the IS-41 registration procedure using ISUP?

6. Which layers are responsible for ISUP and TCAP routing? Do we need GTT for ISUP message routing? Why or why not?

7. In the call release procedure, assume that the calling party hangs up the phone first. After the **REL** message is sent, the originating SSP (that connects to the calling party) cannot release the trunk until it receives the **RLC** message sent from the switch of the called party. An alternative is to allow the originating SSP to release the trunk 0.5–1 second after the **REL** message is sent. Is this alternative appropriate? Give your reason.

8. There are three call release models. In the *calling control model*, the call is disconnected if the calling party hangs up first, and is suspended if the called party hangs up first. In the *called control model*, the call is disconnected if the called party hangs up first, and is suspended if the calling party hangs up first. In the *either control model*, the call is disconnected if any one of the call parties hangs up. The call release model described in Section 5.4 is calling control. Compare these three call release models.

CHAPTER

6

Intersystem Handoff and Authentication in IS-41

In Chapter 5, we discussed two IS-41 applications, location update and call delivery; in this chapter, we address two other IS-41 applications, *intersystem handoff* and *authentication*.

6.1   IS-41 Intersystem Handoff

If the handoff occurs between BSs connected to the same MSC, the procedure typically involves the air interface, not the wireline transport network. This type of handoff is called inter-BS handoff, the details of which were described in Chapters 3 and 4.

If the two BSs involved in handoff are connected to different MSCs, the handoff is referred to as intersystem handoff. In Chapter 2, Section 2.1, four types of intersystem handoff were described: handoff-forward, handoff-backward, handoff-to-third, and path minimization. This section describes how these handoff types can be implemented in IS-41.

6.1.1   Handoff Measurement

Assume that a handoff request has been made for a mobile station (MS) currently connected to BS1 (and thus MSC A), and the target switch is MSC B, as shown in Figure 6.1. Note that SS7 uses out-of-band signaling where the signaling path is different from the voice/data path. In Figure 6.1, the signal link (the dashed line) for delivering the IS-41 TCAP messages is different from the trunk (the solid line) for carrying user information (voice/data). The intersystem handoff measurement procedure at the air interface level was described in Chapter 3, Section 3.1. The measurement procedure at the network level is described here:

Step 1. MSC A sends a query message **HandoffMeasurementRequest** (INVOKE) to MSC B. The message indicates the candidate BS, in this example, BS2, for handoff. MSC A sets the seven-second *location measurement maximum response timer* (LMMRT) and expects to receive a response before the timer expires.

Step 2. When MSC B receives the **HandoffMeasurementRequest** message, it identifies the candidate BS as indicated in the message, and performs signal measurements. If the signal quality of the candidate BS is not good enough, then MSC B may exit the task. If so, MSC A will not hear from MSC B before LMMRT expires. In this case MSC A may exit the task or may try other candidate BSs.

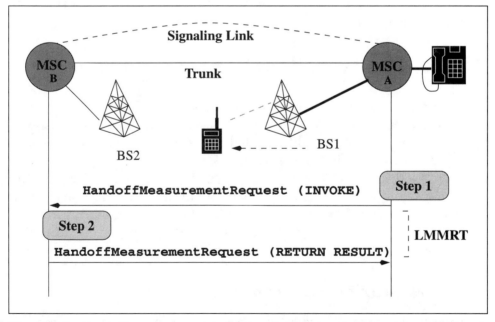

Figure 6.1 Handoff measurement (solid line: the voice path; dashed line: the signaling path).

If MSC B accepts the signal quality of the candidate BS, it sends a response message **HandoffMeasurementRequest** (RETURN RESULT) to MSC A.

If a candidate MSC and BS are identified in handoff measurement, then the intersystem handoff procedure is performed.

6.1.2   Handoff-Forward

In IS-41, the number of "extra" trunks which can be used by intersystem handoff is limited. The number of MSCs to be traversed by a handoff is stored in the InterSwitchCount parameter. This number is limited to no more than a threshold MAXHANDOFF determined by the service provider. The handoff-forward message flow is illustrated in Figure 6.2 and described here:

Step 1. MSC A initiates the handoff-forward procedure if the Inter-SwitchCount value is no more than the MAXHANDOFF threshold and the trunk between MSC A and MSC B is available. MSC A first allocates the trunk and sends a query message, **FacilitiesDirective** (INVOKE), to MSC B. The message includes the InterSwitchCount parameter that is set to the current value, plus one. If MSC A is the anchor MSC, the current InterSwitchCount is 0. MSC A sets the 12-second *handoff order timer* (HOT). If MSC A does not hear from MSC B before the HOT timer expires, MSC A releases the trunk and sends a query message, **FacilitiesRelease** (INVOKE), to MSC B with the "HandoffAbort-not received" indication, and the 4–15-second *clear trunk timer* (CTT) is set. If CTT expires, MSC A repeats the **FacilitiesRelease** message. If MSC A hears from MSC B before the HOT timer expires, Step 2 is executed.

Step 2. When MSC B receives the **FacilitiesDirective** query message, it checks if the voice channel of the designated BS is available.

Step 2.1. If no radio channel is available, MSC B sends the response message, **FacilitiesDirective** (RETURN ER-ROR) with "Resource Shortage" indication to MSC A. When MSC A receives the error message, it stops the HOT timer, exchanges the **FacilitiesRelease** message pair to release the trunk between MSCs A and B, and exits the task.

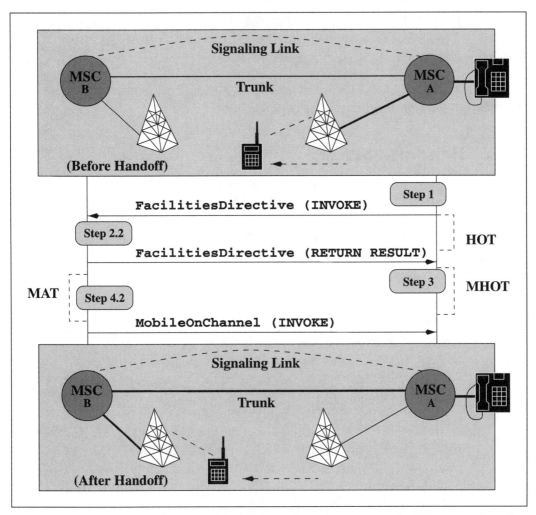

Figure 6.2 Handoff-forward (solid lines: the voice path; dashed lines: the signaling path).

Step 2.2. If a radio channel is available, MSC B returns a response message **FacilitiesDirective** (RETURN RE-SULT) with the selected channel number to MSC A. Then steps 3 and 4 are executed in parallel.

Step 3. When MSC A receives the **FacilitiesDirective** response message, it stops HOT, sets the seven-second *mobile handoff timer* (MHOT). MSC A sends the **handoff execution** message to the MS for transferring to the new radio channel. (Detailed MS-BS handoff interaction was given in Chapter 4, Section 4.2.2.)

Step 4. In parallel with step 3, MSC B sets the seven-second *mobile arrival timer* (MAT), and expects to hear from the MS. There are two possibilities:

Step 4.1. The MAT timer expires, MSC B releases the radio channel, and exits the task. Eventually, the MHOT timer of MSC A will expire, and the trunk will be released.

Step 4.2. The MS responds, MSC B stops timer MAT, and sends a unidirectional message, MobileOnChannel (INVOKE), to MSC A. When the message is received by MSC A, MHOT is stopped. MSC A connects the call path to the inter-MSC trunk. At this point, the MS is switched to the new path.

6.1.3 Handoff-Backward

Suppose that the MS moves from MSC A to MSC B and a handoff-forward is performed. If the MS moves from MSC B back to MSC A again, a handoff-backward occurs. The message flow is illustrated in Figure 6.3, composed of the following steps:

Step 1. MSC B sets the handoff order timer (HOT) and sends a query message, HandoffBack (INVOKE), to MSC A. If MSC B does not hear from MSC A before HOT expires, MSC B aborts the transaction.

Step 2. When MSC A receives the HandoffBack (INVOKE) message, it checks if a radio channel is available on the designated cell. There are two possibilities:

Step 2.1. If no radio channel is available, MSC A sends the response message, HandoffBack (RETURN ERROR), with the "ResourceShortage" indication to MSC B. When MSC B receives the error message, it stops the HOT timer and exits the task.

Step 2.2. If a radio channel is available, MSC A returns a response message, HandoffBack (RETURN RESULT), with the selected channel number to MSC B. Then steps 3 and 4 are executed in parallel.

Step 3. When MSC B receives the HandoffBack response message, it stops HOT, sets the seven-second mobile handoff timer (MHOT),

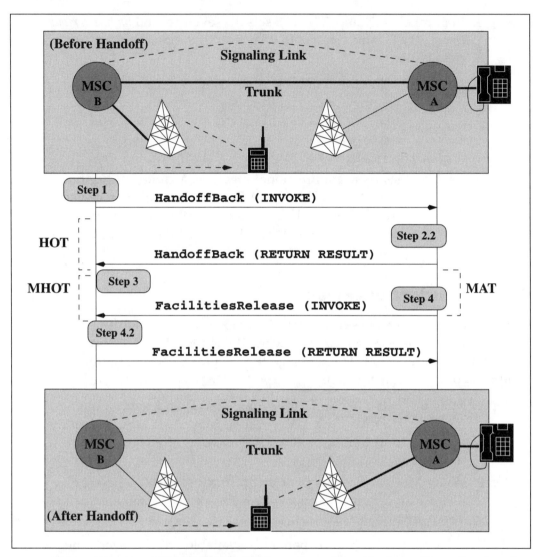

Figure 6.3 Handoff-backward (solid lines: the voice path; dashed lines: the signaling path).

and asks the MS to transfer to the new radio channel. If MSC B does not hear from MSC A before MHOT expires, the task exits.

Step 4. In parallel, MSC A sets the seven-second mobile arrival timer (MAT), and expects to hear from the MS. There are two cases:

Step 4.1. The MAT timer expires, MSC A releases the radio channel, and exits the task. Eventually, the MHOT timer of MSC B will expire.

Step 4.2. The MS responds. At this point, the MS has handed
over to the new voice path. MSC A stops MAT and
sends a query message, FacilitiesRelease (INVOKE),
to MSC B with the indication "HandoffSuccessful."
When the message is received by MSC B, MHOT is
stopped. MSC B sends a response message, FacilitiesRelease (RETURN RESULT), to MSC A and the
trunk between MSCs A and B is released.

6.1.4 Handoff-to-Third and Path Minimization

Suppose that the MS moves from MSC A to MSC B and a handoff-forward
is performed. If the MS moves again from MSC B to MSC C, a handoff-to-
third occurs. Basically, a handoff-forward procedure is executed between
the serving MSC B and the target MSC C.

To reduce the number of extra trunks used in intersystem handoff, *path
minimization* may be performed. The message flow for path minimization
is illustrated in Figure 6.4, and described here:

Step 1. MSC B sets the 18-second *handoff-to-third timer* (HTTT) and
sends a query message, HandoffToThird (INVOKE), to MSC A.
The message identifies the target MSC C for handoff. Note that
if MSC B does not hear from MSC A before HTTT expires, it
aborts the transaction to MSC A, and may optionally initiate the
handoff-forward procedure with MSC C.

Step 2. When MSC A receives the HandoffToThird message, it checks if
the target MSC C is known to MSC A. There are two cases:

Step 2.1. MSC C is not known to MSC A or MSC C is known
to MSC A, but no trunk connection between MSC A
and MSC C is available. MSC A sends a response
message, HandoffToThird (RETURN ERROR) to
MSC B. When MSC B receives the error message,
it stops HTTT, executes recovery procedures, and
exits the task. Optionally, MSC B may initiate the
handoff-forward procedure with MSC C.

Step 2.2. An Interswitch trunk is available, and MSC A sets up
the trunk to MSC C. MSC A sets the handoff or-
der timer (HOT) and sends a query message,
FacilitiesDirective (INVOKE), to MSC C. Then Step 3
is executed. Note that if MSC A does not hear from
MSC Cbefore HOT expires, MSC A will send the

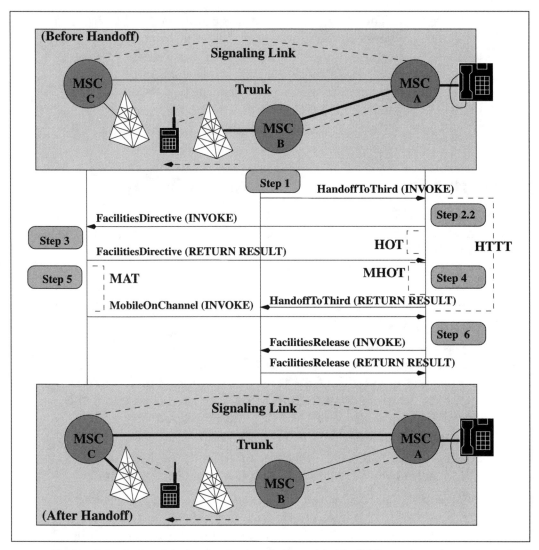

Figure 6.4   Path minimization for handoff-to-third (solid lines: the voice path; dashed lines: the signaling path).

response message, HandoffToThird (RETURN ER-ROR), to MSC B, in which case, the actions described in step 2.1 are taken.

Step 3   When MSC C receives the FacilitiesDirective (INVOKE) message, it checks if a radio channel is available on the designated cell.

Step 3.1.   If no radio channel is available, MSC C sends the response message, FacilitiesDirective (RETURN ER-

ROR), with the "ResourceShortage" indication to MSC A. When MSC A receives the error message, it stops HOT and sends a response message, **HandoffToThird** (RETURN ERROR), to MSC B. When MSC B receives the error message, it stops HTTT and initiates the recovery procedures described in Step 2.1. Trunk release procedures will take place on the trunk between MSCs A and C.

Step 3.2. If a radio channel is available, MSC C returns a response message, **FacilitiesDirective** (RETURN RESULT), with the selected channel number to MSC A. Then steps 4 and 5 are executed in parallel.

Step 4. When MSC A receives the **FacilitiesDirective** (RETURN RESULT) message, it stops HOT and sets the mobile hand-off order timer (MHOT). MSC A sends the response message, **HandoffToThird** (RETURN RESULT), to MSC B. When MSC B receives the response message, it stops HTTT and sets the seven-second *handoff-to-third result timer* (HTTRT). MSC B sends the **handoff execution** message to the MS. (The reader is referred to Chapter 4, Section 4.2.2, for the handoff interaction between the BS and the MS.) The procedure proceeds with step 6. Note that if MSC A does not hear from MSC C before MHOT expires, MSC A initiates the recovery procedures to release the trunk to MSC C.

Step 5. In parallel with step 4, MSC C sets the mobile arrival timer (MAT) after it sends the **FacilitiesDirective** response message to MSC A. MSC C expects to receive the **handoff complete** message from the MS before MAT expires.

Step 5.1. If MAT expires, MSC C releases the reserved radio channel without sending any message to MSC B or A. Eventually, the HTTRT timer at MSC B expires, and MSC B initiates the recovery procedures. MSC A then initiates the recovery procedures to release the trunk between MSCs A and C.

Step 5.2. If the MS responds, MSC C connects the radio channel and the inter-MSC trunk and returns a unidirectional message, **MobileOnChannel** (INVOKE), to MSC A. Then step 6 is executed to clean up unused resources.

Step 6. When MSC A receives the **MobileOnChannel** message from MSC C, the MHOT timer is stopped. MSC A switches the trunk connection from MSC B to MSC C. At this point, the MS has handed over to the new voice path. MSC A exchanges the **FacilitiesRelease** messages with MSC B to release the trunk.

For handoff-to-third without path minimization, MSC C acts as the target MSC, and MSC B acts as the serving MSC, and a handoff-forward is performed. With path minimization, MSC C does not talk to MSC B in the handoff procedure; instead, a handoff-forward is performed between the anchor MSC A and the target MSC C. Communication between MSC A and B is required to remove the unused trunk. Also note that in the design of the timer values, HTTT must be longer than HOT, as indicated in Figure 6.4.

6.1.5   Comments on IS-41 Intersystem Handoff

Several comments are pertinent to the IS-41 intersystem handoff discussion:

- To simplify our discussion, the intersystem handoff procedures in this chapter are based on IS-41 Revision B. In IS-41 Revision C and later versions, the procedures have been modified to include the authentication/encryption information in the TCAP messages for voice path setup. IS-41 authentication is discussed in the next section.

- The mechanism carrying IS-41 TCAP message does not guarantee the FIFO property; that is, the messages may not be delivered in the order they are sent. The high-overhead FIFO delivery mechanism is not required in the IS-41 protocol because the query/response type transactions always preserve the FIFO property. An MSC does not send the next message to the destination MSC before it hears from the destination MSC.

- IS-41 TCAP messages have two priority levels. During heavy traffic situation, low-priority messages are more likely to be discarded. In IS-41, messages that allocate or release resources are assigned the high-priority level. Except for **HandoffMeasurementRequest** messages, all message types described in this section are high-priority messages. Other low-priority messages include those for location registration and cancellation, described in Chapter 5, Section 5.3.

- A TCAP message can have multiple components; each component performs one action. For simplicity, IS-41 TCAP messages are composed of a single component. Some personal communication service implementations under advanced intelligent network platform use multiple component TCAP messages.

6.2   IS-41 Authentication

The EIA/TIA *Telecommunications Systems Bulletins* (TSB) 51 defines protocols for authentication, voice privacy, and signaling message encryption, which have been incorporated into IS-41 Revision C and later versions. The TSB-51 algorithm is based on private key cryptographic techniques in which a secret key, known as *shared secret data* (SSD), is shared between the MS and the authentication center (AuC). This key is known only to these two parties.

Two authentication schemes have been proposed in TSB-51. In the *without-sharing* (WS) scheme, the SSD is shared only between the authentication center and the MS. In the *sharing* (S) scheme, the SSD or some aspect of SSD may be shared with the visited system as well. Since the visited system has the SSD, it can authenticate the MS at call origination or delivery, thereby considerably reducing message flow and call setup time. However, as will be seen later, this scheme requires additional message exchanges during registration. Thus, there is a trade-off between the two schemes, based on the expected number of calls to/from the user between two consecutive registrations. For a user with high call frequency, sharing the SSD with the visited system is beneficial; consequently, the S scheme is preferable. For a user with high mobility rate, sharing SSD with the visited system results in considerably increased traffic; consequently, the WS scheme is preferable. For a given user, the call and the move frequencies may vary from time to time; therefore, it is desirable to switch between the two authentication schemes as the user's behavior changes. We describe two adaptive algorithms to select the authentication scheme for a user. Performance studies indicate that as call or move frequencies of a user change, the adaptive algorithms automatically select the appropriate authentication scheme in real time.

6.2.1   Privacy and Authentication in TSB-51

In AMPS, every MS is associated with a *mobile identification number* (MIN) and an *electronic serial number* (ESN). A MIN is a North American

Numbering Plan (NANP) number that serves as a mobile telephone number. MINs are programmed into MS at purchase, and are known to the customers. An ESN is created at manufacture, and the customers are not supposed to be aware of it. The ESN is a 32-bit serial number where the highest-order 8 bits represent the manufacturer's code. The remaining bits are used as a unique MS number.

When the first AMPS network was built at Bell Labs, few users were expected. ESN was considered sufficient to authenticate a user. Some unscrupulous people figured out that they could receive MINs and ESNs over the air and then reprogram phones so that other cellular users would get the bills. Scanning test equipment for intercepting MIN/ESN combinations is legitimately available. *Cloned phones* can be created following the scanning and reprogramming procedures. To address this serious security issue, this section describes two EIA/TIA TSB-51 schemes for privacy and authentication. We first describe the without-sharing (WS) scheme, then show how it differs from the sharing (S) scheme. To facilitate the discussion that follows, we reiterate notions and terminologies introduced in Chapter 5, Section 5.2. The AuC is a database connected to the HLR, which provides it with the authentication parameters and ciphering keys used to ensure network security. The AuC is solely responsible for maintaining and updating the SSDs. Users move about *location areas* (LAs) belonging to one or more *PCS service providers* (PSPs). Each PSP may provide some combination of BSs for offering wireless access to the MSs. These BSs are controlled by MSCs. Associated with each location area is a visitor location register (VLR). The VLRs may be part of the PSP network. It is likely that the VLRs are collocated with MSCs. For demonstration purposes, we assume that VLRs are separated from the PSP network. Note that the results of this section are not affected by the locations of VLRs. One or more home location registers (HLRs) are maintained by the PSP, which maintain user profiles, current location area, and so on.

6.2.2 Without-Sharing (WS) Scheme

In the WS scheme, the SSD is known to the AuC and the MS only. Message flow for privacy and authentication of the WS scheme is described below.

6.2.2.1 Registration (Location Update)

The authentication message flow for MS registration is shown in Figure 6.5 and is described in the following steps:

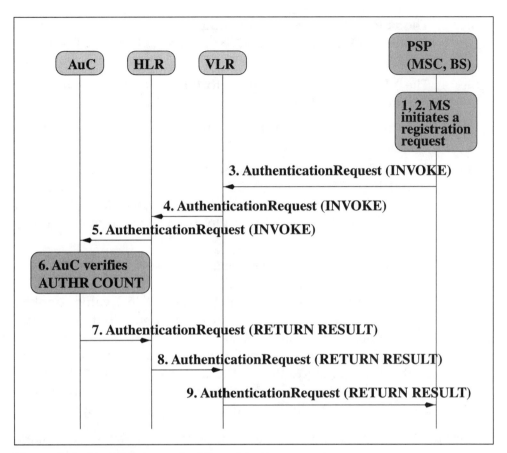

Figure 6.5 The WS scheme for MS registration.

Step 1. An MS determines, based on the signal transmitted by the BS, that it has entered a new LA and that authentication is required to access PSP services. The MS executes the *cellular authentication and voice encryption* (CAVE) algorithm using the SSD; its ESN, MIN, and a random number (RAND) are obtained from the PSP system at that time. The algorithm produces a registration authentication result (AUTHR).

Step 2. The MS requests registration with the PSP by supplying the authentication result AUTHR, ESN, MIN, the most significant 8 bits of RAND denoted as RANDC, and a COUNT value that is the account of the most significant events such as registration, call origination, termination, and so on, initiated by the MS. This call history count is also maintained by the AuC.

Step 3. The PSP system forwards the authentication request in an **AuthenticationRequest** (INVOKE) message to the VLR serving the PSP LA.

Step 4. The VLR forwards the request to the HLR, along with all parameters it received.

Step 5. In turn, the HLR forwards the authentication request to the AuC.

Step 6. The AuC retrieves the SSD associated with the MIN from its database. Then it executes the CAVE algorithm by using the retrieved SSD and the additional parameters (i.e., MIN, ESN, and RAND received from the HLR) to produce the authentication result.

Steps 7–9. After verifying that the generated result matches the AUTHR value received from the MS, the AuC checks if the COUNT value it has stored matches the COUNT value supplied by the MS. Then the AuC provides its response to the authentication request in an **AuthenticationRequest** (RETURN RESULT) message. Note that if authentication fails, the component type of the message is RETURN ERROR. (Throughout this section, we assume that every authentication action is successful.) The message is eventually forwarded to the visited PSP system.

Once the MS has been authenticated, the serving PSP system will start the location update procedure, as described in Chapter 5, Section 5.3.

6.2.2.2   Call Origination

Figure 6.6 illustrates message flow for MS call origination in the visited PSP system. The following steps describe the activities that take place:

Step 1. The MS executes the CAVE algorithm with MIN, SSD, ESN, and a random number RANDC, to produce an authentication request result (AUTHR), a voice privacy mask (VPMASK), and a signaling message encryption key (SMEKEY). Note that VPMASK is applied to voice transmission over the air interface between the MS and the serving PSP system, and SMEKEY is used to encrypt certain fields within the signaling message sent by the MS to the serving PSP system. VPMASK and SMEKEY are generated by the AuC and forwarded to the serving PSP system.

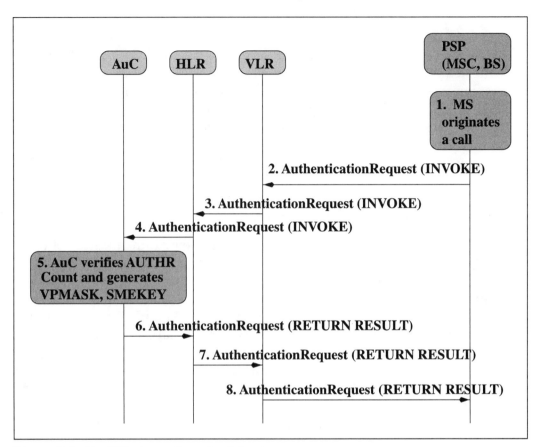

Figure 6.6 The WS scheme for call origination.

Steps 2–4. The MS forwards RAND, AUTHR, COUNT, ESN, and MIN to the serving PSP system, and the serving PSP forwards the **AuthenticationRequest** (INVOKE) message to the AuC.

Step 5. The AuC performs authentication as described in step 6 in the registration procedure.

Steps 6–8. Finally, the AuC generates VPMASK and SMEKEY that get forwarded to the serving PSP system.

Once the MS has been authenticated, the serving PSP system will initiate the **RegistrationNotification** message to determine the called party's current serving PSP. (See Chapter 5, Section 5.3 for details.)

6.2.2.3 Call Termination

The call setup procedure for call termination routes the trunk to the destination MSC, and the MSC pages the MS. The MS responds to the page by executing the CAVE algorithm, sending AUTHR, COUNT, ESN, MIN, and RANDC. The message flow is similar to that of the previous two cases and will not be repeated here. Once the called MS has been successfully authenticated, a voice channel is established for the call between the two calling parties.

6.2.3   Sharing (S) Scheme

When SSD is shared with the visited PSP system, authentication of the MS during registration requires additional steps compared to that in Section 6.2.2. This extra overhead is due to the fact that the old VLR at the previous system has the current value of COUNT, and, therefore, the AuC needs to request COUNT from the previously visited PSP system's VLR. Once the MS is registered with the new VLR, for all other system accesses such as call origination, termination, and flash request for call waiting, the VLR can authenticate the MS without having to forward the authentication request to the AuC. The message flow is therefore considerably reduced when compared with the WS scheme.

6.2.3.1 Registration (Location Update)

Figure 6.7 illustrates the registration message flow when SSD is shared with the visited system, and the following steps describe the process:

Steps 1 and 2. The MS determines that it has entered a new LA and that authentication is required to access PSP services. It executes the CAVE algorithm using SSD, ESN, MIN, and RAND obtained from the PSP system at that time. The algorithm produces a registration authentication result, AUTHR.

Steps 3–6. These steps proceed as in steps 3–6 of the registration procedure in Section 6.2.2. At this point, the AuC has completed verification of the authentication result, AUTHR, generated by the MS. However, it does not have the current value of COUNT, and, therefore, it cannot verify what is supplied by the MS in its registration request. The AuC should obtain the current COUNT value from the VLR of the previously visited PSP system.

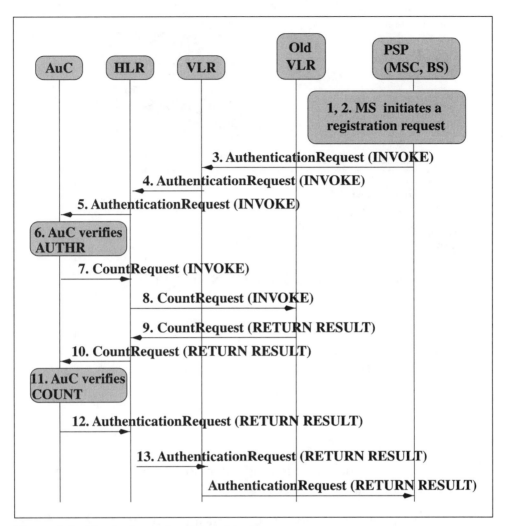

Figure 6.7 The S scheme for MS registration.

Steps 7 and 8. The AuC sends a **CountRequest** (INVOKE) message to the HLR. The message is forwarded to the previously visited VLR.

Step 9. The old VLR responds to the request by sending the COUNT value in a **CountRequest** (RETURN RESULT) message. This message is forwarded from the HLR to the AuC.

Steps 10–13. The AuC verifies the COUNT and sends an authentication result in an **AuthenticationRequest** (RETURN RESULT) message to the requesting system.

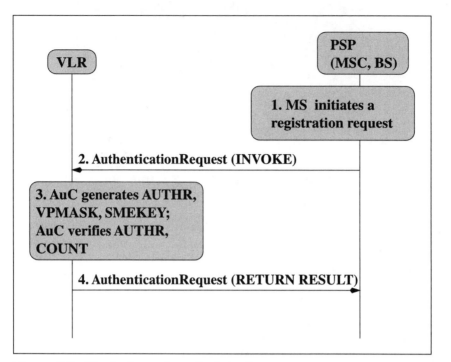

Figure 6.8   The S scheme for call origination.

6.2.3.2   Call Origination

Figure 6.8 illustrates the message flow when an MS in the visited system initiates a call, as detailed in these steps:

Step 1.   The MS executes the CAVE algorithm with SSD, ESN, MIN, and RANDC to generate AUTHR, SMEKEY, and VPMASK. The MS then sends RANDC, AUTHR, COUNT, ESN, and MIN to the visited PSP system.

Step 2.   The visited PSP system sends an authentication request, Au-thenticationRequest (INVOKE), message to the serving VLR.

Step 3.   The VLR executes the CAVE algorithm and generates AUTHR, VPMASK, and SMEKEY.

Step 4.   After verifying AUTHR and COUNT, it includes the result of the verification, along with VPMASK and SMEKEY in its AuthenticationRequest (RETURN RESULT) response message to the visited system.

The message flow for flash request (e.g., for call-waiting service) and SSD update as dictated by administrative needs are not described in this book.

6.2.4   Adaptive Algorithm: AA1

The WS scheme is appropriate when the number of registration operations is larger than the call origination/termination operations. On the other hand, the S scheme is appropriate in the opposite situation. For simplicity, we regard events such as Flash requests and Count updates as being infrequent in comparison to call originations, call terminations, and registrations, and therefore ignore them in the following analysis. However, these events can be easily accommodated in the analysis. Note that the cost of sending a message is determined by the length of the message and the distance between the sender and the receiver locations. To simplify and strengthen the results, we assume that the costs of sending messages from one location (such as the AuC, the HLR, or a VLR) to another are the same. Thus, the number of delivered messages can be considered as the cost of the authentication scheme. To reduce the number of the database (AuC/HLR/VLR) accesses, it is important to choose an appropriate authentication scheme for a user. This subsection describes an adaptive algorithm (AA1) that automatically selects an appropriate authentication scheme for any given user in real time. This adaptive mechanism is based on the user behavior in terms of registration, call origination, and call termination.

We define a *cycle* as the period between two consecutive registrations for a user; we define the *cost* of a cycle as the number of messages sent to access AuC/HLR/VLR due to the call originations and terminations in the cycle and the registration at the beginning of the cycle. Note that the cost does not include the registration at the end of the cycle. The costs of the S scheme and the WS scheme are computed as follows. Let λ be the call arrival rate, and η be the mobility or the rate that a user changes LAs. Then the expected number of call arrivals in a cycle ρ is:

$$\rho = \frac{\lambda}{\eta}$$

In the WS scheme, five database accesses are required to authenticate a registration operation, and five database accesses are required to authenticate a call origination operation or a call termination operation. The cost analysis excludes the messages sent from the the VLRs to the PSP. Note that the number of messages sent from the VLRs to the PSP, as well as the number of messages sent within the PSP system (i.e., between MSC and BS), are the same for both authentication schemes. Thus, including these messages in the cost analysis will not change the results. In the S scheme, nine database accesses are required to authenticate a registration operation (see Figure 6.7) and one database access is required to authenticate a call origination operation or a call termination operation (see Figure 6.8). The expected numbers of database accesses during a cycle for the WS scheme and the S scheme are $C_{ws} = 5 + 5\rho$ and $C_s = 9 + \rho$, respectively. It is interesting to note that:

$$C_{ws} = C_s \Leftrightarrow \rho = 1$$

Also, the S scheme outperforms the WS scheme (i.e., $C_s < C_{ws}$) if and only if $\rho > 1$.

Algorithm AA1 is a $2n$-state finite automaton, with the state diagram shown in Figure 6.9. The WS scheme is exercised if AA1 is in state i for $0 \le i \le n - 1$. The S scheme is exercised if the algorithm is in state j for $n \le j \le 2n - 1$. Let L be the number of call arrivals during the previous cycle. The value for L can be measured by the HLR or the MS through call statistics. If the steady state of the algorithm exists, then the transition probabilities for the finite automaton are:

$$\rho_0 = \Pr[L = 0], \quad \rho_2 = \Pr[L = 1], \quad \text{and} \quad \rho_3 = \Pr[L > 1]$$

AA1 is easily implemented by incorporating the following rules for state transition within the AuC. The AuC needs to maintain $\lfloor \log_2 n \rfloor + 1$ *authentication scheme* (AS) *bits* per user. The VLR needs to maintain an AS bit per user to indicate the type of authentication scheme applicable to that user. When the AuC is accessed for a registration operation, the AuC checks the following: Suppose that the algorithm is in state i.

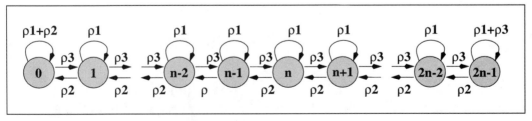

Figure 6.9   The state diagram for AA1.

- If no call arrived during the previous cycle, the algorithm moves to state $i - 1$ for $i > 0$, and remains in the same state i for $i = 0$.

- If exactly one call arrived during the previous cycle, the algorithm remains in the same state i.

- If more than one call arrived during the previous cycle, the algorithm moves to state $i + 1$ for $i < 2n - 1$, and remains in the same state i for $i = 2n - 1$.

When the algorithm moves from state $n - 1$ to state n, the authentication procedure switches from the WS scheme to the S scheme. Similarly, when the algorithm moves from state n to state $n - 1$, the authentication procedure switches from the S scheme to the WS scheme. If $\rho < 1$, the algorithm tends to move to state 0 and the WS scheme is exercised. On the other hand, if $\rho > 1$, the algorithm tends to move to state $2n - 1$, and the S scheme is exercised.

6.2.5 Adaptive Algorithm: AA2

The second adaptive algorithm (AA2) requires only an AS bit in the AuC and VLRs to indicate whether the S scheme or the WS scheme is exercised. At the beginning of a cycle, AA2 always exercises the WS scheme; that is, the AS bit is "WS." After an originating or terminating call arrives, the AS bit is switched to "S," and the S scheme is exercised. The switching from the WS scheme to the S scheme occurs as follows. Without loss of generality, assume that all calls to the user are call originations. Consider the following cycle:

Step 1. When the first call arrives, the authentication message flow follows Figure 6.6, except that when the AuC receives **AuthenticationRequest** (INVOKE), the AS bit at the AuC is switched to "S," and the SSD is sent to the VLR in the **AuthenticationRequest** (RETURN RESULT) message. When the VLR receives the SSD, its AS bit is set to "S." At this moment, the S scheme is exercised.

Step 2. For subsequent call arrivals in this cycle, the message flow in Figure 6.8 is followed.

Step 3. At the end of the cycle—when the MS moves to a new LA, and the authentication/registration occurs, the **AuthenticationRequest** messages are sent to the AuC.

Step 3a. If the AS bit at the AuC is "WS," it implies that no call origination/termination occurs during the cycle, and the message flow follows Figure 6.5.

Step 3b. If the AS bit at the AuC is "S" (i.e., there are call originations/terminations during the cycle), the message flow follows Figure 6.7. The AS bit at the AuC is set to "WS." When the VLR receives the **AuthenticationRequest** (RETURN RESULT) message, its AS bit is set to "WS."

At the end of step 3, the WS scheme is exercised.

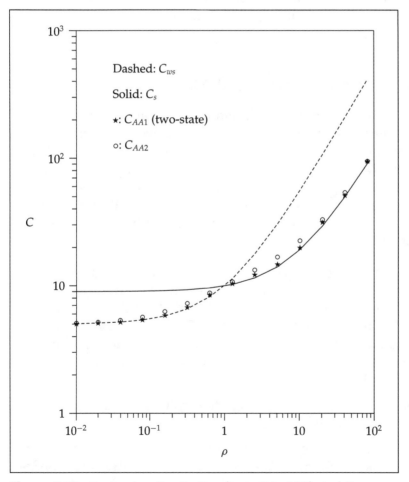

Figure 6.10 Comparing C_{ws}, C_s, C_{AA1} (two-state AA1), and C_{AA2}.

Figure 6.10 compares C_{ws}, C_s, C_{AA1} (two-state AA1), and C_{AA2} where the time that the MS stays in an LA is exponentially distributed. The figure indicates that for $\rho < 1$, $C_{AA2} \simeq C_{AA1} \simeq C_{ws} < C_s$ and for $\rho > 1$, $C_{AA2} \simeq C_{AA1} \simeq C_s < C_{ws}$. In other words, two-state AA1 and AA2 automatically switch to the appropriate authentication scheme, the S scheme or the WS scheme. Note that the performance of AA1 is slightly better than AA2. On the other hand, it is easier to implement AA2 than AA1.

6.3 Summary

This chapter described IS-41 intersystem handoff and authentication. TCAP message flows between MSCs for handoff-forward, handoff-backward, and handoff-to-the-third with path minimization were explained to point out the way to set up and release trunks in these types of intersystem handoffs.

Based on EIA/TIA TSB-51 [EIA93b], we discussed authentication and privacy issues. Two schemes were presented to obtain authentication information in the network. We also proposed algorithms [Lin97j, Lin97i] that make those two schemes adaptive to the user behavior.

Message flows for other applications such as call forwarding, call transfer, call waiting, conference calling, and flexible alerting are not described in this book; readers are referred to [EIA95].

6.4 Review Questions

1. What are the steps of handoff measurements in intersystem handoff?

2. What is the difference between handoff order timer (HOT) and the mobile handoff timer (MHOT)? When are these timers used?

3. In step 4.2 of the handoff backward procedure described in this chapter, the message sent from the MS to MSC A is not shown. What is this message? Add this message to the handoff backward message flow.

4. Include the MS-BS interaction in the intersystem handoff by integrating the message flow in Chapter 4, Figure 4.3, with the message flow in Figures 6.1 and 6.2.

5. Which timeout period of which timer should be longer? HTTT or HOT? Why?

6. What is the maximum elapsed time allowed to perform handoff forward? Suppose that the path minimization procedure fails at step 2, and a handoff forward procedure is exercised. What is the maximum elapsed time to perform the whole procedure?

7. Propose a different procedure to implement path minimization. What are the advantages and disadvantages of your procedure compared with the one described in IS-41?

8. Why is IS-41 registration procedure implemented with low-priority TCAP messages? Why is **HandoffMeasurementRequest** implemented with low-priority TCAP message?

9. Plot the flowcharts for the various IS-41 intersystem handoff types described in this chapter.

10. The sharing sceme may not be implemented if the HLR and the visited PSP are owned by different service providers. Why?

11. In which case would you use the without-sharing scheme for MS authentication? When would you use the sharing scheme?

12. Describe the expected results on raising or lowering the n value in the first adaptive algorithm in Section 6.2.4 (AA1) using engineering terms.

13. Why is the first adaptive algorithm (AA1) we presented more sophisticated than the second (AA2 described in Section 6.2.5)? Why is it more likely for AA2 to be implemented more often than AA1?

14. Show how to integrate the sharing authentication procedure with the registration procedure described in Chapter 5, Section 5.3.

CHAPTER 7

PACS Network Signaling

This chapter describes network signaling for the Personal Access Communications System (PACS). PACS network signaling supports basic call control, roaming, and handoff management. Traditional cellular systems such as AMPS and GSM require specific switches (MSCs), and databases (HLR, VLR) to support PCS services. PACS, in contrast, uses the Advanced Intelligent Network (AIN) protocol, where the general AIN switch and the SCP provide the flexibility to implement PCS network/service applications. With AIN, PCS-related messages for PACS are sent directly from the radio system to the AIN SCP by a sort-of "tunnel" through the AIN switch.

Figure 7.1 shows the PACS architecture, where the *portables* (the PACS term for mobile stations, represented by the pedestrians in the figure) or *fixed-access units* communicate with the network through the *radio ports* (RPs) by using an air interface called *interface A*. This interface takes the signal over the air and converts it to a wire- or fiber-transmittable signal. A group of channels (i.e., time slots) is assigned to each RP. Several RPs are connected to a *radio port control unit* (RPCU) through *interface P*, which separates the RP signal into logical channels. Also, the signal for managing radio functions at multiple RPs is separated logically from the call traffic. The RPCU provides management and control functions between the RP

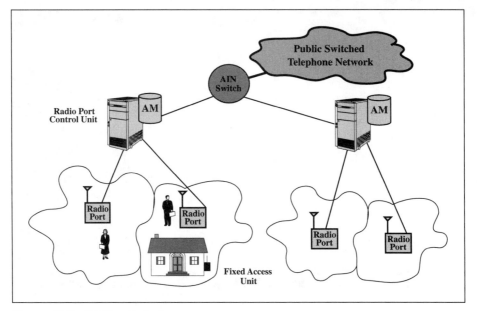

Figure 7.1   PACS architecture.

and the local exchange network. Several RPCUs are connected to a switch of the local exchange network. The *access manager* (AM) residing in the RPCU allows the RPCU to invoke ISDN features. The AM functions include:

- Radio-related service control functions, such as multiple RP management, trunking provision, and RP-to-RP link transfers.

- Nonradio-related service control functions, such as call control, switching, and routing.

Figure 7.2 illustrates the PACS network interfaces. The radio system and the switch communicate via ISDN. The switch and the SCP communicate via the AIN protocol. To be compatible with the existing SS7 network, the AIN switch and the AIN SCP communicate with the PSTN via the SS7 protocol.

The major design goal of PACS network signaling is to utilize the existing AIN network entities, such as AIN SCP and SSP. In this design, there is no need to create new entities, such as MSC, used in other PCS systems. In PACS signaling, the telephony switching functions carried out by the PSTN are separated from the PCS-related signaling carried out by the PCS system. To achieve this goal, a great effort has been devoted to the PACS design. Specifically:

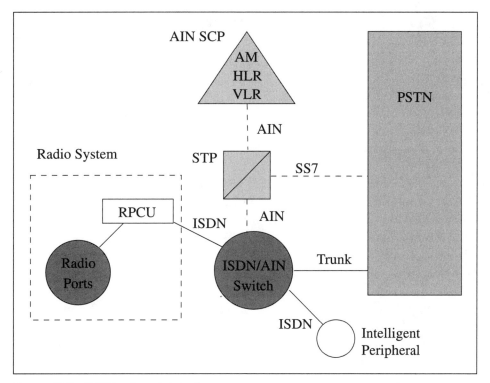

Figure 7.2 PACS network interfaces.

- Noncall-associated signaling is introduced to minimize the modifications to the AIN SSP; that is, the AIN SSP does not interpret the PCS-related or IS-41-like signaling messages.

- Many functions of the MSC have been removed from the SSP and moved to the AM and RPCU. In this chapter, AM is assumed to be colocated with VLR, and thus some of the MSC functions are moved to the VLR.

- The creation of the RPCU introduces a new kind of handoff: inter-RPCU handoff. Inter-RPCU handoff procedure may simply follow the inter-BSC handoff procedure in GSM. However, the GSM procedure requires special functionality in the MSC. In order not to affect the AIN SSP in PACS, complicated anchor-RPCU approaches have been proposed. This chapter describes a simple inter-RPCU approach that utilizes general AIN SSP features.

7.1 PACS Network Elements

This section describes the PACS network elements. The radio characteristics of PACS were described in Chapter 1, Section 1.3.4. In this chapter, we focus on the AIN/ISDN switch and the AIN SCP.

7.1.1 AIN/ISDN Switch

To support PCS application, the AIN switch is equipped with SS7, ISDN, and AIN capabilities. SS7 ISUP is used in the switch to set up the trunks in call control and intersystem handoff. The SS7 TCAP is used to support mobility management, specifically, the IS-41 protocol, and to transport AIN messages between the switch and the SCP. Tables 7.1 and 7.2 provide lists of selected SS7 and AIN messages. Refer to Chapter 5 for complete ISUP and TCAP treatments.

In addition to call control, the ISDN features are used in the switch for *automatic link transfer* (ALT) and noncall-associated signaling (to be described later). A partial list of ISDN messages is given in Table 7.3. The actions taken by these messages will be elaborated later. Two AIN features of the switch are described next:

Triggering and querying. Triggering is the process of identifying calls that need AIN handling. Querying is the process of assembling an AIN message to an AIN SCP at a trigger detection point.

Table 7.1 Selected SS7 Messages

NAME	NOTE
LocationRequest	TCAP (IS-41)
RegistrationCancellation	TCAP (IS-41)
RegistrationNotification	TCAP (IS-41)
RouteRequest	TCAP (IS-41)
ACM (address complete)	ISUP
ANM (answer)	ISUP
IAM (initial address)	ISUP
REL (release)	ISUP
RLC (release complete)	ISUP

Table 7.2 Selected AIN Messages

NAME	NOTE
Analyzed_Route	TCAP (response to Info_Collected)
Forward_Call	TCAP (response to Termination_Attempt)
Info_Collected	TCAP (Off-Hook_Delay trigger)
NCA_Data (P-ALERT)	TCAP
NCA_Data (P-ALERT-ACK)	TCAP
NCA_Data (P-CALL-ORIG)	TCAP
NCA_Data (P-CALL-ORIG-ACK)	TCAP
NCA_Data (P-DISC)	TCAP
NCA_Data (P-INFO)	TCAP
NCA_Data (P-REGNOT)	TCAP
NCA_Data (P-REGNOT-ACK)	TCAP
NCA_Data (P-RELEASE)	TCAP
NCA_Data (P-REL-COM)	TCAP
NCA_Data (RCID-ASSIGN)	TCAP
Termination_Attempt	TCAP (Termination_Attempt trigger)

ISDN/AIN Interworking. *Noncall-Associated* (NCA) signaling provides a generic method for the SCP to communicate with an ISDN-connected device through the switch. The switch essentially provides an appropriate envelope for ISDN and TCAP messages. In PACS, the RPCU communicates with VLR through the switch using NCA signaling for PCS procedures, such as registration and authentication.

Other general AIN features such as *automatic code gaping*, for traffic load control, and *automatic message accounting*, for PCS access charging, are utilized to support PCS applications.

7.1.2 AIN SCP

The AIN SCP provides the service logic, database, and operation capabilities to support HLR, VLR, AM, and other PCS databases such as the authentication center (AuC). The SCP communicates with the switch us-

Table 7.3 Selected ISDN Messages

NAME	NOTE
ALERT	
CALL-PROC (call proceeding)	
CONN (connect)	
CONN-ACK (connect acknowledgment)	
DISC (disconnect)	
FACILITY (ALT request)	
FACILITY (ALT permission)	
REGISTER (P-ALERT)	NCA (envelopNCAData5)
REGISTER (P-ALERT-ACK)	NCA (envelopNCAData)
REGISTER (P-CALL-ORIG)	NCA (envelopNCAData)
REGISTER (P-CALL-ORIG-ACK)	NCA (envelopNCAData5)
REGISTER (P-DISC)	NCA (envelopNCAData)
REGISTER (P-INFO)	NCA (envelopNCAData)
REGISTER (P-REGNOT)	NCA (envelopNCAData)
REGISTER (P-REGNOT-ACK)	NCA (envelopNCAData)
REGISTER (P-RELEASE)	NCA (envelopNCAData)
REGISTER (RCID-ASSIGN)	NCA (envelopNCAData5)
REL (release)	
REL-COM (release complete)	
SETUP	

ing AIN TCAP and the external PCS databases using the IS-41 protocol. The HLR contains a PCS application process, end-user service profiles, and accounting management capabilities. HLR-to-VLR communication is done by IS-41 protocol over SS7. The VLR mediates service requests between the HLR and the AM. The AM controls radio resources. We assume that the VLR and the AM are colocated at the same SCP; and the acronym "VLR" represents VLR/AM.

7.1.3 Intelligent Peripheral

An *intelligent peripheral* is a node that contains functions and resources such as voice announcements or the dual-tone multifrequency digit collection capabilities needed to exchange information with an end user.

The intelligent peripheral can be connected to a switch locally via an ISDN interface or remotely via the SS7 network. Intelligent peripherals may also connect to an SCP via a TCP/IP or ISDN interface. The intelligent peripheral does not play a major role in the current PACS network signaling, but it is anticipated that the intelligent peripheral will be used in PCS-related AIN services.

7.2   PACS Network Interfaces

This section describes the AIN interface, the ISDN interface, and AIN/ISDN interworking for PCS applications.

7.2.1   AIN Interface

The AIN switch and the AIN SCP are like clients and servers in the *remote procedure call* (RPC) model. During the call-processing procedure, the switch may detect the need for AIN processing at *trigger detection points* (TDPs). If so, one or more triggering actions are performed. Triggering is similar to invoking a remote procedure call. The *trigger types* are similar to the RPC procedure names. The trigger action temporarily suspends the switch call processing and launches a parameterized query to the SCP. The SCP performs actions based on the trigger type, and returns some results to the switch. The switch then resumes call processing and determines the next action, based on the results provided by the SCP.

7.2.2   ISDN Interface

Figure 7.3 shows the ISDN interface between the switch and the RPCU. The RPCU communicates with the switch via ISDN basic rate interfaces (BRIs). Every BRI consists of one D channel for signaling and two B channels for voice/data transmission. The switch provides a *terminal service profile* (TSP) for every B channel connected to RPCU. The TSP is associated with a *virtual terminal* (VT) in the RPCU during the terminal initialization process. Every TSP at the switch is assigned a *directory number* (DN) for PCS call origination/termination. Thus, the DN is associated with one VT at the RPCU.

In ISDN signaling, every message contains a common mandatory information element, referred to as the *call reference*. The call reference is unique on a signaling interface; it is used to relate the message to a

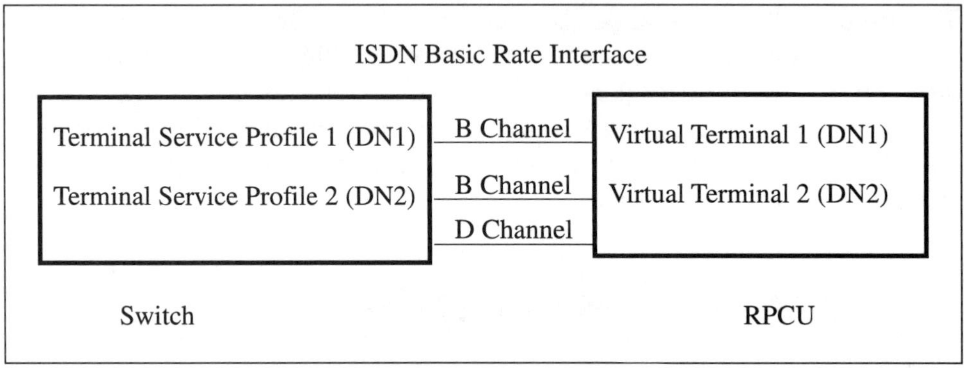

ISDN Basic Rate Interface

Terminal Service Profile 1 (DN1)	B Channel	Virtual Terminal 1 (DN1)
Terminal Service Profile 2 (DN2)	B Channel	Virtual Terminal 2 (DN2)
	D Channel	

Switch   RPCU

Figure 7.3   ISDN interface.

particular call attempt. (The ISDN messages described in this chapter are listed in Table 7.3.)

- The **ALERT** message is used to confirm the B channel selection.

- The Call Proceeding message, **CALL-PROC**, is sent from the called party to the calling party to indicate that the requested call establishment has been initiated and that no more call establishment information will be accepted.

- The Connection message, **CONN**, indicates call acceptance by the called party, and the Connection Acknowledgment message, **CONN-ACK**, indicates that the called party has been awarded the call.

- The Release message, **REL**, requests the other side to clear the B connection. Upon receipt of the **REL** message, the receiver releases the B channel and the call reference, then replies with a Release Complete message, **REL-COM**.

- The **SETUP** message is sent from the calling party to the called party to initiate call establishment.

- In PACS, the AIN switch may send the RPCU a **FACILITY** message to request permission for a handoff operation. The RPCU replies with another **FACILITY** message, to indicate whether or not the handoff request has been granted.

- The **REGISTER** messages are used for NCA signaling. Depending on the information field, the **REGISTER** messages inform the VLR (not the AIN SSP) to carry out various operations. Details of these operations will be described in later sections.

7.3 AIN/ISDN Interworking

With NCA signaling, the switch provides interworking functions between the SCP/VLR (AIN) and the RPCU (ISDN). NCA signaling is a unidirectional communication approach between RPCU and the VLR, and is used for noncall-control procedures such as PCS registration/authentication. Every NCA signaling message contains the information necessary to correlate a request and a response. The RPCU and the VLR keep track of the NCA signaling message exchanges. The ISDN messages exchanged between the switch and the RPCU are of type **REGISTER**. (The operations of the **REGISTER** message are listed in Table 7.3.) A standard ISDN **REL-COM** message sent from the switch to the RPCU is used to close the ISDN transaction. The AIN messages exchanged between the switch and the VLR are of type **NCA_Data**. (The operations of the **NCA_Data** message are listed in Table 7.2.) The switch itself does not interpret the NCA messages; it only forwards the information to the destination node. NCA signaling can be initiated by the RPCU or the VLR, as described in the next two subsections.

7.3.1 NCA Signaling Initiated by the RPCU

The RPCU initiates NCA signaling by sending an ISDN **REGISTER** message to the switch. The **REGISTER** message has a *facility information element* (FIE) to indicate that it is an INVOKE type. The operation is described in the envelopNCAData component.

When the switch receives the **REGISTER** message, it forwards the information to the VLR using an AIN **NCA_Data** message with Unidirectional package type. The component type of the TCAP message is INVOKE, as advised in the ISDN **REGISTER** message. The switch also fills the TCAP component NCAData based on envelopNCAData of the **REGISTER** message, as shown in Figure 7.4. The switch does not expect any acknowledgment from the VLR. The **NCA_Data** message will be handled by the *service logic program* (SLP) in the serving SCP of the VLR. Note that the envelopNCAData operation of the ISDN **REGISTER** messages requires a response to indicate that the switch has successfully forwarded the information to the VLR. An ISDN **REL-COM** message delivers the success/failure indication from the switch to the RPCU, which closes the call reference invoked by the **REGISTER** message. The **REL-COM** message does not return any results corresponding to the **REGISTER** request. The message flow of NCA signaling initiated by the RPCU is illustrated in Figure 7.5(a).

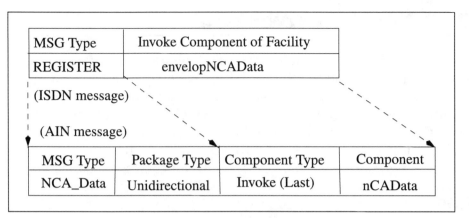

Figure 7.4 NCA message format translation (ISDN to AIN).

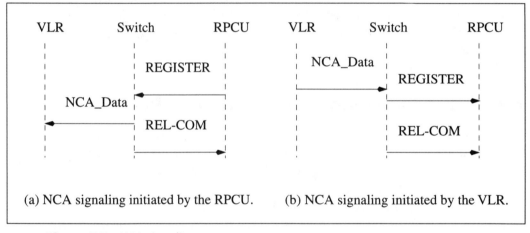

Figure 7.5 NCA signaling.

7.3.2 NCA Signaling Initiated by the VLR

The VLR initiates NCA signaling by sending an AIN **NCA_Data** message to the switch. Based on the **NCA_Data** message, the switch sends an ISDN **REGISTER** message to the RPCU. The message format translation is illustrated in Figure 7.6. The **REGISTER** message may be multicast to a group of RPCUs. After sending the **REGISTER** message, the switch also sends a **REL-COM** message without a FIE to terminate the envelopNCAData5 operation. The purpose of this message is to clear the invocation and the call reference of the **REGISTER** message. Unlike the **REL-COM** message sent in

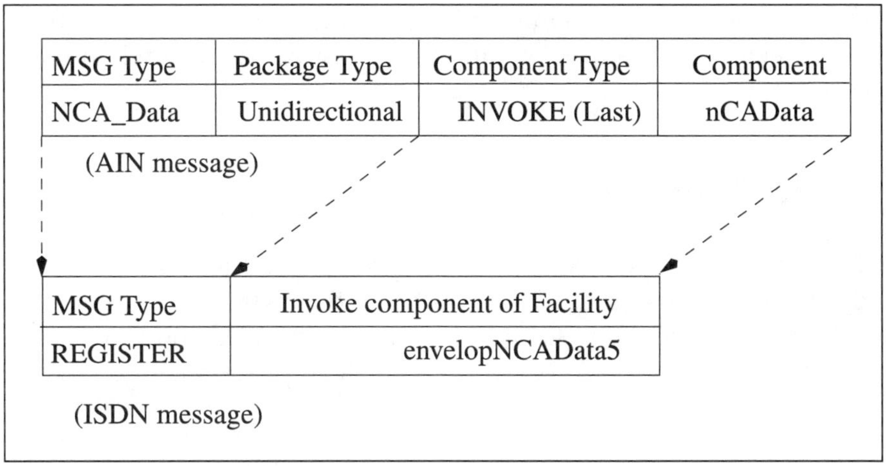

MSG Type	Package Type	Component Type	Component
NCA_Data	Unidirectional	INVOKE (Last)	nCAData

(AIN message)

MSG Type	Invoke component of Facility
REGISTER	envelopNCAData5

(ISDN message)

Figure 7.6   NCA message format translation (AIN to ISDN).

the case initiated by RPCU, this message does not provide success/failure indication of the **REGISTER** message.

The major goal of NCA signaling is to disassociate the AIN SSP from PCS-related signaling so that when the PCS signaling protocol is modified in the future, there will be no need to change the switch. To meet this goal, NCA signaling is designed with the following features:

- The AIN SSP only translates the NCA signaling messages from one format to another, that is, from ISDN to AIN or from AIN to ISDN. The SSP does not interpret the messages.

- In the ISDN interface between the AIN SSP and the RPCU, the call reference is cancelled after every ISDN NCA message so that the switch is not responsible for tracking PCS-related messages.

- In the AIN interface between the AIN SSP and the AIN SCP, the Unidirectional TCAP message format is used instead of the general AIN transaction format—the query/response TCAP format. With the query/response format, the transaction is typically associated with a timer, such as the HOT timer in Chapter 6, Section 6.1, and a timeout period must be specified at the switch. By using the Unidirectional TCAP format, no PCS-related timers need be specified at the switch.

An alternative to NCA signaling is to have the RPCUs communicate with the VLR directly. For example, the RPCUs may be connected to the VLR by a local area network (LAN) using TCP/IP. The advantage of this alternative is that the PCS-related signaling has bypassed the SSP. On the other hand, the technology to connect RPCUs and VLRs must be carefully selected. For example, the LAN solution may not be scalable when the number of RPCUs is large.

7.4   Registration

Figure 7.7 illustrates the PACS registration process. The RPCU communicates with the switch using the ISDN protocol; the switch communicates with the VLR using the AIN TCAP protocol; and the VLR communicates with the HLR using the IS-41 TCAP protocol. The process is described here:

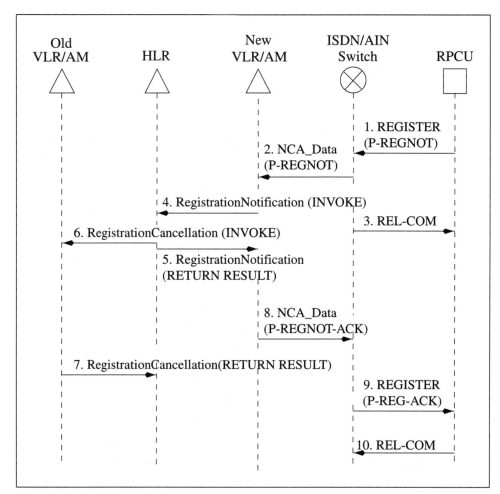

Figure 7.7   Registration process.

Steps 1–3 (registration request). When a portable sends a registration request to the RPCU, information such as the location address and authentication/security data are forwarded to the VLR via NCA signaling messages 1, 2, and 3. The VLR deciphers the portable identification and security. Then it authenticates the portable and performs the registration process. If the portable is in a location area (LA) within the VLR, the HLR is not updated. Otherwise, a message is sent to the HLR as described next.

Steps 4–7. (HLR updating). The VLR sends an IS-41 registration notification message (message 4) to the HLR. The HLR updates the portable location record. The HLR may deny the registration, for example, if the portable has an overdue account. An acknowledgment (message 5) is sent to the VLR to indicate the completion of the HLR update process. A registration cancellation message (message 6) is sent to the old VLR to remove the resource allocated to this portable.

Steps 8–10. (completion of registration). The VLR informs the RPCU of the completion of the registration procedure by NCA signaling messages 8, 9, and 10. These messages may include information such as the identifier, to correlate the VLR and the RPCU and the Alert_ID. The RPCU will pass the Alert_ID to the portable, which is used in the PACS air interface for portable paging.

Note that the portable is authenticated at the VLR, which is different from IS-41 where the authentication is done at the AuC after the HLR is accessed, as described in Chapter 6, Section 6.2. Sharing confidential data in the VLR for authentication may not be an appropriate approach, especially when the VLRs belong to different service providers.

7.5   Call Origination

The following sections describe PACS call setup control. Call release procedures are straightforward, and the reader is referred to Bellcore (Telcordia) GR-2801 for details. Figure 7.8 illustrates the message flow for call origination, which consists of the following three steps:

Step 1. (portable authentication). When a portable requests a call origination, the RPCU selects an idle initialized virtual terminal (and, therefore, a B channel). The RPCU then passes call-related information such as user authentication/security information, radio

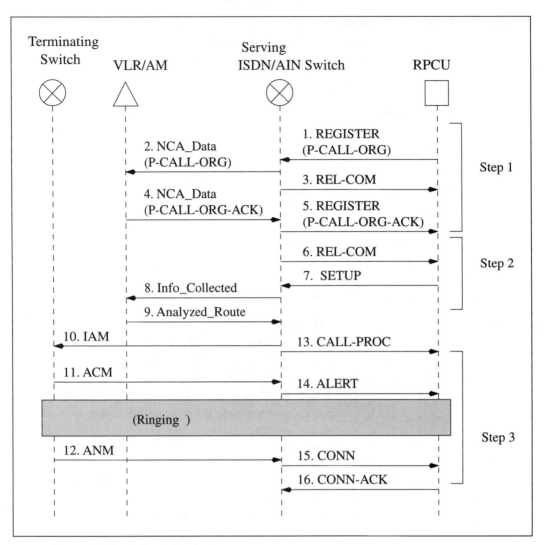

Figure 7.8 Call origination process.

resource and encryption information, the selected interface DN, and so on, to the VLR via NCA signaling messages 1, 2, and 3. The VLR authenticates the portable and returns the result to the RPCU via NCA signaling messages 4, 5, and 6.

Step 2. (service validation). The RPCU includes a progress indicator in the ISDN **SETUP** message (message 7) to inform the serving switch that the caller is not ISDN. The Mobile Identification Number (MIN) is provided in the **SETUP** message, and is not screened by the serving switch. When the serving switch receives the **SETUP** message, it encounters the OffHook_Delay trigger which is assigned on per TSP-basis. The AIN **Info_Collected** (message 8) and **Analyzed_Route** (message 9) messages are exchanged between the serving switch and the VLR. These messages are used for service validation purposes such as verifying that the calling MIN may be delivered to the called party. If the called party is a portable, then the call will retrigger this process at the serving switch to obtain a routable address.

Step 3. (call setup). The serving switch and the terminating switch exchange the ISUP **IAM** (Initial Address) and **ACM** (Address Complete) messages, messages 10 and 11, to set up the trunk connection. The serving switch sends a **CALL-PROC** (Call Proceeding) message (message 13) to the RPCU to indicate that the call setup is in progress. After the serving switch receives the **ACM** message, the serving switch alerts the RPCU using the ISDN **ALERT** message (message 14) to confirm B channel selection. The network then provides audible ringing. After the called party answers, an ISUP **ANM** (Answer) message is sent from the terminating switch to the serving switch, and an ISDN **CONN** (Connect) message is sent from the serving switch to the RPCU (see messages 12, 15, and 16), which stops audible ringing, allowing the conversation to start.

In this call origination procedure, portable authentication at step 1 is separated from the service verification at step 2. Although NCA signaling at step 1 also assists in finding an ISDN BRI and an interface DN for call setup, it would be more efficient if steps 1 and 2 were combined, and if NCA signaling at step 1 was eliminated.

7.6 Call Termination

Figure 7.9 illustrates the call termination process. The call originates at an AIN switch. We assume that the serving SCP of the originating switch is colocated with the HLR. Otherwise, the HLR and the serving SCP need to communicate via IS-41 **LocationRequest** messages. The process consists of these two steps:

Step 1. When the MIN is dialed, the originating switch detects the Info_Analyzed trigger, and an **Info_Analyzed** message (message 1) is sent to the serving SCP, and thus the HLR, to query the routable address for the destination portable. The HLR sends an

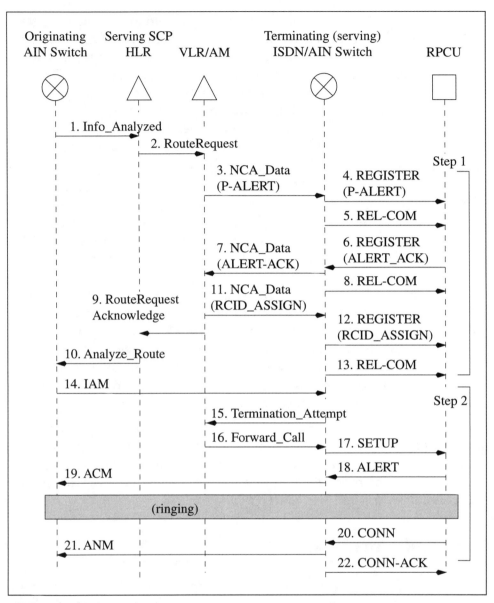

Figure 7.9 Call termination process.

IS-41 **RouteRequest** (INVOKE) message (message 2) to the VLR.
The VLR sends the **P-ALERT** information to a group of RPCUs
via NCA signaling messages 3, 4, and 5. The Alert_ID of the
portable is broadcast. Once the portable replies, the corresponding RPCU selects an interface DN and an initialized virtual

terminal to accommodate the call. The RPCU acknowledges the VLR alerting action by NCA signaling messages 6, 7, and 8.

After portable authentication, the VLR sends the RPCU radio call ID assignment (RCID_ASSIGN) through messages 11, 12, and 13 to provide the session key and other information necessary to establish the call. In parallel, the VLR sends an IS-41 RouteRequest (RETURN RESULT) (message 9) with a routable address to the HLR. The routable address is forwarded to the originating switch by message 10.

Step 2. This step is similar to step 3 of the call origination procedure in Figure 7.8, with two exceptions. First, the Termination_Attempt trigger is detected when the terminating switch receives the IAM message (message 14) with a routable address. Based on the routable address, the serving switch obtains the interface DN from the VLR by the exchange of messages 15 and 16. An alternative to this approach is that the VLR sends the interface DN directly to the HLR, then the originating switch in messages 9 and 10. In this case, there is no need for the Termination_Attempt trigger, and the exchange of messages 15 and 16 is not performed. Second, after the RPCU receives the ISDN SETUP message (message 17) the portable is paged again to establish the radio link. When the portable replies, the RPCU informs the serving switch by sending an ISDN CONN message (message 20), which stops the audible ring tone.

In the PACS call termination procedure, the portable is paged twice. In IS-41 or GSM, the portable is paged only once at step 2, because the paging mechanism is very expensive in these systems. On the other hand, double paging in PACS is justified because the PACS air interface provides an efficient paging mechanism, and the paging cost is insignificant. The advantage of double paging is that if the called party (the portable) is not available, the situation is detected at step 1 of Figure 7.9; step 2 is not executed to avoid the extra trunk setup overhead.

7.7 Intersystem Handoff

PACS intersystem handoff or automatic link transfer (ALT) follows the IS-41 anchor switch approach described in Chapter 6, Section 6.1. Figure 7.10 shows the call path before and after intersystem handoff. (The inter-RPCU handoff will be described briefly at the end of this section. Other types

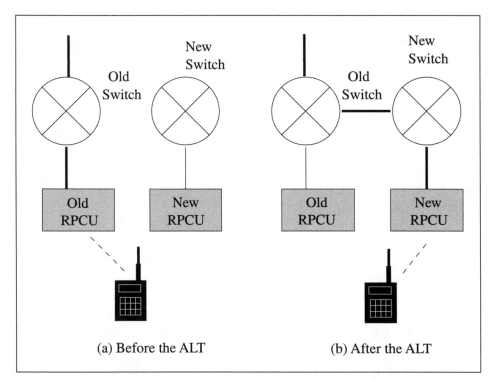

(a) Before the ALT

(b) After the ALT

Figure 7.10 Trunk connection before and after intersystem handoff.

of PACS handoffs were described in Chapter 4.) The message flow of the PACS intersystem handoff procedure is illustrated in Figure 7.11, which consists of the following three steps:

Step 1. The portable sends an ALT request to the new RPCU. The RPCU sends an ISDN **SETUP** message to the new switch to indicate the ALT request. Information such as the DN used by the old RPCU and, optionally, the new DN and the B channel are included in the message. The new switch identifies the ALT request and disables the AIN Off-Hook_Delay trigger. Note that this stage does not involve the VLR. Based on the received old DN, the serving switch determines that it is an intersystem handoff. If the ALT call is accepted, the serving switch replies with an ISDN **CALL-PROC** message (message 2) to the RPCU to establish the B-channel connection. The new switch then sends the old switch an ISUP **IAM** message (message 3) to set up the trunk for the ALT request using the old DN as the called party number and the new DN as the calling party number.

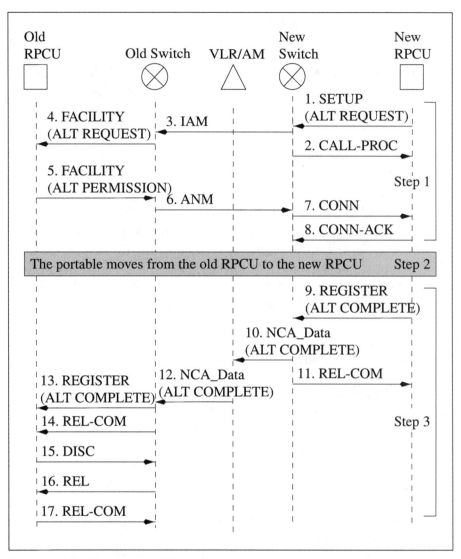

Figure 7.11 Intersystem ALT procedure.

From the IAM message, the old switch identifies the ALT request. Based on the old DN given in the IAM message, the old switch forwards the ALT request to the old RPCU by an ISDN FACILITY message (message 4). If the ALT request is accepted, the old RPCU sends an ISDN FACILITY message (message 5) to provide encryption and other information for the ALT.

The old switch bridges the ALT call into the original call and confirms the trunk setup between the old switch and the new switch by sending an ISUP **ANM** message (message 6) to the new switch. The message also includes PCS-related information such as encryption. The new switch forwards the PCS-related information to the new RPCU by the ISDN **CONN** message (message 7). The RPCU replies with a **CONN-ACK** (Connect Acknowledgment, message 8) to the new switch to confirm the connection of the B channel.

Step 2. The new RPCU asks the portable to transfer to the new radio channel.

Step 3. The new RPCU informs VLR of the ALT completion by NCA signaling through messages 9, 10, and 11. The VLR updates the portable information and informs old RPCU of the ALT completion by NCA signaling messages 12, 13, and 14. Upon receipt of the ALT completion message, the old RPCU and the old switch disconnect the B channel by exchanging the ISDN **DISC/REL/REL-COM** messages (messages 15, 16, and 17).

The addition of RPCUs in the PACS architecture introduces inter-RPCU handoff, which occurs when a communicating portable moves from the RP of a RPCU to the RP of another RPCU, where both the new and the old RPCUs connect to the same switch.

To minimize the impact of inter-RPCU handoff on the AIN SSP, two anchor-RPCU handoff approaches have been proposed. In the *switch loopback* approach, shown in Figures 7.12(a) and (b), the old RPCU dials the new RPCU to make the connection through the switch. For the AIN switch, the action is similar to an ordinary call from the old RPCU to the new RPCU. The disadvantage is that the handoff consumes two more links between the switch and the RPCUs. In the *direct connect* approach, illustrated in Figures 7.12(a) and (c), the RPCUs are connected with trunks. Thus, the handoff is performed without involving the switch. The disadvantage is that extra trunks are required to connect the RPCUs, and an inter-RPCU handoff protocol is required between the RPCUs. A third alternative to inter-RPCU handoff is illustrated in Figures 7.12(a), (d), and (e). The idea is to utilize the existing three-way calling facility of the AIN switch. During the handoff, the old RPCU issues a three-way calling request to connect to the new RPCU, as shown in Figure 7.12(d). After the three-way connection is established, and the portable has moved to the new RPCU, the old RPCU disconnects. For the switch, this operation is just like a normal one-party disconnection in a three-way calling, as shown in Figure 7.12(e). Unlike the anchor approaches, this approach requires

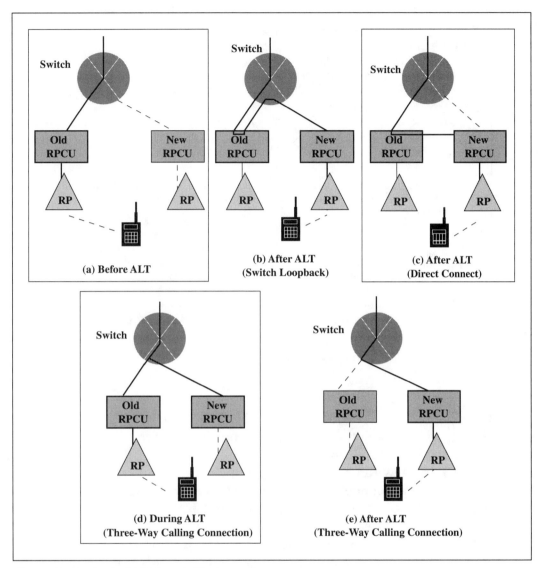

Figure 7.12 Inter-RPCU handoff approaches.

only minor modifications to the RPCU. Additionally, this solution does not consume extra trunks.

7.8   Feature Interactions

In this section, we consider call waiting as an example to illustrate the feature interactions between PCS and existing telephone services.

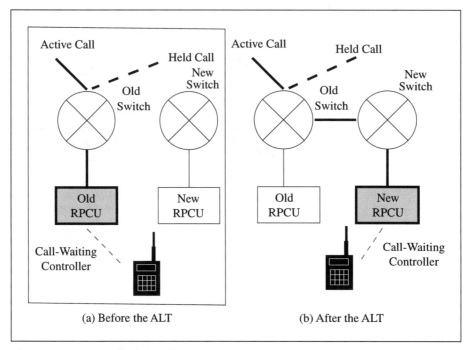

Figure 7.13   ALT during call waiting.

Consider that an ALT occurs when call waiting is active. Figure 7.13 shows the call path for both the active and the held calls before and after the ALT. Before the ALT, the old RPCU is the call-waiting controller. At the end of the ALT, the new RPCU is the call-waiting controller. Both the active and the held calls are connected to the old switch after the ALT. The new RPCU will control the old switch via the new switch to perform call-waiting commands requested by the portable.

   In PACS, the ALT has precedence over call waiting. Thus, during the ALT, the RPCU may delay the call-waiting commands from the portable, or it may reject these commands.

7.9   Summary

Based on [Lin97d], this chapter described PACS network signaling, which supports basic call control, roaming, and handoff management. Details of the PACS radio system is beyond the scope of this book, but can be found in [JTC95, Noe96a].

One of the distinguishing features of PACS is that the Advanced Intelligent Network (AIN) protocol is used, and the general AIN switch and the service control point (SCP) provide the flexibility to implement PCS network/service applications. The PACS radio system connects to a general AIN switch instead of to the specific mobile switching centers used in other cellular systems such as AMPS and GSM. The reader is referred to [Lin97b] for AIN details. In the PACS design, involvement of the AIN switch in most PCS-related features has been minimized. For example, PCS-related messages are sent directly from the RPCU to the AIN SCP by a sort-of "tunnel" through the AIN switch. It is apparent that features such as call setup/release [Bel94d] and intersystem handoff must be built into the AIN switches. In PACS, these features are implemented without modification to the platform of the AIN switch. For PACS inter-RPCU handoff, a performance comparison between switch loopback and direct connect is given in [Lin96a].

The PACS design illustrates a new approach to interconnect the radio system with the PSTN via general AIN switches. However, extra network traffic will be created by the NCA signaling. The performance of PACS network signaling is an open issue for future investigation. The reader is referred to [Bel94d] for a complete treatment of the PACS signaling. A tutorial for PACS radio system can be found in [Noe96b].

7.10 Review Questions

1. Describe the PACS architecture and the network interfaces.

2. What are the functions of the access manager in the PACS network?

3. In which parts of PACS network signaling does ISDN play an important role?

4. To what does noncall-associated signaling refer? Why is it used in PACS?

5. What is the AIN node called that is responsible for voice announcements?

6. What are the main steps in the PACS call origination process?

7. From which procedure can the automatic link transfer procedure be derived?

8. Performance study in [Lin96a] investigated the inter-RPCU handoff in PACS. The study indicated that if users exhibit locality of move-

ment, the switch loopback method is better. Otherwise, the direct connect method should be considered. What is the intuition behind this conclusion?

9. Suppose that VLR/AM and RPCU in PACS are connected directly through TCP/IP. Design the registration procedure for this configuration.

Cellular Digital Packet Data

Cellular digital packet data (CDPD) offers mobile users access to a low-cost, ubiquitous, wireless data network. CDPD can be overlaid on AMPS and IS-136 systems and share its infrastructure equipment on a noninterfering basis. Although it can be assigned to a dedicated RF channel, CDPD's distinctiveness is that it transmits packet data over idle cellular voice channels, and automatically switches to another channel when the current channel is about to be assigned for voice usage. CDPD does not communicate with the underlying cellular network. However, CDPD takes advantage of its knowledge of channel assignment algorithms for cellular system, and predicts the channels available for CDPD use.

CDPD may serve as the wireless extension to a public switched data network or other data networks such as the Internet. It supports *connectionless network services* (CLNS) where every packet, called a *network protocol data unit* (NPDU), is routed individually based on the destination address of the packet and knowledge of the current network topology. Initially, CDPD provides two CLNSs: the standard OSI *connectionless network protocol* and the *Internet protocol*.

This chapter describes the CDPD architecture and protocols, as well as its potential service applications. We provide abstract views of some important features of the CDPD medium access control layer, the mobile data-link protocol layer, and the network layer.

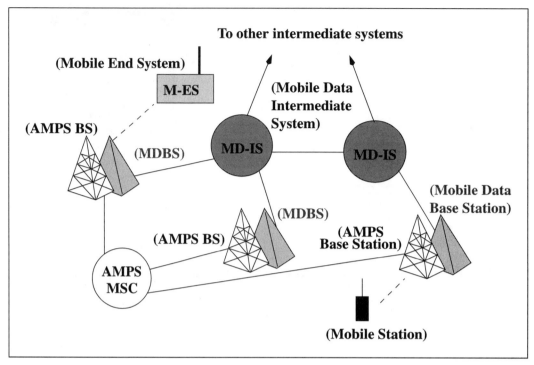

Figure 8.1 The CDPD network reference model.

8.1 CDPD Architecture

There are two basic classes of network entities in the CDPD network:

- End system (ES)
- Intermediate system (IS)

For our purposes, we consider only the mobile parts of the network. That is, we only consider the *mobile end systems* (M-ESs) and the *mobile data intermediate systems* (MD-ISs). Figure 8.1 illustrates the CDPD network reference model.

8.1.1 Mobile End System (M-ES)

A CDPD user communicates with the CDPD network by using the M-ES. Though the physical location of M-ESs may change from time to time, continuous network access is maintained. An M-ES may be a credit card verification unit installed in a taxi, a *personal digital assistant* (PDA), or a CDPD modem for personal computer, palmtop, or laptop, which

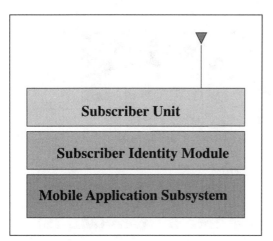

Figure 8.2   Mobile end station architecture.

incorporates a cellular transceiver in a palm-sized, serially connected unit to a PC. The M-ES consists of three parts, as shown in Figure 8.2:

- *Subscriber unit*, used to access the radio interface.
- *Subscriber identity module*, which contains information to identify a subscriber.
- *Mobile application subsystem*, which provides the M-ES application functionality, and can be a personal computer or a simple data gathering/telemetric tool.

8.1.2   Mobile Database Station (MDBS)

The MDBS is responsible for detailed control of the radio interface, such as radio channel allocation, interoperation with cellular voice channel usage, and radio media access control. As shown in Figure 8.3, an MDBS consists of several modem-transceivers, each of which supports one channel pair. The user data received by the modem-transceiver are processed by control computers before being delivered to the MD-IS. In order to share radio resources with the cellular system, MDBSs are expected to be colocated with the cell site transceivers that provide cellular telephone service. MDBSs may also share other cell site hardware, such as antennas to communicate with the M-ESs. M-ESs can communicate only with the outside world through MDBSs; there is no direct communication path between M-ESs. Because of a short 2-bit synchronization delay between the MDBS and the M-ES, the radius of a CDPD is typically limited to less than 10 miles.

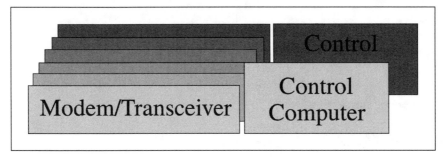

Figure 8.3   Mobile database station architecture.

8.1.3   Mobile Data-Intermediate System (MD-IS)

An MD-IS connects to several MDBSs via wired links (e.g., multiple DS0 trunks) or via microwave. The MD-IS consists of a frame relay switch, a packet router, and a workstation. It receives data from one network entity and forwards it to another network entity. The MD-IS supports user mobility by operating a CDPD-specific *mobile network location protocol* to maintain location information for CDPD users.

8.2   CDPD Air Interface

An M-ES communicates with an MDBS via a 19.2 Kbps raw duplex wireless link, referred to as a *CDPD channel stream*. A CDPD channel stream can be accessed simultaneously by several M-ESs. CDPD channel streams use idle cellular RF channels to transmit data to and from M-ESs. However, CDPD systems are designed to use idle cellular capacity without direct communication with the cellular system. A strict requirement of CDPD is that CDPD transmission must not interfere with cellular voice calls. We will describe how this goal is achieved in the following sections.

The link from the MDBS to the M-ES is called the *forward link*; the link from the M-ES to the MDBS is called the *reverse link*. The MD-IS queues all frames, and sends them to the corresponding MDBS for transmission on the forward link. The MDBS broadcasts frames in its radio coverage area. Thus, the transmission on the forward link is contentionless. Only M-ESs that have valid *network entity identifiers* (NEIs) can decode the received data.

CDPD follows the traditional *slotted, nonpersistent digital sense multiple access* (DSMA) protocol for the reverse link access. The protocol works as follows: On the forward link, an MDBS broadcasts the availability of the reverse link by an idle/busy control flag. If there are no transmissions on the reverse channel, the MDBS sets the control flag "idle." Upon detecting the idle status, an M-ES may transmit the data on the reverse link. If the M-ES detects a "busy" status, it waits for a random period of time, then rechecks the status of the control flag. It is possible that two M-ESs detect the "idle" status, and try to access the reverse link at the same time. In this case, a collision occurs and the M-ESs follow an exponential backoff procedure for retransmission.

A single M-ES may repeatedly transmit long bursts. To prevent this *channel-hogging* situation, a minimum time period is defined between two bursts by one M-ES to ensure that other M-ESs have a fair opportunity to access the reverse link.

When an M-ES in communication moves from one cell to another, a radio link transfer process is required to reconnect the M-ES in the new cell. The CDPD link transfer process is controlled by the M-ES. The M-ES monitors the radio link quality. If the quality falls below the predefined thresholds for the radio signal strength and error rates, the M-ES initiates link transfer by searching for a better quality channel from a list of available channels broadcast by the MDBSs. The M-ES tunes to the new channel and informs the new MDBS that it has entered the cell. The new MD-IS updates its *registration directory* (to be elaborated later) so that the future data for the M-ES are directed to the current cell. If the old MDBS and the new MDBS connect to different MD-ISs, transport layer retransmission is required to reestablish the end-to-end connection.

Sleep mode is provided in CDPD to allow an idle M-ES to shut off power for a predefined period. To "wake up" the M-ES, the MD-IS periodically broadcasts a notification message to provide the list of M-ESs that are recipients of the frames queued in the MD-IS. The M-ES periodically activates its receiver to listen to the broadcast notification message. If its name is found in the list, the M-ES leaves sleep mode and sends a notification message to the MD-IS. With this mechanism, the battery life of the M-ES can be extended. Sleep mode operation is requested during the *temporary equipment identifier* (TEI) assignment procedure. Within the serving area of an MD-IS, each M-ES requests a TEI to become a legal client. The TEI will be contained in every frame transmitted on the channel stream. During the TEI assignment phase, the value of the *element inactivity timer* (T203) is negotiated by the ID Request messages. A zero value of T203 implies no sleep mode operation by this M-ES. The default value is 30 seconds. Both the MD-IS and the M-ES maintain T203 timers. The M-ES triggers T203 at the end of a frame transmission on the reverse link, and the MD-IS starts the corresponding T203 timer upon receipt of the reverse frame from the M-ES. If no frame is transmitted before both T203 timers expire, the sleep management procedures are executed at both the M-ES and the MD-IS.

The MD-IS maintains a *TEI notification timer* (T204) for each channel stream. The MD-IS broadcasts a TEI notification frame when T204 expires. This frame contains the TEI values of the M-ESs that have pending frames in the MD-IS. Even if no sleeping M-ES is using the channel stream, the TEI notification frame is sent to allow all M-ESs to synchronize with the T204 timer. A recommended T204 value is 60 seconds.

Each sleeping M-ES should wake up during the TEI notification message broadcast time. If the TEI value of the M-ES is not in the notification message, it simply reenters sleep mode. Otherwise, after the M-ES exits sleep mode it sends a Receiver Ready (RR) frame to notify the MD-IS that it is ready to receive the pending frames. If the MD-IS does not receive an RR frame from the sleeping M-ES, it triggers the corresponding T204 again. The selection of T203 and T204 values affects CDPD performance. A large T204 value and a small T203 value can effectively reduce the power consumption, but at the cost of degrading the frame transmission performance—more lost frames, longer frame waiting times, and larger waiting time variance.

8.3   Radio Resource Allocation

With *channel sniffing* and *channel hopping*, CDPD allows M-ESs to use idle voice channels without interrupting the cellular system. The concept is described shortly. An MDBS periodically scans the channels within its radio coverage area and generates a candidate list of available channels for CDPD traffic. This list is then forwarded to the MD-IS. The MD-IS collects channel lists from all the associated MDBSs, and determines the CDPD channel streams based on its knowledge of the voice channel allocation algorithm.

During the monitoring phase, the MDBS determines the availability of channels in two ways. If a communication link between the cellular system and the CDPD system exists, information about voice channel usage can be obtained directly from the cellular system. If such a communication link does not exist, the MDBS detects channel usage through the cellular transmission path by using a forward power monitor called a *sniffer*. Since every cell may contain as many as 60 voice channels, it is critical that the MDBS find the available channels in real time.

With the channel monitoring mechanism, the MDBS should be able to change channels before a voice assignment is made on the current CDPD channel. This action should be completed in 40 msec. When the MDBS detects that the CDPD channel is about to be assigned for a voice call by the cellular system, it performs an *emergency*, or *forced hop*, by switching the channel without informing its M-ESs. When an M-ES loses contact with the forward link, it searches the likely hop channel list broadcast earlier by the MDBS to reestablish the radio link.

The MDBS may periodically perform channel switching called *timed hop* or *planned hop* to avoid *channel sealing* or *channel stealing*. When the cellular system notices interference on a channel, the channel is sealed and becomes unavailable to a voice user. Since the cellular system cannot recognize CDPD, it may seal a channel used by CDPD, preventing the channel from being used by cellular users. If so, CDPD *steals* the channel from the cellular network, which violates the rule that CDPD should not affect the voice system. To avoid stealing a CDPD channel, the MDBS uses timed hops to switch a CDPD channel stream periodically, where the hop period is of the order of 10 seconds. In a timed hop, the MDBS broadcasts a control message to all M-ESs using the channel, instructing them to move to a new channel if one is available. Channel hopping will not be performed if dedicated channels are assigned for CDPD use.

In the timed hop mechanism, a *dwell timer* is defined for each shared RF channel to specify the period that the CDPD channel stream can use the RF channel before a timed hop is performed. On the expiration of this timer, the MDBS invokes the planned hop procedure to switch the CDPD channel stream to another RF channel. Specifically, the MDBS sends a switch channel message to the M-ESs of the CDPD channel stream through the old RF channel. Then it ceases transmission on the channel stream and tunes to the new frequency within 40 msec. The shared RF channels are also configured using a *layoff timer*. After a planned hop, the released RF channel cannot be used for CDPD before its layoff timer expires. This timer prevents a blacked-out CDPD channel stream from selecting an RF channel just released by another CDPD stream (i.e., whose dwell timer has just expired).

Consider a CDPD MDBS that shares RF channels with a cellular BS. The maximum number of RF channels that can be simultaneously used by the CDPD channel streams is $N_{CDPD} \leq N$ where N is the number of RF channels in a BS. When the dwell timer of a CDPD channel stream expires, the utilized RF channel is released. This RF channel will not be used by CDPD until its layoff timer expires. The CDPD channel stream then hops to another idle RF channel. If no such channel exists, the CDPD channel stream is blacked out. In some implementations, the CDPD channel stream may keep the old RF channel if no other RF channel is available. When a voice conversation is complete, there are two possibilities: If the number of CDPD channel streams is less than N_{CDPD} and the layoff timer of the RF channel has already expired, the released RF channel is assigned to a blacked-out CDPD channel stream; otherwise, the RF channel is returned to the idle channel pool. When the layoff timer of the RF channel expires, the system checks if the number of CDPD channel streams is less than N_{CDPD}. If so, this idle RF channel is assigned to a CDPD channel stream that had been blacked out.

The effects of T_d (the dwell time), T_l (the layoff time), and N_{CDPD} (the maximum number of CDPD channel streams) on the output measures (i.e., P_b representing the voice-call blocking probability and A_v representing CDPD channel availability) are described as follows:

- If T_d is sufficiently large, increasing T_d degrades P_b without improving A_v.

- If the call arrival rate λ is sufficiently small, increasing T_l significantly degrades A_v without improving P_b.

- If T_l is sufficiently large, increasing T_l degrades A_v without improving P_b.

- If the sniffer mechanism is effective, then P_b can be significantly improved without degrading A_v.

These observations indicate that the dwell and layoff timers should not be engineered at large values, and that an efficient sniffer is essential to good CDPD performance.

8.4 Roaming Management

CDPD roaming management is achieved by two functions: the *mobile home function* (MHF) and the *mobile serving function* (MSF).

An M-ES is identified by a distinct NEI. Every NEI is associated with a home MD-IS. The home MD-IS maintains a *location directory* to record the address of the current serving MD-IS for each of its homed M-ESs. This procedure is called the *location directory service* in the MHF. The M-ES may roam away from its home MD-IS and visit other MD-IS. The visited MD-IS maintains a registration directory to keep track of all visiting M-ESs. This procedure is called the *registration directory service* in the MSF.

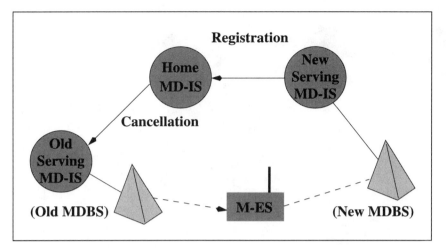

Figure 8.4   Location registration procedure.

Location registration. From the channel stream, an M-ES identifies its location, which is the address of the serving MD-IS. When the M-ES moves to another serving area, it registers at the registration directory of the current serving MD-IS via the registration service in the MSF. This MD-IS then notifies the home MD-IS of the current location of the M-ES, and the location directory of the home MD-IS is updated using the registration service in the home MHF. The home MD-IS then sends a message to the old serving MD-IS to delete the M-ES record of the registration directory in the old MD-IS. The location registration procedure is illustrated in Figure 8.4.

NPDU forwarding. To route an NPDU to an M-ES, the NPDU is first routed to the home MD-IS according to the NEI of the M-ES, as shown in step 1, Figure 8.5. If the M-ES is not in the home area, the address of the current serving MD-IS of the M-ES is identified in the location directory. The NPDU is then encapsulated and tunneled to the current serving MD-IS, as shown in step 2, Figure 8.5. This process is referred to as the *redirection and forwarding service* in the MHF at the home MD-IS. Note that encapsulation encloses the data within an NPDU inside another NPDU header. This process is also known as tunneling, since it can be used to hide the original NPDU header information during delivery to the new NPDU destination specified in the encapsulated NPDU. As shown in step 3 of Figure 8.5, upon receipt of the forwarded NPDU, the current serving MD-IS decapsulates the NPDU and routes

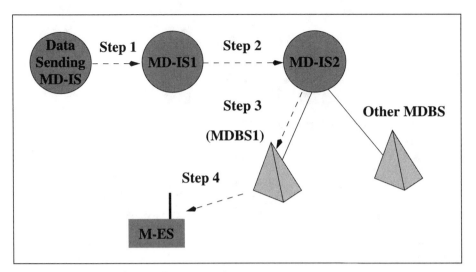

Figure 8.5 NPDU forwarding procedure.

it to the cell where the M-ES resides. This process is called the *readdress service* in the MSF at the serving MD-IS.

8.5 Summary

Both the CDPD application and the manufacturing technologies are well developed. Practical customer applications and markets have been identified. Several CDPD applications under consideration are:

Location-related services. The MD-IS is able to track an M-ES because the identifier of the MDBS where the M-ES resides is stored in the MD-IS as part of the registration or link transfer procedures. Location information can be used for services such as electronic road map, emergency service (e.g., E911), and M-ES/vehicle theft recovery. If an M-ES or a vehicle where the M-ES is mounted is reported stolen, the CDPD network can send a query message to the M-ES, asking the M-ES to report its current location for police usage. Some applications may deliver different messages to an M-ES based on its current location, for example, to provide the nearest restaurant location to the CDPD user.

Broadcast service. Since the MDBS communicates with M-ESs through broadcasting, broadcast services add little implementation complexity to CDPD compared with its wireline counterparts. Examples of the broadcast services are news report, weather, and traffic advisories.

Other transaction-type services. Several obvious CDPD services include:

- Credit card verification, especially for businesses that are mobile by nature, such as taxi services.

- Job dispatch services, for example, for field service, maintenance, or taxis.

- Messaging services, such as e-mail, voice mail, reply to incoming mail, and bidirectional paging.

For further reading about CDPD, the reader is referred to [Tay97, CDP95, Paw94, Mas94, Sre96b], and [Qui93]. The default values of CDPD timers are described in [Sre96b]. Performance studies of CDPD can be found in [Bud95, Jai94a, Tsa99, Nan95]. Specifically, effects of timed hop and emergency hop can be found in [Lin99d, Chu98]. A comprehensive comparison between CDPD and circuit switched data is given in [Sur95].

8.6 Review Questions

1. What are the main architecture entities in a CDPD network? What is the major concept behind CDPD in terms of using cellular radio resource?

2. How does DSMA work in CDPD?

3. How does CDPD sleep mode work? Compare it with GSM sleep mode.

4. What is the TEI notification timer used for?

5. To prevent the channel hogging situation, a minimum time period is defined between two bursts by one M-ES to ensure that other M-ESs have a fair opportunity to access the reverse link. Design a model to investigate how the length of this minimum time period affects the performance of CDPD. (What are the output measures?) Also, design an adaptive algorithm to dynamically adjust this minimum time period. What are the factors that trigger the adjustment in your design?

6. CDPD utilizes the sleep mode mechanism to conserve the power of mobile end systems (M-ESs). A large T204 value and a small T203 value can effectively reduce the power consumption at the cost of

degrading the frame transmission performance (more lost frames, longer frame waiting times, and larger waiting variance). Design an adaptive algorithm that can dynamically adjust the T203 and T204 based on the data traffic.

7. To what does the term channel stealing refer? Why is it important to avoid this phenomenon?

8. What are planned hop and emergency hop? What are dwell time and layoff time?

9. How does NPDU routing work?

10. Who are the potential subscribers to CDPD services?

11. In many CDPD networks, dedicated RF channels are reserved for CDPD services. This approach avoids complex mechanisms such as timed hop and emergency hop. If you are an AMPS/CDPD operator, will you take this approach?

GSM System Overview

Global System for Mobile Communications (GSM) is a digital wireless network standard designed by standardization committees from major European telecommunications operators and manufacturers. The GSM standard provides a common set of compatible services and capabilities to all mobile users across Europe and several million customers worldwide. The basic requirements of GSM have been described in five aspects:

Services. The system will provide service portability; that is, mobile stations (MSs) or mobile phones can be used in all participating countries. The system will offer services that exist in the wireline network, as well as services specific to mobile communications. In addition to vehicle-mounted stations, the system will provide service to MSs used by pedestrians and/or onboard ships.

Quality of services and security. The quality for voice telephony of GSM will be at least as good as the previous analog systems over the practical operating range. The system will be capable of offering information encryption without significantly affecting the costs to users who do not require such facility.

Radio frequency utilization. The system will permit a high level of spectrum efficiency and state-of-the-art subscriber facilities. The system will be capable of operating in the entire allocated frequency band, and coexist with the earlier systems in the same frequency band.

Network. The identification and numbering plans will be based on relevant ITU recommendations. An international standardized signaling system will be used for switching and mobility management. The existing fixed public networks should not be significantly modified.

Cost. The system parameters will be chosen with a view to limiting the cost of the complete system, in particular the MSs.

This chapter provides an overview of the GSM system. We first introduce the GSM architecture, then give details of the radio interface in the architecture. We discuss how the locations of the MSs are tracked, and how phone calls are delivered to these MSs in a GSM network. Finally, we describe the security and data service aspects of GSM.

9.1 GSM Architecture

Figure 9.1 illustrates the GSM architecture. In this architecture, a *mobile station* (MS) communicates with a *base station system* (BSS) through the *radio interface*. The BSS is connected to the *network and switching subsystem* (NSS) by communicating with a *mobile switching center* (MSC) using the *A interface*.

9.1.1 Mobile Station

The MS consists of two parts: the *subscriber identity module* (SIM) and the *mobile equipment* (ME). In a broader definition, the MS also includes a third part called *terminal equipment* (TE), which can be a PDA or PC connected to the ME. In this case, the first two parts (i.e., ME and SIM) are called the *mobile terminal* (MT). An SIM can be:

- A smart card, usually the size of a credit card
- A smaller-sized "plug-in SIM"
- A smart card that can be perforated, which contains a plug-in SIM that can be broken out of it

The SIM is protected by a *personal identity number* (PIN) between four to eight digits in length. The PIN is initially loaded by the network operator at the subscription time. This PIN can be deactivated or changed by the

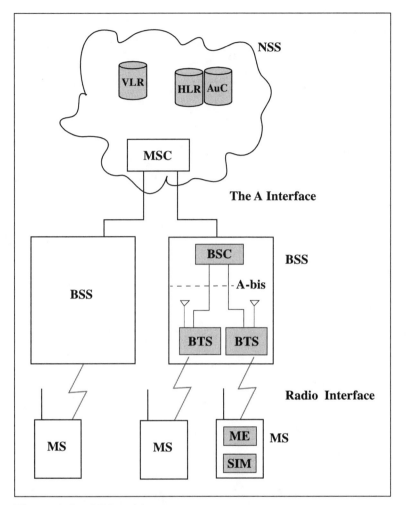

Figure 9.1 GSM architecture.

user. To use the MS, the user is asked to enter the PIN. If the number is not correctly entered in three consecutive attempts, the SIM is blocked and the MS cannot be used. To unblock the SIM, the user is asked to enter the eight-digit *PIN unblocking key* (PUK).

A SIM contains the subscriber-related information, including the PIN and PUK codes. The subscriber-related data also include a list of abbreviated and customized short dialing numbers, short messages received when the subscriber is not present, and names of preferred networks to provide service, and so on. Parts of the SIM information can be modified by the subscriber either by using the keypad of an MS or a personal computer using an RS232 connection. Figure 9.2 illustrates an example of the

```
              GSM SIM SCAN v1.00 by xxxx 1998
*****************************************************************
                    Answer To Reset Info
----------------------------------------------------------------
ATR => 3B 82 00 55 19
TS = 3B   Direct convention
T0 = 82   TD = 00
F = 372   Baud rate = Clock * D/F [Hz]
D = 1
I = 50 mA Maximum programming current
P = 5 V   Programming voltage
N = 0     Extra guardtime (Stop bit = 2+N)
T = 0     Protocol type
The Historical Characters: 55 19
*****************************************************************
               Smart Card CLASSES and INSTRUCTIONS Info
----------------------------------------------------------------
CLA:INS  A0:04 => GSM: Invalidate
   P1:P2:P3 00 00 00
   9400  No EF selected
   9804  Access condition not fulfilled!
   CHV (PIN) UNBLOCK-Verification failed
CLA:INS  A0:28 => GSM: Enable  CHV (PIN)
   P1:P2:P3 00 01 08
   6B00  Incorrect parameter P1 or/and P2
   6708  Incorrect parameter P3
CLA:INS  A0:FA => GSM: Sleep
   P1:P2:P3 00 00 00      9000  OK
*****************************************************************
                         Files   Info
----------------------------------------------------------------
3F00:           *** GSM Master File ***
----------------------------------------------------------------
Response: 00 00 00 12 3F 00 01 00 00 44 44 ...
-----------------------------------------
Allocated memory  :0012    CHV1(PIN1)        :Disabled
File ID           :3F00    CHV1(PIN1) Status :3 Tries left
Type of file      :MF      CHV1(PUK1) Status :10 Tries left
Number of DF      :3       CHV2(PIN2) Status :3 Tries left
Number of EF      :5       CHV2(PUK2) Status :10 Tries left
Number of CHV's   :4       ...
3F00:7F20:6F07:   IMSI
----------------------------------------------------------------
Response: 00 00 ...
-----------------------------------------
File ID            :6F07       Type of file  :EF
Structure of File :Transparent File Size     :0009
Read Access       :CHV (PIN) 1 Write Access  :CHV (PIN) 4
Increase Access   :CHV (PIN) 15 Rehabilitate :CHV (PIN) 1
Invalidate        :CHV (PIN) 4 File Status   :Not Invalidated
...
```

Figure 9.2   SIM data retrieved from a software tool (edited version).

SIM data retrieved by using software on a PC. Subscriber-related data are sent to the ME during operation, which are deleted after the removal of the SIM or deactivation of the MS.

The SIM card can be updated *over the air* through *SIM Toolkit*, with which network operators can remotely upgrade an MS by sending codes through short messages described in Chapter 12. These messages are issued from a SimCard server and are received by MSs equipped with SIM-Toolkit capability. SIM Toolkit provides security-related functions so that SIM cards are not falsely modified. In some networks, for example D1 T-Mobil in Germany, every new MS connected to the network is SIM Toolkit-compliant, and will be used for high-security applications such as mobile banking.

The ME contains the noncustomer-related hardware and software specific to the radio interface. When the SIM is removed from an MS, the remaining ME cannot be used for reaching the service, except for emergency calls. SIMs may be attached to MEs with different characteristics. At every new connection between MS (SIM) and the network, the characteristic indication of the ME, called *classmark*, is given to the network. This SIM-ME design supports portability, as well as enhancing security. Usually, the ME is the property of the subscriber. The SIM, although loaned to the subscriber, is the property of the service provider.

9.1.2 Base Station System

The BSS connects the MS and the NSS. The BSS consists of two parts: the *base transceiver station* (BTS) and the *base station controller* (BSC). Figures 9.3 and 9.4 illustrate GSM BTS and BSC products, respectively. The BTS contains transmitter, receiver, and signaling equipment specific to the radio interface in order to contact the MSs. An important part of the BTS is the *transcoder/rate adapter unit* (TRAU) that carries out GSM-specific speech encoding/decoding and rate adaption in data transmission. The BSC is responsible for the switching functions in the BSS, and is in turn connected to an MSC in the NSS. The BSC supports radio channel allocation/release and handoff management (to be described in Section 9.3). A BSC may connect to several BTSs and maintain cell configuration data of these BTSs. The BSC communicates with the BTSs using ISDN protocols via the *A-bis* interface. In GSM BSS design, a BSC may connect to only one BTS, in which case they are likely to be colocated. In this scenario, the BSC and the BTS may be integrated without the A-bis interface.

Capacity planning for BSC is very important. In busy hours, the processor load of a BSC is roughly distributed over call activities (around 20–25

Figure 9.3 GSM BTS (by courtesy of Nortel).

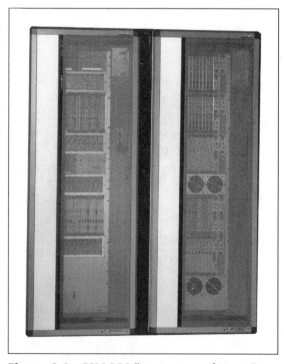

Figure 9.4 GSM BSC (by courtesy of Nortel).

percent), paging and short message service (around 10–15 percent), mobility management (handoff and location update; around 20–25 percent), and hardware checking/network-triggered events (around 15–20 percent). A BSC is typically engineered at 80 percent utilization. When a BSC is overloaded, it first rejects location update, next MS originating calls, then handoffs.

9.1.3 Network and Switching Subsystem

The NSS supports the switching functions, subscriber profiles, and mobility management. The basic switching function in the NSS is performed by the MSC. This interface follows a signaling protocol used in the telephone network. The MSC also communicates with other network elements external to GSM utilizing the same signaling protocol. The current location of an MS is usually maintained by the HLR and VLR (as described in Chapter 2, Section 2.2). When an MS moves from the home system to a visited system, its location is registered at the VLR of the visited system. The VLR then informs the MS's HLR of its current location. The *authentication center* (AuC) is used in the security data management for the authentication of subscribers. The AuC may be colocated with the HLR.

An incoming call is routed to an MSC, unless the fixed network is able to interrogate the HLR directly. That MSC is called the *gateway MSC* (GMSC). An MSC can function as a GMSC by including appropriate software and HLR interrogation functions, and by provisioning interface and the signaling link to the HLR. The GMSC obtains the location information and routes the calls to the visited MSC of the subscribers to receive the calls. (The details will be elaborated in Chapter 11, Section 11.1.)

9.1.4 Radio Interface

The GSM radio link uses both FDMA and TDMA technologies. The 900-MHz frequency bands for the GSM downlink signal and the uplink signal are 935–960 MHz and 890–915 MHz, respectively. The frequency band is divided into 124 pairs of frequency duplex channels with 200-KHz carrier spacing. Note that, for a given distance, less power is required to transmit signal over a lower frequency. To save MS power, uplink frequencies in mobile systems are always the lower band of frequencies. *Discontinuous transmission* is used in GSM to save the power consumption of the MS. With this function, an MS turns the transmitter on only while voice is present. When there is no voice input, the transmitter is turned off. GSM also supports *discontinuous reception* where the MS needs to listen only to its subchannel for paging.

The length of a GSM frame in a frequency channel is 4.615 msec. The frame is divided into eight bursts (time slots) of length 0.577 msec. The time slots in the uplink are derived from the downlink by a delay of three time slots. This arrangement prevents an MS from transmitting and receiving at the same time. However, due to propagation delays, especially when the MS is far away from the BTS, the three time-slot delay cannot be accurately maintained. The solution is to compute the *timing advance value* so that the exact shift between downlink and uplink seen by the MS is three time slots minus the timing advance value. This timing advance value is calculated by the BSS, based on the bursts received from the MS, and is signaled to the MS twice per second to inform the MS of the appropriate timing value.

The GSM burst structure is illustrated in Figure 9.5. Every burst contains 148 bits (0.546 msec), followed by 0.031 msec guard time (8.25 bits). The burst begins with three head bits, and ends with three tail bits, all of which are logical zeros. Two groups of data bits are separated by an equalizer training sequence of 26 bits. Each data group consists of 57 information bits and one flag that indicates whether the information bits are for user speech/data or signaling. Depending on the information carried by a time slot—the information bits in Figure 9.5—two types of *logical channels* are defined: *traffic channels* (TCHs) and *control channels* (CCHs). TCHs are intended to carry user information (speech or data). Two kinds of TCHs are defined:

Full-rate TCH (TCH/F). Provides transmission speed of 13 Kbps for speech or 9.6, 4.8, or 2.4 Kbps for data. *Enhanced full-rate* (EFR) speech

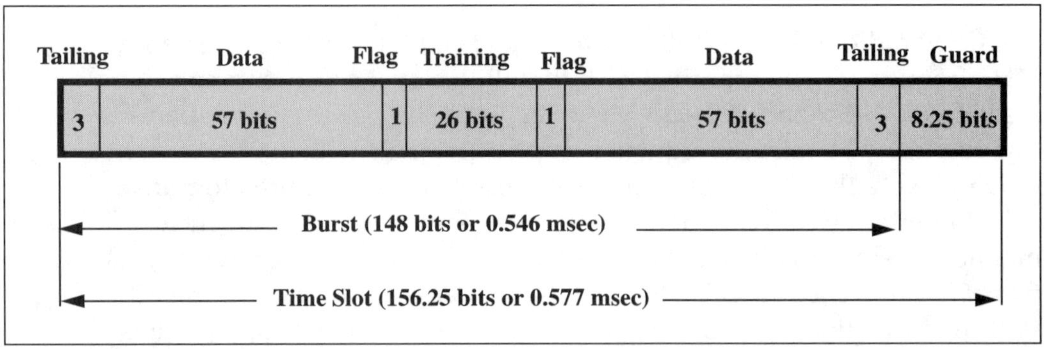

Figure 9.5 GSM burst structure.

coders have been implemented to improve the speech quality of a TCH/F.

Half-rate TCH (TCH/H). Allows transmission of 6.5 Kbps speech, or 4.8 or 2.4 Kbps of data.

The CCHs are intended to carry signaling information. Three types of CCHs are defined in GSM:

Common control channels (CCCHs). Include the following channel types:

- *Paging channel* (PCH), used by the network to page the destination MS in call termination.

- *Access grant channel* (AGCH), used by the network to indicate radio link allocation upon prime access of an MS.

- *Random access channel (RACH)*, used by the MSs for initial access to the network.

Several MSs may access the same RACH, potentially resulting in collisions. The slotted Aloha protocol is adopted in GSM to resolve access collision. PCH and AGCH are delivered from the BSS to the MSs by the downlink. RACH utilizes the uplink.

Dedicated control channels. Supported in GSM for dedicated use by a specific MS.

- *Standalone dedicated control channel* (SDCCH), used only for signaling and for short messages.

- *Slow associated control channel* (SACCH), associated with either a TCH or an SDCCH. The SACCH is used for nonurgent procedures, mainly the transmission of power and time alignment control information over the downlink, and measurement reports from the MS over the uplink. A TCH is always allocated with a control channel SACCH to transport both user information and signaling data in parallel.

- *Fast associated control channel* (FACCH), used for time-critical signaling, such as call-establishing progress, authentication of subscriber, or handoff. The FACCH makes use of the TCH during a call; thus, there is a loss of user data because the FACCH "steals" the bandwidth of the TCH.

- *Cell broadcast channel* (CBCH), carries only the short message service cell broadcast messages, which use the same time slot as the SDCCH.

The CBCH is used on the downlink only. SDCCH, SACCH, and FACCH are used in both downlink and uplink.

Broadcast channels (BCHs). Used by the BTS to broadcast information to the MSs in its coverage area.

- *Frequency correction channel* (FCCH) and *synchronization channel* (SCH) carry information from the BSS to the MS. The information allows the MS to acquire and stay synchronized with the BSS.

- *Broadcast control channel* (BCCH) provides system information such as access information for the selected cell and information related to the surrounding cells to support cell selection and location registration procedures in an MS.

Figure 9.6 shows the radio aspect of *mobile call origination*, which describes how the logical channels are involved in the call setup procedure. To initiate call setup, the MS sends a signaling channel request to the network through RACH. The BSC informs the MS of the allocated signaling channel (SDCCH) through AGCH. Then the MS sends the call origination request via SDCCH. The MSC instructs the BSC to allocate a TCH for this call. Then the MS acknowledges the traffic channel assignment through FACCH. Finally, both the MS and the BTS tune to the TCH.

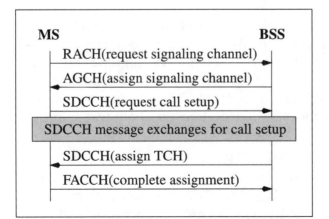

Figure 9.6   GSM call origination (radio aspect).

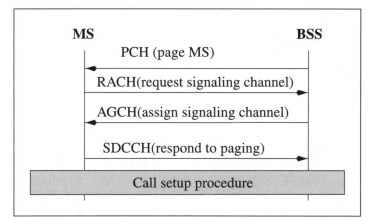

Figure 9.7 GSM call termination (radio aspect).

Figure 9.7 shows the radio aspect of *mobile call termination*. In this case, the MSC requests the BSS to page the MS. The BSCs instruct the BTSs in the desired LA to page the MS by using PCH. When the destination MS receives the paging message, it requests an SDCCH through RACH. The BTS assigns the SDCCH through AGCH.

The MS responds the paging through the SDCCH. This SDCCH is also used to set up the call as in the call origination case.

9.2   Location Tracking and Call Setup

The current location of an MS is maintained by a two-level hierarchical strategy with the HLR and the VLRs. When an MS visits a new location, it must register in the VLR of the visited location.

The HLR must also be informed about this registration. To access the MS, the HLR is queried to find the current VLR of the MS. (The details follow.) The registration process of the MS moving from one VLR to another VLR is illustrated in Figure 9.8, and is described in the following steps:

Step 1. The MS periodically listens to the BCCH broadcast from the BSS. If the MS detects that it has entered a new location area, it sends a registration message to the new VLR by using the SDCCH channel.

Step 2. The new VLR communicates with the old VLR to find the HLR of the MS. (Details of this operation will be elaborated in

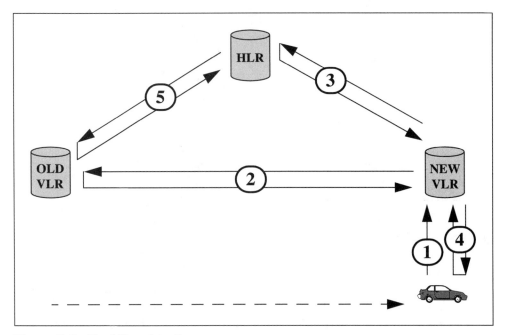

Figure 9.8   The MS registration process.

Section 11.1.) The new VLR then performs the authentication process to be described in the next section.

Step 3. After the MS is authenticated, the new VLR sends a registration message to the HLR. If the registration request is accepted, the HLR provides the new VLR with all relevant subscriber information for call handling.

Step 4. The new VLR informs the MS of the successful registration.

Step 5. After step 3, the HLR sends a deregistration (cancellation) message to the old VLR. The old VLR cancels the record for the MS and sends an acknowledgment to the HLR for the cancellation.

When the MS is inactive, due to switching off or SIM removal, it transmits a *detach* to deregister from the network. The MS may also periodically send registration messages to the network. The period may range from six minutes to slightly more than 24 hours. Periodic registration is useful for fault-tolerance purposes, as described in Chapter 11. If the VLR or HLR fails, periodic registration will speed up the recovery of the databases.

The GSM call control is similar to IS-41. The radio aspect of mobile

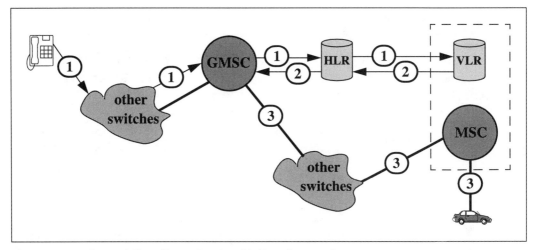

Figure 9.9 The mobile call termination (delivery) procedure.

call origination was described in Section 9.1.4. The network aspect of this procedure is described in Chapter 11, Section 11.1.2. For a GSM *mobile call termination* or *call delivery*, the *MS ISDN number* (MSISDN) of the subscriber is dialed. MSISDN is part of the ISDN numbering plan defined in ITU-T Recommendation E.164. This number points to the subscriber's record in the HLR. The HLR record contains the information to locate the MSC where the subscriber is currently located. Details of the information fields maintained in the HLR are described in Chapter 11, Section 11.2. The basic call termination procedure is described in the following steps, and is shown in Figure 9.9:

Step 1. When the MSISDN is dialed, the call is forwarded to the GMSC, a switch that has the capability to interrogate the HLR for routing information. The HLR requests the current VLR of the MS to provide the routable address, called a *mobile station roaming number* (MSRN).

Step 2. The VLR returns the MSRN to the GMSC through the HLR.

Step 3. The GMSC uses the MSRN to route the call to the MS through the visited MSC.

The MS may already be engaged in another communication when a call arrives. If the mobile user has subscribed to the *call-waiting* service, the MSC proceeds directly to connect the call to the MS. Different communication sessions may be associated with an MS at the same time. These sessions are distinguished by their *transaction identifiers*.

9.3 Security

GSM security is addressed in two aspects: *authentication* and *encryption*. Authentication avoids fraudulent access by a cloned MS. Encryption avoids unauthorized listening.

A secret key, K_i, is used to achieve authentication. K_i is stored in the AuC as well as in the SIM. The K_i value is unknown to the subscriber. To initiate the authentication process, the home system of the MS generates a 128-bit

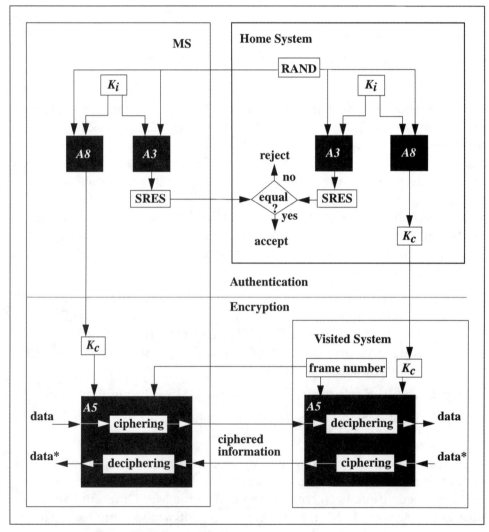

Figure 9.10 Authentication and encryption.

random number called *RAND*. This number is sent to the MS. By exercising an algorithm, *A3*, both the network (AuC) and the MS (SIM) use K_i and RAND to produce a *signed result* (SRES), as shown in Figure 9.10. The SRES generated by the MS is sent to the home system and is compared with the SRES generated by the AuC. If they are not identical, the access request is rejected. Note that if the SRES and RAND generated by the AuC are sent from the HLR to the visited VLR in advance, the SRES comparison can be done at the visited VLR. Algorithm A3 is dependent on the GSM service provider. Since the visited system may not know the A3 algorithm of a roaming MS, authentication result SRES is generated at the home system of the MS. In IS-41, the authentication process may be done locally in the visited system as in the S scheme explained in Chapter 6, Section 6.2.3.

If the MS is accepted for access, an encryption key K_c is produced by an algorithm, *A8*, with K_i and RAND as inputs, shown in Figure 9.10. Like A3, *A8* is specific to the home system. After the home system has generated K_c, this encryption key is sent to the visited system. K_c and the TDMA frame number encoded in the data bits are used by an algorithm, *A5*, to cipher and decipher the data stream between the MS and the visited system. The same A5 algorithm may be used in all systems participating in the GSM service.

9.4 Data Services

GSM Phase 2 standard supports two data service groups: *short message services* and *bearer services*. (GSM short message services will be elaborated in Chapter 12.) GSM bearer services are similar to the ISDN services (data circuit duplex, data packet duplex, and so on), except that the maximum data rate is limited to 9.6 Kbps. These services can be employed on notebook PCs or PDAs connected to the MS via a PCMCIA card. Most mobile operators offer short message service as part of the basic subscription package. In contrast, subscription of bearer service was typically less than 10 percent in Taiwan by 2000 (including facsimile, asynchronous data, and synchronous data).

To offer bearer service, a circuit-switched connection is established in the GSM network to connect the MS and an interface of the PSTN. To do so, the wireline circuit and radio channel resources are reserved even if the data are not transferred. An alternative is to release the resources when the data are not transferred. The disadvantage is that the GSM call setup time is too long, and extra signaling traffic for circuit setup is generated. Many applications cannot tolerate a long setup delay.

Since Phase 2 GSM systems do not support fast access to radio resources on demand and packet-switched transmission, the short message and bearer data services in GSM are insufficient to support Internet applications, such as large volume FTP or World Wide Web, in an efficient manner. To provide efficient data capabilities for GSM, new GSM data protocols have been developed by the European Telecommunications Standards Institute (ETSI) as part of the GSM Phase 2+ standard. These protocols include:

- High-Speed Circuit-Switched Data (HSCSD) for high-speed file transfers and mobile video applications

- General Packet Radio Service (GPRS), for bursty data applications such as e-mail and WWW

The data rates are expected to be raised from 9.6 Kbps to 28.8 Kbps or higher. In the near term, the baseline standard for mobile professionals will probably be 19.2 Kbps.

9.4.1 HSCSD

HSCSD is a circuit-switched protocol for large file transfer and multimedia applications. The physical layer of HSCSD is the same as that for the Phase 2 GSM data services. The data rate of HSCSD has been increased by using multiple TDMA time slots (up to eight) instead of one time slot in the current data applications. The data rate can also be increased by data compression techniques. The HSCSD architecture is illustrated in Figure 9.11. The data computing session is performed at a terminal equipment (TE), such as a computer connected to the MS. The *network interworking function* (IWF) supports adaption between GSM and the external networks. Thus, TAF and IWF are sensitive to the end-to-end services. On the other hand, the GSM entities between TAF and IWF are independent of the services. They provide only the bearer capabilities required to transport the corresponding data flow.

The radio interface is the same as that of the current GSM system except that multiple, independent time slots can be utilized to provide high-speed links, as previously described. The *radio link protocol* (RLP) has been enhanced in HSCSD to support multilink (time-slot) operation. The protocol may or may not recover the frame errors between TAF and IWF.

The problem of multiple time-slot assignment is that the blocking rate of the system will be increased; that is, fewer customers can share the GSM services if more radio resources are assigned to individual customers.

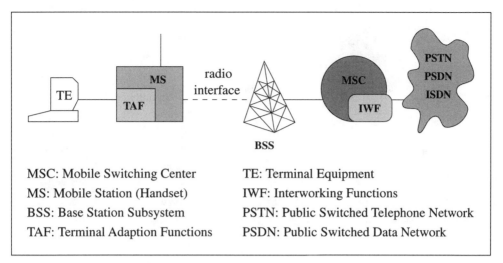

Figure 9.11   HSCSD architecture.

This problem can be reduced by flexible resource assignment where the service or the customers specify the maximum capacity and the minimum capacity. Based on the currently available capacity of a BS, a customer will be assigned any rate between the maximum and the minimum capacities.

9.4.2   GPRS

GPRS is a packet-switched protocol for applications such as the Web, where the user spends most of the time reading information, and the bursty data are transferred through the link only when necessary. Unlike HSCSD, the GSM circuit-switching architecture cannot satisfy the packet-switching nature of GPRS. Thus, GPRS requires its own transport network. Figure 9.12 illustrates the GPRS architecture.

GPRS introduces two new entities, namely, *serving GPRS support node* (SGSN) and *gateway GPRS support node* (GGSN), to the GSM architecture. SGSN receives and transmits packets between the MSs and their counterparts in the *public-switched data network* (PSDN). GGSN interworks with the PSDN using connectionless network protocols, such as the Internet protocol and the OSI connectionless network protocol, or connection-oriented protocols such as X.25. SGSN and GGSN interact with the GSM location databases, including the HLR and the VLRs, to track the location of the MSs. The GPRS data units are routed to the destination MSs based on location information. Both SGSN and GGSN may be equipped with caches containing location information to speed up the routing procedure.

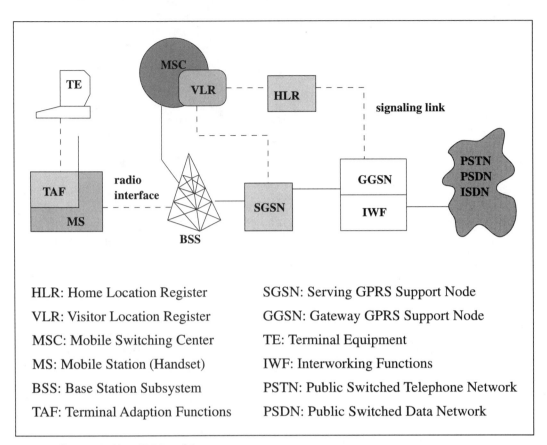

Figure 9.12   GPRS architecture.

Like HSCSD, GPRS air interface requires a new radio link protocol to guarantee fast call setup procedure and low-bit error rate for data transfer between the MSs and the BSs. Furthermore, GPRS needs to implement a *packet radio media access control* (MAC) for packet switching (see Chapter 18).

Based on the preceding discussion, HSCSD and GPRS have very different cost and revenue profiles. GPRS typically supports up to 100 users with one to eight channels, while HSCSD typically supports fewer users, where a user may utilize two to eight channels. GPRS supports broadcast and multisessions, while HSCSD supports point-to-point sessions. GPRS requires an investment in new infrastructure. On the other hand, HSCSD needs to address handoff issues.

In June 1999, Nokia announced its Card Phone 2.0 for HSCSD with transmission speed up to 43.2 Kbps without data compression. Card Phone 2.0 is a PC card with a built-in GSM phone. Compared with a standard MS, HSCSD MS consumes more power to support multiple time-slot transmission. Thus, Nokia Card Phone derives its power source from the laptop computer to which it is connected. Currently, equipment suppliers are committing more to GPRS than HSCSD.

9.5 Unstructured Supplementary Service Data

During the evolution of GSM, supplementary services have been introduced in various stages. These new services may not be recognized by older MSs. To support these new services in old MSs, *unstructured supplementary service data* (USSD) was introduced in GSM 02.90, 03.90, and 04.90 specifications. When the MS cannot recognize the text string entered by the user, it utilizes USSD to deliver the text to the network, and leaves the interpretation of the text to the network. Both the MS and the network can exchange multiple USSD messages in a dialogue manner. Thus, USSD is used as a GSM transparent bearer for old MSs. When a new supplementary service is introduced, the MSs support this service following the standard GSM supplementary model. For older MSs, USSD functions as a transport mechanism to deliver the new service. Chapter 19, Section 19.5, will illustrate how USSD can serve as a bearer service for the Wireless Application Protocol (WAP).

USSD is flexible in terms of message length and content. It uses all digits plus the asterisk (*) and pound (#) keys. A USSD string is a command code (typically two or three digits) followed by several parameters. The parameters (supplementary information) have variable lengths and are separated by an asterisk. The whole string ends with the pound symbol. For example, if we specify command code 159 for call forwarding, the USSD string:

$$*159*5288128\#$$

sent by the MS will instruct the network to forward all incoming calls to that MS to the phone number 528-8128. This USSD string is sent out in the same manner as placing a call. Furthermore, most MSs can store several USSD strings, and allow sending these strings through speed-dialing keys.

The USSD architecture is illustrated in Figure 9.13. The USSD provides interaction between a GSM node (MSC, VLR, or HLR) and the MS. If the USSD service node is an MSC, the USSD messages are exchanged through path (1) in Figure 9.13. If the service node is a VLR (or HLR),

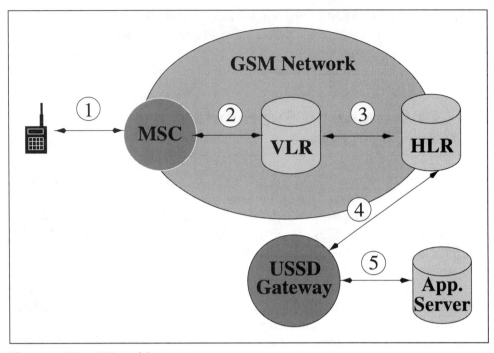

Figure 9.13 USSD architecture.

the messages are exchanged through path (1)↔ (2) (or (1) ↔ (2) ↔ (3)) in Figure 9.13. Suppose that a new USSD service that enables subscribers to obtain real-time stock quotes is implemented at the home network. To utilize this service, USSD messages would be exchanged between the MS and the HLR. Since the MS communicates directly with the HLR, the subscriber can monitor stock values even when roaming to another country. However, it is probably not practical to support this stock query service in the HLR. The HLR is expensive to modify, maintain, and test, and may not have extra processing power required to handle additional services. Thus, a reasonable solution is to introduce a *USSD gateway* that connects to the application (i.e., stock query) server. The USSD gateway connects to the HLR using GSM MAP and to application servers by TCP/IP. When the subscriber issues a stock query request encoded in a USSD string, the MS sends it to the HLR via SS7. The HLR routes the USSD message directly to the USSD gateway ((4) in Figure 9.13) without any interpretation. The USSD gateway translates the USSD format and sends the query to the application server ((5) in Figure 9.13). The server then returns the results to the MS for display.

In terms of turnaround time for interactive applications, USSD is better than SMS. According to Nokia, USSD can be up to seven times faster than SMS for performing a two-way transaction.

9.6   Summary

This chapter introduced the GSM system. Details of the GSM network signaling will be discussed in subsequent chapters. Other GSM references can be found in [Lyc91, Hau94, Mou92].

Descriptions of GSM 1800, the GSM system operated at 1.8 GHz, can be found in [Ram94]. The radio interface of PCS 1900, the GSM version at 1.9 GHz, was standardized in the Joint Technical Committee (JTC) [Coo94]. The network portion of PCS 1900 was introduced into TR46 for adaption to meet ANSI standards. MSISDN numbering is defined in ITU-T Recommendation E.164 [CCI91]. Solutions for flexible resource assignment in HSCSD can be found in [Jen97, Jen97c]. Details of GPRS are described in Chapter 18. Details of USSD can be found in [ETS97i, ETS96b], and [ETS97j]. GSM SIM Toolkit is specified in [ETS97h].

The whole set of official GSM specifications generated by ETSI is structured in 12 series [Mou92]: (1) General, (2) Service Aspects, (3) Network Aspects, (4) MS-BSS Interface and Protocols, (5) Physical Layer on the Radio Path, (6) Speech Coding Specification, (7) Terminal Adaptors for Mobile Stations, (8) BSS to MSC Interfaces, (9) Network Interworking, (10) empty (originally planned for service interworking specifications), (11) Equipment and Type Approval Specification, (12) Operation and Maintenance. GSM documents can be downloaded without charge from the ETSI Web site at www.etsi.org.

9.7   Review Questions

1. What are the major parts of an MS in GSM? Describe them.

2. Describe the possible connection configurations for BTSs and BSCs in GSM.

3. What is the AuC used for in GSM?

4. What does it mean that GSM uses both FDMA and TDMA techniques? Explain.

5. How is the exact three time-slot delay between the uplink and the downlink maintained?

6. What is the training sequence used for in the GSM bursts?

7. What are the different types of control channels in GSM?

8. Why is the GSM Phase 2 system not well suited for bursty data services?

9. Do HSCSD and/or GPRS introduce new handoff issues to GSM?

10. By whom and to what is the MSISDN number transferred in the case of a mobile-terminated call?

11. How is the GSM system secured against fraudulent use?

12. Which of A3, A5, and A8 are specific to GSM operators? Why?

13. Compare the authentication procedures in IS-41 and GSM.

14. Show how to integrate the registration and the authentication procedures in GSM.

15. Some operators consider reimplementing SMS by using USSD. Since standard MSs support SMS, what is the motivation for doing so?

16. Implement the IS-41C-significant event COUNT checking (described in Section 6.2.2.1) in GSM authentication.

17. Priority call is a service offered in GSM network. In this service, a priority call request is buffered in a waiting queue if no free channel is available. The buffered request can be served as soon as free channels become available. Develop a model to evaluate the performance for the priority call service. Do you think priority calls can significantly reduce the probability of call blocking? (Hint: See the model in [Yan99].)

18. In GSM HSCSD, the data rate can be increased by using multiple time slots instead of a single time slot. Multiple time-slot assignment results in a high blocking rate. To accommodate more users, design a flexible resource allocation strategy that negotiates the resources requested by the users. That is, during heavy traffic, the network only allocates partial resources to the users (Hint: See the model in [Jen98b].)

GSM Network Signaling

This chapter discusses GSM network signaling. Based on the GSM architecture described in Chapter 9, Section 9.1, Figure 10.1 shows various network signaling protocols used by the entity interfaces in GSM. We will focus on the software platform for implementing the GSM network signaling protocol called GSM MAP (Mobile Application Part). GSM MAP is used in the B, C, D, E, F, and G interfaces illustrated in Figure 10.1. In terms of network signaling, the GSM architecture can be partitioned into three parts:

Databases. GSM utilizes databases such as VLR, HLR, and AuC, which were discussed in Chapter 9. In addition, an *equipment identity register* (EIR) is used to maintain a list of legitimate, fraudulent, or faulty mobile stations. EIR works with HLR to block calls from illegitimate MSs. (Note that when the GSM network bars an MS, it does not bar the subscriber.) EIR is optional in a GSM network, and often is not used. AuC and EIR are implemented either as standalone nodes or as a combined AuC/EIR node. Alternatively, the AuC may be integrated with the HLR. To accomplish mobility management, the HLR communicates with VLRs through the D interface. VLRs communicate with each other through the G interface.

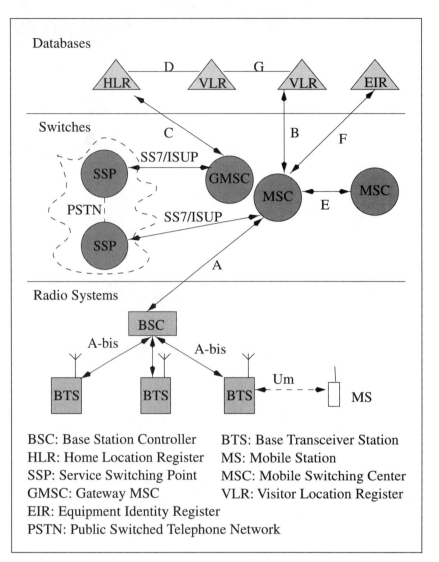

Figure 10.1   GSM protocol interfaces.

Switches. The GSM MSC performs necessary switching functions for mobile stations within the geographical area it controls. This geographical area is called an MSC area. An MSC area is partitioned into several *location areas* (LAs). Every LA consists of several BTSs. The LAs are not shown in Figure 10.1. (The LA hierarchy will be discussed in Chapter 11.) To originate a call from a mobile station (MS) to a wireline user the MSC communicates with an SSP in the PSTN using the SS7 ISUP protocol described in Chapter 5, Section 5.4.

To deliver a call from a PSTN user to an MS, the originating SSP in the PSTN communicates with a gateway MSC (GMSC) using SS7 ISUP, described in Chapter 9, Section 9.2. During the intersystem handoff procedure, two MSCs are required to communicate with each other through the E interface. To perform mobility management and call-handling tasks, the MSC needs to communicate with HLR using the C interface and with a VLR using the B interface. To prevent fraudulent handset usage, the MSC communicates with the EIR using the F interface.

Radio system. The GSM radio system consists of base station controllers (BSCs), base transceiver stations (BTSs), and MSs. The BSC connects to an MSC through the A interface using a signaling protocol compatible with signaling in the telephone network. The BSC also connects to one or more BTSs through the A-bis interface using the ISDN link access protocol for the D channel (LAPD). A BTS communicates with the MSs through the radio interface U_m.

This chapter describes the software platform for the GSM MAP implementation that supports interfaces B, C, D, E, and F. The GSM MAP is an

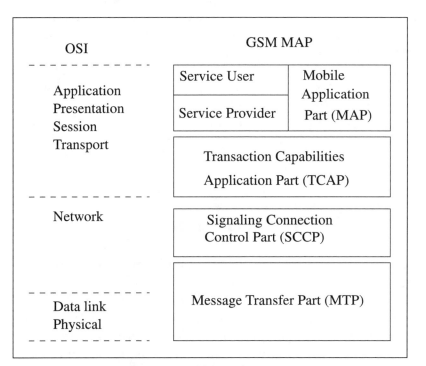

Figure 10.2 GSM MAP protocol hierarchy.

Table 10.1 GSM MAP SCCP Subsystem Numbers

APPLICATION SERVICE ELEMENT	SUBSYSTEM NUMBER
Reserved	00000101
HLR	00000110
VLR	00000111
MSC	00001000
EIR	00001001
(Possible) AuC	00001010

application of the SS7 protocol described in Chapter 5, Section 5.1, which consists of four layers, shown in Figure 10.2. In this figure, the Signaling Connection Control Part (SCCP) layer merits further discussion. GSM MAP uses SCCP classes 0 and 1 connectionless services that provide efficient routing with or without maintaining message sequencing between two or more messages. The network entities may consist of several application service elements (ASEs). The SCCP addresses these ASEs with *subsystem numbers* (SSNs). The SSNs for GSM MAP ASEs are listed in Table 10.1. For intra-GSM network message delivery, the destination address of the message may be a simple *destination point code* (DPC) that can be used by the MTP for direct routing. For inter-GSM network message delivery, the originating node does not have enough knowledge to identify the actual address of the destination. In this case, the SCCP translates the actual destination address by *Global Title Translation* (GTT), as described in Chapter 5, Section 5.2.

10.1 GSM MAP Service Framework

The GSM network entities (such as HLR, VLR, and MSC) communicate with each other through MAP dialogues by invoking MAP service primitives. A service primitive can be one of four types: Request, Indication, Response, and Confirm. The service primitive is initiated by a MAP service user of a network entity called the dialogue initiator, as shown in Figure 10.3. The service type is Request. This service request is sent to the MAP service provider of the network entity.

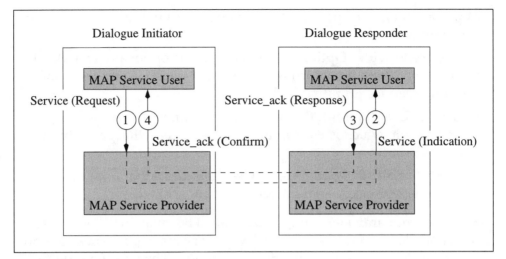

Figure 10.3 GSM MAP service model.

NOTE In this chapter, the terms *service provider* and *service user* are used in the context of the MAP client/server model. The reader should not be confused with *server provider* used to refer to the mobile operator, and *user* used to refer to the mobile subscriber in other chapters of this book.

The service provider delivers the request to the peer network entity, the dialogue responder, by using a lower-layer protocol such as TCAP. When the MAP service provider of the peer network entity receives the request, it invokes the same service primitive with type Indication to inform the destination MAP service user. In most cases, the information (parameters) of the service with type Indication is identical to that with type Request. The primitive is typically a query, which asks the dialogue responder to perform some operations.

A corresponding service acknowledgment, with or without results, may be sent from the dialogue responder to the dialogue initiator. The same service primitive with type Response is invoked by the MAP service user of the dialogue responder. After the MAP service provider of the dialogue initiator receives this response, it invokes the same service primitive with type Confirm. The parameters of the Confirm and the Response services are identical in most cases, except that the Confirm service may include an extra provider error parameter to indicate a protocol error.

The parameters of a service primitive type can be one of the four categories:

M (Mandatory). The parameter must be present in the indicated primitive type.

O (Service Provider Option). The parameter is optionally included by the service provider, which is used in the Indication and the Confirm types of service primitives.

U (Service User Option). The parameter is optionally included by the service user, which is used in the Request and the Response types of service primitives.

C (Conditional). The parameter is used to indicate that one of a number of mutually exclusive parameters must be included.

Examples for parameter category usage will be given in Section 10.4.

A MAP dialogue consists of several MAP services to perform a common task. The services are either specific or common. The specific services include:

- Mobility services
- Operation and maintenance services
- Call-handling services
- Supplementary services
- Short message service management services

The common MAP services are used to establish and clear MAP dialogue between peer MAP service users. They invoke functions supported by TCAP and report abnormal situations. Six common MAP services are defined in GSM MAP, as follows:

MAP-OPEN. Used to establish a MAP dialogue. This service is confirmed by the service provider; that is, **MAP-OPEN** has Request/Indication and Response/Confirm types.

MAP-CLOSE. Used to clear a MAP dialogue. This service is not confirmed by the service provider; that is, the service primitive only has the Request/Indication types, not the Response/Confirm types.

MAP-DELIMITER. Used to explicitly request the TCAP to transfer the MAP protocol data units to the peer entities. This service does not have any parameters and is not confirmed by the service provider.

MAP-U-ABORT. Used by the service user to abort a dialogue. This service is not confirmed by the service provider. The reason for aborting the dialogue can be resource limitation due to congestion, application procedure error, and so on.

MAP-P-ABORT. Used by the service provider to abort a dialogue. This service primitive has only the Indication type. The reason for aborting the dialogue can be provider malfunction, resource limitation, maintenance activity, and so on.

MAP-NOTICE. Used by the service provider to inform the service user of protocol problems such as abnormal event detected by the peer and response rejected by the peer. This service primitive has only the Indication type.

10.2   The MAP Protocol Machine

When a MAP user issues a service request, the request is processed by the *MAP protocol machine* (PM) in the service provider, which is illustrated in Figure 10.4. The MAP PM consists of four components:

Dialogue state machine (DSM). Coordinates the *service state machines* (SSMs). For every MAP dialogue, an instance of DSM is created to handle the dialogue. An SSM is either an RSM or a PSM, to be described next.

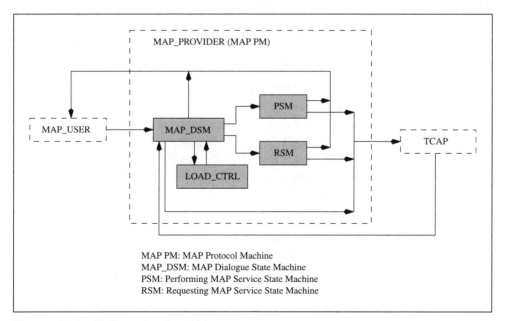

Figure 10.4   MAP protocol machine.

Requesting service state machine (RSM). Handles a MAP-specific service requested during a dialogue. This SSM is created by the DSM for each requested service.

Performing service state machine (PSM). Handles a MAP service performed during a dialogue. This SSM is created by the DSM for each service to be performed.

Load Control. Monitors the traffic generated by the service activities. There is only one instance of this process in each system. If an overload situation is detected, low-priority MAP operations may be ignored. The suggested priority levels from high to low for the MAP service primitives are handoff, mobility management, short message services, and subscriber-controlled inputs (i.e., supplementary services such as call waiting and call forwarding).

When the service provider receives a **MAP-OPEN** Request from the service user or a **TC-BEGIN** Indication from the TCAP, the MAP PM is invoked and an instance of DSM is created. For every service primitive issued during the MAP dialogue, an instance of PSM is created by the DSM at the performer's side, and an instance of RSM is created by the DSM at the initiator's side.

10.3   The MAP Dialogue

Figure 10.5 illustrates an example of a MAP dialogue message flow; the detailed steps are described here:

Step 1. A service user initiates a MAP dialogue by invoking the **MAP-OPEN** Request service primitive, followed by one or more specific service (user request) primitives, then the **MAP-DELIMITER** Request service. In Figure 10.5, **MAP-OPEN** is followed by one specific service primitive, **MAP_Service1**. **MAP_Service1** represents a GSM service primitive such as **MAP_SEND_ROUTING_INFORMATION**, to be elaborated in Section 10.4.

Step 2. The MAP PM creates an instance of DSM to handle the **MAP-OPEN** Request primitive. For every one of the following user request primitives, an RSM is created. The RSM uses the **TC-INVOKE** (transaction capabilities invoke) procedure to set the operation code and TCAP parameters for the service request. Then the control is passed back to the DSM. The DSM continues

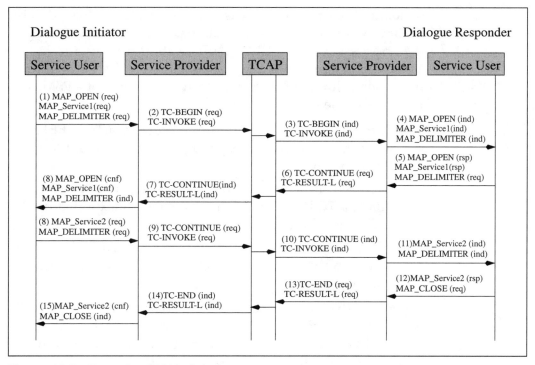

Figure 10.5 Example of MAP dialogue.

to process the user request primitives until the **MAP-DELIMITER** Request primitive is encountered. The MAP PM enables the **TC-BEGIN** primitive at the TCAP layer, and waits for a response from TCAP. The TCAP layer generates the SS7 TCAP message with the appropriate package and the component types, described in Chapter 5, Section 5.3, and sends it to the dialogue responder, possibly though the SS7 network.

Before the MAP PM receives a response from TCAP, it refuses to accept any new requests from its service user except for a **MAP-U-ABORT** or a prearranged **MAP-CLOSE**.

Step 3. The **TC-*** Request primitives will be delivered by the TCAP and the lower-layer protocols of SS7 to the peer MAP PM; the primitives are now of type Indication.

Step 4. When the MAP PM of the dialogue responder receives the **TC-BEGIN** Indication, a DSM is invoked. If the DSM identifies any error from the received **TC-BEGIN** Indication, a **TC-U-ABORT** Request is sent back to the dialogue initiator to terminate the dialogue. The DSM also checks if the system is overloaded. If so, **TC-BEGIN** will not be processed. Otherwise—that is, normally—the DSM issues the **MAP-OPEN** Indication primitive to its MAP service user. The DSM then encounters the **TC-INVOKE** Indication primitive, which results in the creation of a PSM. The PSM checks the following:

- If the received arguments are not correct, a **TC-U-REJECT** with problem code "mistyped parameter" is sent to the dialogue initiator.

- If the service (**Service1** in our example) cannot be identified, a **TC-U-ERROR** with error code "unexpected data value" is sent to the dialogue initiator.

- If the service parameters are not available, a **TC-U-ERROR** with error code "data missing" is sent to the dialogue initiator.

If any of these events occurs, the PSM sends a **MAP-NOTICE** to its MAP service user. Assuming that no error occurs, the PSM issues a **MAP-Service1** Indication primitive to be passed to its service user, and the control is passed back to the DSM.

After the DSM has processed all received components, it informs its MAP service user by the **MAP-DELIMITER** Indication primitive. The MAP PM then waits for a **MAP-OPEN** Response primitive from its MAP service user. During the waiting period, the MAP PM will not accept any primitives from the dialogue initiator, except for a **TC-P-ABORT** Indication.

Step 5. The MAP service user processes the Indication primitives received from the MAP service provider, and returns the results with the **MAP-OPEN** and the **MAP-Service1** Response primitives, followed by the **MAP-DELIMITER** Request primitive.

Step 6. When the MAP service provider receives the **MAP-OPEN** Response primitive, the DSM first checks if the response is negative. If so, it generates a MAP_Refuse_PDU (protocol data unit) to be delivered by the Indication primitive **TC-END**.

Assuming that the response is positive, a MAP_Accept_PDU is generated. The DSM proceeds to receive the **MAP-Service1** Response primitive and passes the control to the PSM. The PSM checks if any user error is present. If so, depending on the type of error, either a **TC-U-ERROR** or a **TC-U-REJECT** Indication primitive is issued. Otherwise—that is, normally—the PSM issues a TC-RESULT-L Request primitive and passes the control back to the DSM. If the user-specific parameters of the Response primitives cannot be transferred in a single signaling frame, the PSM issues a TC-RESULT-NL instead of a TC-RESULT-L.

The DSM continues to process the specific service primitives until the MAP-DELIMITER Request primitive is encountered. The DSM issues a TC-CONTINUE Request primitive with the MAP_Accept_PDU. A TCAP message is generated by the TCAP layer and is delivered to the dialogue initiator. At this point, the MAP dialogue is considered established at the dialogue responder's side.

Step 7. The TC-CONTINUE/TC-RESULT-L Indication primitives are received by the MAP service provider of the dialogue initiator. When the DSM receives the TC-CONTINUE, it performs tests, as described in step 4. In the normal case, it accepts the dialogue and passes the control to the RSM to handle the specific service primitives. Our example assumes that the RSM processes the TC-RESULT-L primitive. If the result parameter is not defined for the specific service primitive, the RSM requests to transfer the TC-U-REJECT with the problem code "mistyped parameter" to the dialogue responder, and issues the MAP-Service1 Confirm primitive to its MAP service user with the provider-error parameter code "invalid response received."

In the normal case, the RSM maps the TC-RESULT-L parameters to the MAP-Service1 Confirm primitive and passes the control back to the DSM. After all components have been processed, the DSM informs the MAP service user. At this point, the dialogue is considered established at the dialogue initiator's side.

Step 8. The MAP service user of the dialogue initiator handles the Confirm primitives and, possibly, makes new requests.

Steps 9–11. These steps are similar to steps 2–4.

Steps 12–15. These steps are similar to steps 5–8, except that the dialogue termination is driven by the MAP-CLOSE primitives and the TC-END primitives.

10.4   Examples of MAP Service Primitives

This section uses *retrieval of routing information* (see the call setup procedure described in Section 9.2 and Section 11.1.2) to illustrate the information

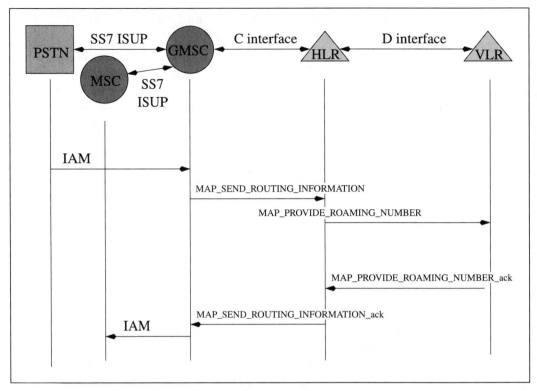

Figure 10.6 Retrieval of routing information.

delivered in the specific service primitives. Consider the call delivery process where a PSTN user calls a GSM subscriber. The message flow is illustrated in Figure 10.6. When the MSISDN number of the GSM subscriber is dialed, the trunk is set up by the SS7 ISUP message IAM to a specific GMSC that has the capability to interrogate the HLR for routing information.

The HLR requests the current VLR of the MS to provide the roaming number. The VLR allocates a roaming number, and sends this number to the GMSC through the HLR. (Details for them are provided in Chapter 11, Section 11.1.) With the roaming number, the trunk is set up from the GMSC to the destination MSC by the IAM message. Two services, **MAP_SEND_ROUTING_INFORMATION** and **MAP_PROVIDE_ROAMING_NUMBER**, are used for routing information retrieval. Table 10.2(a) lists the parameters for the four **MAP_SEND_ROUTING_INFORMATION** primitives. In this table, the notation (=) means that the parameter on the right takes on the same value as the parameter appearing immediately to its left. The parameters are described as follows:

Table 10.2 Primitives for Routing Information Retrieval

PARAMETER NAME	REQUEST	INDICATION	RESPONSE	CONFIRM
Invoke ID	M	M(=)	M(=)	M(=)
MSISDN	M	M(=)		
CUG Interlock	C	C(=)	C	C(=)
CUG Outgoing Access	C	C(=)	C	C(=)
Number of Forwarding	C	C(=)		
Network Signal Info	C	C(=)		
IMSI			C	C(=)
MSRN			C	C(=)
Forwarding Data			C	C(=)
User Error			C	C(=)
Provider Error				O

(a) MAP_SEND_ROUTING_INFORMATION Parameters

PARAMETER NAME	REQUEST	INDICATION	RESPONSE	CONFIRM
Invoke ID	M	M(=)	M(=)	M(=)
IMSI	M	M(=)		
MSC Number	M	M(=)		
MSISDN	C	C(=)		
LMSI	C	C(=)		
GSM Bearer Capability	C	C(=)		
Network Signal Info	C	C(=)		
MSRN			C	C(=)
User Error			C	C(=)
Provider Error				O

(b) MAP_PROVIDE_ROAMING_NUMBER Parameters

Invoke ID. A unique number generated by the MAP service user to identify the corresponding service primitives in the MAP service user-provider interface.

MSISDN. The mobile station ISDN number of the called party; that is, the "telephone number" of the called mobile subscriber. For GSM 900 and GSM 1800 deployed in Europe and Asia, an MSISDN consists of a country code (CC), national destination code (NDC), and subscriber number (SN). The SN is the address to the serving MSC/VLR. To make a call from the United States to a GSM user in Taiwan, the caller dials, for example, 011-886-93-105401. In this number, 11 is the international switch access (ISCA) code in the United States; 886 is the CC for Taiwan; 93 is the NDC; and 105401 is the SN. To call the same GSM subscriber from Taiwan, the ISCA and the CC codes are not dialed.

For PCS 1900 deployed in North America, the MSISDN follows the North American Number Plan (NANP) format, which consists of the CC, a three-digit number planning area (NPA) code plus a seven-digit SN code. A caller in Taiwan makes a phone call to a PCS 1900 user in the United States by dialing, for example, 002-1-206-528-8128. In this number, 02 is the ISCA in Taiwan; 1 is the CC for the United States; 206 is the NPA code; and 528-8128 is the SN.

CUG Interlock. The *closed user group* (CUG) interlock code defined in ETS 300-138 specification, which is included in the Request/Indication primitives if this information is received from IAM. This parameter is present only in the Response/Confirm primitives if the call is interpreted by the HLR as a CUG call.

CUG defines a group of users (e.g., employees of a company) with specific network services. With CUG, it is possible to limit the incoming/outgoing calls inside the group. The statistics in Taiwan indicate that CUG subscription is around 4–6 percent and the CUG size is typically small, for example, three to five members.

CUG Outgoing Access. Represents the outgoing access of a closed user group. It is present only if the CUG Interlock parameter is provided. This parameter is present only in the Response/Confirm primitives if the call is interpreted by the HLR as a CUG call.

Number of Forwarding. Counts the number of times the call has been forwarded. This information is provided by ISUP—the IAM message.

Call forwarding is more likely to occur to roaming users. Statistics indicate that a home MSC experiences 0.4–0.5 percent of call forwarding and a visited MSC typically experiences 10 percent of call forwarding.

Network Signal Info. Provides external signal information, that is, the signaling protocol between the GSM network and the PSTN, such as ISDN bearer capabilities.

IMSI (International Mobile Subscriber Identity). Used to identify the called MS. Unlike MSISDN, IMSI is not known to the GSM user, and is used by GSM networks only. Specifically, IMSI is stored in the SIM, the HLR, and the serving VLR. The IMSI consists of three parts: A three-digit mobile country code (MCC), a two- or three-digit mobile network code (MNC), and a mobile station identification number (MSIN). The length of IMSI is no more than 15 digits.

MSRN (Mobile Subscriber Roaming Number). The routing number that identifies the current location of the called MS. MSRN is a temporary network identity assigned during the call establishment to a mobile subscriber. MSRN consists of a CC, an NDC, and an SN. The SN is the address to the serving MSC/VLR.

Forwarding Data. Used to invoke the call-forwarding service. If the MSRN parameter is present, this parameter will not be included, and vice versa. This parameter consists of:

1. The address to which a call is to be forwarded.
2. Forwarding options such as notification to forwarding party, notification to calling party, or forwarding reason.

User Error. Sent by the responder when an error is detected. The reason for an error can be:

- Unknown subscriber
- Telephone number changed
- Call barred (e.g., incoming calls are barred by the called MS)
- CUG reject
- Bearer service not provisioned
- Teleservice not provisioned
- Facility not supported
- Absent subscriber
- Forwarding violation
- System failure
- Data missing
- Unexpected data value

Table 10.2(b) lists the parameters for the four **MAP_PROVIDE_ROAMING_NUMBER** primitives, some of which are the same as those listed in Table 10.2(a), and will not be reiterated. The remaining parameters are described here:

MSC Number. The ISDN number of the MSC where the called MS resides.

LMSI (local mobile station identity). Used by the VLR for internal data management of the called MS.

GSM Bearer Capability. Included if the connection is for nonspeech services such as short message services.

User Error. Sent when an error is detected. The reason can be absent subscriber, no MSRN available, facility not supported, system failure, data missing, or unexpected data value.

In Table 10.2, the four primitives of a service have the same Invoke ID. The parameters of the Indication (Confirm) primitive have the same values as that of the Request (Response) primitive (this is true for most MAP services). The Provider Error parameter is optionally included in the Confirm primitive only.

The **MAP_SEND_ROUTING_INFORMATION** service is used by the initiator (i.e., GMSC) to request the responder (HLR) to provide the routing address, MSRN, for the called MS with the phone number MSISDN. The GMSC receives the desired MSRN, forwarding data (if the MS is not available and the call can be forwarded), or an error message. If the MSRN is received, this routing number is used to deliver **IAM** message for trunk setup to the destination MSC.

When the HLR receives the **MAP_SEND_ROUTING_INFORMATION** Request, it invokes **MAP_PROVIDE_ROAMING_NUMBER** service to obtain the MSRN from the VLR. Note that the MSC Number parameter is redundant in the sense that the VLR already has the same information. Normally, the MSRN is produced by using the MSC Number stored in the VLR. If the MSC Number in the VLR is lost due to database failure (described in Chapter 11), the MSRN is created by using the MSC Number provided by the HLR.

10.5 Summary

This chapter provided an overview to the MAP protocol used in the GSM interfaces B, C, D, E, and F. The general platform of the MAP service primitives were described, and examples were provided. We showed how GSM MAP dialogue is carried out by the MAP protocol machine. Network signaling messages for GSM MAP are delivered by SS7, as that for IS-41, described in Chapter 5. The reader is encouraged to compare the SS7 message flows for both GSM MAP and IS-41. GSM CUG is defined in [ETS92a] and [ETS92b]. GSM MAP uses SCCP classes 0 and 1 connectionless services defined in [ANS92c]. Other GSM network signaling protocols and interfaces are beyond the scope of this book. Readers are referred to the GSM 09 series [ETS94f, ETS94e, ETS94d, ETS92c] for additional information.

10.6   Review Questions

1. What is the EIR used for in GSM networks?
2. Which network entities use GSM MAP to communicate with each other?
3. What are the four categories a service primitive can be?
4. What are the parts of the MAP protocol machine (PM)?
5. Why are there several instances of RSMs and PSMs in a MAP PM?
6. The suggested GSM load control priority from high to low are hand-off, mobility management, short message services, and subscriber controlled inputs. Why?
7. How is the routing information retrieved using GSM MAP?
8. Include **MAP-OPEN, TC-BEGIN,** and other common MAP services into the message flow of routing information retrieval in Figure 10.6.
9. Does GSM MAP use the same SS7 signaling mechanism as IS-41? Explain.
10. Describe the code formats for MSRN and MSISDN. Explain why they have the same format.
11. How many mobile subscribers can be accommodated in a GSM network? Is the number of MSISDNs issued in a GSM network always equal to the number of IMSIs issued in that GSM network?

CHAPTER 11

GSM Mobility Management

GSM networks track the locations of the MSs so that incoming calls can be delivered to the subscribers. To exercise location tracking, a mobile service area is partitioned into several location areas (LAs) or registration areas. Every LA consists of a group of base transceiver stations (BTSs) that communicate with the MSs over radio links. The major task of mobility management is to update the location of an MS when it moves from one LA to another. The location update procedure is referred to as *registration*, which is initiated by the MS as follows: The BTSs periodically broadcast the corresponding LA addresses to the MSs. When an MS receives an LA address different from the one stored in its memory, it sends a registration message to the network. The location information is stored in the mobility databases such as the HLR and the VLR described in Chapter 9, Section 9.1.3. Every VLR maintains the information of a group of LAs. When an MS visits an LA, a temporary record of the MS is created in the VLR to indicate its location, that is, the LA address. For every MS, a permanent record is maintained in the HLR. The record stores the address of the last VLR visited by the MS. Figure 11.1 shows the GSM location area hierarchy, where the BTSs of an LA are connected to the corresponding MSC. Thus, an MSC covers several LAs. One or more MSCs are connected to a VLR, which exchange location information with the VLR through the

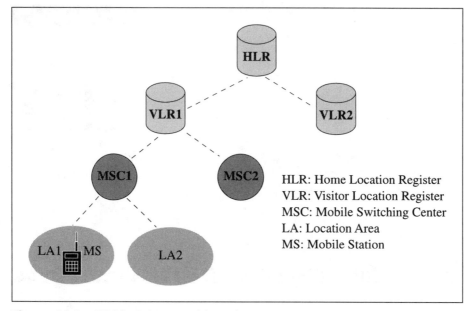

Figure 11.1 GSM location area hierarchy.

SS7 network, as described in Chapter 5, Section 5.1. Similarly, the VLR communicates with the HLR to exchange location information using SS7 messages.

In this chapter, we first describe the GSM location update procedures, then consider two issues of GSM mobility databases: fault tolerance and database overflow.

Fault tolerance. If the location databases fail, the loss or corruption of location information will seriously degrade the service offered to the subscribers. Thus, fault tolerance of location databases becomes one of the most important issues for mobile network management. This chapter describes the failure restoration procedures in GSM and proposes an algorithm to speed up the HLR failure recovery procedure.

Database overflow. The VLR may overflow if too many mobile users move into the VLR-controlled area in a short period. If the VLR is full when a mobile user arrives, the user fails to "register" in the database, and thus cannot receive cellular service. This phenomenon is called *VLR overflow*. To resolve this problem, we propose a VLR overflow control scheme that allows users to receive services when a VLR is full.

11.1   GSM Location Update

In GSM, registration or location update occurs when an MS moves from one LA to another. This procedure was briefly introduced in Chapter 9, Section 9.2. This section provides details of the GSM location update procedure.

11.1.1   Basic Location Update Procedure

The basic location update procedure handles inter-LA, inter-MSC, and inter-VLR movements without considering fault tolerance and VLR overflow. Note that an MS cannot distinguish the types of movement. Thus no matter which kinds of movement occur, location update request messages with the same format are sent from the MS to the network.

11.1.1.1   Case 1: Inter-LA Movement

The MS moves from LA1 to LA2, where both LAs are connected to the same MSC (see Figure 11.2). In the GSM 04.08 specification, there are nine message exchanges between the MS and the MSC and ten message exchanges between the MSC and the VLR. To simplify the description, only four major steps are listed here, as follows:

Step 1. A location update request message is sent from the MS to the MSC through the BTS. This message includes the addresses of the previously visited LA, MSC, and VLR. In this case, the addresses of previous MSC and VLR are the same as those for the new MSC and VLR. Furthermore, the MS identifies itself by the *temporary mobile subscriber identity* (TMSI), which is an alias for IMSI. As described in Chapter 10, Section 10.4, IMSI is the unique subscriber identity that identifies the HLR of the MS. TMSI is used to avoid sending the IMSI on the radio path. This temporary identity is allocated to an MS by the VLR at inter-VLR registration, and can be changed by the VLR, for example, after every call setup.

Step 2. The MSC forwards the location update request to the VLR by a TCAP message, **MAP_UPDATE_LOCATION_AREA**. This message includes:

   ■ Address of the MSC
   ■ TMSI of the MS

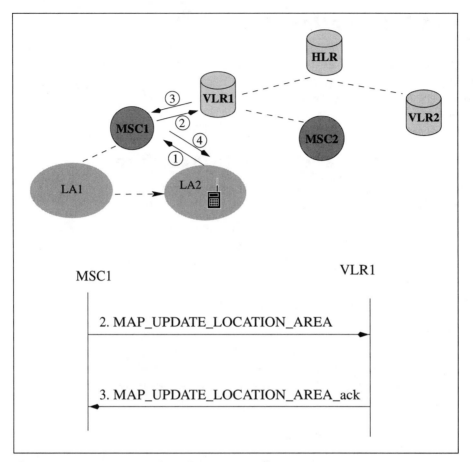

Figure 11.2   Inter-LA registration message flow.

- Previous *location area identification* (LAI); for example, the ID for LA1 in Figure 11.2

- Target LAI; for example, the ID for LA2 in Figure 11.2

- Other related information listed in Section 6.1.1 of GSM 09.02 and GSM 03.12

Note that the LAI is used for paging the MS in the call termination procedure.

Steps 3 and 4. The VLR notices that both LA1 and LA2 belong to the same MSC. It updates the LAI field of the VLR record, and replies with an acknowledgment to the MS through the MSC.

NOTE Messages 2 and 3 are TCAP messages of package type IN-VOKE, and messages 4 and 5 are TCAP messages of package type RETURN RESULT. In the remainder of this book, we use the notations Message and Message_ack to represent the Message (INVOKE) and Message (RETURN RESULT) message pair.

11.1.1.2 Case 2: Inter-MSC Movement

The two LAs belong to different MSCs of the same VLR, as shown in Figure 11.3. The simplified procedure is described in the following steps:

Steps 1 and 2. The location update request is sent from the MS to the VLR, as described in the first two steps of Case 1, Section 11.1.1.1.

Step 3. The VLR notices that the previous LA and the target LA belong to MSC1 and MSC2, respectively. Both MSCs are connected to the same VLR. The VLR updates the LAI and the MSC fields of

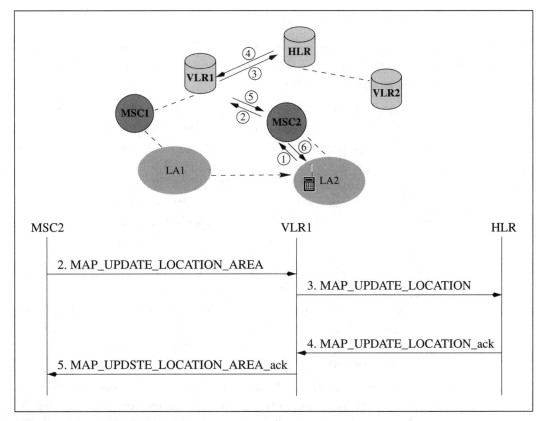

Figure 11.3 Inter-MSC registration message flow.

the VLR record, and derives the HLR address of the MS from the MS's IMSI stored in the VLR record. The VLR sends the **MAP_UPDATE_LOCATION** message to the HLR. The message includes:

- IMSI of the MS
- Address of the target MSC (i.e., MSC2)
- Address of the target VLR (i.e., VLR1)
- Other related information, as listed in Section 6.1.2 of GSM 09.02

Step 4. By using the received IMSI, the HLR identifies the MS's record. The MSC number field of the record is updated. An acknowledgment is sent to the VLR.

Steps 5 and 6. Similar to steps 3 and 4 in Case 1, the acknowledgment is forwarded to the MS.

11.1.1.3   Case 3: Inter-VLR Movement

The two LAs belong to MSCs connected to different VLRs, as illustrated in Figure 11.4. A simplified Inter-VLR location update procedure (that omits authentication) is described next.

Step 1. The location update request is sent from the MS to the VLR, as described in the first two steps of Case 1, Section 11.1.1.1.

Steps 2 and 3. Since the MS moves from VLR1 to VLR2, VLR2 does not have a VLR record of the MS, and the IMSI of the MS is not known. From the **MAP_UPDATE_LOCATION_AREA** message, VLR2 identifies the address of the previous VLR (VLR1). It sends the message **MAP_SEND_IDENTIFICATION** to VLR1. Details concerning this message can be found in Section 6.1.4 of GSM 09.02. Basically, the message provides the TMSI of the MS, which is used by VLR1 to retrieve the corresponding IMSI in the database. The IMSI is then sent back to VLR2.

To enhance security, confidential data (IMSI) typically is not sent over air in GSM location updating. In IS-41, on the other hand, the subscriber identity is sent directly from the MS to the new VLR to reduce signaling traffic.

Steps 4 and 5. VLR2 creates a VLR record for the MS, and sends a registration message to update the HLR, as described in step 3 of Case 2, Section 11.1.1.2. The HLR updates the record of the

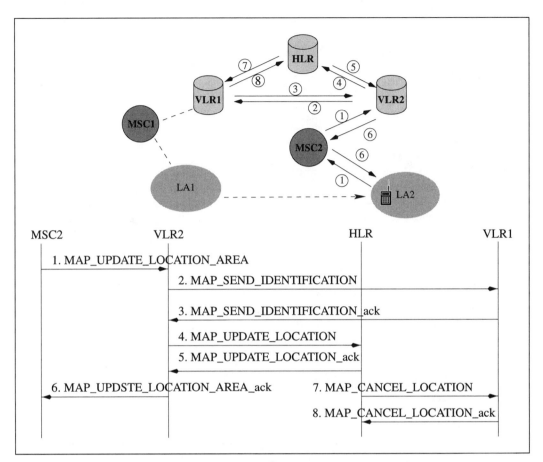

Figure 11.4   Inter-VLR registration message flow.

MS in the same way as in step 4 of Case 2 except that the VLR address field of the record is also updated. An acknowledgment is sent back to VLR2.

Step 6.   VLR2 generates a new TMSI and sends it to the MS. In GSM, the TMSI is changed from time to time to avoid fraudulent usage.

Steps 7 and 8.   The obsolete record of the MS in VLR1 is deleted.

11.1.2   Basic Call Origination and Termination Procedures

Figure 11.5 illustrates the basic call origination procedure; the algorithm is described in the following steps:

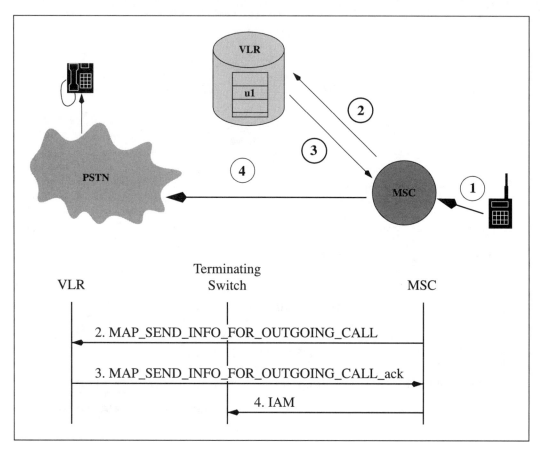

Figure 11.5 Call origination operation.

Step 1. The MSu1 sends the call origination request to the MSC.

Step 2. The MSC forwards the request to the VLR by sending MAP_SEND_INFO_FOR_OUTGOING_CALL.

Step 3. The VLR checks the *u1*'s profile and sends MAP_SEND_INFO_FOR_OUTGOING_CALL_ack to the MSC to grant the call request.

Step 4. The MSC sets up the trunk according to the standard PSTN call setup procedure.

For call termination to a GSM subscriber, routing information must be obtained from the serving VLR (see Figure 11.6). Details of the basic call termination procedure are given as follows:

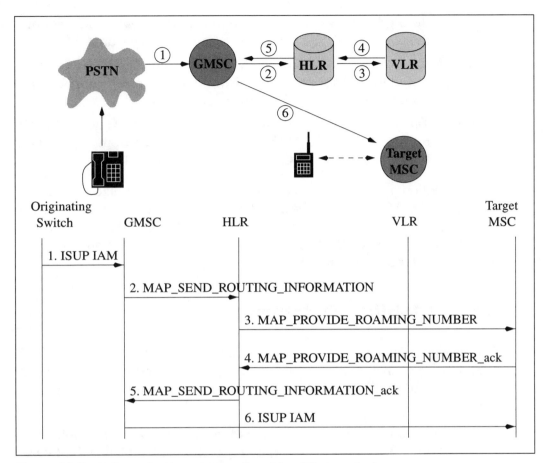

Figure 11.6   Call termination message flow (simplified version).

Step 1.   When the mobile station ISDN number (MSISDN) is dialed by a PSTN user, the call is routed to a gateway MSC by an SS7 ISUP IAM message, described in Chapter 5, Section 5.4.

Step 2.   To obtain the routing information, the gateway MSC or ISDN exchange interrogates the HLR by sending **MAP_SEND_ROUTING_INFORMATION** to the HLR. This message consists of the MSISDN of the MS and other related information, listed in Section 8.3 of GSM 09.02.

Step 3.   The HLR sends a **MAP_PROVIDE_ROAMING_NUMBER** message to the VLR to obtain the mobile subscriber roaming number (MSRN). The message consists of the IMSI, the MSC number, and other related information. Note that at inter-MSC and inter-VLR location update, the MSC number is maintained in the HLR during location update. This number provides the address of the target MSC, and is used to set up the voice trunk.

Steps 4 and 5. The VLR creates the MSRN by using the MSC number stored in the VLR record of the MS. This roaming number is sent back to the gateway MSC through the HLR.

Step 6. The MSRN provides the address of the target MSC where the MS resides. An SS7 ISUP IAM message is directed from the gateway MSC to the target MSC to set up the voice trunk.

The location update and the call-delivery procedures utilize the location information in HLR/VLR. If the mobility databases fail, the system will not be able to track the MS. In the next section, we describe the information maintained in the HLR/VLR, and show how the information can be recovered after database failures.

11.2   Mobility Databases

The *home location register* (HLR) is a database used for mobile user information management. All permanent subscriber data other than the secret key are stored in this database. An HLR record consists of three types of information:

- *Mobile station information*, such as the IMSI used by the mobile station to access the network, and the MSISDN, which is the ISDN number—the "phone number" of an MS.

- *Location information*, such as the ISDN number (address) of the VLR where the MS resides and the ISDN number of the MSC where the MS resides.

- *Service information*, such as service subscription, service restrictions, and supplementary services.

The visitor location register (VLR) is the database of the service area visited by an MS. The VLR contains all subscriber data of an MS required for call handling and other purposes. Similar to the HLR, the VLR information consists of three parts:

- *Mobile station information*, such as IMSI, MSISDN, and TMSI, as defined in GSM 03.03.

- *Location information*, such as MSC number and the location area ID (LAI).

- *Service information*, which is a subset of the service information stored in the HLR.

In the MS-related fields, TMSI structure can be determined by each operator, but its length should not be longer than eight digits. LAI consists of a three-digit mobile country code (MCC), a two- or three-digit mobile network code (MNC), and a location access code of up to 16 digits.

11.3 Failure Restoration

This section describes failure restoration procedures for both the VLR and the HLR.

11.3.1 VLR Failure Restoration

After a VLR failure, the service information of a VLR record is recovered by the first contact between the VLR and the HLR of the corresponding MS. The location information is recovered by the first radio contact between the VLR and the MS. The mobile station information is recovered either by contact with the HLR or the MS. VLR record restoration is initiated by one of the following three events: MS registration, MS call origination, and MS call termination.

MS registration. Since the VLR record was erased by the failure, the VLR considers the registration as a case of inter-VLR movement. Following the normal registration procedure defined in inter-VLR movement, the VLR record is recovered. In this case, TMSI sent from the MS to the VLR cannot be recognized, and the MS is asked to send IMSI over the air.

MS call origination. When the VLR receives the call origination request MAP_SEND_INFO_FOR_OUTGOING_CALL from the MSC, the VLR record for the MS is not found. The VLR considers the situation as a system error, with the cause "unidentified subscriber." The request is rejected, and the MS is asked to initiate the location registration procedure in Section 11.1.1. After the registration procedure, the VLR record is recovered.

MS call termination. The call termination message flow is illustrated in Figure 11.7 and is detailed in the following procedure:

Steps 1–3. Similar to the first three steps of the basic call termination procedure, the VLR is queried to provide the MSRN. (Note

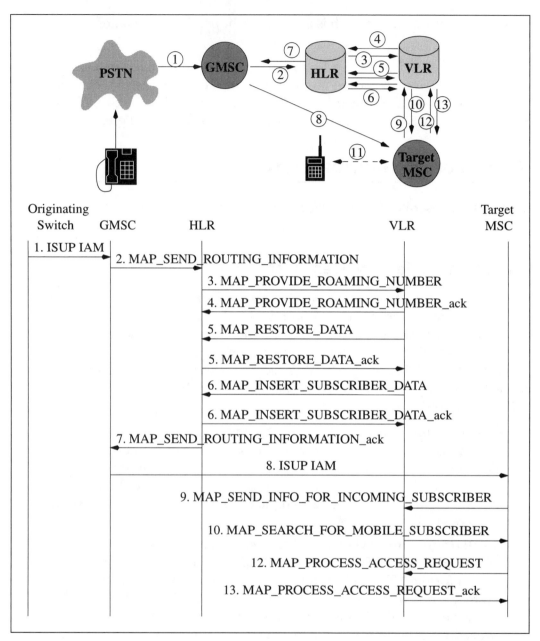

Figure 11.7 Call termination message flow (failure restoration).

that the IMSI and the MSC number are provided in the MAP_PROVIDE_ROAMING_NUMBER message sent from the HLR to the VLR.) The VLR searches the MS record by using the received IMSI. Since the record has been erased after the failure, the search fails. The VLR creates a VLR record for the MS. Neither the service nor the location information is available in this record. Steps 4 and 5 are executed in parallel.

Steps 4 and 7. Since the VLR does not have the routing information, it uses the MSC number provided by the MAP_PROVIDE_ROAMING_NUMBER message to create the MSRN. The number is sent back to the gateway MSC to set up the call in step 8.

Steps 5 and 6. The VLR recovers the service information of the VLR record by sending a MAP_RESTORE_DATA message to the HLR. The HLR sends the service information to the VLR using the MAP_INSERT_SUBSCRIBER_DATA message described in Section 6.8.1 of GSM 09.02. At this point, the service information of the VLR record has been recovered. However, the location information, specifically, the LAI number, still is not available. This information will be recovered at step 11.

Step 8. After the gateway MSC receives the MSRN in step 7, the SS7 ISUP message IAM is sent to the target MSC, as described in step 6 of the basic call termination procedure, Section 11.1.2.

Steps 9–11. The target MSC does not have the LA information of the MS. In order to proceed to set up the call, the MSC sends the message MAP_SEND_INFO_FOR_INCOMING_CALL to the VLR. Unfortunately, the VLR does not have the LAI information either. Hence the VLR asks the MSC to determine the LA of the MS by sending a MAP_SEARCH_FOR_MOBILE_SUBSCRIBER message.

Steps 12 and 13. The MSC initiates paging of the MS in all LAs. If the paging is successful, the current LA address of the MS is sent back to the VLR by the MAP_PROCESS_ACCESS_REQUEST message. At this point, the location information of the VLR record is recovered.

Note that MAP_SEARCH_FOR_MOBILE_SUBSCRIBER is an expensive operation because every BTS connected to the MSC must perform the paging operation. To avoid this "wide area paging," the GSM system may periodically ask the MSs to reregister. Using periodic location updating, after a VLR failure, there is a better chance that the location information will be recovered by the periodic location confirmation before the first call termination occurs, thereby avoiding an expensive MS search operation.

11.3.2 HLR Failure Restoration

For a GSM HLR, it is mandatory to save the updates into nonvolatile storage. Changes of service information are saved into the backup storage device immediately after any update. The location information is periodically check-pointed, that is, the information is periodically transferred from the HLR into the backup. Updating the service information is done infrequently since most subscribers rarely change their service profiles after subscription, and the immediate backup update operations do not cost too much.

After an HLR failure, the data in the backup are reloaded into the HLR. We define an *uncovered period* as the time interval after the last backup operation and before the restart of the HLR. Data that have been changed in the uncovered period cannot be recovered. The following HLR restoration procedure is executed (see Figure 11.8):

Step 1. The HLR sends an SS7 TCAP message **MAP_RESET** to the VLRs where its MSs are located. Details of **MAP_RESET** are given in Section 6.10.1 of GSM 09.02.

Step 2. All the VLRs derive all MSs of the HLR; and for each MS, they send an SS7 TCAP message, **MAP_UPDATE_LOCATION**, to the

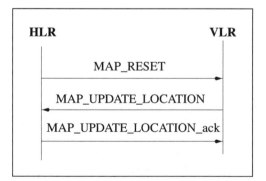

Figure 11.8 HLR restoration procedure.

HLR. After the location update operation, the HLR record is recovered.

The HLR restoration procedure is not robust because an MS may move into a VLR (which does not have any other MSs from the given HLR residing) during the uncovered period, and the new location is not known to the HLR at the last check-pointing time. If so, the HLR will not be able to locate the VLR of the MS during step 1 of HLR restoration procedure. We describe an algorithm to resolve this problem in the next section.

11.4   VLR Identification Algorithm

This section describes an algorithm to identify the exact VLRs to be contacted by the HLR after an HLR failure. To simplify the description, we assume that every VLR covers exactly one MSC. Extension of our algorithm to accommodate multi-MSCs is trivial. To implement the VLR Identification Algorithm (VIA), extra data structures are required in the HLR, as shown in Figure 11.9. This figure shows only the fields of the HLR record required to exercise the VIA. In the backup, the extra data structure is a set *VLR_List** of VLRs that have been modified during the uncovered period. After an HLR failure, the HLR only needs to send the **MAP_RESET** messages to the VLRs listed in *VLR_List**.

In HLR, every record includes two extra fields, as illustrated in Figure 11.9.

- The *ts* field indicates the last time of location update. In some GSM implementations, this field already exists for other purposes.

- The *PVLR* field contains the address of the VLR where the MS resided at the last check-pointing time. Thus, for any MS *p*, we have:

$$HLR^*[p] \cdot VLR = HLR[p] \cdot PVLR$$

Two extra data structures are introduced to the HLR:

- *TS* is the last check-pointing or backup time.

- *VLR_Counter* is a set of (*VLR*, *Count*) pairs, where *Count* represents the "effective number" of MSs entering the VLR *VLR* during the uncovered period. An MS is not effective to a VLR if it entered the VLR area then left the area during the uncovered period. For example, in Figure 11.9, there are three effective MSs in VLR V_1. Note that the VLRs recorded in *VLR_Counter* are the VLRs in *VLR_List**.

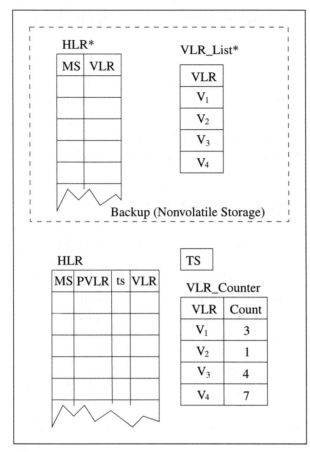

Figure 11.9 HLR architecture.

In VIA, information of the HLR is periodically saved into the backup by using the following check-pointing procedure.

VIA Procedure 1: Check-pointing

Step 1. **For** every location entry p in HLR^* **do**:

$$HLR[p]^* \cdot VLR \leftarrow HLR[p] \cdot VLR;$$

Step 2. $TS \leftarrow$ current time;

Step 3. **For** every location entry p in HLR **do**:

$$HLR[p] \cdot ts \leftarrow TS; \;\; HLR[p] \cdot PVLR \leftarrow HLR[p] \cdot VLR;$$

Step 4. *VLR_Counter* ← ∅, *VLR_List** ← ∅;

In procedure 1, every location entry is saved into the backup at step 1. The clock *TS* is set to the time of check-pointing at step 2. The timestamp field, *ts*, of every location entry in HLR is set to *TS* to indicate that the last location of the MS was updated no later than the latest check-pointing time *TS* at step 3. The *PVLR* is set to the current VLR address of the MS. Finally, at step 4, both *VLR_Counter* and *VLR_List** are set to empty to indicate that no VLR has new roaming MS at *TS*.

Suppose that MS p moves into VLR area V_{new} at time t. Then a message **MAP_UPDATE_LOCATION** is sent from V_{new} to the HLR. Procedure 2 at the HLR is triggered to perform the registration operation.

VIA Procedure 2: Registration

Step 1. Update *HLR*:

$$V_{old} \leftarrow HLR[p] \cdot VLR;$$

Send message, **MAP_CANCEL_LOCATION**, to cancel the VLR entry of p at V_{old}:

$$HLR[p] \cdot VLR \leftarrow V_{new};$$
$$t_{old} \leftarrow HLR[p] \cdot ts;$$
$$HLR[p] \cdot ts \leftarrow t;$$

Step 2. Update the V_{new} *Count* field in *VLR_Counter*: **If**

$$HLR[p] \cdot VLR \neq HLR[p] \cdot PVLR$$

then:

Step 2.1. **If** $VLR\_Counter[V_{new}]$ exists, **then**:

$$VLR\_Counter[V_{new}] \cdot Count \leftarrow VLR\_Counter[V_{new}] \cdot Count + 1;$$

Step 2.2. **Else** create $VLR\_Counter[V_{new}]$ and $VLR\_List^*[V_{new}]$:

$$VLR\_Counter[V_{new}] \leftarrow 1;$$

Step 3. Update the V_{old} counter entry: **If** $t_{old} > TS$ **and** $V_{old} \neq HLR[p] \cdot PVLR$ **then**:

Step 3.1.

$VLR\_Counter[V_{old}] \cdot Count \leftarrow VLR\_Counter[V_{old}] \cdot Count - 1;$

Step 3.2. **If** $VLR\_Counter[V_{old}].Count = 0$ **then**:

Step 3.2.1. Delete $VLR\_Counter[V_{old}]$ and $VLR\_List^*[V_{old}]$;

At step 1 of procedure 2, the location information of the MS is updated and its location record at the old VLR, V_{old}, is cancelled by the deregistration message **MAP_CANCEL_LOCATION**. The last update time, t_{old}, is saved to be used in step 3.

At steps 2 and 3 of procedure 2, $VLR\_Counter[]$ is used to count the "effective" number of MSs that enter the VLRs during the period $[TS, t]$. Note that if the MS was in V_{new} before TS (i.e., $HLR[p] \cdot VLR = HLR^*[p] \cdot VLR = HLR[p] \cdot PVLR$), then the HLR may consider that the MS never moves out of the VLR, and there is no need to increment the VLR counter, and step 2 is skipped.

If the MS moved into V_{old} during the uncovered period—that is, $ts_{old} > TS$—it implies that the movement into V_{old} is not effective because the MS has moved out of V_{old} at t. Thus, the V_{old} counter should be decremented by 1, as described in step 3.

When $VLR\_Counter[V] \cdot Count > 1$, then any update to $VLR\_Counter[V]$ will not invoke modification to $VLR\_List^*[]$. In other words, access to the HLR backup is avoided. The purpose of procedure 2 is to avoid updating the backup for every registration operation.

After an HLR failure, procedure 3 is executed to restore the HLR. In this procedure, the HLR restores the location entries from the backup and requests current status of the MSs from all VLRs that have updated MS information between the last check-pointing time and the HLR failure time.

VIA Procedure 3: Restore

Step 1. $TS \leftarrow$ current time;

Step 2. **For** every location entry p in HLR, **do**:

$HLR[p] \cdot PVLR = HLR[p] \cdot VLR \leftarrow HLR[p]^* \cdot VLR;$

$HLR[p] \cdot ts \leftarrow TS;$

Step 3. **For** every VLR entry *V* in *VLR_List**, send an SS7 TCAP
         MAP_RESET message to *V*;

After the **MAP_RESET** messages are sent, the HLR will follow the
GSM HLR restoration procedure in Section 11.3.2 to recover the location
information as described previously.

In the VIA, the backups—specifically *VLR_List**—are modified only at
steps 2.2 and 3.2.1 of procedure 2. Our experience indicates that the MSs
are likely to move within certain VLRs, and the frequency of accessing
*VLR_List** in VIA is relatively low compared with the frequency of location
update operations. Thus, the cost, mainly the access to the backup of VIA,
is low, and the execution of the VIA is expected to be efficient.

11.5   VLR Overflow Control

Mobile users of different cellular systems may visit an LA (e.g., GSM users
from England and Taiwan may visit Hong Kong); therefore, the number of
records in the VLR can change dynamically. Specifically, new records are
created when users move in, and obsolete records are deleted when the
corresponding users move out. It is possible that the number of the records
in the corresponding VLR may be larger than that of the HLR, and the VLR
may overflow if too many mobile users move into the LA in a short period.
If the VLR is full when a mobile user arrives, the user fails to "register" in
the database, and thus cannot receive cellular service. This phenomenon is
called *VLR overflow*. To resolve this problem, this section proposes a VLR
overflow control scheme that allows users to receive services when a VLR
is full.

When a VLR is full, the incoming mobile users cannot register using the
registration procedure described in Section 11.1.1, and thus cannot receive
cellular services. To resolve this problem, overflow control algorithms
O-I, O-II, O-III, and O-IV are presented, which allow new users to receive
services when the VLR is full. In the overflow control scheme, an extra flag
(1 bit) is required in the HLR records. No modifications are made to the
MS.

11.5.1   Algorithm O-I: Registration

Suppose that an MS moves into the area controlled by the VLR *V2*. If
V2 is not full, then the registration procedure described in Section 11.1.1

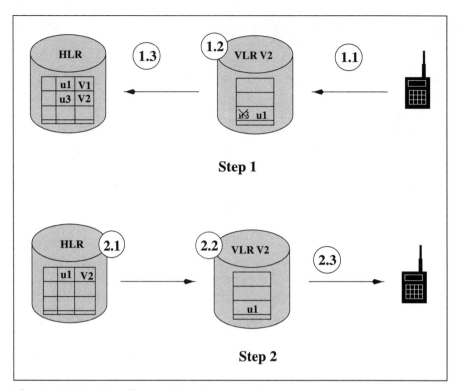

Figure 11.10 Overflow registration operation.

is executed. If *V2* is full, then the following steps are executed (see Figure 11.10):

Step 1. Registration Request:

Step 1.1. This is the same as step 1 of the normal registration procedure.

Step 1.2. The database is full. *V2* follows a replacement policy to select a record to be deleted (*u3* in Figure 11.10). The storage for the deleted record is used to store the *u1*'s information. The selected user (i.e., *u3*) is called the *overflow user*.
The replacement policy may be based on various heuristics. For example, *V2* may select a record randomly, select the oldest record, or select an inactive record (i.e., the user has not had call activities re-

cently). *V2* may select *u1* as the overflow user (i.e., *u3 = u1*), and does not create a VLR record for *u1*.

Step 1.3. *V2* forwards the registration request to the HLR with the indication that *u3*'s record is deleted due to database overflow.

Step 2. Registration Response:

Step 2.1. The HLR updates the location of *u1*, and sets the overflow flag in *u3*'s record (to indicate that *V2* does not have a VLR record for *u3*). Note that *u3* may be identical to *u1*, as pointed out in step 1.2.

Step 2.2. The HLR acknowledges the registration operation and sends *u1*'s profile to *V2*. If *u1* is the overflow user, then the message does not include the profile information.

Step 2.3. *V2* sends an acknowledgment to the MS.

11.5.2 Algorithm O-II: Cancellation

If *u1* is not an overflow user at VLR *V1*, then steps 7 and 8 of the inter-VLR registration procedure are executed to cancel *u1*'s VLR record in *V1*. If *u1* is an overflow user at *V1*, then *u1* does not have a record in *V1*. The cancellation operation simply resets the overflow flag of *u1*'s HLR record if *u1* is not an overflow user in *V2* (as shown in Figure 11.11). The call origination for an overflow user is described next.

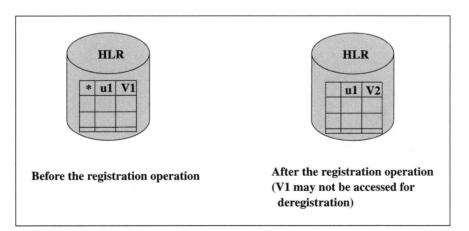

Before the registration operation

After the registration operation (V1 may not be accessed for deregistration)

Figure 11.11 Cancellation operation with overflow VLR.

11.5.3 Algorithm O-III: Call Origination

This procedure is shown in Figure 11.12; here are its steps:

Step 1. The MS sends the call origination request to *V2*.

Step 2. *V2* cannot find *u1*'s record, and denies the call request.

Steps 3 and 4. The MS initiates the registration procedure; Algorithm O-I is executed.

Steps 5 and 6. The MS reissues the call origination request, and the normal call origination procedure is executed.

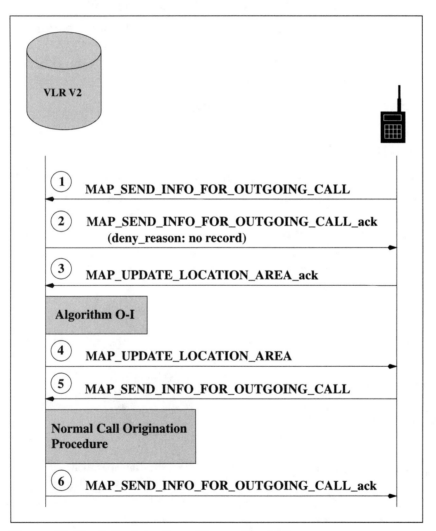

Figure 11.12 Call origination with overflow VLR.

To deliver a call to an overflow user, the algorithm O-IV is exercised, as described in the next section.

11.5.4   Algorithm O-IV: Call Termination

This algorithm is shown in Figure 11.13; it follows these steps:

Step 1. Location query:

> Step 1.1. The calling party dials the phone number of *u1*. The request is sent to the originating switch in the PSTN.
>
> Step 1.2. The originating switch sends a location query message to the HLR.
>
> Step 1.3. The HLR determines that *u1* is an overflow user and sends a query message to obtain the routing information. The user profile information is attached in the message.

Step 2. Location response:

> Step 2.1. If *V2* is not full, a record for *u1* is created. If *V2* is full, a user record is deleted and is used to store *u1*'s information. *V2* creates the routable address of *u1* and sends it back to the HLR. If the VLR record is not available, refer to the details of the routable address creation as described in GSM 09.02. If a record is replaced (*u3* in Figure 11.13), the replacement information is included in the message.
>
> Step 2.2. The HLR returns the routable address to the originating switch. If a record is replaced, the overflow flags (for *u1* and *u3* in Figure 11.13) are updated at the HLR.
>
> Step 2.3. The originating switch sets up the trunk to the MSC based on the routable address.
>
> Step 2.4. The MSC pages the mobile phone and the call path is established.

NOTE The preceding description has been simplified. The actual message flow of Algorithm O-IV is very similar to that in Figure 11.7.

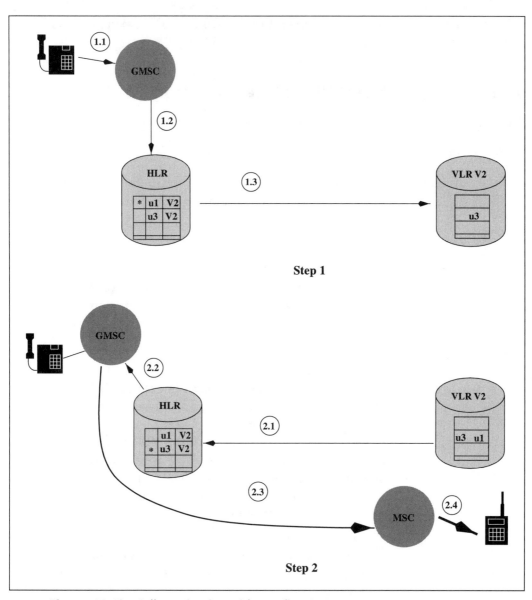

Figure 11.13   Call termination with overflow VLR.

With Algorithms O-I through O-IV, an LA can accommodate an unlimited number of mobile users as long as the number of simultaneous phone calls to these users is no larger than the size of the database. This situation should never occur in the real world.

11.6   Summary

This chapter presented mobility management in GSM. The MS registration procedure, the call delivery procedure, and the location database failure restoration procedure were described. The SS7 message exchanges between MSC, VLR, and HLR in these procedures were also specified. The MS location registration procedures were described for three cases of MS movement: inter-LA movement, inter-MSC movement, and inter-VLR movement [ETS93i]. Information stored in VLR and HLR is defined in [ETS94f, ETS93h, ETS93j, ETS93k]. Also in this chapter, an efficient VLR identification algorithm to speed up HLR failure restoration was outlined. The algorithm maintains timestamped HLR records and counts the effective number of MSs entering each VLR since the last HLR check-pointing. As a result, during an HLR failure recovery, the VLRs that need to be contacted for MS location update can be accurately identified. The selection of the frequency for location registration was studied in [Lin95a]. Further reading for mobility database failure restoration can be found in [Fan00a, Fan00b, Haa98, Cha98, ETS93l, ITU93a].

Based on [Lin00a], we also proposed an approach to resolve the VLR overflow problem. With the overflow mechanism, an LA can accommodate an unlimited number of mobile users as long as the number of simultaneous phone calls to these users is no larger than the size of the database. Note that the procedures described in Sections 11.1 and 11.3 are standard GSM procedures. We invented the VIA and VLR overflow algorithms that are not accommodated in GSM specifications. The VLR overflow algorithm was granted a patent in the United Kingdom (patent number 2328119).

11.7   Review Questions

1. Consider two MSCs, A and B. Suppose the BTSs connected to MSC A are partitioned into two groups A_1 and A_2, and that the BTSs of MSC B are grouped into B_1 and B_2. Is it reasonable to group A_1 and B_1 into an LA, and group A_2 and B_2 into another LA?

2. TMSI is operator-dependent. In the location update procedure, does it cause a problem when a VLR receives a TMSI of a unknown format (i.e., the TMSI is defined in another GSM network) from a roaming MS? Does it make sense to define an operator-independent TMSI?

3. Compare the formats of TMSI and IMSI. Is it appropriate to design the code structures so that TMSI is longer than IMSI? (Hint: Consider the space complexity of a paging message.)

4. Compare the formats of IMSI and LAI. How many LAs can be defined in a GSM network? What does it imply when the IMSI and the LAI for a mobile user have the same MCC and MNC?

5. What is the information stored in the HLR? What is the information stored in the VLR? Why are the pieces of information in HLR and VLR different?

6. Describe three events that recover a VLR record after a VLR fault restoration. Before a VLR record is recovered, how does the VLR route the MS terminated call to the corresponding MS?

7. What are the two main steps of a HLR restoration procedure in GSM?

8. Can you recover a GSM system if both the HLR and VLR fail at the same time?

9. What is a VLR database overflow and why is it a big issue?

10. Describe the VLR overflow control procedure in the case of MS registration. In Figure 11.10, if $u3$ is not marked in HLR (as being replaced), can you modify Algorithms O-II, O-III, and O-IV so that the overflow mechanism still works?

11. Can IS-41 use the same fault-tolerance and database-overflow mechanisms for GSM described in this chapter? Why or why not?

12. Consider the HLR failure restoration for IS-41. To restore the data of an HLR after a failure, the HLR needs the help of all the VLRs where its mobile phones are located. In EIA/TIA IS-41 [EIA91a], the HLR recovery procedure works as follows:

    (a) After a failure, the HLR initiates the recovery procedure by sending an **Unreliable Roamer Data Directive** message to all of its associated VLRs. The VLRs then remove all records of the mobile phones associated with that HLR from their memory.

    (b) At some future point in time, a "lost" mobile phone contacts the VLR for call origination or location confirmation (to be described). The VLR then sends a registration message to the HLR associated with that mobile, allowing the HLR to reconstruct its internal data structures in an incremental fashion.

After the HLR failure, if the first event of a mobile phone is a call origination (a request from the mobile phone) then the VLR detects the existence of the mobile phone and the HLR record of the mobile phone is restored through the registration process. If the first k events of a mobile phone are call deliveries (someone attempts to call the mobile subscriber), then the k calls are lost because the HLR cannot identify the location of the mobile phone.

The delay to confirm the location of a mobile phone after a HLR failure depends on the traffic from the mobile phone. If a mobile phone is silent for a long time, all call deliveries during this period will be lost.

The *periodic location update* mechanism described in GSM 03.07 [ETS93l] can be used to reduce this delay and loss. In this approach, a mobile phone periodically establishes radio contact with the network to confirm its location. Design a performance model to investigate how the frequency of periodic location update affects the IS-41 failure restoration. (Hint: See the model in [Haa98].)

12

GSM Short Message Service

The GSM *short message service* (SMS) provides a connectionless transfer of messages with low-capacity and low-time performance. In December 1992, the first short message, sent from a PC to an MS, was delivered in the Vodafone GSM network in the United Kingdom.

Every GSM short message can contain up to 140 octets, or 160 characters, of GSM default alphabet, as defined in GSM 03.38. To allow messages longer than 160 characters, *SMS concatenation* (that delivers a long message by concatenating several individual standard short messages) and *SMS compression* have been defined and incorporated in the GSM SMS standards. The SMS operates like a paging service, with the added capability that messages can pass in both directions. The short messages are transported on the GSM SDCCH signaling channel described in Chapter 9, Section 9.1.4. Thus, messages can be received while the mobile users are in conversation. Two types of GSM short message services have been defined:

- *Cell broadcast* service, which periodically delivers short messages to all subscribers in a given area.

- *Point-to-point* service, which sends short messages to a specific user. This GSM feature can be considered as an enhanced two-way paging service.

This chapter will focus on the point-to-point service. We describe the SMS architecture, protocol hierarchy, mobile-originated messaging, mobile-terminated messaging, and AT commands.

12.1   SMS Architecture

An example of the GSM short message service network architecture is illustrated in Figure 12.1. In this architecture, the short message is first delivered from the message sender (e.g., a GSM MS or a paging input device, described in Chapter 22, Section 22.1) to a *short message service center* (SM-SC). The SM-SC is connected to the GSM network through a specific GSM MSC called the short message service gateway MSC (SMS GMSC). The SM-SC may connect to several GSM networks and to several SMS GMSCs in a GSM network. Following the GSM roaming protocol, the SMS GMSC locates the current MSC of the message receiver and forwards the message to that MSC. The MSC broadcasts the message to the base station systems, and the base transceiver stations (BTSs) page the destination MS. The MS used for short message services must contain special software to enable the messages to be decoded and stored. Messages can be stored either in the SIM or in the memory of the mobile equipment (ME) for display on the standard screen of the MS.

An MS may send or reply to a short message. The message is delivered to a *short message service interworking MSC* (IWMSC) and then to the SM-SC, as explained in the subsequent sections. The recipient of the short message can be an MS, a fax machine, or a PC connected to the Internet. Experience indicates that mobile-originating traffic is around 20 percent of mobile-terminating traffic. Note that SMS is a store-and-forward service. Short messages cannot be sent directly from the sender to the recipient without passing through the SM-SC.

To simpify the generation of a short message in an MS, several technologies have been proposed. *Predictive text input algorithms* installed in an MS reduce the number of input keystrokes by predicting the next word the user will generate. New features, such as the QWERTY keyboard, can be built in the MS to provide simpler access to messaging services.

There are three types of short messages: *user-specific*, *ME-specific*, and *SIM-specific*. A user-specific message is displayed to the user. An ME-specific message is processed by the mobile equipment instead of showing to the user. A special function created by the handset vendor can be triggered by the ME-specific message. For example, a Nokia smart message is an ME-specific message. The vendor-defined special functions include

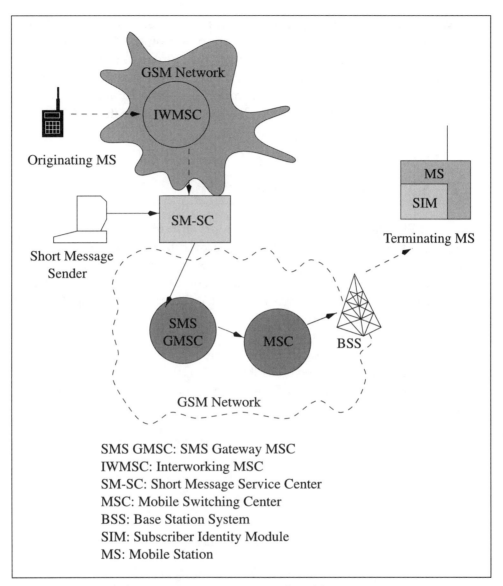

SMS GMSC: SMS Gateway MSC
IWMSC: Interworking MSC
SM-SC: Short Message Service Center
MSC: Mobile Switching Center
BSS: Base Station System
SIM: Subscriber Identity Module
MS: Mobile Station

Figure 12.1   GSM short message service network architecture.

playing a ringing tone, displaying a business card, modifying the default icon, and so on. Similarly, a SIM-specific message is processed at the SIM card. If a GSM operator designs a special function in the SIM card, the SIM-specific message can trigger this function.

The SM-SC plays an important role in supporting high-quality SMS service. An SM-SC should be scalable, with high availability and reliability.

The SM-SCs are typically implemented on high-speed server platforms. For example, the Sema SM-SC products are based on the Compaq Alpha server; the Ericsson SM-SC is based on the Sun SPARC station; and the Nokia SM-SC utilizes Hewlett-Packard's 9000 server. Existing SM-SC products support TCP/IP access, and many of them can accommodate new data protocols, such as the Wireless Application Protocol (WAP), described in Chapter 19.

12.2   SMS Protocol Hierarchy

Figure 12.2 illustrates the SMS protocol hierarchy for mobile-originated messaging, as defined in GSM 04.11. The architecture for mobile-terminated messaging is similar, with the exception that the IWMSC is replaced by the GMSC. The SMS protocol hierarchy consists of four layers: short message application layer (SM-AL), short message transfer layer (SM-TL), short message relay layer (SM-RL), and connection management sublayer (CM-sub). In this hierarchy, the protocol between the IWMSC and the SM-SC below the transfer layer is not specified in GSM. Some example protocols are described in GSM 03.47. Other potential protocols include Telocator Alphanumeric Input Protocol and Telocator Data Proto-

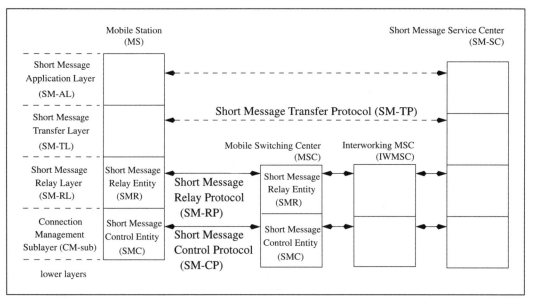

Figure 12.2   SMS MS-MSC protocol hierarchy (mobile origination).

col, described in Chapter 22, Section 22.2. The protocol between the MSC and IWMSC is GSM MAP, utilizing SS7 TCAP, as described in Chapter 5, Section 5.1.

The layers below the CM-sublayer are the *mobility management* (MM) sublayer and the *radio resource* (RR) management sublayer. At the RR-sublayer, the short message service is supported by a control channel such as SDCCH or SACCH. The upper layer protocols are described next.

12.2.1 Short Message Transfer Layer

The SM-TL provides services to transfer SM-AL short messages and the corresponding delivery reports described in GSM 03.40. These SM-TL-supported service primitives generate a reference number called the *short message identifier* (SMI) for every short message associated with the primitives. This SMI at the MS is not carried between the peer entity at the SM-SC. That is, a short message may have different SMIs at the MS and the SM-SC sides.

The Transfer Protocol SM-TP consists of four types of *transfer protocol data units* (TPDUs), as described in Section 9.2.2 in GSM 03.40 and summarized here:

SMS-SUBMIT. Conveys a short message, referred to as *transfer protocol-user data*, or TP-UD, from the MS to the SM-SC. TP-UD optionally specifies the *validity period* that the short message can be buffered in the SM-SC if it cannot be delivered to the recipient immediately.

SMS-DELIVER. Conveys a short message from the SM-SC to the MS. This TPDU includes a *service center timestamp*. The SM-SC uses this timestamp to inform the recipient MS about the arrival time of the short message at the SM-TL of the SM-SC. A Boolean parameter, More-To-Send, is used to indicate if one or more messages are waiting in the SM-SC for delivery to the recipient MS.

SMS-STATUS-REPORT. Conveys a report from the SM-SC to the MS. The report describes the status of the previously sent mobile-originated short message. If the previous short message is not delivered successfully, this TPDU may report permanent errors, such as validity period expiration or incompatible destination, or temporary errors, such as congestion. This TPDU is optionally initiated by **SMS-SUBMIT**.

SMS-COMMAND. Conveys a command from the MS to the SM-SC. The command can be a query about the previous submitted short message, cancellation of the status report, or deletion of the submitted message.

We elaborate more on the TPDU format by using **SMS-SUBMIT** as an example. The **SMS-SUBMIT** TPDU includes the following parameters:

Message Type Indicator (MTI). Specifies the TPDU type. MTI is 01 for **SMS-SUBMIT**.

Reject Duplicates (RD). Indicates if the SM-SC should reject the duplicated **SMS-SUBMIT** TPDU.

Validity Period Format (VPF). Specifies the format of validity period field. Validity period indicates the time interval that the short message can be buffered in the SM-SC if it cannot be delivered to the recipient immediately.

Status Report Request (SRR). Indicates whether a status report should be sent back to the sender.

User Data Header Indicator (UDHI). As its name implies.

Reply Path (RP). Indicates whether the reply path is used.

The **SMS-DELIVER** TPDU is similar to the **SMS-SUBMIT** TPDU, except that **SMS-DELIVER** includes fields, such as More-to-Send, to indicate whether there are more messages to be received, and Status Report Indication (SRI), to indicate whether the MS should return a status report to the SM-SC. Every TPDU, except for **SMS-STATUS-REPORT**, has a *protocol identifier* that identifies the layer protocol above SM-TL. For an unsuccessful delivery due to temporary absence of the MS, *messages-waiting* information may be stored in the HLR/VLR of the recipient MS. The TPDUs are either of priority or nonpriority. A nonpriority TPDU will not be attempted again if the MS is absent.

12.2.2 Short Message Relay Layer

The short message relay layer (SM-RL) provides services to transfer TPDUs and the corresponding delivery reports for SM-TL. These SM-RL-supported service primitives generate SM-RL SMI for every short message associated with the primitives. Similar to the SM-TL SMI, the SM-RL SMI at the MS is not carried at the peer entity in the SM-SC. For every short message, the SM-RL SMI is mapped to and from the SM-TL SMI.

At this layer, the short message relay (SMR) entity at the MS communicates with the peer SMR at the MSC by using the short message relay protocol (SM-RP). SM-RP provides the networking functions between MS and SM-SC, which interworks with TCAP/MAP in the MSC.

SM-RP consists of the following *relay protocol data unit* (RPDU) types:

RP-DATA. Invoked by the SM-RL-DATA service primitive, which passes the TPDU and necessary control information from the MS to the network or from the network to the MS. **RP-DATA** contains the originating address (MS or SM-SC), the terminating address (SM-SC or MS), and the user data containing TPDU. A mobile-terminated (MT) **RP-DATA** may indicate if there are more waiting messages in the SM-SC.

RP-SM-MEMORY-AVAILABLE. Invoked by the SM-RL-MEMORY-AVAILABLE primitive, which passes the necessary control information from the MS to the network to indicate that the MS has memory available to receive one or more short messages.

RP-ACK. Invoked by the SM-RL-REPORT primitive to acknowledge the corresponding **RP-DATA** or **RP-SM-MEMORY-AVAILABLE** data units.

RP-ERROR. Invoked by the SM-RL-REPORT primitive to report any error of a corresponding **RP-DATA**. An error may occur if (1) the message is too short to contain complete message type information and the message should be ignored, (2) the message reference is unknown, (3) the message type is unknown, or (4) the message content is semantically incorrect.

12.2.3 Connection Management Sublayer

The connection management sublayer (CM-Sub) for SMS provides services to support the SM-RL. In this layer, the short message control (SMC) entity at the MS communicates with the peer SMC at the MSC by using the short message control protocol (SM-CP). The MS has two SMC entities. One handles the MS-originated (MO) short message service and the other handles the MS-terminated (MT) short message service. Note that the SMC entities cannot simultaneously perform messaging in both directions.

The SM-CP consists of the following protocol elements:

CP-DATA. Invoked by the SM-CP service primitives MNSMS-DATA or MNSMS-ESTablish, which deliver RPDU between the MS and the MSC.

CP-ACK. Acknowledges the corresponding **CP-DATA**. **CP-ACK** does not contain any specific information elements.

CP-ERROR. Invoked by the SM-CP service primitives MNSMS-ABORT or MNSMS-ERROR, which provide the cause of the messaging procedure error.

Before any CP message is delivered, an MM-connection must be established. The SMC uses the MNSMS-ESTablish primitive to establish an MM-connection and then transfer an RPDU on that MM-connection. Note that the primitives with prefix MNSMS are between SMC and SMR, as indicated in Figure 12.3. The primitives between SMC and MM are prefixed with MMSMS. The SMC uses the MNSMS-DATA primitive to transfer an RPDU on an established MM-connection. When the short message delivery is completed, the MM-connection is released by the SMC using the MNSMS-RELease service primitive. In abnormal cases, such as RR-connection failure or SM-CP protocol error, the SMC releases an MM-connection by using the MNSMS-ABORT service primitive. When an error occurs, the causes are similar to that reported by **RP-ERROR**. In this case, the SMC releases an MM-connection by using the MNSMS-ERROR service primitive.

12.3   **Mobile-Originated Messaging**

In mobile originated (MO) messaging, an MS sends a short message to the SM-SC. Depending on the destination of the message, the SM-SC may deliver the message to another MS or to a normal pager through the traditional paging system described in Chapter 22. The logical message path is MS→ originating MSC→IWMSC→SM-SC. Note that the IWMSC can be the originating MSC. For illustration purposes, we divide the message flow of MO messaging into three parts: Figure 12.3 illustrates part 1 for MO messaging, which is described in the following steps:

Step 1.   The SM-TL entity issues an **SMS-SUBMIT** TPDU to the SM-RL by the SM-RL-DATA(Request) primitive.

Step 2.   The SMR entity creates an **RP-DATA(MO)** RPDU, and invokes the MNSMS-ESTablish(Request) primitive to transfer the RPDU. The SMR sets the timer $TR1M$ and expects to receive the **RP-ACK** before $TR1M$ expires. If the timer expires, the CM-connection, and thus the MM-connection, are aborted, and a report indication is passed to SM-TL.

Step 3.   The SMC entity first establishes the MM-connection, as illustrated in Figure 12.4.

Step 3a.   The MS sends a **CM_SERVICE_REQUEST** message to the MSC. The service type of this message is "short

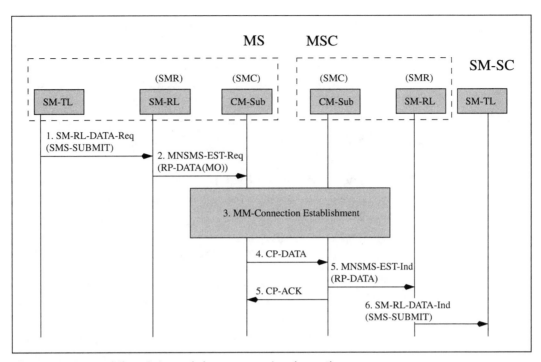

Figure 12.3   Mobile-originated short messaging (part 1).

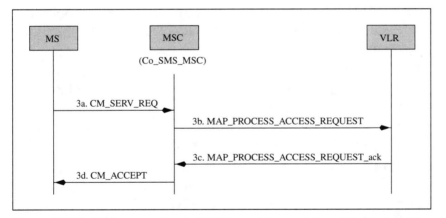

Figure 12.4   MM-connection establishment for mobile-originated short messaging.

message service," to be distinguished from the voice call transmission.

Step 3b. The SMS coordinating process in the MSC—Co_SMS_MSC—is invoked, which sends the **MAP_PROCESS_ACCESS_REQUEST** message to the VLR. This message and other messages with prefix **MAP_** are GSM MAP, delivered through the SS7 network by using the SS7 TCAP protocol.

Step 3c. The VLR checks to determine if the MS is legal to receive the short message service. If so, it acknowledges the MSC request.

Step 3d. The MSC forwards the acceptance to the MS by sending the message **CM_SERVICE_ACCEPT**.

Step 4. After the connection to the MSC has been established, the SMC creates the **CP-DATA** containing the RPDU and sends the message to the MSC. It sets a timer $TC1^*$, and expects to receive the result before $TC1^*$ expires. The value of the timer may vary with the length of **CP-DATA** and the type of the radio channel (SDCCH or SACCH) used for the transmission. If $TC1^*$ expires, the **CP-DATA** message may be retransmitted for, at most, three times. If the attempt is not successful, the error is reported to SM-RL, and the CM-connection is released. If the attempt succeeds, step 5 is executed.

Step 5. The MSC acknowledges the **CP-DATA** message by returning a **CP-ACK**. When the SMC of the MS receives the **CP-ACK**, the $TC1^*$ timer is reset. The **SMS-SUBMIT** request is forwarded from the SMC entity to the SMR entity of the MSC by the MNSMS-ESTablish(Indication) primitive.

Step 6. The **SMS-SUBMIT** request is forwarded from the SMR entity to the SM-TL of the MSC by the SM-RL-DATA(Indication) primitive. The SMR sets a timer, $TR2N$, and expects to receive the **SMS-STATUS-REPORT** (see step 13) before $TR2N$ expires. If the timer expires, the SMR requests the SMC to abort the CM-connection. It also sends a report indication to the SM-TL. Note that the transfer layer protocol involves only the MS and the SM-SC.

Figure 12.5 illustrates part 2 for MO messaging, which is described in the following steps:

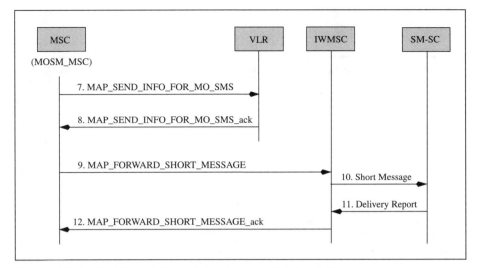

Figure 12.5   Mobile-originated short messaging (part 2).

Step 7. After the SM-TL of MSC receives the TPDU, the mobile-originated short message service process in the MSC—MOSM_MSC—is invoked. The MOSM_MSC sends the **MAP_SEND_INFO_FOR_MO_SMS** message to the VLR to request subscriber-related information, such as the MSISDN of the MS. This message is used to check whether the request violates supplementary services invoked or if any restrictions have been imposed.

Step 8. The VLR either acknowledges the request positively or provides the following error causes: teleservice not provisioned, call barred, unexpected data value, or data missing.

Step 9. If the VLR response is positive, the MSC sends the GSM MAP message **MAP_FORWARD_SHORT_MESSAGE** to the IWMSC, the gateway to the SM-SC. Note that if the originating MSC is the IWMSC, this message is saved. The message includes the SM-SC address provided by the MSC (this address is an E.164 number), the sender's MSISDN, and the short message, that is, the TPDU.

Steps 10–12. The short message is delivered to the SM-SC, and the SM-SC returns a delivery report to the IWMSC. This report is included in the GSM MAP message, **MAP_FORWARD_SHORT_MESSAGE_ack** sent from the IWMSC to the MSC.

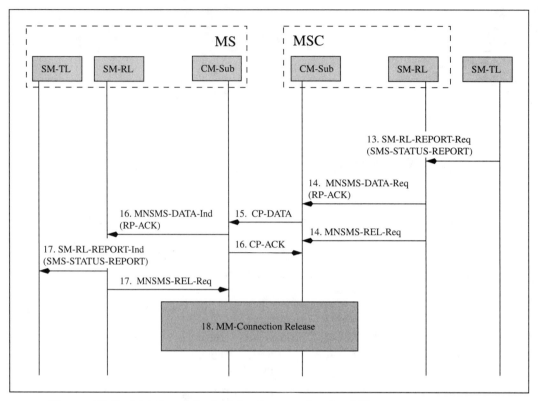

Figure 12.6 Mobile-originated short messaging (part 3).

Figure 12.6 illustrates part 3 for MO messaging, which is described in the following steps:

Steps 13 and 14. The SM-TL entity sends the TPDU **SMS-STATUS-REPORT** to the SMR entity at SM-RL, and the *TR2N* timer is stopped. The SMR generates **RP-ACK** and sends it to SMC at CM-Sub.

Step 15. The SMC entity generates the **CP-DATA** and sends it to the MS. The *TC1** timer is set, as in step 4.

Step 16. When the SMC entity of the MS receives the **CP-DATA**, it forwards the **RP-ACK** to the SMR entity at the SM-RL. It also sends the **CP-ACK** to the MSC.

Step 17. The SMR stops the *TR1M* timer, forwards **SMS-STATUS-REPORT** to SM-TL, and invokes the MNSMS-RELease primitive to release the CM-connection.

Step 18. The CM-connection and the MM-connection are released. If the short message transfer is not successful, the status report provides the cause of error to the MS. The error can be one of the following: unknown service center address, service center congestion, invalid short message entity address, subscriber not service center subscriber, or protocol error.

Note that the MO messaging procedure is similar to that for GSM call origination, as described in Chapter 11, Section 11.1, with one major difference: MO messaging needs IWMSC to interwork to SM-SC. On the other hand, in GSM call origination, the originating MSC processes the call request just like a typical central office in PSTN.

12.4 Mobile-Terminated Messaging

In mobile terminated (MT) messaging, an MS receives a short message from the SM-SC. The message sender can be another MS in the GSM network or an input device in the traditional paging system. The logical message path is SM-SC→GMSC→terminating MSC→MS, where the GMSC can be the terminating MSC. The 22-step message flow is shown in three figures Figure 12.7 illustrates steps 1–10 for MT messaging. Note

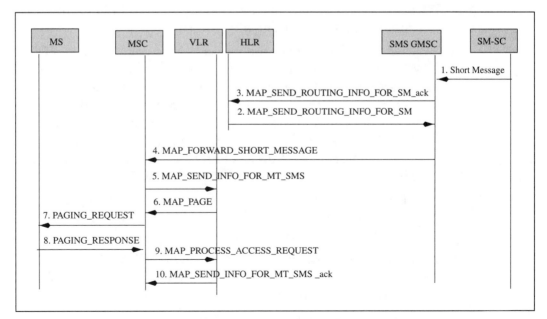

Figure 12.7 Mobile-terminated short messaging (part 1).

that in this procedure, the GMSC needs to query the HLR to locate the terminating MSC. The procedure is described in the following steps:

Steps 1 and 2. The SMS GMSC receives a short message (RP user data) from the SM-SC. The SMS GMSC requests the routing information by sending the message **MAP_SEND_ROUTING_ INFO_FOR_SM** to the HLR. The message includes the MSISDN of the recipient MS.

Step 3. The HLR uses the received MSISDN to retrieve routing information for the MS. The HLR returns **MAP_SEND_ROUTING_ INFO_FOR_ SM_ack** to the SMS GMSC. If the operation fails, an error is indicated in the message. The error causes are similar to those listed in step 8 of the MO messaging. If the operation is successful, the message includes the IMSI and the serving MSC address of the recipient MS.

Step 4. The SMS GMSC delivers the short message to the MSC by sending the message **MAP_FORWARD_SHORT_MESSAGE**. This message is described in step 9 of MO messaging, with one major exception: In MT messaging, the message should specify the More-To-Send parameter to indicate if there are more messages to send. This parameter is not used in MO messaging. Also, the destination address is IMSI in MT messaging.

Step 5. The MSC sends **MAP_SEND_INFO_FOR_MT_SMS** to the VLR to obtain the subscriber-related information.

Step 6. When the VLR receives the message **MAP_SEND_INFO_FOR_ MT_SMS**, a micro-procedure, Check_Indication, is invoked to verify the data value of the message. If the tests are passed, the VLR initiates the paging procedure. If the VLR knows the location area (LA) of the recipient MS, then **MAP_PAGE** is sent to page the MS in the LA. Otherwise, **MAP_SEARCH_FOR_SUBSCRIBER** is sent to page all LAs in the MSC. For simplicity, assume that **MAP_PAGE** is sent.

Steps 7–9. The MSC performs the paging operation. If the operation is successful, the MSC sends the **MAP_PROCESS_ACCESS_ REQUEST** message to the VLR.

Step 10. The VLR sends **MAP_SEND_INFO_FOR_MT_SMS_ack** to the MSC, and the MSC is allowed to initiate forwarding of the short message to the MS.

Figure 12.8 illustrates steps 11–20 for MT messaging.

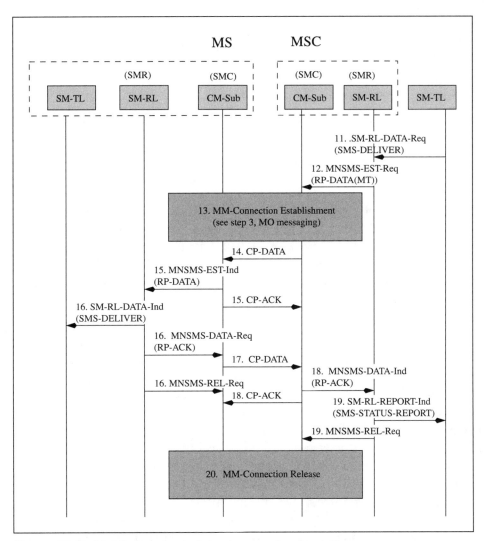

Figure 12.8 Mobile-terminated short messaging (part 2).

Step 11–20. The SMR entity of the MSC generates **RP-DATA** from the TPDU **SMS-DELIVER** and relays it to the MS. These steps are similar to steps 1–6, and 13–19 in MO messaging.

Figure 12.9 illustrates steps 21 and 22 for MT messaging.

Step 21. After the MSC has received the **SMS-STATUS-REPORT** at step 19, the result is included in the message **MAP_FORWARD_SHORT_MESSAGE_ack** to acknowledge the message sent in step 4.

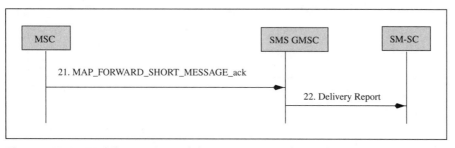

Figure 12.9 Mobile-terminated short messaging (part 3).

Step 22. If the result sent from MSC to SM-SC indicates that the recipient MS is absent, the SMS GMSC may invoke the procedure MAP_REPORT_SM_DELIVER_STATUS, and informs the HLR the status for further processing. The SMS GMSC may take actions for other failures/errors. In any case, it forwards the result to the SM-SC.

The MT messaging procedure is similar to GSM call termination with one major difference: In MT messaging, when the HLR is queried by the GMSC, the destination MSC number stored in the HLR is sent back to the GMSC directly. In GSM call termination, the HLR always queries the VLR to obtain the MSC number and the related routing information. Note that the MSC number stored in the VLR is more up to date than that in the HLR. Since a voice call is circuit oriented, and the voice trunk must be set up from the GMSC to the terminating MSC, accurate routing information must be obtained from the VLR to avoid unnecessary trunk reservation due to misrouting. In contrast, MT messaging is packet oriented, and trunk setup is not needed; thus, the MSC number is obtained directly from the HLR to simplify the routable address query procedure. If the MSC number is out of date (which is not very likely), the SMS protocol considers the MS to be absent.

12.5 The DTE-DCE Interface

As we described in Chapter 9, Section 9.1.1, an MS includes two parts:

- Mobile terminal (MT), which consists of SIM and ME.
- Terminal equipment (TE), which may be a PDA or PC.

Table 12.1 AT Commands and Status Indications

AT COMMAND	DESCRIPTION
+CNMI	New Message Indication to TE
+CBM	New CBM (Cell-Broadcast Message)
+CMGC	Send Command
+CMGD	Delete Message
+CMGL	List Message
+CMGR	Read Message
+CMGS	Send Message
+CMGW	Write Message to Memory
+CMT	SMS Message Received
+CNMA	New Message Acknowledgment to ME/TE
+CPMS	Preferred Message Storage
+CSCA	Service Center Address
+CSCB	Select Broadcast Message Types
+CSDH	Show Text Mode Parameters
+CSMP	Set Text Mode Parameters
+CRES	Restore Setting

The MT and TE are connected either by an RS232 port, an Infrared port (e.g., IrDA), or a PCMCIA interface through the Data Terminal Equipment (DTE)-*Data Circuit Terminating Equipment* (DCE) protocol. The DTE-DCE interface defines a set of *AT commands*, some of which are listed in Table 12.1.

The TE can instruct the MT to send a short message by issuing the AT command +CMGS, as follows.

$$AT+CMGS = <\text{length}><CR><\text{pdu}>$$

where $<\text{length}>$ is the length of the actual data unit in octets and $<\text{pdu}>$ is the **SMS-SUBMIT** TPDU. If the MT transmits the packet successfully, it will reply to the TE with the following command.

$$+CMGS :<\text{ref-no}><CR><LF><CR><LF> OK <CR><LF>$$

where <ref-no> is the message reference sent from the SM-SC. When the MT receives a short message, it will notify the TE with the SMS message received command +CMT:

$$+CMT:, < length > < CR > < LF > < pdu > < CR > < LF >$$

where <length> is the number of octets of the TPDU and <pdu> is the **SMS-DELIVER** TPDU. The following example given in GSM 07.05 illustrates a session to restore the message parameters from the ME to the TE, and to set up the cell broadcast number (CBN) identifiers that TE would like to receive:

Line 1. AT+CRES

Line 2. OK

Line 3. AT+CSMP?; +CSCA?

Line 4. +CSMP: 17, 167, 0, 0

Line 5. +CSCA: "358501234567"

Line 6. OK

Line 7. AT+CSDH=1

Line 8. OK

Line 9. AT+CSCB=0

Line 10. OK

At line 1, the TE restores setting from nonvolatile memory to volatile memory. At line 3, the TE queries short message parameters. At lines 4 and 5, the MT returns the default values for **SMS-SUBMIT** and the SM-SC address. At lines 7 and 9, the TE specifies to show all message headers in text mode (code 0: do not show message headers; code 1: show message headers) and to accept all cell broadcasting messages (CBMs) (code 0: accept CBMs; code 1: reject CBMs).

12.6 Summary

This chapter described GSM point-to-point short messaging. The short message protocol hierarchy was introduced, and the mobile-originated and mobile-terminated messaging procedures were described. Inter-MSC handoff may occur during short message delivery. Other procedures, such as the memory-available notification procedure, follow the same rules described in the mobile-originated/terminated messaging, but are not covered by this book. Details on these topics can be found in [ETS94h]. The reader is referred to [ETS93m] for detailed short message information flow. The protocol between the IWMSC and the SM-SC below the transfer layer is not specified in GSM. Some example protocols are described in [ETS93a, ETS94g, ETS94f]. Further reading for GSM short messaging can be found in [ETS97a]. Detailed specifications of AT commands are documented in [ETS97k].

12.7   Review Questions

1. Describe the following types of short message: user-specific, ME-specific, and SIM-specific.

2. What are the main parts of the GSM SMS protocol stack?

3. Describe the TPDU types defined in the GSM SMS protocol. Can you add new TPDU types or remove existing TPDU types so that the features and performance of the SMS protocol can be improved?

4. Describe the SM-RL. In the SMS protocol, is it a good idea to keep the same SM-RL SMI (short message identifier) in the peer entities?

5. What must be done before delivering a short message control protocol message?

6. What is the major difference between the main functionality of the mobile-originated messaging and the GSM call-origination procedures?

7. What is the major difference between the main functionality of the mobile-terminated messaging and the GSM call-termination procedures?

8. How would you solve the case where inter-MSC handoff occurs during SMS delivery?

9. Since the protocol between the SM-SC and the GSM network is not specified, is short message service available to an MS roaming around GSM networks with various SM-SC implementations?

10. Based on the existing GSM SMS protocol, can you implement multicast of short messages?

11. We have developed an end-point SMS-IP integration solution called iSMS system, whose architecture is shown in Figure 12.10. In this system, the GSM MSs can access the IP services through the iSMS gateway. The iSMS gateway serves as a TE, which connects to a

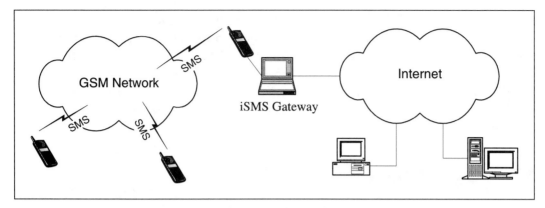

Figure 12.10 iSMS system architecture (an end-point SMS-IP integration solution).

standard GSM handset that serves as a GSM-compliant modem (i.e., an MT) and communicates with other MSs through the short message service. A major advantage of iSMS is that the whole system is built without the involvement of a GSM operator and SM-SC equipment vendors. Following the iSMS concept, design an e-mail forwarding mechanism that forwards e-mails from a PC (i.e., the iSMS gateway in Figure 12.10). When the PC receives an e-mail from the Internet, it instructs the MT (wireless modem) to send a short message to a specific MS, where the short message contains the e-mail received by the PC. In your design, the PC uses AT commands to communicate with the MT, as described in Table 12.1. Which AT commands are required to implement this mechanism?

CHAPTER
13

International Roaming
for GSM

GSM supports roaming services that allow a subscriber in a GSM network to receive mobile telephony service when the user visits a different GSM network. If both GSM networks are within the same country, call setup for a roamer can be done efficiently, as described in Chapter 9, Section 9.2. However, if the networks are located in different countries, the current GSM implementation for call delivery to the roamer can be very expensive. Before we examine the technical aspects of GSM network operation, let us describe the international roaming issue from the customer's perspective.

Consider the following scenario: John is a subscriber of GSM service in Taiwan. Suppose that he travels from Taiwan to Singapore, which have a GSM roaming agreement. When John arrives at the airport, he uses his GSM handset (mobile station) to call his friend Jenny to meet him at the airport. A few minutes later Jenny calls John (by dialing John's GSM phone number) to let him know that she will be late due to a traffic jam. Finally, they meet and have a very nice get-together. At the end of the month, John receives the GSM service bill, and finds that he was charged for a local GSM call for the first phone call and an international call from Taiwan to Singapore for the second phone call; Jenny notices that she has been charged for an international call from Singapore to Taiwan for the same second phone call. Both John and Jenny are unhappy. What happened?

In current GSM international roaming implementations, call delivery (call termination) to a GSM roamer results in one or two international calls. Suppose that a GSM user from Taiwan (John, in this example) roams to Singapore. There are three scenarios for call delivery to John:

Scenario 1. If a person in Taiwan calls John, the result is a local call and an international call. The caller is charged for a local GSM call; John is charged for an international call from Taiwan to Singapore.

Scenario 2. If the caller is from a third country (say, Hong Kong), the call delivery to John results in two international calls. The caller is charged for an international call from Hong Kong to Taiwan, and John is charged for an international call from Taiwan to Singapore.

Scenario 3. If the caller (Jenny, in our previous example) is in Singapore, the call delivery results in two international calls, even though both Jenny and John are in Singapore! This scenario is in fact a special case of scenario 2, and is referred to as *tromboning*.

The tromboning effect in scenario 3 discourages call terminations to a GSM roamer. Most likely, John will ask Jenny not to dial his GSM number when he visits Singapore again.

In this chapter, we explain why call delivery (specifically, scenario 3) to a GSM roamer is so expensive in the current implementation. Then we present solutions that reduce the network cost for GSM calls to international roamers. Basically, these solutions redefine the GSM network signaling procedure for call delivery to roamers so that the unnecessary international circuits in scenario 3 are avoided.

13.1 International GSM Call Setup

The call delivery procedure to a GSM roamer is basically the same as the procedure described in Chapter 9, Figure 9.9, or Chapter 11, Figure 11.6, except that two *international switch centers* (ISCs) are involved in the voice path. In telecommunications, all countries have a national network, which is connected to an international network. ISCs offer interworking functions between the national networks and the international network. The call path of every international call is composed of three segments: one in the origination country, another in the international network, and the third in the destination country. These circuit segments are interconnected by two ISCs: one in the origination country and the other in the destination country.

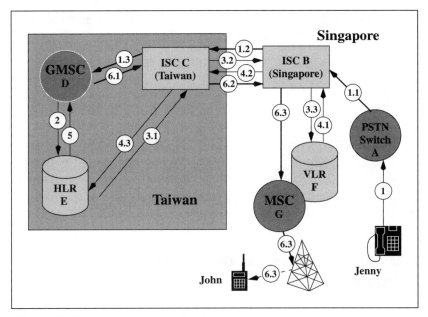

Figure 13.1   International call setup procedure.

Consider the previous example where Jenny places a call to John, who has roamed from Taiwan to Singapore. The call setup message flow is illustrated in Figure 13.1; the steps involved are as follows:

Step 1. John's GSM home system is in Taiwan, so Jenny first dials the *international switch center access code* (ISCA), then the *country code* (CC). Then she dials John's MSISDN. As described in Chapter 10, Section 10.4, an MSISDN in Taiwan is a *national destination code* (NDC), 93, followed by a six-digit *subscriber number* (SN). When Switch A interprets the ISCA, the first portion of the dialed digits, it identifies the call as an international call, then sets up the call using the IAM message (see 1.1 in Figure 13.1) to Singapore's International Switch Center, that is, ISC B. Based on the country code, ISC B routes the call to Taiwan's International Switch Center, ISC C (see 1.2 in Figure 13.1). ISC C interprets the prefix of the remaining digits, and sets up the voice trunk to GMSC D.

Step 2. GMSC D queries HLR E to obtain the MSRN.

Steps 3 and 4. HLR E queries VLR F. Note that these messages travel between Taiwan and Singapore (see 3.1, 3.2, 3.3, 4.1, 4.2, and 4.3 in Figure 13.1).

Step 5. The MSRN is returned to GMSC D.

Step 6. Based on the MSRN, GMSC D uses the IAM message to set up the trunk to MSC G, and, therefore, connects to John.

In this call setup procedure, the voice circuit path is:

$$(1) \rightarrow (1.1) \rightarrow (1.2) \rightarrow (1.3) \rightarrow (6.1) \rightarrow (6.2) \rightarrow (6.3)$$

which requires two international trunk connections. As a result, Jenny is charged for the international call from Singapore to Taiwan (1.2 in Figure 13.1) and John is charged for the international call from Taiwan to Singapore (6.2 in Figure 13.1). Since both John and Jenny are in Singapore, the call delivery is supposed to be local. Thus, it is desirable to remove the two international circuits from the call delivery in scenario 3.

13.2   Reducing the International Call Delivery Cost

To avoid unnecessary international trunk setups, an IAM message should not travel across country boundaries before the destination is known. We propose four solutions that follow this guideline. A basic restriction is that we should not introduce any new message types to the GSM MAP protocol defined in GSM specification 09.02, that is, the solutions utilize only existing messages with the prefix **MAP_** (see Chapter 10, Section 10.1). In the first three solutions, we utilize the concept of *roamer location cache* (RLC). The RLC in a visited system maintains a database containing the records of all international roamers who are presently in that visited system. From the perspective of a VLR in the visited system, RLC functions as the HLR of a roamer. From the perspective of the HLR in the home system of the roamer, RLC serves as the VLR in a visited system. In solution 4, we introduce a special dialing code that leads the call to the GMSC of the visited GSM system. Since the GMSC is a general-purpose switching system, it can perform routing translations to access the HLR of the roamer and route the call to the destination MSC directly.

13.2.1   Solution 1

In this solution, the RLC is colocated with the ISC in the visited system. The registration procedure is shown in Figure 13.2. (The reader is referred to Chapter 11, Section 11.1 for the basic GSM inter-VLR location update process.) To simplify our discussion, steps 2 and 3 (MAP_SEND_IDENTIFICATION), steps 7 and 8 (MAP_CANCELLATION_

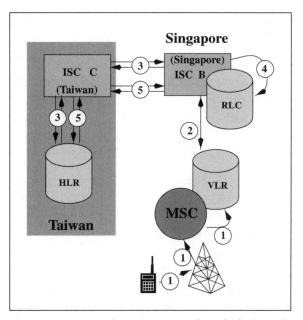

Figure 13.2 Registration procedure (solution 1).

LOCATION) in Chapter 11, Figure 11.4, and the authentication procedure have been omitted. The location update procedure is described in the following steps:

Step 1. The MS registers to the VLR.

Step 2. The VLR sends **MAP_UPDATE_LOCATION** to the roamer's HLR. Since the HLR is in a foreign country, the message is routed to ISC B.

Step 3. ISC B interprets the message, identifying it as a roamer registration operation. The message is forwarded to Taiwan (ISC C) as usual.

Step 4. At the same time, ISC B duplicates the message and forwards it to the RLC. RLC creates a record to store the IMSI and VLR/MSC address.

Step 5. After the registration operation has been completed, the RLC does not have the MSISDN of the roamer. (Only IMSI is delivered in the standard GSM location update operations.) Without the MSISDN information, the RLC cannot handle call delivery to the roamer. Thus, the RLC requests this information from the HLR using the **MAP_RESTORE_DATA** message, as described in Chapter 11, Section 11.3.1. The roamer's

MSISDN will be returned from the HLR to the RLC through the **MAP_INSERT_SUBSCRIBER_DATA** message.

If the roamer leaves the visited system, the VLR will receive a **MAP_CANCEL_LOCATION** message, as described in step 7 of Figure 11.4 (Chapter 11, Section 11.1.1). After removing the obsolete VLR record of the roamer, the VLR will forward the cancellation message to RLC to cancel the obsolete location record in the RLC. Call delivery for scenario 3 under solution 1 is illustrated in Figure 13.3. The steps are described here:

Step 1. Jenny first dials the ISCA code, the CC code, then John's MSISDN, as before. When Switch A interprets the first portion of the dialed digits (i.e., ISCA + CC), it identifies the call as an international call, then routes the trunk (using the IAM message; see 1 in Figure 13.3) to ISC B.

Step 2. Based on the CC code and the prefix of the remaining digits, ISC B recognizes that the called party is a potential roamer. ISC B searches RLC using the MSISDN provided by the IAM message. If there is no such entry, the call delivery is for scenario 2, and ISC B forwards the IAM message to Taiwan.

Step 3. If an entry for John is found, the call delivery follows Figure 13.3. RLC serves as John's HLR to obtain the MSRN.

Step 4. By using the MSRN, ISC B routes the IAM message to John, and the two international circuits are avoided.

The advantage of solution 1 is that only ISC B needs to be modified. Other network elements, such as the VLR and HLR, remain the same. The

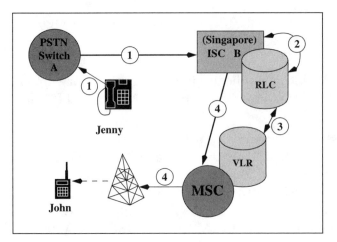

Figure 13.3 Call delivery (solution 1).

disadvantage of this approach is that most ISCs are not equipped with the GSM MAP protocol, and thus may not be able to interpret the GSM MAP messages in step 2. Also, ISCs typically belong to an international telephone carrier different from that of the GSM service providers. An agreement may have to be made between the two service providers. The transfer of charging and billing information is also more difficult.

13.2.2 Solution 2

The GSM service provider may want to build its own RLC without involving an ISC. In this case, call delivery to a foreign GSM user should not be forwarded to the ISC. Instead, the caller would dial into a switch (colocated with the RLC) in the local GSM system for call forwarding.

The location update in this solution is illustrated in Figure 13.4, and the steps are described as follows:

Step 1. The MS registers to the VLR.

Step 2. The VLR recognizes that the registration is for an international roamer. The VLR sends the **MAP_UPDATE_LOCATION** message to the RLC. The RLC creates a record to store the IMSI and the VLR/MSC address.

Step 3. The RLC sends the **MAP_UPDATE_LOCATION** message to the roamer's HLR through the international switch centers.

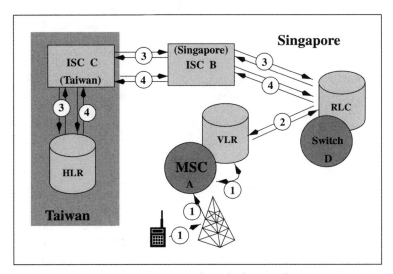

Figure 13.4 Registration procedure (solution 2).

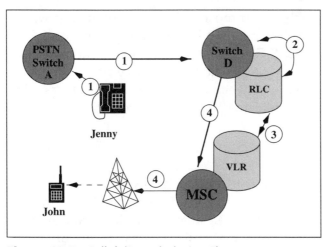

Figure 13.5   Call delivery (solution 2).

Step 4.   After the registration operation has been completed, RLC obtains the MSISDN of the roamer using the **MAP_RESTORE_DATA** message, as described in solution 1.

Call delivery for scenario 3 under solution 2 is illustrated in Figure 13.5. The steps are the same as those for solution 1, except that Jenny dials the number of Switch D instead of the country code. After Switch D is connected, Jenny will be asked to dial John's MSISDN. If the MSISDN is not found in the RLC, scenario 2 applies to this call delivery, and Switch D routes the call to the ISC. If the MSISDN is found in the RLC, it is a scenario 3 call delivery, and the call is processed locally, as illustrated in Figure 13.5. The advantage of this approach is that the modifications are made only within the GSM network; they do not involve an international carrier. The disadvantages include the extra modifications to the VLR; also, the caller must dial the number of Switch D, then the MSISDN. Moreover, the dialing process is different from the ordinary international call dialing procedure with which users are already familiar. Sophisticated billing procedures are also required, since the calling party can be charged either with a GSM call or with an international call.

13.2.3   Solution 3

As we pointed out, solution 2 may not be attractive because the VLR must be modified. An alternative is to introduce an *extractor*, as illustrated in Figure 13.6. The extractor monitors (but does not modify) the messages passing through the signaling links of the VLR and takes action when a

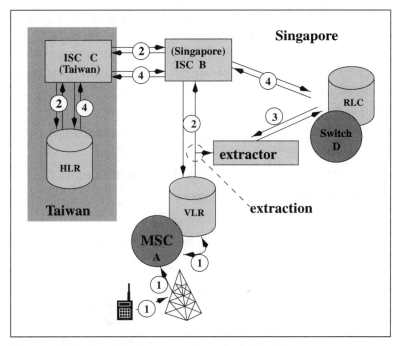

Figure 13.6 Registration procedure (solution 3).

location update message is sent to the HLR in the foreign country. In the registration procedure for solution 3, when the **MAP_UPDATE_LOCATION** message is delivered from the VLR to the ISC B at step 2, the extractor will also send a registration message to the RLC, and the RLC will create a roamer record, as in solution 2. Then the RLC obtains the roamer's MSISDN from the HLR, as in step 4 of solution 2.

The call delivery procedure for solution 3 is exactly the same as that for solution 2. The advantage of solution 3 over solution 2 is that it is transparent to the VLR. The disadvantage is that a new network component (i.e., the extractor) is introduced. Solution 3 can be deployed based on Lucent Technologies' 5ESS MSC 2000 system. The extractor can be an HP E4250 ACCESS7 (this system is an innovative platform for collecting and analyzing the SS7 data in the network in real time) and the RLC/Switch D can be WinComm's Jupiter PBX.

13.2.4 Solution 4

In this solution, the registration procedure is the same as that illustrated in Chapter 11, Figure 11.4. The basic idea of this solution is to divert the mobile call termination (incoming call to the mobile) into the visited GSM system before it reaches the ISC. The operator of the visited GSM system reserves an *international roamer access code* (IRAC) in its numbering plan, and announces to the public that it is a cheaper way to call visiting roamers. To make a call to a visiting GSM roamer, one should dial NDC1 + IRAC + CC + NDC2 + SN, where:

- NDC1 is the NDC or mobile network access code to the visited GSM system.
- IRAC is the international roamer access code just mentioned.
- CC is the country code of the home country.
- NDC2 is the NDC of the home GSM system.
- SN is the subscriber number for the roamer (given by the home GSM system).

According to NDC1, the PSTN routes the call to a GMSC of the visited GSM system. From IRAC, the GMSC recognizes it as an international roaming call. Instead of querying the HLR of the visited system, the GMSC translates CC + NDC2 + SN into MSISDN and uses it as the address to reach the roamer's HLR. If there is a bidirectional signaling path between the GMSC and the roamer's HLR, the call would follow the normal GSM call delivery procedure. That is, the GMSC in the visited system would query the HLR of the roamer's home system to obtain the MSRN. Since the roamer registered to a VLR in the visited system, the MSRN would be located at one of the MSCs in the visited system. The GMSC would route the call to the MSC and, eventually, reach the destination MS.

In this scheme, we assume that a signaling path between the GMSC in the visited system and the HLR in the home system already exists. Due to the fact that the GMSC and the HLR are located in different countries, the fulfillment of the signaling relationship would become an implementation issue. Basically, if an international STP does not exist (which is true in many countries in Europe and the Asia Pacific region), every node involved in the international roaming process must have a *point code* (PC) in the International SS7 Signaling Network. To fulfill this implementation, the GMSC must: (1) be able to connect to more than one SS7 signaling network; (2) be equipped with the Global Title Translation that translates MSISDNs into *network indicator*, point code, and *subsystem number* for all HLRs with roaming agreement; and (3) be able to route an international MSRN into the national network.

The advantages of this solution are that the GSM call delivery procedure (and thus the VLR software) is not modified, and no new network elements are required. Furthermore, the implementation is cost-effective because no new network elements such as RLC are introduced. If the GMSC is implemented by a general-purpose switching system, such as Lucent Technologies' 5ESS, the functions listed previously could be achieved at a reasonable cost. A potential limitation is that many MSCs may not have the required functionality to implement this solution.

13.3   Summary

Our experience indicates that most call terminations to a GSM user occur when the GSM user is in his or her home system or when the GSM user is in a visited system and the caller is also in the same visited country (i.e., scenario 3 call delivery, described in the beginning of this chapter). For the second case, both the caller and the GSM roamer are charged for an international call in the current GSM implementation. It is desirable to resolve this problem so that two international calls are processed as a local call.

This chapter proposed four approaches to reduce two potential international calls into one local phone call. In the first three solutions, a roamer location cache called RLC is introduced. These approaches do not introduce any new message types to GSM MAP protocol. Solution 1 requires modifications to the international switch center. Solution 2 requires modifications to the VLR. Solution 3 utilizes a new network element, an extractor, without modifying any existing network elements. The extractor can be an HP E4250 ACCESS7 [Hew95]. Solution 4 does not modify the GSM roamer call delivery procedure; however, extra features at the GMSC are required. This solution assumes that the GMSC in the visited system is powerful enough to access the roamer's HLR for call delivery. Such powerful switch systems already exist (e.g., Lucent Technologies' 5ESS MSC 2000 system described in [Luc97]). Based on the capability and availability of the existing PSTN/GSM system, one may choose an appropriate solution (among the four solutions) to address scenario 3. The solutions may significantly reduce the network traffic and the customer costs.

13.4   Review Questions

1. What is the function of ISC? What is the number called and what is the number in your country to call it?

2. Why is it a problem with solution 2, described in Section 13.2.2, if the given country has more than one GSM provider? Does solu-

tion 3, described in Section 13.2.3, solve the problems mentioned at solution 2?

3. What is the function of RLC? Which tromboning-elimination solutions described in this book utilize RLC?

4. Let's assume that the company running the ISC in a country has the majority of the stocks of the GSM provider. Which solution would you recommend them to implement for tromboning elimination?

5. What are the reasons and the counterreasons from the service provider's view to implement a tromboning-elimination solution for scenario 3 in its systems?

6. Design a mechanism to eliminate international tromboning as follows: Suppose that a mobile user of country A visits country B. When someone in country B calls this roamer, the call is set up back to country A. However, the HLR of the roamer will detect that the user is visiting country B. The HLR instructs the GMSC to release the international link and ask the originating switch (at country B) to forward this call to a special MSC C of country B. Then this special MSC C connects the call locally. Describe the modifications required to implement this scheme. Can an existing switching platform and SS7 capability support the originating switch to forward the call to the special MSC?

7. Suppose that tromboning-elimination solutions 1–4 are implemented in GSM networks of four different countries (one solution for each of the countries). If a GSM user roams among these countries, would this person's MS have problems working in these countries to eliminate the tromboning effect?

8. Consider the following service: When someone in country A attempts to call a mobile user of country B, this person first dials a special number, then the mobile phone number (including the ISCA and CC). If the mobile user is in country A, it is a local or national call within country A. If the mobile user is in a country other than country A, the call is connected as a standard international call to the mobile user. Which solutions described in this chapter can be used to implement this service? What are the possible business models for this service? Can the provider of this service be different from the GSM operator and the fixed network Telco?

9. Consider feature interaction that may occur in solutions 1–4. For example, can voice mailbox for a roaming user be implemented with these solutions?

GSM Operations, Administration, and Maintenance

This chapter discusses operations, administration, and maintenance (OA&M) for GSM. To manage the network, GSM requires OA&M functions that are similar to the ones supported in wireline telecommunications systems. To be compatible with other telecommunication systems, GSM OA&M follows the standard Telecommunication Management Network (TMN) concept developed by ITU-T. First, we briefly describe the general TMN concept, then we focus on the GSM-specific features that are implemented on top of the TMN platform.

The TMN architecture is illustrated in Figure 14.1. Several components are identified in the TMN model:

Operations system (OS). With the *operations system function* (OSF), the OS is responsible for the overall TMN management. An OSF can be billing, accounting, management of mobile equipment, HLR measurement, and so on. An OS may reside in an *operations and maintenance center* (OMC), and depending on the network size, a GSM network may have one or more OMCs.

Network element (NE). The NEs in GSM are HLR, VLR, MSC, EIR, AuC, BSC, and BTS. The NEs are monitored or controlled by the OS. The *network element functions* (NEFs) in the NE represent the telecommunications and support functions to be managed by the OS.

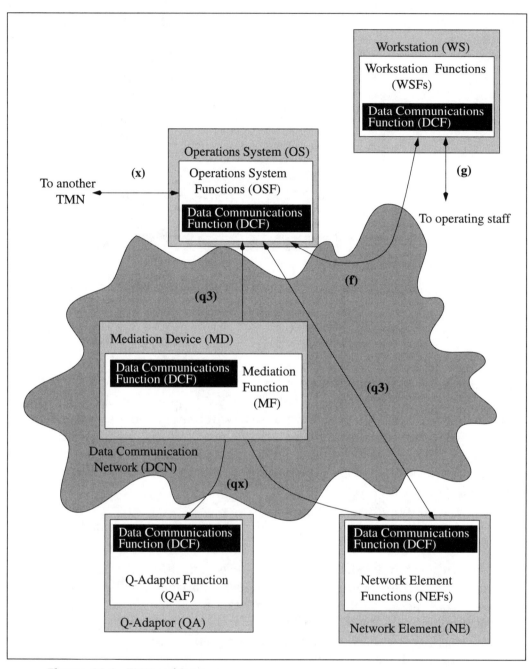

Figure 14.1 TMN architecture.

Data communication network (DCN). The OSs, NEs, and other TMN elements communicate through DCN by using the *data communication function* (DCF). The DCN technology can be WAN, LAN, or others. The GSM OMC typically connects to MSCs and BSCs by X.25.

Mediation device (MD). The MD adapts the OS to the specific NEs. It uses the *mediation function* (MF) to route or pass information between standardized interfaces. For example, consider the GSM architecture in Chapter 10, Figure 10.1. Under TMN, a BTS is connected to the management network through its BSC, as shown in Figure 14.2, and the BSC acts as the MD for all BTSs under its control.

Q-Adaptor (QA). The QA uses the *Q-adaptor function* (QAF) to connect the non-TMN entities that are either NEF-like or OSF-like.

Workstation (WS). The WS interacts the operations/maintenance personnel with the OS through the *workstation functions* (WSFs). With WSFs, staff access the status of the network and monitor the system parameters.

The relationship between components of TMN functions are defined by using the *reference points*:

- The q_3 point connects an OSF to an MF or an NEF. In Figure 14.2, q_3 connects GSM OA&M OSF and MF/NEF in BSC.

- The q_x point connects an MF to an NEF or a QAF. In Figure 14.2, q_x connects MF in BSC and NEF in BTS.

- The x point connects an OSF to another OSF or an OSF-like functionality in a different TMN.

- The f point connects an OSF to a WSF.

- The g point connects a WSF to the operating staff.

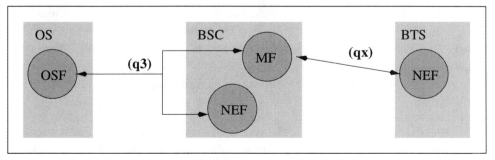

Figure 14.2 TMN connection for the base station system.

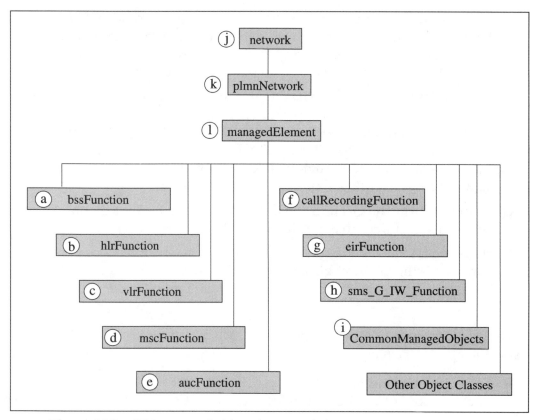

Figure 14.3   GSM-managed object class containment.

Every GSM network has a *network management center* (NMC) for controlling the OMCs in the network. Staff in the NMC handle long-term systemwide issues. On the other hand, local operators at an OMC work on short-term regional issues. In GSM TMN, some common management functions (see (i) in Figure 14.3) are used to support other specific functions, such as *hlrFunction* and *vlrFunction* (see (a)–(h) in Figure 14.3). All these functions are derived from the *managedElement* class defined in ITU-T M.3100 (see (l) in Figure 14.3). The *managedElement* class is derived from the *plmnNetwork* class (see (k) in Figure 14.3), and the *plmnNetwork* class is derived from the *network* class (see (j) in Figure 14.3). The *common management functions* for GSM are classified into the following three categories:

Forwarding of event notifications. GSM-managed object classes in NE emit event notifications to the OS following the *Event Report Systems Management Function* defined in ITU-T X.734. The object class *Event*

Forwarding Discriminator (EFD) in the NE manages forwarding of event notifications, to be elaborated later.

Information logging. Information generated by the NE may be stored in a record filestore in the NE. The information can be subsequently retrieved by the NE or the OS. The GSM NE follows the standard *Log Control Systems Management Function* defined in ITU-T X.735, which allows the OS to control the logging of selective event notifications.

Bulk data transfer between the OS and the NE. The data transfer between the OS and the NE uses the *Common Management Information Service Element* (CMISE) control of *File Transfer Access and Management* (FTAM), defined in GSM 12.01. The data transfer is controlled by the OS.

Figure 14.3 illustrates the specific GSM network management functions listed here:

(a) bssFunction for BSS management

(b) hlrFunction for HLR management

(c) vlrFunction for VLR management

(d) mscFunction for MSC management

(e) aucFunction for AuC management

(f) callRecordingFunction for call recording management

(g) eirFunction for EIR management

(h) sms_G_IW_Function for short message service management

This chapter will use *callRecordingFunction* and *hlrFunction* as examples to illustrate GSM network management.

14.1   Call-Recording Functions

In GSM operation, the billing of mobile subscribers, statistics of service usage, and roaming traffic must be monitored by the OS, as described in GSM 12.05. This information is provided by the NEs, such as the MSCs, BSSs, and location registers (VLR/HLR), and is managed by the *tariff and charging administration*, as defined in ITU-T M.3200. The administration includes the following services:

Service provision. This OSF ((a) in Figure 14.4) introduces new or modified services to the GSM network. The modifications to the

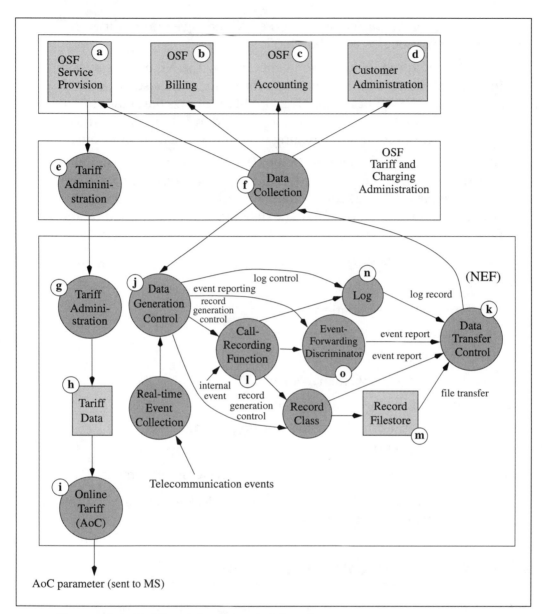

Figure 14.4 Tariff and charging administration.

existing services may be based partly on the service usage statistics provided by the NEs such as MSC.

Billing. Based on the data collected from the NEs, this OSF ((b) in Figure 14.4) determines the charge for the services.

Accounting. The GSM accounting service ((c) in Figure 14.4) consists of two parts:

- *Inter-PLMN (Public Land Mobile Network) accounting.* Required for roaming traffic management, which is settled by means of the *transfer account procedure* (TAP). TAP records are regularly exchanged between a GSM network and the other networks. For a visitor from another GSM network, the mobile-originated call charges are calculated and converted to an agreed accounting currency, such as *Special Drawing Rights* (SDRs), before they are stored in the TAP. Mobile-terminated calls for a visitor may or may not be charged, but the associated rerouting charges must be considered. The GSM network receives the TAPs of its customers roaming at the other networks. These TAPs are processed by the billing OSF.

- *Fixed-network accounting.* Manages the call traffic between the mobile stations and the fixed networks and the signaling traffic for functions such as location updates. The charges of the aforementioned traffic are defined based on the call records provided by the NEs, generally MSCs.

Customer administration. This OSF ((d) in Figure 14.4) handles customer queries such as billing complaints.

An important aspect of the tariff and charging administration OS is that the normal operation of the system should not be interrupted when it is modified. This goal is achieved by creating a duplicate copy of the OSF using the tsCopyTariffSystem action, defined in GSM 12.24.

14.1.1 Tariff Administration

In Figure 14.4(e), the OSF tariff administration function provides the tariff administration information to the NEs (specifically, the MSCs). The information is then passed from the MSC to the MS following the path (g)→(h)→(i) in Figure 14.4 to support the *advice of charge* (AoC), described in GSM 12.24 and GSM 12.86.

The OSF uses the *tariff class management functions* to assign a *tariff class* with service, distance, and time-based tariff-dependent charging parameters. These dependencies are elaborated next:

- The service-charging dependencies are defined based on the customized AoC. The AoC service definition may consist of one or more service types (basic and/or supplementary), radio channel types, connection type (call origination or call termination), and so on.

- The distance dependencies are defined based on the origins, destinations, and charging zones.

- The time-based tariff dependences are determined by the tariff periods, such as holiday/working day, off-peak/on-peak, and so on.

14.1.2 Data Collection

Figure 14.4(f) illustrates the *data collection functions* in the OSF. These functions provide the specifications of the collected data to the NEs through the *data generation control* in the NEF (see (j) in Figure 14.4), including record generation, event reporting, and log control. The OSF data collection functions collect the data from these NEs through the *data transfer control* ((k) in Figure 14.4) in the NEF. In the NEF, the *call-recording function* ((l) in Figure 14.4) generates potential call and event records based on the internal telecommunication events of the NE. The record generation control determines where the records are sent; there are three possibilities:

- The records may be forwarded to the record filestore (see Figure 14.4(m)), then transferred to the OSF via FTAM in real time. One or more class types (billing, accounting, and so on) are defined for the transferred records.

- The records may be saved in a log file (see Figure 14.4(n)), to be accessed later by the OSF using the log control, defined in ITU-T X.735.

- The records may also be passed to the EFDs controlled by the event-reporting function, defined in ITU-T X.734, for short-term event reporting in Figure 14.4(o).

14.2 Performance Measurement and Management

To support future cellular network planning, the operator must check the performance of the current network operation. With performance management, it is possible to collect and receive statistics based on both short-term and long-term measurements.

The performance of the GSM network should be evaluated based on the data provided by the NEs. The data include the user/signaling traffic levels, network configuration verification, resource access measurements, and quality of service (QoS), defined in GSM 12.04.

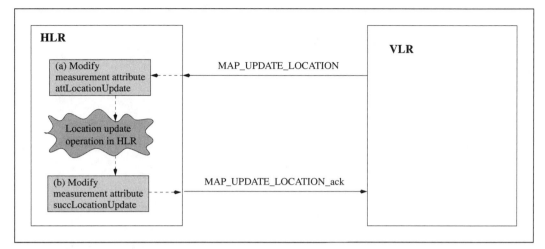

Figure 14.5 Measurement attribute modifications in location update.

The measurement task is achieved by administering the *measurement jobs*. A measurement job is created, modified, displayed, suspended, resumed, and deleted in the OS. This job is scheduled in a period to accumulate the measurement data for inspection. The measurement job instructs the *measurement function* objects in the NEs to collect the data. In measurement management, the data exchanges between the OS and the NEs follows the mechanisms illustrated in Figure 14.4.

Consider the location update measurements of an HLR. The procedure is illustrated in Figure 14.5. In this example, the VLR sends a GSM MAP message **MAP_UPDATE_LOCATION** to the HLR. The HLR updates the location information as well as two measurement attributes, and sends the GSM MAP message **MAP_UPDATE_LOCATION_ack** back to the VLR. The measurement job created in the OS is implemented as a simpleScanner object, defined in ITU-T X.738.

As illustrated in Figure 14.6, both the HLR measurement job (the simpleScanner) and the *hlrMeasurementFunction* are derived from the *hlrFunction* class. The *hlrFunction* class is derived from the *managedElement* class in Figure 14.3. The simpleScanner object has the following attributes:

Measurement types. For the example in Figure 14.5, the measurement types include:

- *attLocationUpdate*, the number of the attempted location updates
- *succLocationUpdate*, the number of the successful location updates

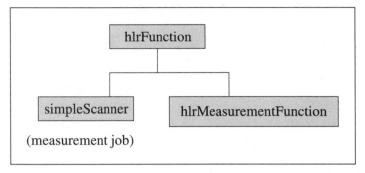

Figure 14.6 HLR measurement object class containment.

Both attributes are single-integer values. In Figure 14.5(a), the attLocationUpdate value is incremented by 1 when the **MAP_UPDATE_LOCATION** service indication is received. In Figure 14.5(b), the succLocationUpdate value is incremented by 1 when the **MAP_UPDATE_LOCATION** service response is received without the "user error" parameter value.

Measured network resources. For the example in Figure 14.5, the network resource is HLR.

Measurement function. The simpleScanner specifies one or more measurement functions in the NEs to collect the desired data. For the example in Figure 14.6, this attribute is *hlrMeasurementFunction* in the HLR. The measurement functions must be created before the simpleScanner is instantiated. For the example in Figure 14.5, the *hlrMeasurementFunction* has a conditional package called *locationUpdatePackage*. This package consists of two attributes, attLocationUpdate and succLocationUpdate, which are the measurement types of the simpleScanner.

Measurement schedule. This attribute specifies the start time and the stop time of the active measurement period. The measurement should be started within 90 days after the measurement job is created.

Granularity period. This attribute specifies the periodic interval of sending measured data from the NE, which is the HLR in Figure 14.6, to the OS. The granularity period should be longer than five minutes, and cannot be changed during the lifetime of the simpleScanner. If this attribute is not specified, or is set to the value 0, then the measured data are gathered under the request of the OS.

Scan report. At the end of every granularity period, a scan report is sent from the NE to the OS. The report includes the timestamp to indicate when it is sent to the OS, and the measurements collected by all measurement functions defined in simpleScanner. For the example in Figure 14.5, the measurements include the numbers of the attempted and successful location updates.

Other performance management and measurement functions include those for BSC, BTS, MSC, GMSC, VLR, and EIR. Details on these functions can be found in GSM 12.04.

14.3 Subscriber and Service Data Management

The GSM subscriber and service data management in GSM 12.02 defines the management for NEs such as AuC, HLR, VLR, and EIR. Under this management, the managed data in different NEFs may depend on each other. For example, to create a subscriber profile in the HLR, the subscriber data should already exist in the AuC. If it does not, the creation in the HLR fails. We use HLR as an example to illustrate the GSM subscriber and service data management. Figure 14.7 shows the HLR subscriber administration object class hierarchy. Basically, the mobile station ISDN numbers (MSISDN) and the subscribers represented by the international mobile subscriber identities (IMSIs) are managed in HLR.

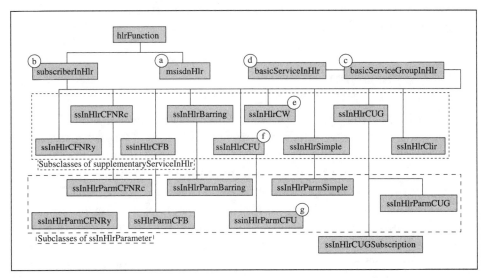

Figure 14.7 HLR subscriber administration object class containment.

Blocks of available MSISDNs are provided in an HLR. Information about the MSISDN is stored in *msisdnHlr*, shown in Figure 14.7(a). An MSISDN may be connected to a subscriber (IMSI), and can be disconnected when the IMSI is removed from the service. An MSISDN can associate with several basic services. The association is established between the *msisdnHlr* object and the *basicServiceInHlr* objects shown in Figure 14.7(d).

When a customer subscribes to the GSM services, a subscriber profile, and thus the *subscriberInHlr* object ((b) in Figure 14.7), is created in the HLR, and an IMSI is assigned to the customer. One or more MSISDNs are allocated to the IMSI. The association is made between the *msisdnHlr* objects and the *subscriberInHlr* object. For every basic service the customer subscribes to, a *basicServiceGroupInHlr* object and the relevant *basicServiceInHlr* object ((c) and (d) in Figure 14.7) are created. Similarly, for every supplementary service, such as call waiting or call forwarding, a *supplementaryServiceInHlr* object (*ssInHlrCW* or *ssInHlrCFU*; see (e) and (f) in Figure 14.7) is created. Some supplementary services are specified with parameters. In this case, the *supplementaryServiceInHlr* object will contain the *ssInHlrParameter* object. For example, the *ssInHlrCFU* object contains the *ssInHlrParmCFU* object ((g) in Figure 14.7), with attributes such as forwardedToNumber. The subscriber data may be modified, for example, when a basic or a supplementary service is withdrawn or when a new service is added. When a subscriber is deleted from the HLR, the corresponding *subscriberInHlr* object and all its contained objects are removed. The attribute of the corresponding *msisdnHlr* is modified, and the MSISDN is no longer associated with the IMSI.

Other subscriber and service data management functions include the functions for AuC, VLR, and EIR. The details can be found in GSM 12.02.

14.4 Summary

Based on [Lin97c] this chapter provided an overview to the GSM OA&M management, following the TMN concept [ETS93e]. Two important OA&M functions not elaborated in this chapter are configuration management and fault management. Configuration management allows staff to configure the network elements (HLRs, VLRs, MSCs, BSCs, BTSs, and so on) connected in a GSM network. A user-friendly interface typically provides a graphical view of the entire network, which can be zoomed-in to get more detailed information of a particular network element. When a failure occurs in the network, fault management provides one or more alarms to attract the attention of the staff.

For further reading, complete descriptions for GSM TMN common management functions are given in [ITU92b]. Specific GSM network management functions are described in [ETS93g, ETS93f, ETS94c, ETS93d]. The Event Report Systems Management Function and Log Control Systems Management Function are defined in [ITU96a] and [ITU93b]. Transfer Access and Management for GSM and Tariff and Charging Administration are elaborated in [ETS93b] and [ITU96b], respectively. The Transfer Account Procedure is defined in [ITU88]. The log control to access NEF and the event reporting function in NEF are defined in [ITU93b] and [ITU96a]. We specifically discussed call recording and HLR management. In this example, the measurement job created in the OS is implemented as a simpleScanner object, defined in [ITU92a]. The complete descriptions (e.g., network security [ETS94b], network configuration [ETS94a] and others) of the GSM OA&M management can be found in the 12 series of the GSM technical specifications. An introduction and the history of GSM TMN is given in [Tow95].

14.5   Review Questions

1. What is TMN? Why was it adapted in GSM?

2. What is the function of the operations system in the OA&M architecture?

3. Which part of GSM OA&M is responsible for determining the charge for the services?

4. How does charging work in the case of international roaming?

5. What are the "measurement jobs" good for?

6. What are the major differences between the OA&M for the PSTN and a GSM network?

7. Based on GSM OA&M, design a measurement job for GSM MS call termination.

8. Compare the GSM OA&M functions and the WLL OAM, described in Chapter 23, Section 23.6. Is it appropriate to implement the WLL OAM using TMN platform?

CHAPTER

15

Mobile Number Portability

Number portability is a network function that allows a subscriber to keep a "unique" telephone number. Number portability is one of three important mechanisms to enhance fair competition among telecommunication operators and to improve customer service quality. (The other two mechanisms for fair competition are equal access and network unbundling.) Three kinds of number portability are discussed: location portability, service portability, and operator portability.

- With *location portability*, a subscriber may move from one location to another location without changing his or her telephone number. This type of portability is already implied in mobile phone service.

- With *service portability*, a subscriber may keep the same telephone number when changing the telecommunication services. In the United States, service portability between fixed telephone service and mobile phone service is implementable because both services follow the "NPA-NXX-XXXX" telephone number format. In Taiwan, the service code "093" for mobile service is distinguished from the area codes of fixed telephone service. As a result, service portability is not available in Taiwan unless the numbering plan is modified.

- With *operator portability*, a subscriber may switch operators or service providers without changing his or her telephone number.

In most countries, location portability and service portability are ignored, and only operator portability is implemented in a fixed network. The reason is twofold: First, operator portability is considered essential for fair competition among operators, while location portability and service portability are typically treated as value-added services; second, the implementation and operation costs can be significantly reduced if we ignore service portability and location portability.

Many countries, including Australia, China, Hong Kong, Japan, Taiwan, the United Kingdom, the United States, and numerous others in Europe, have implemented, or are in the process of implementing, fixed-network number portability. In these countries, the implementation schedule for mobile number portability typically follows fixed-network number portability. Survey studies by the Office of Telecommunications (OFTEL) United Kingdom and DGT/Taiwan indicated that most mobile operators are not enthusiastic about implementing number portability. They questioned whether there was a real demand for mobile number portability and whether it would provide significant benefits. Note, however, that number portability is considered a mechanism that will help a new operator or competitive local exchange carrier (CLEC) to compete with the existing operator or incumbent local exchange carrier (ILEC). In Taiwan, the licenses for mobile service are limited, and our 1999 survey indicated that none of the mobile operators in Taiwan were interested in implementing mobile number portability.

Some mobile operators also claimed that the absence of number portability may not deter customers from switching operators. In the United States, a *called-party-pays* policy is exercised, whereby mobile subscribers typically pay for the air-time usage and mobility for both incoming and outgoing calls. In order not to receive undesirable calls, customers are unlikely to distribute their numbers widely. From this aspect, number portability may not be an important factor when the customers decide to change mobile operators. Thus, in the United States, "Most mobile operators fought number portability kicking and screaming, and expressed amazement that the FCC would do such an evil thing to them" [Ame97].

On the other hand, in Taiwan or the United Kingdom, a *calling-party-pays* policy is exercised whereby mobile subscribers pay only for outgoing calls; incoming calls are paid by the callers. In this scenario, mobile customers, especially businesspeople who have high mobility (such as salespeople, plumbers, electricians, and builders), are likely to widely distribute their numbers. Furthermore, compared with fixed-network telephone numbers, few mobile numbers are published in telephone directories. Therefore, the benefits of number portability for mobile customers are more numerous than those for fixed-network customers. According to a U.K. survey, without number portability, only 42 percent of corporate subscribers are willing to change mobile operators. This percentage will increase to 96 percent if number portability is introduced. Changing numbers becomes a barrier to switching mobile operators, which turned out to be a major reason that mobile operators were against mobile number portability, specifically, "The mobile service providers know that customer loyalty with the hold of a unique number will be even harder to keep"[Che99].

An OFTEL analysis showed that there will be a net gain to the United Kingdom economy of $147 million USD with the introduction of mobile number portability. NERA's analysis indicated that by introducing mobile number portability, the net benefit for Hong Kong economy will range from $160 million USD to $188 million USD. Thus, they concluded that to improve a country's economy, mobile number portability should be enforced by the government.

This chapter introduces fixed-network number portability, then mobile number portability. We discuss number portability mechanisms, the costs incurred by number portability, and the cost recovery issues. We begin by defining some number portability terms.

Originally, a telephone number is assigned to a switch, called the *donor switch* or *release switch*. If the telephone number is moved from this switch to another switch, the new switch is called the *recipient switch*. The "moved" number is referred to as a *ported number*. Note that the ported number indicates the routing information to the donor switch.

15.1 Fixed-Network Number Portability

Four basic solutions have been proposed to support fixed-network number portability: call forwarding, call drop-back, query-on-release, and all-call-query. Call setup for these approaches is illustrated in Figure 15.1. In the subfigures, dashed lines represent signaling paths and solid lines represent trunk setup paths.

The call-forwarding call setup procedure is illustrated in Figure 15.1(a); the steps are as follows:

Step 1. The originating switch routes the call to the donor switch according to the dialed telephone number. In Figure 15.1(a), a solid arrow between two switches represents a trunk set up by using an SS7 ISUP Initial Address Message (IAM), as described in Chapter 5, Section 5.4.

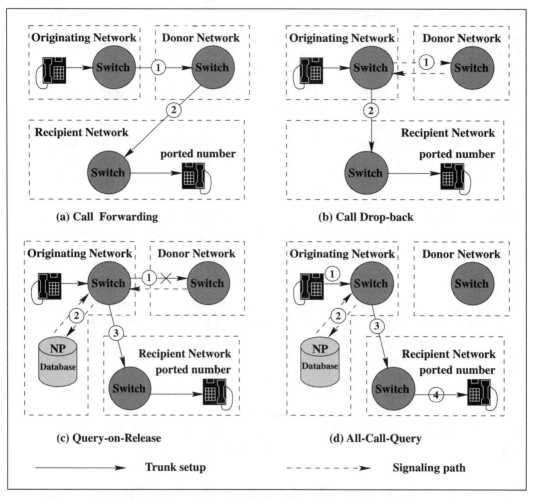

Figure 15.1 Number portability solutions for a fixed network.

Step 2. If the dialed number has been ported, the donor switch forwards the call to the recipient switch. For a nonported number, the recipient switch is the donor switch in this step, and no forwarding action is performed.

The call drop-back call setup procedure is illustrated in Figure 15.1(b):

Step 1. The originating switch queries the donor switch to obtain the routing information of the recipient switch. In Figure 15.1, dashed arrows represent SS7 TCAP signaling message exchange without involving trunk setup.

Step 2. The originating switch sets up the trunk to the recipient switch based on the obtained routing information.

The query-on-release (QoR) call setup procedure is illustrated in Figure 15.1(c):

Step 1. As in call forwarding, the originating switch sets up the trunk to the donor switch using an SS7 ISUP **IAM** message. If the dialed number has been ported, the donor switch replies with an SS7 ISUP **Release Message (REL)** with the QoR cause value.

Step 2. When the donor switch receives the **REL** message, the trunk to the donor switch is released. Since the QoR cause value indicates that the called party number is ported, the originating switch sends an SS7 TCAP message to query the number portability database for the routing address of the recipient switch.

Step 3. The originating switch sets up the trunk to the recipient switch based on the obtained routing information.

The all-call-query call setup procedure is illustrated in Figure 15.1(d):

Step 1. The originating switch sends an SS7 TCAP message to query the number portability database for the routing address of the recipient switch.

Step 2. The originating switch sets up the trunk to the recipient switch based on the obtained routing information.

In the remainder of this section, we discuss the fixed-network number portability overhead for extra call setup costs, initial system setup costs, and customer transfer costs.

15.1.1   Extra Call Setup Costs

Column 3 of Table 15.1 lists the extra costs required to set up a call after number portability has been introduced. In this table, p represents the percentage of call terminations to ported numbers. The variable c_t represents the cost for switching and transmission elements. OFTEL estimated c_t to be \$.50/min for British Telecom's (BT's) fixed network and \$.90/min for a mobile network. OFTEL also estimated the signaling cost to be \$.07/min. For trunk drop-in query-on-release, the cost, c_d is estimated to be \$.18/min. Following these estimations, we assume that $c_t = 6c_s$ and $c_d = 2c_s$. The extra call setup costs for various fixed-network number portability solutions are illustrated in Figure 15.2. The figure

Table 15.1 Comparison of Fixed-Network Number Portability Solutions

NUMBER PORTABILITY SOLUTION	ROUTING INDEPENDENCE	EXTRA CALL SETUP COST	INITIAL SYSTEM SETUP COST
Call Forwarding	low	pc_t	low
Call Drop-back	medium	c_s	medium
Query-on-Release	medium	$p(c_s + c_d)$	high
All-Call-Query	high	c_s	high

indicates that, in terms of reducing extra call setup costs, all-call-query or call drop-back should be selected when p is large, and query-on-release should be selected when p is small.

A study of number portability regulations in Taiwan indicated that if the government enforces the number portability database mechanism, at the early stage, the new operators or CLECs prefer all-call-query, while existing operators or ILECs prefer query-on-release. The reason is that all-call-query allows CLECs to independently set up the calls without the involvement of the ILEC, which provides more flexibility for CLECs

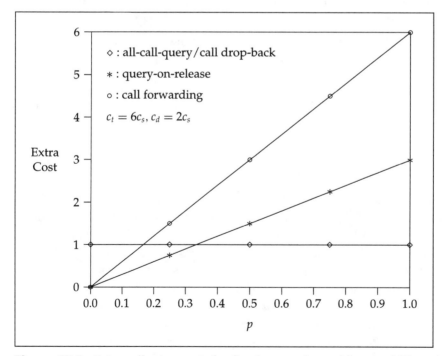

Figure 15.2 Extra call setup costs for fixed-network number portability solutions.

to compete. (Column 2 of Table 15.1 indicates that all-call-query is the best in terms of routing independence.) Furthermore, the CLECs tend to purchase advanced switches that are already equipped with database querying capability. Therefore, the implementation costs for all-call-query can be significantly reduced. On the other hand, when the ILEC originates a call at the early deployment stage of number portability, the portion, p, is expected to be small, and the donor switch is likely to belong to ILEC itself. Thus, for a nonported call termination, no extra cost is incurred to the ILEC. For a ported call termination, the ILEC is unlikely to reimburse any CLEC because both the originating and the donor switches belong to the ILEC.

Similar to query-on-release, call forwarding and call drop-back involve the donor network resources during call setup. Sepcifically, both query-on-release and call drop-back require signaling interactions with the donor switch, and call forwarding utilizes trunk/transmission resources of the donor switch. Column 2 of Table 15.1 lists the degree of independence of call setup routing for the four solutions.

15.1.2   Initial System Setup Costs

To support number portability, initial system setup is required. This setup includes the costs for number portability systems development, network management, line testing, operator services, billing information, exchanges overlay, maintenance, and support. Initial system setup costs were estimated to be $52 million USD for BT's fixed-network number portability and $12 million USD for mobile number portability.

The system setup costs for various fixed-network number portability solutions are listed in Column 4 of Table 15.1. Since call forwarding is a function already built into existing switches, system setup costs are the lowest among the four solutions. In call drop-back, a new signaling protocol between the originating switch and donor switch must be implemented, requiring extra system setup effort compared with call forwarding. In all-call-query, significant system setup cost is required to implement the number portability database mechanism. Besides the cost for the database mechanism, query-on-release must also implement a new signaling protocol between the originating switch and the donor switch.

15.1.3   Customer Transfer Costs

Customer transfer costs or per-line setup costs are incurred when moving a ported number from the donor operator to the recipient operator. The costs include closing down an old account, opening up a new account, and coordinating physical line switching. The transfer cost for fixed-network ported number is estimated to be around $45, and the cost for mobile ported number is estimated to be $29 USD. Some number portability studies considered the customer transfer costs as part of number portability overhead. We feel that a major portion of the customer transfer costs exists even if number portability is not implemented. However, extra coordination between the donor and the recipient operators is required to move a ported number. Futhermore, issues such as "allowing a customer who left bad debt to the donor operator when this customer moves to the recipient operator with the ported number" should be carefully resolved.

For both call forwarding and call drop-back, when a customer switches service from the donor network to the recipient network with number portability, the routing information of the recipient switch is stored in the donor switch. For query-on-release, when a customer switches service with number portability, the donor switch records that the number has been ported (but does not need to memorize the address of the recipient switch). The recipient network needs to create or modify the number portability database entry to record routing information for the ported number. The number portability database may be a centralized database maintained by a third party other than the telecommunication operators. Alternatively, the mechanism can be a distributed database maintained by the telecommunication operators themselves. Like query-on-release, when a customer switches service in all-call-query, the recipient network needs to create or modify a number portability database entry to record routing information for the ported number.

15.1.4 Cost Recovery

It has long been argued who should cover the costs for number portability. Some contend that the ported customers should cover the costs for number portability, while others believe that the number portability costs should be borne by all telecommunication users, for two reasons:

- Number portability should be treated as a "default function" instead of an added-value service. Since all users have the opportunity to reach ported numbers, they all benefit from number portability.

- If the cost for a ported number is significantly higher than for a nonported number, the users will be discouraged from utilizing this capability. If so, the original goal of number portability to provide fair competition and service quality improvement will not be achieved.

Table 15.2 Cost Recovery for Fixed-Network Number Portability Solutions

NUMBER PORTABILITY SOLUTION	CUSTOMER TRANSFER COST	EXTRA CALL SETUP COST	INITIAL SYSTEM SETUP COST
Call Forwarding	$r \rightarrow d; c \rightarrow r$	$o \rightarrow d$	own
Call Drop-back	$r \rightarrow d; c \rightarrow r$	$o \rightarrow d$	own
Query-on-Release	$r \rightarrow d, db; c \rightarrow r$	$o \rightarrow d, o \rightarrow db$	own
All-Call-Query	$r \rightarrow db; c \rightarrow r$	$o \rightarrow db$	own

Depending on telecommunication policies, different countries may have different decisions for cost recovery. Table 15.2 lists the cost recovery alternatives. In this table, r, d, o, and c represent recipient operator, donor operator, originating operator, and customer, respectively. The initials db represent the party who manages the number portability database. The relation $r \rightarrow d$ means that the recipient operator needs to reimburse the donor operator, and "own" means that the operators should bear their own costs. (Note that the cost recovery suggestions in Table 15.2 are given based on technical viewpoints. The reader should bear in mind that rules for cost recovery are also affected by the business and regulation factors that vary from country to country.)

Most studies have suggested that the operators should bear their own costs for initial system setup; for customer transfer costs, the donor operator should bear the cost for closing down an account, and the recipient operator should bear the cost for opening up a new account. For physical line switching, cost recovery should follow the same rules as for nonported numbers. In call forwarding, call drop-back and query-on-release, the recipient operator needs the donor operator's assistance to transfer the ported customers. Thus, reimbursement from the recipient operator to the donor operator is required. In query-on-release and all-call-query, the recipient operator needs to cover the costs for modifying the number portability database. The recipient operator may charge the customers for importing their numbers. The donor operators are not expected to charge customers with ported numbers who move out.

In call forwarding and call drop-back, to set up calls to ported numbers, an originating operator utilizes the donor switch's resources. The originating operators should pay the access fees to the donor operators according to telecommunications regulations. For query-on-release and all-call-query, the call setup procedure involves a database query. There are two alternatives: First, if the number portability database is maintained by a third party, the originating operators should reimburse the database access costs. In this case, the originating operators typically download the routing information from the third-party database into their local databases, and call routing is done by querying the local databases. Second, the operators may distribute the ported number routing information among themselves. In this case, the operators are expected to bear their own costs.

As mentioned earlier, different countries may have different approaches for cost recovery. In Taiwan, we recommend that the database mechanism should be built, and the operators are encouraged to utilize all-call-query. In this scenario, the donor and the recipient operators should bear their own costs; the ported numbers should not be treated differently from the nonported numbers—except for a customer transfer cost that the recipient operators may charge ported customers.

15.2 Number Portability for Mobile Networks

Although most mobile operators are not enthusiastic about implementing mobile number portability, they cannot avoid the impact of fixed-network number portability. When a mobile station (MS) originates a call to a ported number in the fixed network, the originating mobile switching center (MSC) needs to route the call to the correct destination by using one of the four fixed-network number portability solutions described in the previous section. Alternatively, the MSC may direct the call to a switch in the fixed network, which then routes the call to the recipient switch. In this case, the mobile operator should reimburse the fixed-network operator for extra routing cost.

Before we describe mobile number portability, we point out that a mobile phone is associated with two numbers: the *directory* number and the *identification* number. In GSM, the MSISDN (mobile station ISDN number) is the directory number, which is dialed to reach the MS; in other words, MSISDN is the telephone number of the MS. The IMSI (international mobile subscriber identification) is a confidential number that uniquely identifies an MS in the mobile network. IMSI is hidden from the mobile user, which is used to authenticate/identify the MS during location update and call origination, as described in Chapter 9. When a mobile user switches operators, a new MSISDN and IMSI pair is assigned to the user. When mobile number portability is introduced, the mobile user keeps the MSISDN (the ported number) while being issued a new IMSI.

For mobile systems based on EIA/TIA IS-41, the identification number and the directory number are referred to as the *mobile identification number*

(MIN) and the *mobile directory number* (MDN), respectively. The mobile operators typically assume that both MIN and MDN have the same value, and so are used interchangeably. The MIN/MDN is of the format NPA-NXX-XXXX. The first six digits, NPA-NXX, identify the home system of the MS. Without this home network identification, roaming is not possible. The MDN is used as the calling-party number parameters in signaling and billing records. If mobile number portability is introduced, the MIN will be different from the MDN, in which case, using the MIN as the calling party number will result in misrouting in services such as automatic callback and calling number/calling name. Similarly, using MDN for location update will result in errors when performing the registration procedure. Thus, to support portability, separation of MIN and MDN is required for the IS-41-based systems. This means that extra costs are incurred to modify mobile software in the MSC, home location register (HLR), and visitor location register (VLR).

Following the preceding discussion, the impact of number portability on mobile network is considered in three aspects:

Location update. The identification number (IMSI or MIN) is used in the location update procedure. Since the assignment of this number is not affected by the introduction of number portability, location update is not affected by portability—except that MIN/MDN separation is required for the IS-41-based systems.

Mobile call origination. As mentioned in the beginning of this section, to originate a call to a ported number, the MSC needs to be equipped with a routing mechanism.

Mobile call termination. To deliver or terminate a call to a ported mobile number, the standard mobile call termination procedure is modified to accommodate the portability mechanism.

In the United States, number portability is introduced to the mobile operators in two phases. In phase 1, mechanisms for mobile to (ported) fixed-network calls are implemented. In phase 2, the MIN/MDN separation, as well as mobile call termination mechanism, is implemented.

15.3   Mobile Number Portability Mechanisms

In mobile service, the network tracks the location of every MS. The location information is stored in two mobile databases, the HLR and the VLR. To deliver a call to an MS, the databases are queried for routing information via the MSC where the MS resides. Figure 15.3 illustrates a simplified GSM

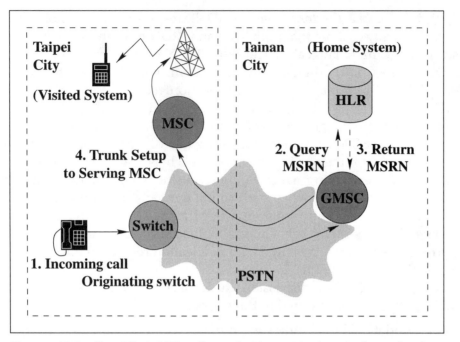

Figure 15.3 Simplified GSM call termination procedure and tromboning routing (dashed arrows: signaling; solid arrows: voice trunk).

call termination procedure where the interaction between HLR and VLR is omitted. (The reader is referred to Chapter 9, Section 9.2 for the detailed call termination procedure.) In Figure 15.3, the visited system (where the MS resides) may be different from its home system. Call termination to the MS must be routed to the GMSC at the home system due to the following restrictions:

Restriction 1. The GMSC must be in the call path for the provision of special features and services, as well as for billing.

Restriction 2. The originating switch does not have the capability to query the HLR database, which must be done by the GMSC.

A tromboning effect may occur if both the calling party and the called MS are in the same city (say, Taipei) and the GMSC is located in a different city (say, Tainan). The cost for tromboning can be highly significant, especially for international roaming described in Chapter 13.

To support mobile number portability, call termination in Figure 15.3 is modified. We describe four mobile number portability solutions as follows.

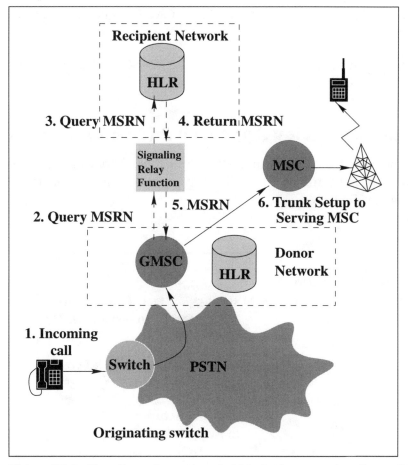

Figure 15.4   Signaling relay approach 1 (dashed arrows: signaling; solid arrows: voice trunk).

15.3.1   Signaling Relay Approach 1 (SRA 1)

SRA 1 utilizes a *signaling relay function* (SRF) mechanism to provide routing information for ported numbers. The call setup procedure consists of the following steps (shown in Figure 15.4):

Step 1.   The originating switch routes the incoming call to the donor GMSC of the ported MS.

Step 2.   The donor GMSC sends the MSRN query message to the SRF.

Steps 3–5.   The SRF determines the HLR of the destination MS. If the MS is not ported, the original HLR is queried. If the MS is ported, the recipient HLR is queried.

Step 6. Upon receipt of the MSRN, the donor GMSC routes the call to the serving MSC.

This approach violates restriction 1; that is, the GMSC of the recipient network is not in the call path.

15.3.2   Signaling Relay Approach 2 (SRA 2)

SRA 2 makes sure that the recipient GMSC is in the call path for call termination to a ported number. The call setup procedure is described as follows (see Figure 15.5):

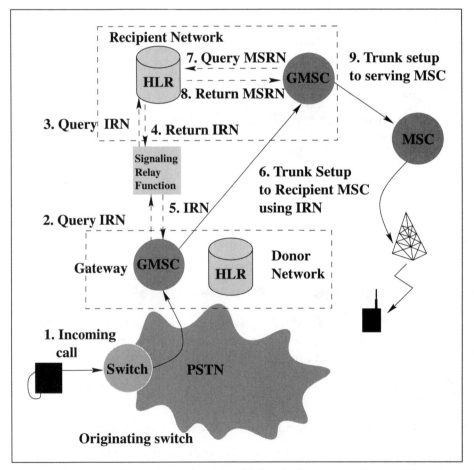

Figure 15.5   Signaling relay approach 2 (dashed arrows: signaling; solid arrows: voice trunk).

Step 1. The originating switch routes the incoming call to the donor GMSC of the ported MS.

Step 2. The donor GMSC sends the MSRN query message to the signaling relay function (SRF).

Steps 3–5. If the MS is ported, then the SRF queries the recipient HLR. In this case, the recipient HLR returns an *intermediate routing number* (IRN) instead of the MSRN. In the UK, the IRN consists of the called party numer with a prefix that indicates the recipient GMSC.

Step 6. Upon receipt of the IRN, the donor GMSC routes the call to the recipient GMSC.

Steps 7–9. The recipient GMSC routes the call using the standard GSM call termination procedure.

Inefficient tromboning call setup may occur in SRA 2. Suppose that an MS p is ported from a donor network A to a recipient network B. When an MS q in the recipient network makes a phone call to p, tromboning setup between GMSCs A and B occurs as shown in Figure 15.6. The tromboning trunks can be eliminated if the called number is screened at the originating MSC before being routed out of the originating mobile network. This screening could be effected either by interrogating the HLR or a mobile number portability database.

In the United States, T1P1 committee's proposal, the originating MSC interrogates the number portability database to have the called number translated into a routing number. The called party number is sent in the Generic Address Parameter and the Forward Call Indicator is set to "number translated." The call is then routed using the routing number.

The OFTEL study concluded that the tromboning cost is cheaper than screening, and therefore did not recommend the introduction of the screening mechanism.

15.3.3 All-Call-Query Approach 1 (ACQ 1)

ACQ 1 utilizes the existing fixed-network, all-call-query mechanism to route the calls to a ported MS (see Figure 15.7).

Steps 1 and 2. The originating switch queries the mobile number portability database to obtain the IRN of the recipient GMSC.

Step 3. The originating switch sets up the trunk to the recipient GMSC.

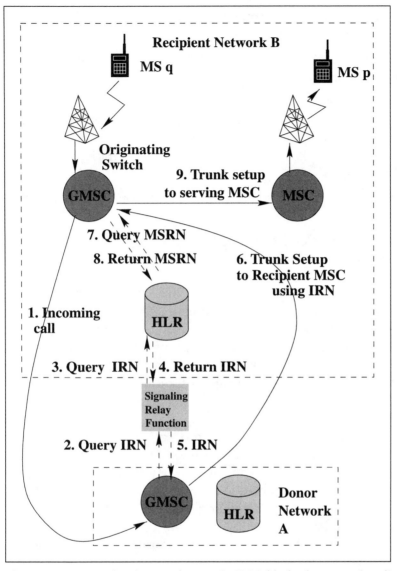

Figure 15.6 Tromboning trunk setup in SRF 2 (dashed arrows: signaling; solid arrows: voice trunk).

Steps 4–6. The recipient GMSC routes the call according to the standard GSM call termination procedure.

Like the standard GSM call termination without number portability, tromboning may occur if both originating and serving MSCs are at the same location while the recipient GMSC is located at a different place.

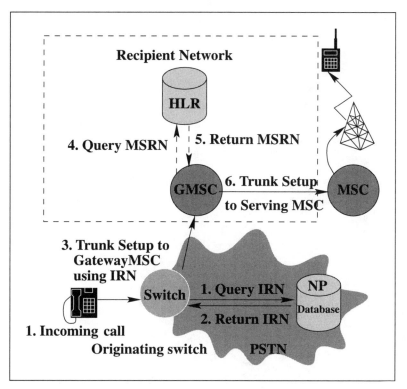

Figure 15.7 All-call-query approach 1 (dashed arrows: signaling; solid arrows: voice trunk).

15.3.4 All-Call-Query Approach 2 (ACQ 2)

ACQ 2 bypasses the recipient GMSC as follows (see Figure 15.8):

Step 1. The originating switch queries the mobile number portability database.

Steps 2–4. The number portability database utilizes the signaling relay function to identify the HLR of the called MS, and launches a query message to the recipient HLR to obtain the MSRN.

Step 5. The originating switch sets up the trunk to the serving MSC based on the IMSI.

Similar to SRA 1, this approach violates restriction 1. Thanks to fixed-network number portability, the originating switch is assumed to be equipped with database querying capability, and restriction 2 is relaxed in ACQ 2.

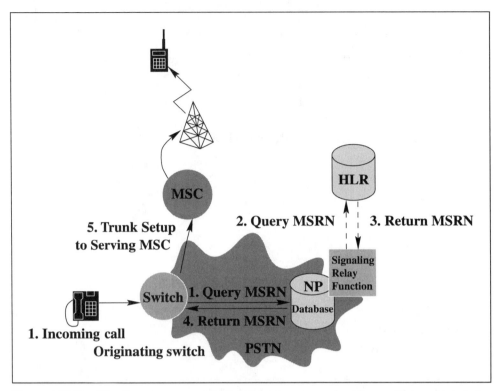

Figure 15.8 All-call-query approach 2 (dashed arrows: signaling; solid arrows: voice trunk).

15.4 Implementation Costs for Mobile Number Portability

Column 2 of Table 15.3 shows to what degree the originating network depends on the donor network for routing calls to the ported MSs. Both

Table 15.3 Comparison of Mobile Number Portability Solutions

NUMBER PORTABILITY SOLUTION	ROUTING INDEPENDENCE	EXTRA CALL SETUP COST	INITIAL SYSTEM SETUP COST
SRA 1	low	c_s	medium
SRA 2	low	$2c_s + pc_t$	medium
ACQ 1	high	c_s	medium
ACQ 2	high	$c_s - c_t$	medium

SRA 1 and 2 route calls to donor networks, and their routing independence is low. On the other hand, donor networks are not involved in call routing in ACQ 1 and 2, and their routing independence is high. Thus, in terms of the routing independence, ACQ 1 and 2 are better than SRA 1 and 2.

Both SRA 1 and ACQ 2 reduce the routing overhead by eliminating the GMSC of the recipient network from the call path, but they violate restriction 1, which requires the originating operators and the recipient operators to work out cost recovery agreements (including billing and service provision).

Table 15.4 lists cost recovery alternatives for mobile number portability. Mobile operators are expected to bear their own initial system setup costs (column 4, Table 15.4). Since the MSCs already have the capability to query databases, the intial system setup costs are expected to be lower than those for fixed-network number portability. For ACQ 1, the mobile network can reuse the fixed-network, all-call-query mechanism, and the initial system setup cost can be significantly reduced.

Guidelines for mobile transfer cost recovery are similar to those for fixed networks, except that no physical line switching is required. If the signaling relay functions (SRFs) are maintained by the third party, the recipient operators should reimburse the third party for routing information modifications (column 2, Table 15.4). If the SRFs are maintained by the donor operators, the recipient operators should reimburse the donor operators. The recipient operators may charge the ported customers for the transfer overhead.

In SRA 1 and 2, the donor networks are involved in call setup. Therefore, the originating operators should reimburse the donor operators for the additional call setup cost. If the mobile number portability databases and SRFs are maintained by the third party, the originating operators should reimburse the third party directly or indirectly for the extra call setup cost. Column 3 of Table 15.3 lists the extra call setup costs for the four

Table 15.4 Cost Recovery Mobile Number Portability Solutions

NUMBER PORTABILITY SOLUTION	CUSTOMER TRANSFER COST	EXTRA CALL SETUP COST	INITIAL SYSTEM SETUP COST
SRA 1	$r \to d(db); c \to r$	$o \to d, d \to db$	own
SRA 2	$r \to d(db); c \to r$	$o \to d, r, d \to db$	own
ACQ 1	$r \to db; c \to r$	$o \to db$	own
ACQ 2	$r \to db; c \to r$	$o \to db$	own

mobile number portability solutions. Compared with the standard GSM call setup procedure in Figure 15.3, SRA 1 incurs extra number portability querying and SRF signaling (steps 1–4, Figure 15.4). SRA 2 incurs extra SRF signaling (steps 2 and 5, Figure 15.5) for querying IRN, and an extra trunk setup (step 6, Figure 15.5) if the destination MS is ported. As in all-call-query in fixed networks, ACQ 1 requires one number portability database query (steps 1 and 2, Figure 15.7). ACQ 2 assumes that restriction 2 can be relaxed so that the cost for trunk setup from the originating switch to the GMSC of the home system is eliminated. On the other hand, this solution incurs extra SRF signaling (steps 2 and 3, Figure 15.8).

15.5 Summary

This chapter introduced fixed-network number portability and mobile number portability based on the materials in [TEL95, Tot95, INP97, ETS99]. We described number portability mechanisms and their implementation costs. Cost-recovery issues for number portability were discussed from a technical perspective. We point out here that rules for cost recovery also depend on business and regulatory factors that vary from country to country. The reader is referred to [FCC96, Lin99e, Att98, Oft97b] for the details. Several suveys for number portability have been conducted by OFTEL [Oft97a, Oft97b], NERA [Att98], DGT/Taiwan [Yu 99] and OVUM [Hor98]. Service portability between fixed telephone service and mobile phone service is discussed in [NAN98]. A new signaling protocol, call drop-back, is described in [One98]. The MDN/MIN issues for mobile number portability are elaborated in [NAN98]. The SRF mechanism is discussed in [Att98].

For further information, the reader is referred to the following Web sites for the most up-to-date content:

- Office of the Telecommunications Authority (Hong Kong): www.ofta.gov.hk/numbering
- Office of Telecommunications (UK): www.oftel.gov.uk/numbers
- Number Portability Administration Center: www.npac.com
- Ported Communications: www.ported.com
- FCC: www.fcc.gov/ccb/nanc
- Lockheed Martin: www.numberpool.com
- North American Number Plan Administration: www.nanpa.com

15.6   Review Questions

1. What is number portability? Describe three types of number portability. Which kind of number portability is affected by the numbering plan?

2. Describe the four solutions for the fixed-network number portability. If you are a switch vendor, which solution is most profitable? What are the best solutions for ILEC and CLEC? Why?

3. What are the differences between fixed-network number portability and mobile number portability?

4. How are the mobile identification number and the mobile directory number affected by mobile number portability? In terms of mobile number portability implementation, which protocol is better, GSM MAP or IS-41?

5. Describe the solutions for mobile number portability.

6. Assume that service portability is available in a country, and that a customer would like to switch from fixed-network service to GSM service. What actions should be taken to transfer this customer?

7. Does mobile number portability raise a *feature interaction* issue that affects other telecommunication services? For example, is a call-forwarding service affected by number portability?

8. When a customer terminates telephone services, the assigned telephone number is reclaimed. This reclaimed number is reassigned to a new customer after an aging period. The process is called *number recycling*. Does number portability reduce the telephone number recycling problem?

9. Propose a performance model to investigate the screening mechanism described in SRA 2. What are the input parameters and output measures?

10. Can a mobile voice mailbox be provided with ACQ 2? If your answer is yes, explain how. If your answer is no, show how to modify ACQ 2 to accommodate this service.

11. Do we need to implement location portability for mobile phone service?

VoIP Service for Mobile Networks

Supporting telephony services over an Internet Protocol (IP) network, better known as voice over IP (VoIP), is considered as a promising trend in telecommunications. Integrating mobile phone services with VoIP in particular has become an important issue, one that has been studied intensively. *Telecommunications and Internet Protocol Harmonization over Network* (TIPHON) specifies the mechanism (i.e., a mediation gatekeeper) to provide the service control functions for convergence of IP networks, mobile networks, fixed wireless networks, and the public switched telephone network (PSTN). Several scenarios are defined in TIPHON to illustrate different ways of integrating IP and mobile networks. In this chapter, we use GSM as an example of mobile networks to describe mobile/IP integration, where the mobile signaling protocol is GSM MAP, described in Chapter 10.

Our discussion also applies to other mobile signaling protocols, such as IS-41 (ANSI-41), described in Chapter 7. The elements in the GSM network include the mobile station (MS), base transceiver station (BTS), base station controller (BSC), mobile switching center (MSC), home location register (HLR), and visitor location register (VLR). Details of the GSM system were discussed in Chapter 9.

A TIPHON scenario that integrates mobile and IP networks to support terminal mobility is illustrated in Figure 16.1, where the mediation gatekeeper serves as a VLR to support roaming management. The BSC/BTS in

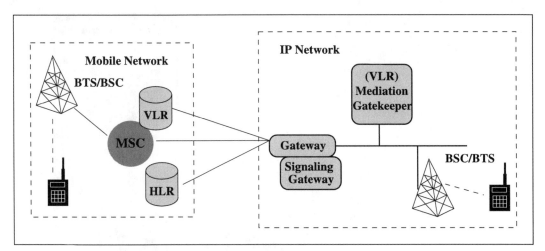

Figure 16.1 TIPHON IP and mobile integration scenario.

the IP network provides wireless access to the IP network. In the first section, 16.1, we describe GSM on the Net, an example of the scenario given in Figure 16.2. Then we elaborate on another TIPHON scenario, one that describes mobile and IP integration to support user mobility. An example of this scenario, iGSM, is proposed in Section 16.2 to integrate GSM and VoIP services.

16.1 GSM on the Net

Based on a concept similar to TIPHON, Ericsson's GSM on the Net [Gra98] utilizes a corporate intranet to integrate an enterprise communication network with the public GSM network. This system supports both *terminal mobility* (whereby a terminal can be moved around the service area without losing contact with the system) and *user mobility* (whereby, using various types of terminals, a user can move around the service area without losing contact with the system). The GSM on the Net architecture is illustrated in Figure 16.2, which consists of GSM and corporate networks. Each of the elements in the corporate network is connected to a switched Ethernet with 10 Mbps bandwidth. They communicate with each other using the H.323 family of protocols (see Section 16.2.1). The network elements of GSM on the Net are described here:

Service node. Enables user mobility, controls calls among different types of terminals, and translates addresses between PSTN and GSM on the Net. It also provides authentication, resource management,

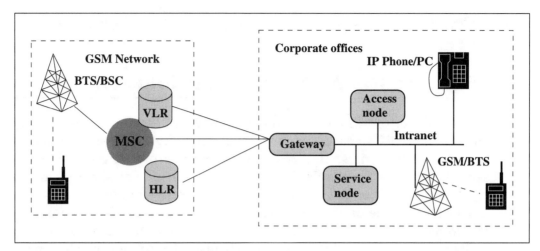

Figure 16.2   GSM on the Net architecture.

least-cost routing, and administration for user identity and service profile.

Access node. Resembles the MSC, VLR, and BSC to manage connection, mobility, and radio resources. It does not provide trunks for user information transmission; instead, this node controls only the communication between the endpoints. The access node consists of the network access controller (NAC), responsible for all tasks related to the core network, and the radio network server (RNS), responsible for the tasks related to the BTS nodes.

GSM/BTS. Provides wireless access for a GSM MS in the IP network. This node consists of BTS and the A-bis gateway connected to RNS.

Gateway. Provides interfaces between GSM on the Net and other networks (particularly the GSM network). It consists of both voice and SS7 gateway functionality.

Terminal equipment. Can be an IP phone, PC (for video phone calls), DECT phone, or GSM mobile station (MS).

The service node and the access node are implemented on standard servers. Based on the user identity, the service node keeps the profiles of the registered users to indicate the services (call forwarding, call waiting and so on) subscribed to by the users. The access node is responsible for call handling of the GSM MS. The location update and call control procedure of GSM on the Net can be established by utilizing the radio protocol, described in Chapter 9, Section 9.1.4, and the H.323 family of protocols described in Section 16.3. The reader is encouraged to design these procedures.

16.2   The iGSM Wireless VoIP Solution

The remainder of this chapter proposes the iGSM service that realizes another TIPHON scenario supporting user mobility for GSM subscribers to access VoIP services. That is, a GSM subscriber ordering the iGSM service can enjoy the standard GSM services when he or she is in the GSM network. When the person moves to the IP network (without a GSM mobile station), he or she can utilize an H.323 terminal (IP phone or a PC) to receive an incoming call to his or her MSISDN (mobile station ISDN number). The GSM roaming mechanism determines whether the subscriber is in the GSM network or the IP network. The iGSM solution is different from GSM on the Net in the following aspects: Unlike GSM on the Net (which integrates a corporate network with the public GSM network), iGSM is a value-added service to the public GSM networks. The iGSM network does not introduce wireless access equipment (i.e., GSM BTS) in the IP network; rather, iGSM service is implemented using standard platforms (general IP gateway/gatekeeper).

In this section, we describe the iGSM architecture and the protocols for location update and call delivery. We discuss how the tromboning effect (see Chapter 13) in standard GSM systems can be avoided when accessing the IP network. Then we investigate the problem of misrouting a call caused by user mobility.

16.2.1   The H.323 Network

The iGSM system consists of the GSM and H.323 (IP) networks. Although we consider H.323 as the VoIP protocol, our results can be generalized to accommodate other protocols such as the Media Gateway Control Protocol.

We briefly introduce H.323 as follows: ITU-T H.323 covers the technical requirements for multimedia communications over packet-based networks that may not provide a guaranteed quality of service. Figure 16.3 illustrates an H.323 system, where the terminal, gateway, gatekeeper, and multipoint control unit are called *endpoints*.

Terminal. Customer premises equipment (CPE) that provides audio, video, and data communications capability for point-to-point or multipoint conferences in the H.323 network.

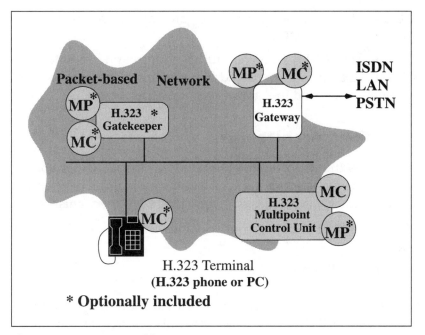

Figure 16.3   H.323 architecture.

Gateway. Performs call control functions (setup and release) and the communication protocol translation mechanism between an H.323 endpoint and an endpoint of a circuit-switched network, such as PSTN, ISDN, or LAN. It also translates the transmitted media from one format to another between the IP network and a circuit-switched network. Two H.323 endpoints in the same network can communicate without involving the gateway.

Gatekeeper. Optional in an H.323 network. The gatekeeper may be physically colocated with a terminal, gateway, or multipoint control unit. A gatekeeper provides call control services to the H.323 endpoints. The functions of the gatekeeper include address translation, admissions control, bandwidth control, and zone management. The gatekeeper may also perform optional functions such as call control signaling, call authorization, call management, and so on.

Multipoint control unit (MCU). Utilizes multipoint controllers (and, optionally, multipoint processors) to support multipoint conferences.

Multipoint controller (MC). Provides control functions to support conferences between three or more endpoints in a multipoint conference.

Every MCU contains an MC. Terminals, gateways, and gatekeepers may or may not contain MCs.

Multipoint processor (MP). Receives audio, video, and/or data streams from the endpoints involved in a multipoint conference. An MP is optionally included in a gateway, gatekeeper, or MCU.

16.2.2   The iGSM Architecture

Figure 16.4 illustrates the iGSM architecture, where the GSM network is not modified. In the IP network, an iGSM gateway is implemented to perform two major functions besides the standard H.323 mechanisms:

- GSM MAP and H.225 RAS (*registration, admission, and status*) protocol translation
- GSM/PSTN/IP call setup and release

NOTE In H.323, the signaling gateway (which manages signaling protocols such as SS7 ISUP/TACP, GSM MAP, and ISDN) is separated from the media gateway. To simplify our discussion, we assume that both signaling and media gateways are integrated into an iGSM gateway.

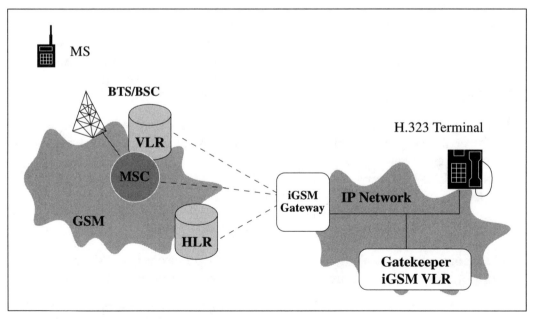

Figure 16.4   iGSM architecture.

An iGSM gatekeeper is implemented to serve as the VLR for iGSM subscribers who visit the IP network. Thus, every iGSM gatekeeper is assigned an ISDN number that can be recognized by the HLR. The iGSM gatekeeper also maintains a list of all iGSM subscribers (whether they visit the IP network or not). Based on this list, the gatekeeper performs MSISDN-to-transport address translation (using the standard H.323 alias address-into-transport address translation mechanism) and GSM roaming management procedures for the iGSM subscribers.

The iGSM architecture is scalable. We can add iGSM gateways and gatekeepers into the system in the same way that multiple VLRs and MSCs exist in a GSM network.

16.3   iGSM Procedures and Message Flows

This section describes registration, deregistration, and call delivery procedures for iGSM service. Logically, the iGSM gatekeeper maintains an iGSM database that stores information for all iGSM subscribers. Physically, the database can be distributed among several gatekeepers. Every iGSM subscriber has a record in the database, which consists of the following fields:

- MSISDN of the MS

- Transport address of the H.323 terminal for the subscriber in the IP network

- Password of the iGSM subscriber

- HLR address (ISDN number) of the iGSM subscriber

- IMSI (international mobile station identity) of the MS

- User profile, which indicates the service features and restrictions of the iGSM subscriber

- Presence indication of the iGSM subscriber in the IP network

Unlike a traditional GSM VLR, the iGSM database does not maintain information such as the MSC address, LAI (location area identity), TMSI (temporary mobile station identity), or authentication/encryption information, such as K_c, signed result (SRES), and RAND.

To implement GSM MAP messages in the RAS protocol, the nonStandardData field of a RAS message is used to indicate the "type" and parameters of a GSM MAP operation. Alternatively, GSM MAP messages can be implemented by the RAS nonstandard messages. In this chapter, we utilize the nonStandardData field of RAS messages.

16.3.1 Registration

If an iGSM user moves around the location areas within the GSM network, the registration procedure follows GSM MAP. When the iGSM user moves from the GSM network to the IP network (see Figure 16.5), the registration procedure is described in the following steps (the message flow is given in Figure 16.6):

Step 1. The iGSM user moves from the GSM network to the IP network.

Step 2. When the H.323 terminal is turned on, the user enters the MSISDN and the password to activate the iGSM VoIP service. The H.323 terminal initiates endpoint registration to inform the iGSM gatekeeper of its transport address and alias address (i.e., MSISDN). The RAS RRQ (Registration Request) message sent from the H.323 terminal to the iGSM gatekeeper includes the password in the nonStandardData field of the message.

Step 3. The iGSM gatekeeper validates the subscriber with the password. Then it initiates the GSM registration procedure by

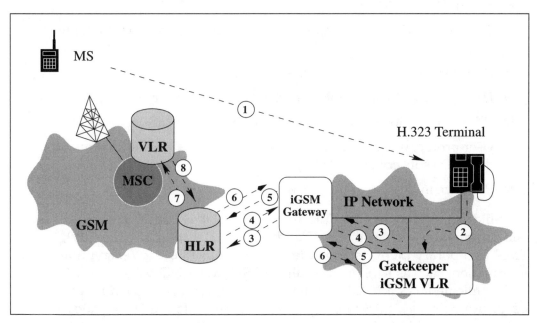

Figure 16.5 Movement from the GSM network to the IP network.

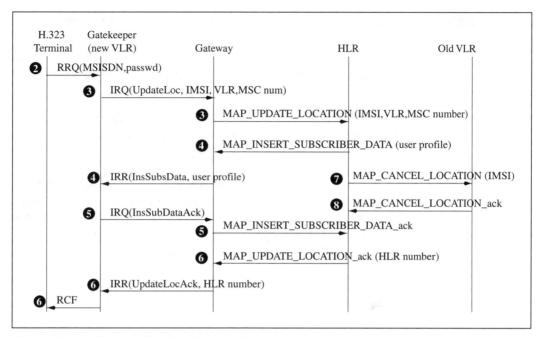

Figure 16.6   Message flow for iGSM registration.

sending an **IRQ** (Information Request) message to the iGSM gateway. The **nonStandardData** field of the message carries the type of the GSM operation (i.e., **UpdateLoc**), the IMSI, the VLR address (the address of the gatekeeper), and the MSC address (the address of the H.323 terminal). Based on the **UpdateLoc** type indicated in the message, the iGSM gateway translates the **IRQ** message into the GSM MAP message **MAP_UPDATE_LOCATION** and forwards it to the HLR.

Step 4. Based on the received IMSI, the HLR retrieves the user profile and sends it back to the iGSM gateway using the GSM MAP message **MAP_INSERT_SUBSCRIBER_DATA**. The gateway forwards the user profile to the iGSM gatekeeper using the RAS **IRR** (Information Request Response) message with type **InsSubsData**.

Step 5. The iGSM gatekeeper records the user profile and acknowledges the operation by sending an **IRQ** message with type **InsSub-DataAck**. The iGSM gateway translates the **IRQ** message into the **MAP_INSERT_SUBS_DATA_ack** message and forwards it to the HLR.

Step 6. The HLR completes the registration operation by sending the GSM MAP message **MAP_UPDATE_LOCATION_ack** that contains the HLR address. The gateway translates it into the **RCF** (Registration Confirm) message with type **UpdateLocAck**, and forwards it to the gatekeeper.

Steps 7 and 8. The HLR informs the old VLR of deregistration by sending the **MAP_CANCEL_LOCATION** message. The old VLR deletes the VLR record for the iGSM MS.

GSM authentication and encryption mechanism is disabled in this message flow, to avoid distributing GSM secret information (such as K_i) to equipment other than the SIM (subscriber identity module) card on the user side. This argument is especially important when the ISP service is provided by a different operator than the GSM service.

16.3.2   Deregistration

When an iGSM subscriber moves from the IP network to the GSM network, he or she performs registration in the GSM network (or misrouting may occur, as described in Section 16.4.2). The standard GSM registration procedure is exercised. In this case, the iGSM gatekeeper is the "old VLR," and the deregistration actions—steps 7 and 8 described in Section 16.3.1—are modified. The message flow for iGSM deregistration is illustrated in Figure 16.7, with the following steps:

Step 1. When the iGSM gateway receives the **MAP_CANCEL_LOCATION** (with parameter IMSI), it translates this message into an unsolicited **IRR** message with type **CanLoc**, and forwards it to the

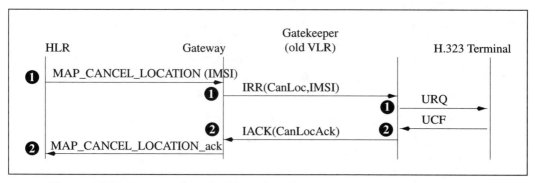

Figure 16.7   Message flow for iGSM deregistration.

gatekeeper. The gatekeeper updates the iGSM database to indicate that the subscriber is no longer in the IP network, and sends the URQ (Unregister Request) message to the terminal.

Step 2. The terminal responds with a UCF (Unregister Confirmation) message. The gatekeeper responds with an IACK (Information Request Acknowledgement) message with type CanLocAck, to the gateway; the gateway forwards this information to the HLR via the MAP_CANCEL_LOCATION_ack message.

After sending the UCF message, the terminal may change the alias address associated with its transport address, or vice versa, for other IP applications.

16.3.3   Call Delivery to the IP Network

When an iGSM subscriber is in the IP network, call origination to the H.323 terminal follows the standard H.323 call setup procedure. When the iGSM subscriber is in the GSM network, call originations from the MS and call deliveries to the MS follow standard GSM procedures, described in Chapter 11. Figure 16.8 illustrates call delivery from PSTN to an iGSM subscriber visiting the IP network. The call setup procedure is described in the following steps (the message flow is given in Figure 16.9):

Step 1. The caller dials the MSISDN of the iGSM subscriber. Consider an MSISDN number 0-936105401 in Taiwan. The first digit, 0, indicates a special service. The next three digits, 936, are used to identify the gateway MSC (GMSC) of the MS associated with the MSISDN. The originating switch sends an SS7 IAM (Initial Address Message) to the GMSC to reserve the trunk.

Step 2. The GMSC queries the location of the iGSM subscriber by sending the GSM MAP message MAP_SEND_ROUTING_ INFORMATION to the HLR. Based on the received MSISDN, the address in the HLR record indicates that the iGSM subscriber is in the IP network. The HLR sends the MAP_PROVIDE_ ROAMING_NUMBER message to the gateway. The gateway translates the GSM MAP message into an RAS LRQ (Location Request) message, with type RoamNo, and sends it to the gatekeeper.

Step 3. The gatekeeper generates the mobile station roaming number (MSRN) based on the address of the gateway and the

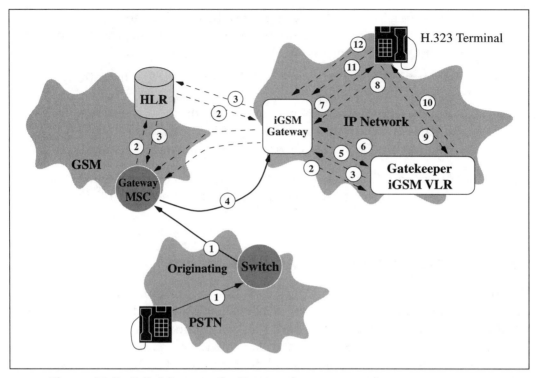

Figure 16.8   Call delivery to the IP network.

H.323 terminal. An RAS **LCF** (Location Confirm) message, with type **RoamNoAck**, is sent to the gateway; the gateway translates this message into the GSM MAP message **MAP_PROVIDE_ROAMING_NUMBER_ack** with MSRN. The HLR forwards the MSRN to the GMSC through the GSM MAP message **MAP_SEND_ROUTING_INFORMATION_ack**.

Step 4.   Based on the received MSRN, the GMSC sets up the trunk to the gateway using the **IAM** message.

Steps 5 and 6.   The gateway receives the MSRN of the iGSM subscriber. Through the **ARQ** (Admissions Request) and **ACF** (Admissions Confirm) message pair exchange, the gateway uses the MSRN to obtain the terminal's call-signaling channel transport address from the gatekeeper.

Steps 7 and 8.   The gateway sends the H.225 (Q.931) **Set-up** message to the H.323 terminal. If the H.323 terminal accepts this call, it replies with the **Call Proceeding** message to indicate that

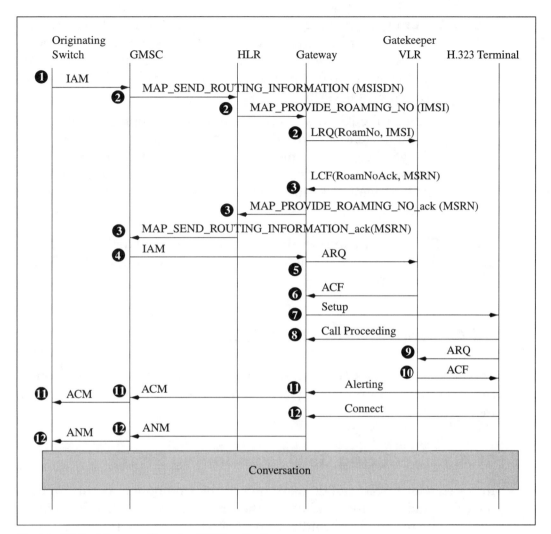

Figure 16.9 Message flow for iGSM call setup.

enough routing information has been received and that it does not expect to receive more routing information from the gateway.

Steps 9 and 10. The H.323 terminal exchanges the **ARQ** and **ACF** message pair with the gatekeeper. It is possible at this point that an **ARJ** (Admission Reject) message will be received by the terminal and that the call will be released.

Step 11. A ringing tone is generated at the H.323 terminal to alert the iGSM subscriber. The H.225 **Alerting** message is sent to the gateway. The gateway translates the message into an SS7 **ACM** (Address Complete) message, and forwards it to the originating switch via the GMSC.

Step 12. When the iGSM subscriber answers the phone, the H.323 terminal generates the RAS **Connect** message and sends it to the gatekeeper. This message is translated into the SS7 **ANM** (Answer) message and is forwarded to the originating switch. At this point, the call path is established and the conversation begins.

PSTN-IP call release follows the standard procedures defined in H.323. There is no need to create a new call release procedure for iGSM. The details are omitted.

16.4   Implementation Issues

This section discusses two issues regarding the iGSM implementation: reducing the GSM tromboning effect and investigating misrouting of user mobility.

16.4.1   Reducing GSM Tromboning Effect

In the standard GSM call delivery procedure, tromboning occurs when the caller and the called MS are in the same city but the GMSC is in another city (or another country, as described in Chapter 13). We assume that both GSM MSCs and iGSM gateways can serve as GMSCs for iGSM subscribers. If an iGSM subscriber is assigned a GSM MSC as his or her GMSC, call delivery follows the procedure described in Section 16.3.3, and tromboning occurs. On the other hand, if the iGSM gateway is assigned as the GMSC of the iGSM subscriber, call delivery tromboning can be avoided. Figure 16.10(a) illustrates a PSTN-to-iGSM (IP network) call with the following steps:

Steps 1 and 2. The originating switch routes the call to the iGSM gateway based on the dialed MSISDN.

Step 3. The iGSM gateway first queries the iGSM gatekeeper to check if the iGSM subscriber is in the IP network. If not, the iGSM

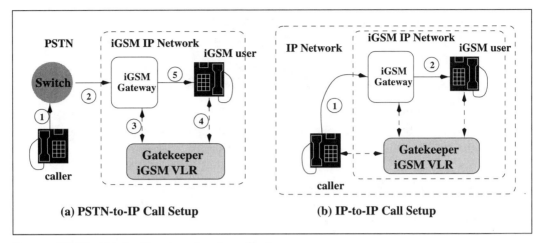

(a) PSTN-to-IP Call Setup   (b) IP-to-IP Call Setup

Figure 16.10   Eliminating tromboning effect.

gateway queries the HLR, and performs the standard GSM call delivery procedure.

Steps 4 and 5. If the iGSM subscriber is in the IP network, the iGSM gateway sets up the call to the H.323 terminal following the standard H.323 call setup procedure.

It is clear that no resources in the GSM network are consumed at steps 4 and 5, and that the call setup cost is cheaper compared with the case in Figure 16.9. Figure 16.10(b) illustrates an IP-to-iGSM (IP network) call. In this case, the call setup cost is exactly the same as that for a traditional VoIP call, which is even cheaper than the PSTN to iGSM call. Thus, two kinds of subscribers are anticipated in iGSM:

■ The GMSCs of the subscribers are standard GSM MSCs. In this case, the subscribers typically subscribe to the standard GSM services at the beginning, and determine to include the iGSM service later.

■ The GMSC of the subscribers is the iGSM gateway. In this case, the subscribers typically subscribe to the iGSM service from the beginning.

For the first kind of subscriber, call delivery follows the standard GSM procedure. When a subscriber visits the IP network, tromboning may occur as in traditional GSM networks. The GSM operator would prefer this scenario if the iGSM gateway and gatekeeper are owned by other ISPs. For the second kind of subscribers, call-delivery tromboning can be avoided when the subscriber visits the IP network. In this scenario, the GSM operator is likely to own the iGSM gateway and gatekeeper.

16.4.2   Misrouting Due to User Mobility

To support user mobility, the subscriber needs to explicitly perform registration to inform the system in which location area he or she resides when the terminal has been changed. If the subscriber forgets to take this action when he or she changes terminals, call deliveries to the subscriber may be misrouted. This problem can be eliminated if the subscriber always turns off the MS when he or she moves to the H.323 terminal. The turn-off action results in a GSM detach message, which deregisters the MS. For an iGSM subscriber, misrouting may occur in the following scenario:

Step 1.   The subscriber is in the GSM location area (LA) A and the HLR indicates that the person is in LA A. The subscriber then moves to the IP network (LA B) without turning off the GSM MS (see (1) in Figure 16.11(a)).

Step 2.   The subscriber registers in the IP network following the procedure described in Section 16.3.1. After registration, the HLR record is modified (see (2) in Figure 16.11(b)) and the subscriber's record in VLR A is removed (see (3) in Figure 16.11(b)).

Step 3.   The subscriber moves back to the GSM MS at LA A. Since the GSM MS is still on, the subscriber does not notice that an explicit registration is required. Thus, the HLR indicates that the subscriber is still in LA B (Figure 16.11(c)), and when someone attempts to call this subscriber, the call is misrouted to LA B.

The misrouting problem is avoided if the subscriber explicitly or implicitly registers with the GSM MS at step 3. Implicit registration occurs in two cases:

Case 1.   The subscriber originates a call. In this case, VLR A finds that the VLR record for the subscriber does not exist. VLR A will ask the MS to perform a registration operation, as described in the VLR failure restoration procedure in Chapter 11.

Case 2.   The subscriber moves to another LA in the GSM network. Registration is automatically initiated by the GSM MS.

In both cases, after the HLR has modified the subscriber's record, it also cancels the subscriber's VLR record in VLR B, as described in Section 16.3.1.

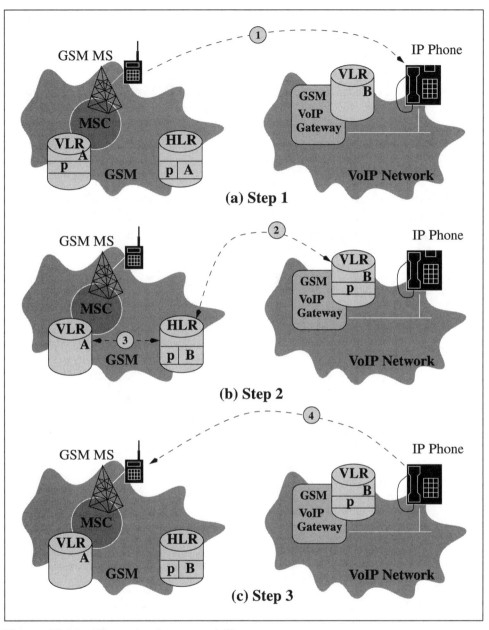

(a) Step 1

(b) Step 2

(c) Step 3

Figure 16.11 Misrouting in user mobility.

Next we will investigate how serious misrouting can be if the subscriber does not perform an explicit registration. (Readers not interested in analytical derivation can skip the following parts and jump to the last paragraph of this section.)

To begin, call originations and deliveries will be Poisson processes, and τ_o and τ_t will be the interarrival times for call originations and deliveries, respectively. Then τ_o and τ_t will have exponential distributions, with rates λ_o and λ_t; $\tau_{t,n}$ will be the interarrival time for n consecutive call deliveries, and $\tau_{t,n}$ will have an Erlang distribution with mean n/λ_t.

With that in mind, let τ_r be the time that the iGSM subscriber stays in an LA. Suppose that τ_r is a random variable with the density function $f_r(\cdot)$, distribution function $F_r(\cdot)$ and Laplace transform $f_r^*(s)$. Any call deliveries that occur during the period $\min(\tau_o, \tau_r)$ are misrouted. Let K be the number of misrouted call deliveries; then, for $n \geq 0$:

$$\Pr[K \geq n] = \Pr[\tau_o > \tau_{t,n}, \tau_r > \tau_{t,n}]$$

$$= \int_{\tau_{t,n}=0}^{\infty} \left\{ \left[\frac{\lambda_t^n}{(n-1)!} \right] \tau_{t,n}^{n-1} e^{-\lambda_t \tau_{t,n}} \right.$$

$$\left. \times \left[\int_{\tau_o=\tau_{t,n}}^{\infty} \lambda_o e^{\lambda_o \tau_o} d\tau_o \right] \left[\int_{\tau_r=\tau_{t,n}}^{\infty} f_r(\tau_r) d\tau_r \right] \right\} d\tau_{t,n}$$

$$= \left[\frac{\lambda_t^n}{(n-1)!} \right] \left\{ \int_{\tau_{t,n}=0}^{\infty} \tau_{t,n}^{n-1} e^{-(\lambda_t+\lambda_o)\tau_{t,n}} [1 - F_r(\tau_{t,n})] d\tau_{t,n} \right\}$$

$$= \left(\frac{\lambda_t}{\lambda_t + \lambda_o} \right)^n + \left[\frac{(-\lambda_t)^n}{(n-1)!} \right] \left\{ \frac{d^{n-1} \left[\frac{f_r^*(s)}{s} \right]}{ds^{n-1}} \right\} \Bigg|_{s=\lambda_t+\lambda_o}$$

$$= \left(\frac{\lambda_t}{\lambda_t + \lambda_o} \right)^n + \left[\frac{(-\lambda_t)^n}{(\lambda_t + \lambda_o)(n-1)!} \right]$$

$$\times \left\{ \frac{d^{n-1} f_r^*(s)}{ds^{n-1}} - (n-1) \left\{ \frac{d^{n-2} \left[\frac{f_r^*(s)}{s} \right]}{ds^{n-2}} \right\} \right\} \Bigg|_{s=\lambda_t+\lambda_o} \tag{16.1}$$

where, by convention:

$$\frac{d^0 f_r^*(s)}{ds^0} = f_f^*(s), \text{ and } \frac{d^{-1} f_r^*(s)}{ds^{-1}} = \frac{d^{-2} f_r^*(s)}{ds^{-2}} = 0$$

For $n \geq 0$, we have:

$$\Pr[K = n] = \Pr[K \geq n] - \Pr[K \geq n + 1] \qquad (16.2)$$

where $\Pr[K \geq 0] = 1$.

If τ_r has a Gamma distribution with mean m and variance v, then:

$$f_r^*(s) = \left[\frac{(1/m)}{(1/m) + (v/m^2)s} \right]^{\frac{m^2}{v}} \text{ and}$$

$$\frac{d^k f_r^*(s)}{ds^k} = \left(\frac{1}{m} \right)^{\frac{m^2}{v}} \left[\prod_{i=0}^{k-1} \left(-\frac{m^2}{v} - i \right) \right] \left(\frac{1}{m} + \frac{vs}{m^2} \right)^{-\frac{m^2}{v} - k} \left(\frac{v}{m^2} \right)^k \qquad (16.3)$$

Figure 16.12 plots $\Pr[K = 0]$, $\Pr[K = 1]$, $\Pr[K = 2]$, and $\Pr[K \geq 3]$, where call originations occur every 30 minutes and call deliveries occur every 60 minutes. The solid curves are for analytic analysis and the dashed curves are for simulation. It is clear that our analytic analysis is consistent with the simulation results. The figure indicates that the misrouting probabilities increase as the variance v of the user LA residence time decreases. The figure also indicates that if the subscribers originate calls much more frequently than they receive calls, the misrouting effect can be ignored. But if the user LA residence times, the intercall origination times, and the intercall delivery times are of the same order, the misrouting effect cannot be ignored. This problem exists for all approaches, based on the concept of *universal personal telecommunication* (UPT) that supports user mobility. To eliminate the misrouting problem, iGSM subscribers must perform an explicit registration; specifically, a subscriber should turn off his or her MS when moving to the IP network, and turn the MS back on when he or she moves back to the GSM network.

NOTE Misrouted calls are not necessarily lost. With call forwarding on no reply, these calls can be forwarded to an appropriate destination or mailbox.

16.5 Summary

This chapter described iGSM, a VoIP value-added service for GSM that supports user mobility. That is, iGSM allows a GSM user to access VoIP services when he or she moves to an IP network. iGSM tracks the locations of an iGSM subscriber as long as the subscriber turns off/on the terminal

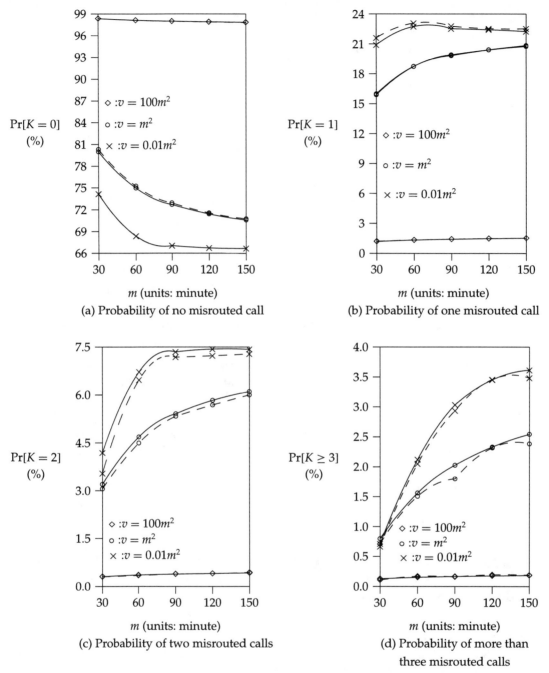

Figure 16.12 Misrouting probabilities (dashed lines: simulation; solid lines: analytic analysis).

(GSM MS or IP terminal) when he or she leaves/arrives at the network. To interwork GSM and IP networks, we proposed the iGSM protocol translation mechanism between GSM MAP and H.323. Based on this mechanism, we showed how iGSM registration, deregistration, and call delivery procedures work. The implementation of iGSM does not require modifications to the GSM network. The iGSM protocol translation mechanism can be implemented using a standard H.323 gateway and gatekeeper. We studied how tromboning in GSM systems can be avoided when accessing an IP network. Then we investigated the misrouting problem caused by user mobility.

If the iGSM service is provided by an ISP other than the GSM operator, security issues must be addressed to determine what kinds of GSM subscriber data can be accessed and modified by the ISP. Other iGSM issues such as billing and supplementary services are for further study. The TIPHON documents can be found in [ETS98a] and the series references therein. Details of GSM on the Net are given in [Gra98]. The Media Gateway Control Protocol is defined in [Ara98]. ITU-T H.323 and H.225 specifications can be found in [ITU99, ITU98]. Universal personal telecommunication is elaborated in [ITU93c].

16.6   Review Questions

1. What is terminal mobility? What is user mobility?

2. What is voice over IP? What are the advantages and the disadvantages of this approach?

3. Describe an MS-to-MS call between two GSM networks connected to an IP network.

4. How could conference calls be supported in the iGSM architecture?

5. How can GSM tromboning be avoided in iGSM?

6. Describe the misrouting issue caused by user mobility. How can this problem be resolved?

7. Reimplement the message flows in Figures 16.6, 16.7, and 16.9 for an IS-41-based mobile network.

8. Consider a group of Ericsson GSM on the Nets connected through the Internet. Implement the mobility management protocol for this network by using H.323/H.225. Describe the issues to be considered for inter-BS handoff within a net and the handoff crossing the net boundary.

9. To enhance security, should we distribute authentication and encryption keys to an H.323 network? If not, what are the alternatives?

10. For the wireless VoIP scheme described in this chapter, design a mechanism that guides the user to perform registration as appropriate so that misrouting due to user mobility can be avoided. (Hint: The mechanism may involve SIM card.)

Mobile Prepaid Phone Services

Prepaid phone is a telecommunication service that requires a customer to pay before making calls. Traditionally, coins played an important role in prepaid phone service, until the telephone companies realized that coins presented a range of problems. For one, extra overhead was incurred from periodic collection of coins. Two, coin payphones were more likely to be damaged by vandalism. To avoid equipment damage and revenue loss, prepaid cards were invented, and have become the fastest-growing prepayment method. The average availability of so-called smart card–based payphones is more than 95 percent, while the comparable figure for coin phones is less than 70 percent. Prepaid telecommunication services were offered in Europe and Asia in 1982; they became popular in the United States in 1992, where more than 30 prepaid solution vendors are currently competing for carrier business.

During the past few years, mobile prepaid service has been growing exponentially all over the world. In 1997, there were about 60 million GSM subscribers worldwide, of which 8 percent subscribed to prepaid service. The Philippines, Australia, Hong Kong, Singapore, and Taiwan have already experienced success with prepaid services, and it is estimated that worldwide prepaid revenue will be $102.8 billion (U.S. dollars) annually by the year 2007 (source: www.baskerville.co.uk).

The opposite of prepaid service is *postpaid* service, whereby the customers pay the telecommunication services after a period of time, typically a month. Postpaid services are limited by (1) the high deposit required when setting up service, and (2) the risk of bad debt. These disadvantages can be removed or reduced using prepaid services that allow a smaller prepayment that immediately goes toward the customer's usage.

Initially, prepaid cards used in payphone applications were simply token cards whose main benefit was to address the theft and vandalism issues associated with the use of cash. Recently, more advantages have been exploited. From the service provider's viewpoint, prepaid service can significantly reduce the business operation costs. Because no service is provided if the end users do not deposit enough money in the accounts, the additional costs of credit checking and collections departments can be eliminated. In other words, service can be offered to people with bad credit (which can be as high as 40 percent of the prepaid customer population); typically, revenue is received one and a half months earlier, compared with the postpaid service. And, because it is not necessary to bill prepaid subscribers, printing invoices or managing accounts can be avoided.

From the customer's perspective, prepaid services provide immediate service without the need for long-term contracts, allowing better control of spending. Particularly, many end users (especially the young) just want to enjoy the service; they do not want to fill in subscription forms. Their needs can be satisfied by prepaid service. Imagine buying a prepaid GSM subscription in the supermarket! Furthermore, prepaid service eliminates the monthly subscription charge and reduces the perceived risk of stolen or lost cards. The preceding discussion for prepaid telephone services implies that customer-imposed barrier to entry is relatively low. This conclusion is particularly true for mobile phone service. In Taiwan, FarEasTone reported that in May 1999, more than 40 percent of its 1.2 million customers subscribed to prepaid service in one year after the company launched prepaid service in mid-1998.

Although fixed and mobile prepaid services share many characteristics, they have two major differences: First, a fixed telephone service provider knows nothing about the prepaid customers; second, fixed prepaid service allows outgoing calls only, whereas mobile prepaid service allows both incoming and outgoing calls. Thus, no account management is required in the fixed prepaid service. A subscriber simply buys a calling card and starts making calls. As soon as the prepaid balance is used, the card becomes inactive. To provide mobile prepaid service, a prepaid service center is required to perform account management and other functions, as we will discuss later.

This chapter describes and compares four mobile prepaid service solutions. We first identify the requirements for mobile prepaid service. Then we describe mobile prepaid service approaches, including wireless intelligent network, service node, hot billing, and handset-based. These approaches are compared to guide service providers in selecting their prepaid service platforms.

17.1 Mobile Prepaid Services

We use GSM as an example to illustrate how the prepaid service works. In GSM prepaid service, a customer subscribes with prepaid credit. This credit is either coded into the subscriber identity module (SIM) card or kept in the network. In many service areas, initialization of a prepaid customer must be completed within a certain number of days after subscription. In Taiwan, prepaid service is available immediately after purchasing the service. Whenever the customer originates a prepaid call, the corresponding payment is decremented from the prepaid credit. A status report showing the credit balance can be obtained from the SIM card or the network.

If the balance is depleted, the customer cannot originate calls, but may be allowed to receive phone calls for a predetermined period (e.g., six months). To recover the prepaid service, the balance has to be recharged by purchasing a *top-up card*, which is similar to a lottery scratch card. When the seal is scratched off, a secret code appears. The customer dials a toll-free number and follows the instructions of an interactive voice response (IVR) to input the mobile station ISDN number (MSISDN) and the secret code. The system verifies and refreshes the account if it is a valid code. If, on the other hand, the prepaid balance is not depleted at the end of a valid period, the balance is automatically reset to zero. After a designated period of time, the unused prepaid credit may be considered abandoned, and becomes the service provider's (or government's) property.

Several mechanisms in the mobile prepaid service are not found in the fixed prepaid service:

- An extra billing system for mobile prepaid service is required. Various rate plans must be maintained based on destination of call (local, national, international), particular numbers (premium rate or free phone number), partitioning of airtime versus land network usage, call-forwarding charges, and so on. Tariff switching is required when a customer moves among different service areas during the prepaid calls.

- A real-time usage metering function must be built in the prepaid service system to monitor the amount of remaining credit on the customer account. This function measures the services provided to the customer, and decrements the balance during the service or immediately after the service is completed.

- Sales taxes are generally collected at the *point of sale* (POS) for prepaid service. Other taxes (universal service fees, relay service fees, presubscribed line charges, and federal access charges) are embedded in the cost of the prepaid product, then allocated by the service provider accordingly. Due to the mobility of the prepaid customers, mobile service providers must understand usage that originates from the various tax jurisdictions based on mobility databases such as HLR and VLR.

- A customer care mechanism maintains items including customer activation and deactivation times, credit value, remaining time period, PIN information, deletion time, reason for subscriber deletion, and so on. An easy credit-refresh mechanism is essential to encourage the customers to continue the prepaid service. The mechanism should also generate solicited responses to customer balance inquiries, and generate unsolicited warnings when the customer's remaining balance drops below a predetermined threshold.

Four solutions have been proposed to implement prepaid services: the wireless intelligent network approach, the service node approach, the hot billing approach, and the handset-based approach. In the remainder of this chapter, we describe these service solutions and show how they implement the prepaid mechanisms just discussed.

17.2 Wireless Intelligent Network Approach

The *Wireless intelligent network* (WIN) approach is considered a complete solution to prepaid service. In this approach, a *prepaid service control point* (P-SCP) communicates with the MSC through an intelligent network protocol over the SS7 signaling network. This intelligent network protocol follows the same concept as the AIN protocol described in Chapter 7. Several WIN triggers are defined. At prepaid call setup, and during the call-holding period, the MSC encounters WIN triggers at different stages, which remotely instruct the P-SCP to carry out decisions about how that call should be processed based on the prepaid applications. All billing information for a prepaid customer is stored in the P-SCP. The mobile network may need extra SS7 links to accommodate signaling traffic generated by the WIN prepaid mechanism.

17.2.1   WIN Call Origination

Figure 17.1 illustrates the WIN call origination process, which comprises the following steps:

Step 1. The prepaid customer initiates a call by dialing the called party's telephone number.

Step 2. The MSC encounters the WIN call setup trigger. The call setup process is suspended, and a prepaid call request message is sent to the P-SCP. The message includes the MSISDN, location information of the MS, and the called party telephone number. The P-SCP determines whether or not the customer can make the call by querying its database. Based upon threshold processing parameters defined in the prepaid billing system, the P-SCP may deny or accept the call. (In this example, assume that the call is accepted.)

Step 3. The P-SCP instructs the MSC to establish an ISDN (voice) link to the intelligent peripheral.

Step 4. The P-SCP instructs the intelligent peripheral to provide *account status notification*, such as the balance and the charging rate for the call to be made to the prepaid customer.

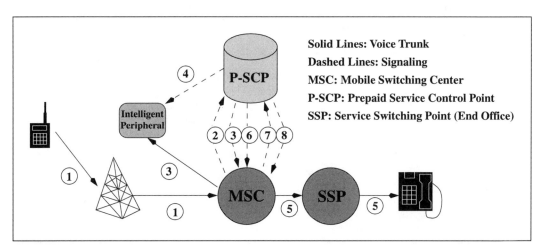

Figure 17.1 WIN prepaid call origination.

NOTE In this procedure, steps 3 and 4 are optional.

Step 5. The P-SCP asks the MSC to resume the call setup procedure, and the call is eventually connected. The P-SCP starts a countdown timer. The amount of credit decrement (from the current balance) is derived from carrier-defined threshold parameters, the rate plan, the destination, and time/date dependency.

Step 6. The call terminates when either the balance depletes or the call completes. If the countdown timer ends before the customer terminates the call, the P-SCP instructs the MSC to terminate the call. For normal call completion, this step does not exist.

Step 7. Once the call is terminated, the MSC encounters a WIN call-release trigger, which sends a disconnect message to P-SCP indicating the completion time of the call.

Step 8. The P-SCP rates the completed call and updates the customer's prepaid balance accordingly. Then it sends the current balance and cost of the call to the MSC. The MSC releases the call.

17.2.2 WIN Call Termination

For calling-party-pays billing (which is used in Europe and Taiwan), call termination to a prepaid customer is exactly the same as that for postpaid call termination. For called-party-pays billing (which is used in the United States), a mobile user pays for the air usage and mobility of incoming and outgoing calls. The message flow of a WIN prepaid call termination is illustrated in Figure 17.2, and described in the following steps:

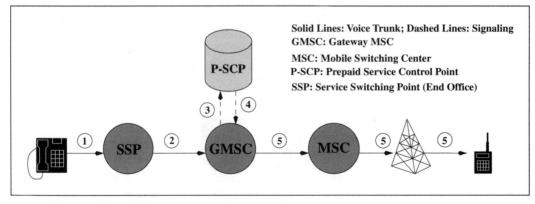

Figure 17.2 Prepaid call termination in IN.

Step 1. The calling party dials the prepaid customer's MSISDN.

Step 2. The call is forwarded to the gateway MSC (GMSC) of the prepaid MSISDN.

Step 3. The GMSC encounters a WIN call setup trigger. The call setup process is suspended and a prepaid call request message is sent to the P-SCP. The message includes the MSISDN and related information.

Step 4. The P-SCP determines whether or not the prepaid customer is eligible to receive the call. Assuming that the call is accepted, the P-SCP instructs the MSC to resume the call-setup procedure.

Step 5. Following the GSM standard mobile station roaming number (MSRN) retrieval and call-setup procedures described in Chapter 9, Section 9.2, the call is eventually connected. The P-SCP monitors the prepaid customer's balance, as described in step 5 of the prepaid call origination procedure.

For called-party-pays billing, the call release procedure for prepaid call termination is exactly the same as that for prepaid call origination.

17.2.3 WIN Prepaid Recharging

The message flow of WIN prepaid recharging is illustrated in Figure 17.3; the steps are as follows:

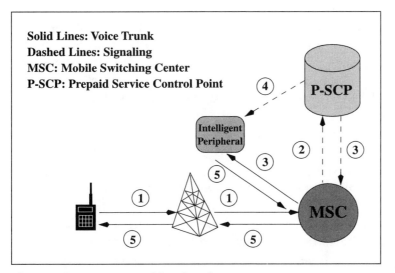

Figure 17.3 WIN prepaid recharging.

Step 1. A prepaid customer initiates the recharging procedure by dialing a designated number.

Step 2. The MSC encounters the WIN trigger, and a query message is sent to the P-SCP. The message includes the MSISDN of the prepaid phone and related information.

Step 3. The P-SCP instructs the MSC to establish a voice channel to the intelligent peripheral.

Step 4. The P-SCP interacts with the intelligent peripheral to (1) play an announcement and (2) ask the prepaid customer to enter his or her PIN number and related information for recharging. Then the P-SCP checks to determine if the voucher is valid.

Step 5. After credit updating, the P-SCP asks the intelligent peripheral to play a new balance announcement. Then it instructs the MSC to disconnect the intelligent peripheral. The MSC releases the call, and the recharging procedure completes.

17.3 Service Node Approach

The service node approach is the most widely deployed prepaid service solution at the initial stage of prepaid service provisioning. Many major switching infrastructure providers have predefined call models within their switching architectures. To deploy the prepaid service without interrupting the existing call models, most mobile service providers implement service nodes in their networks to externally control prepaid billing. As shown in Figure 17.4, a service node typically colocates with an MSC, and is connected to the MSC using standard T1/E1 trunks assigned to a particular block of prepaid numbers. To improve the efficiency of the call setup procedure, high-speed trunks may be considered for connection.

The service node can be implemented by using *computer telephony integration* (CTI) techniques or PC-controlled *private branch exchange* (PBX) techniques. The idea behind CTI is to utilize computer intelligence to manage telephone calls. With *application programming interfaces* (APIs) such as the Telephony Applications Programming Interface (TAPI) and Telephone Services Application Programming Interface (TSAPI), the prepaid applications for service node can be developed for small installations (e.g., several hundreds of lines). In a PC-controlled PBX, the software (typically written in a high-level language such as C++) in the call control layer can be modified to implement various telecommunication applications. The

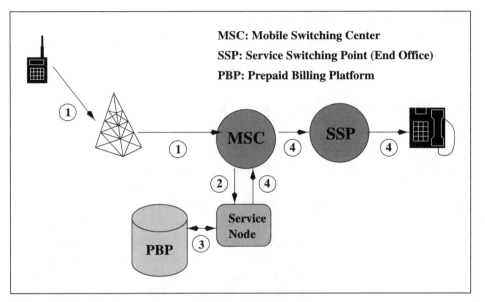

Figure 17.4   Service node prepaid call origination.

same platform can be used to implement the prepaid service node effectively. PC-controlled PBXs provide larger and more cost-effective solutions (in terms of telephone line capacity) than CTI switching. On the other hand, CTI platforms support general APIs that allows fast deployment compared with the PC-controlled PBX platform. The prepaid call origination based on the service node approach is illustrated in Figure 17.4; it comprises these steps:

Step 1. The prepaid customer initiates a call by dialing the called party's telephone number.

Step 2. The MSC identifies that the caller is a prepaid customer. The MSC sets up the trunk to the service node.

Step 3. The service node authorizes the call request by consulting the prepaid billing platform.

Step 4. If the call request is granted, the service node sets up a trunk back to the MSC, and the trunk is eventually connected to the called party. The service node starts credit decrement.

One may argue that at step 4, the service node should set up the call directly to the public switched telephone network (PSTN) without passing through the MSC again. By doing so, two ports in the MSC are saved. Typically, this alternative is not considered due to the extra overhead incurred for interworking to the PSTN. In general, small switches such as service nodes are not allowed to connect to the PSTN POI (point of interface).

17.4   Hot Billing Approach

Hot billing uses *call detail records* (CDRs) to process prepaid usage. The prepaid CDR is created in the MSC. The information in a CDR includes type of service, date/time of usage, user identification, the destination of the call, and location information. These records are generated when the calls are completed, and are transported from the MSC to the prepaid service center. The balance of the customer's account is decremented according to the CDRs. When a customer uses up the prepaid credit, the HLR and the authentication center (AuC) are notified to prevent further service access; the prepaid service center instructs the network to route the next prepaid call attempt to an IVR to play an announcement indicating that the balance has been depleted. The IVR can also communicate with the customer to replenish the prepaid credit by using a top-up card, a credit/debit card, or a credit transfer from a bank account.

Figure 17.5 illustrates the interfaces that may be used in the hot billing architecture. In this architecture, a call record is sent from the MSC to

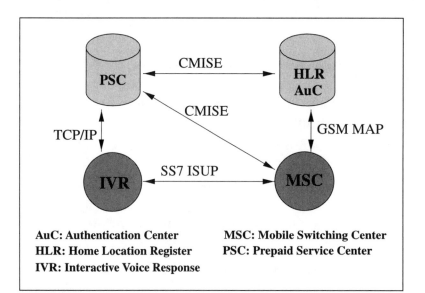

Figure 17.5   Hot billing architecture and interfaces.

the prepaid service center using protocols such as Common Management Information Service Element (CMISE). The same protocol can be used for communication between the prepaid service center and the HLR. The HLR communicates with the MSC by invoking GSM MAP service primitives, as described in Chapters 9 and 10. The IVR generates automatic messages that allow the customer accounts to be queried and reloaded. The voice trunks between the IVR and the MSC are set up by SS7 ISUP (ISDN User Part) messages.

Hot billing depends on real-time data collectors/routers to transport the CDRs from the MSC to the prepaid service center. The HLR/AuC is updated to allow/prevent prepaid customer access.

17.4.1 Hot Billing Prepaid Service Initialization and Call Origination

This subsection discusses service initialization and call origination for the hot billing approach. Note that other prepaid service approaches share the similar service initialization procedure described in the following steps:

Step 1. The customer subscribes to the prepaid service center at the POS or by calling the customer care center.

Step 2. The prepaid service center creates a subscriber data record including IMSI, MSISDN, account of credit, period of validity, tariff model, and other authentication-related information.

Step 3. The prepaid service center activates the prepaid service by sending the customer data to the HLR, which then creates a record for the customer.

To remove a customer from prepaid service, the prepaid service center simply sends a request to the HLR to delete the customer's record.

The hot billing prepaid call origination procedure is illustrated in Figure 17.6; it has the following steps:

Step 1. When a customer originates a prepaid call, the IMSI is sent to the MSC.

Step 2. Based on the IMSI, the MSC instructs the HLR to determine whether or not it is a valid service request.

Step 3. If the verification is successful, the HLR downloads the customer data and a prepaid tag to the MSC. The call is connected.

Step 4. When the call terminates, a CDR is created and sent to the prepaid service center.

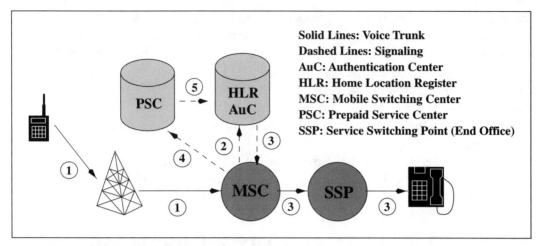

Figure 17.6   Hot billing prepaid call origination.

Step 5. The prepaid service center decrements the prepaid credit based on the received billing record. If the balance is negative, the prepaid service center instructs the HLR to suspend the prepaid service or to delete the customer's record.

17.4.2   Hot Billing Customer Query and Recharging

A customer can query his or her current balance through the following steps (see Figure 17.7):

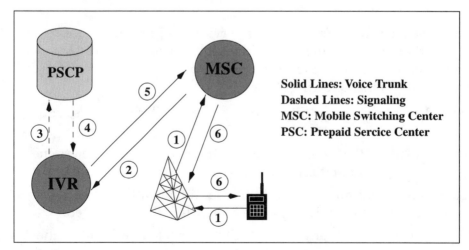

Figure 17.7   The hot billing prepaid credit query procedure.

Step 1. The customer makes a service query call that, typically, is free of charge.

Step 2. The MSC sends the request, together with the MSISDN of the customer, to the IVR, and sets up a voice path to the IVR.

Steps 3 and 4. The IVR queries the prepaid service center for account balance information.

Steps 5 and 6. The IVR plays an announcement to answer the customer.

When the prepaid credit has been decremented below a threshold, the prepaid service center automatically calls the customer and plays a warning message to remind the customer for credit recharging. The customer may recharge the prepaid credit using the top-up card, described in Section 17.1. This recharging procedure is similar to the credit query procedure illustrated in Figure 17.7.

If the prepaid credit depletes during a phone call, the credit becomes negative at the end of the phone call. The negative credit is potentially a bad debt. If the customer does not recharge the credit, it becomes a real bad debt to the service provider. Thus, the "one-call exposure" becomes a major concern of the hot billing approach. A prepaid customer may place the last call and stay connected while the account balance becomes negative. This occurs because most wireless switches do not release the CDR until the call has completed. Some service providers, however, argue that one-call exposure may not be a problem. If the purchased prepaid credits are large enough, the fraudulent user has to exhaust the credit before he or she can overrun the account, which may not be cost-effective for fraud usage. Still, one-call exposure may be a serious problem, especially when called-party-pays billing is exercised and parallel call-forwarding service is available. In this scenario, the MS is used as the call-forwarding mechanism and the fraudulent user consecutively initiates several calls to the MS in parallel with different forwarding destinations. Consequently, some prepaid solution vendors suggest that call forwarding should not be offered to the prepaid service customers.

To avoid bad debt, the other three approaches described in this chapter decrement the prepaid credit by seconds during a phone call. In the hot billing approach, sending these "real-time" CDRs by seconds to the prepaid service center and processing these CDRs at the center may incur heavy overhead to the network. Practically, the CDRs are delivered and processed on a per-call basis and, in some cases, on a multiple-call basis. Thus, in the hot billing approach, it is important to select the CDR sending frequency such that the sum of the CDR sending/processing cost and the bad debt is minimized. Also, the service providers may have guarded against one-call exposure by using appropriate call-barring classes. Based on the thresholds under consideration, the network determines when to warn and deny service to a customer.

17.5 Handset-Based Approach

In the handset-based approach, the MS performs credit deduction during the call and determines when the credit limit is reached. In this approach, the prepaid credit is stored in the MS. In the United States, special phones are required. For GSM, the credit is stored in the SIM card. We use GSM as an example to describe how a handset-based approach works.

17.5.1 SIM Card Issues

In a typical implementation, the memory size of a SIM card is 8 Kbps. In later SIM versions, this is upgraded to 16 Kbps. SIM memory is partitioned into two areas. One area stores information such as abbreviated and customized dialing numbers, short messages received, a menu of subscribed services, names of preferred networks to provide service, and so on. Another area stores programs that can be executed to carry out simple commands.

The handset-based approach utilizes the GSM phase 2 supplementary message Advice of Charge (AoC) to transfer the prepaid balance information and the tariff schemes. AoC provides information for the MS to produce a cost estimate of the services used. AoC consists of two service types: *advice of charge charging* (AoCC) and *advice of charge information* (AoCI). To utilize handset-based prepaid service, the MS must support AoCC. Older MSs that support only AoCI do not work. The supplementary service AoCC is activated for every prepaid customer in an HLR, which will be used in call setup and tariff switching.

Several data fields in a SIM card are used to provide charging information of prepaid service: *accumulated call meter* (ACM), *accumulated call meter maximum* (ACM*) and *price per unit and currency table* (PUCT). The ACM parameter accumulates the used prepaid units. The ACM* parameter records the amount of purchased prepaid credit. When the MS receives the AoC message from the MSC, it converts AoC into a sequence of SIM commands that modify the SIM data fields (i.e., ACM), thereby debiting the customer. The PUCT parameter is the value of the home unit in a currency chosen by the subscriber. The value of the PUCT can be set by the subscriber and may exceed the value published by the mobile network. The PUCT value does not have any impact on the charges raised by the network.

A prepaid service center is required in the handset-based prepaid system, which utilizes the short message service to download executable programs to the SIM card. In call setup and tariff switching, the MSC provides the tariff-charging parameters to the MS, and the MS executes the programs with these parameters for call debiting.

In the SIM card, an extra software filter is required to distinguish prepaid-related short messages from normal short messages. To enhance security, a prepaid-related short message may be authenticated by the SIM card. The GSM specification allows customers to access ACM and ACM* data fields in the SIM card by using a password, PIN2. To support prepaid SIM card, the PIN2 must be disabled by the card manufacturer when the card is personalized. When the prepaid customer becomes a postpaid customer, the PIN2 will be activated by a short message triggered by the subscription switching process.

The SIM Toolkit specification supports proactive commands that enable the SIM card to execute application programs. For GSM phase 2 SIM cards with larger memory, the cards can run applets downloaded from the SIM Toolkit service. These applets can run security-checking algorithms and simple rating algorithms. The 16 Kbps memory allows the SIM cards to hold tariff table data for various rate plans.

17.5.2   Handset-Based Prepaid Call Origination

The prepaid call origination for the handset-based approach is described in the following steps (see Figure 17.8):

Step 1. The prepaid customer initiates a call by dialing the called party's telephone number.

Step 2. Based on the rate plan and other parameters (such as the destination and time/date dependency), the MSC sends the AoC e-parameter (including charging information such as ACM and ACM*) to the MS.

Step 3. If the MS supports AoCC, then it acknowledges the reception of the e-parameters. If this acknowledgment is not received by the MSC, the call is denied. Otherwise, the call is connected.

Step 4. During the call, the MS uses the AoC e-parameters for tariff information. It decrements the credit on the SIM card by incrementing the used units in the ACM. If the MS determines that

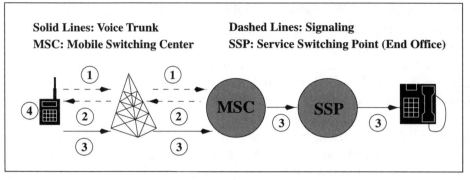

Figure 17.8   Prepaid call origination in handset-based approach.

the value of ACM has reached that of ACM*, the MS disconnects the call and informs the MSC that call release has occurred. This AoC disconnection mechanism works autonomously in the MS without any involvement from the network.

Besides call setup, the AoC e-parameters are transferred to the MS at tariff switching (e.g., billing rate changing, because the MS roams to another area). To reduce the risk of fraud, the handset-based approach may be combined with the hot billing approach. In this case, the prepaid service center in the hot billing approach is included in the prepaid architecture. Figure 17.9 shows the message flow of the the prepaid call origination for the combined approach; its steps are as follows:

Steps 1–3.   These steps are the same as those for call origination for the handset-based approach. Some of the details (i.e., steps 2 and 3 in Figure 17.6) in the hot billing call setup are not shown here.

Step 4.   The call is released when the call completes normally or when the MS notices that the prepaid credit is used up. In either case, the MS sends a message to the MSC for call release.

Step 5.   The MSC generates a prepaid CDR, which is then transferred to the prepaid service center. Unlike the regular CDR, the prepaid CDR includes the AoC e-parameters. The prepaid service center updates the prepaid credit as in the hot billing approach. When ACM is above a threshold, the prepaid service center may automatically send a warning message to the MS for recharging the prepaid credit.

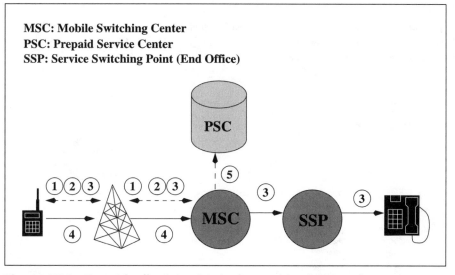

MSC: Mobile Switching Center
PSC: Prepaid Service Center
SSP: Service Switching Point (End Office)

Figure 17.9   Prepaid call origination in the combined approach.

From the viewpoint of the handset-based approach, this combination provides better fraud protection. When the credit in the prepaid service center is different from the MS, the service provider may terminate the service for further fraud investigation. From the viewpoint of the hot billing approach, this combination eliminates the possibility of one-call exposure. As soon as the credit is used up, the MS terminates the call, and the situation is reported to the prepaid service center.

Besides the additional implementation complexity, a potential issue for the combined approach is that the charging information (e.g., ACM and ACM*) may not be consistent for reasons other than fraudulent usage. Thus, synchronization between the prepaid service center and the MS is important.

17.5.3   Handset-Based Prepaid Recharging

Like the hot billing approach, in this process, a customer recharges the prepaid credit by purchasing a scratch card, as described in these steps (see Figure 17.10):

Step 1. The customer makes a toll-free call that connects to an IVR. The prepaid service center validates the secret code (obtained from the scratch card) and the MSISDN of the prepaid customer. If validation is successful, the prepaid service center resets ACM to zero; ACM* is set to the amount of the new credit.

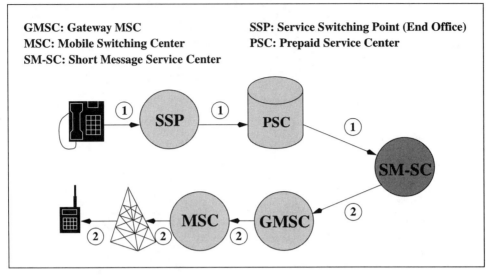

Figure 17.10 Prepaid call recharging in handset-based approach.

Step 2. If the recharging procedure is successful, the prepaid service center generates a reload short message. This message is delivered to the MS through the short message service center (SM-SC) in a few minutes, as described in Chapter 12. If the SM-SC fails to deliver the message (e.g., the MS is turned off), it repeats the message delivery action until it succeeds.

17.6 Comparison of the Prepaid Solutions

Based on the descriptions in the previous sections, we compare the four prepaid service approaches in the following aspects: roaming, scalability, fraud risk, initial setup, service features, and real-time rating.

17.6.1 Roaming to Other Networks

Assume that the home and the visited systems belong to different service providers. To provide roaming to prepaid customers, an agreement (which can be a part of the roaming agreement) must be made between the home system and the visited system. This agreement is required so that the visited system can (and is willing to) distinguish prepaid calls from the postpaid calls generated by roamers. In most existing scenarios, GSM service providers assign special MSISDN number blocks to prepaid customers. The visited system then identifies a prepaid call based on the MSISDN. There are potential disadvantages to using the MSISDN for prepaid call identification. First, operator number portability (described in Chapter 15) will not be allowed. (With number portability, a customer can switch mobile service providers without changing the MSISDN.) Second, service number portability will not be allowed; that is, for the same GSM system, a prepaid customer cannot switch to postpaid service without changing the MSISDN. It seems that identifying prepaid calls by IMSIs will be a better alternative to address these issues. However, the MSC at the visited system may need to be modified so that it can perform call routing based on IMSIs.

Prepaid charging cannot be performed at the visited system because the home system and the visited system may exercise incompatible prepaid service solutions. Thus, most (if not all) networks require the visited MSC to route the prepaid call back to the home network. This operation is achieved by using the standard "alternate" routing or "optimal" routing that can be easily implemented by setting up routing parameters in the MSC. That is, in the call model of a visited MSC, if the prepaid MSISDN is recognized, the visited MSC routes the call based on the MSISDN instead of the called party number. Figure 17.11 uses the service node approach as an example to illustrate how prepaid call origination is preformed in

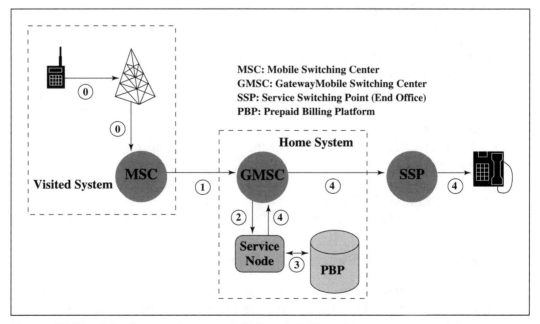

Figure 17.11   Roaming to other networks for prepaid service.

the visited system. When the visited MSC receives the prepaid call at step 0, the MSC routes the call directly to the GMSC of the prepaid MS. The remaining steps are the same as those described in Section 17.3. An extra trunk connection is required in this call setup procedure. Prepaid calls are charged more than postpaid calls, due, in part, to this reason. It is clear that the preceding procedure is too expensive for international roaming, described in Chapter 13.

17.6.2 Scalability

It is apparent that both the handset-based and the WIN approaches have good scalability. In the hot billing approach, the size of prepaid customer population is limited to the MSC's capability to process and deliver CDR messages.

In the service node approach, the capacity of the trunks between the service node and the MSC limits the prepaid customer population that can be accommodated in the system. Interestingly enough, in Taiwan, statistics from some service providers exercising the service node approach indicate that GSM network traffic congestion is caused by incoming calls to the prepaid customers, not outgoing prepaid calls. That is, traffic congestion is not caused by the limited capacity of the service node.

17.6.3 Fraud Risk

In the handset-based approach, AoC communication is not encrypted. It is a fairly straightforward exercise to tamper with or ignore AoC by intercepting the debit commands. Also, it is possible to modify the credit illegally in the MS. Thus, it turns out that the handset-based approach has poor fraud protection. Several manufacturers are working on SIM encryption.

The risk of fraud can be high for the hot billing approach due to one-call exposure. As we pointed out, this occurs because most wireless switches do not release the CDRs until the calls have completed. Fraud risk can be reduced if mid-call CDR sending is exercised.

Both the service node and the WIN approaches exhibit low fraud risk.

17.6.4 Initial System Setup

The initial system setup cost and setup time for the handset-based approach is average. This approach does not require changes to the mobile network infrastructure, except that the MSC must support AoC. On the other hand, the prepaid MSs must be GSM phase 2-compliant to receive AoC messages. Furthermore, special SIM software is required to execute rate plans in the MS. The GSM service providers may be locked to a single-source SIM supplier. This situation is undesirable, especially when the SIM card market is unpredictable.

The initial system setup cost and setup time for the hot billing approach is average. This approach requires the integration of the prepaid service center, the IVR recharging mechanism, and the MSC/HLR.

System setup for the service node approach can be done quickly. The mobile network infrastructure is not modified. The only system setup cost is for the establishment of the service node. For this reason, up to the end of 2000, service node was the only working prepaid solution in Taiwan.

The initial system setup time for the WIN approach is long, and the setup cost is very high. Furthermore, this approach does not provide a fully developed model for other mobile networks to follow. The design of services and switch software development for intelligent network is complex. For small- and medium-sized service providers, a full implementation of a WIN architecture may not be a realistic option.

17.6.5 Service Features

The handset-based approach supports limited service features because the number of rate plans that can be stored in the SIM card is limited and cannot be conveniently updated. The SIM card also relies on the MSC to provide the tariff charging model.

The service feature provisioning for the hot billing approach is better than average, which is typically limited by the per-post call charging mechanism.

Both the service node and the WIN approaches support flexible service features. For WIN, many service features can be integrated with the prepaid service under the intelligent network platform.

None of the four approaches can support prepaid short message service, because the short message is delivered by the SS7 TCAP, which cannot not be identified by the MSC for charging purposes. Instead, charging for the short message is done at the SM-SC. One solution is to modify SM-SC such that, before delivering a prepaid short message, the SM-SC sends a charging message to MS, PSC, or P-SCP (depending on the approach exercised) for decrementing the prepaid credit of the customer (see (1) in Figure 17.12). If the SM-SC receives a positive response (see (2) in Figure 17.12), the short message is sent (see (3) in Figure 17.12).

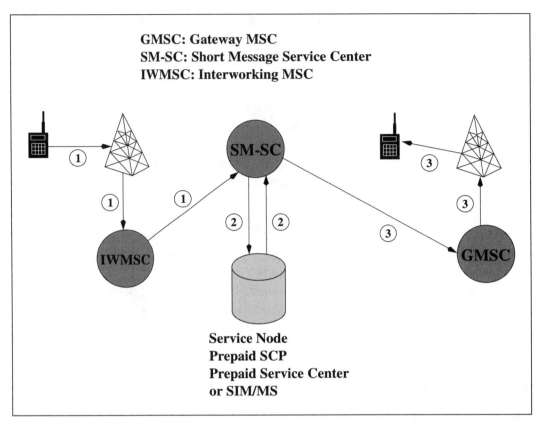

Figure 17.12 Prepaid short message service.

17.6.6   Real-Time Rating

In the handset-based approach, real-time rating is performed at the MS. In the service node approach, real-time rating is performed at the service node. In the WIN approach, real-time rating is performed at the P-SCP. The hot billing approach cannot support real-time rating. The credit information update depends on the MSC capability of sending CDRs.

17.7   Summary

This chapter described four mobile prepaid service approaches and compared their weaknesses and strengths. Among the four approaches, the handset-based approach is a low-cost, high-risk solution. The wireless intelligent network approach is a high-cost, low-risk solution. The service node approach is a quick, but dirty, solution, which allows rapid deployment with limited capacity. The hot billing approach is an average solution that cannot provide real-time service.

To supplement the technical discussion for the prepaid service approaches, we point out that the business case for packaging prepaid services is very important. Recently, prepaid service has been over-promoted in Mexico, resulting in the loss of postpaid revenues because the prepaid service was introduced with more favorable rates. Thus, it is important for service providers to balance their prepaid and postpaid marketing and distribution strategies through segmentation (for example, targeting prepaid service for high-risk customers, or packaging the service as gifts). As mentioned in Section 17.1, though service providers may know why customers purchase prepaid services, our experience indicates that they may not know why customers stop using prepaid service, nor when customers switch to another service provider.

In Taiwan, prepaid service is considered to be a niche market, and the strategy is to promote program loyalty to convert prepaid customers into postpaid customers. As a final remark, credit transfer for mobile prepaid service is clearly an application for electronic commerce, which transfers electronic cash over digital networks in real time. Prepaid billing systems are beginning to influence existing billing systems, where the payment-processing components will need to be tailored for the online nature of the new medium. For further reading, the CTI technologies that can be utilized for implementing the service node prepaid approach can be found in [D'H96, Ans96, Cro96, Fle96, Sul96]. For the PBX-based service node technologies, the reader is referred to [Lin99b]. Details of TAPI and TSAPI are elaborated in [Mic96] and [Cro96, Nov96], respectively. CDR for prepaid service is introduced in [INF98]. The CMISE standard is specified in [ETS93c]. The tax jurisdictions based on mobility databases are discussed in [Sla98].

17.8   Review Questions

1. What is prepaid telephone service? What is postpaid telephone service? What are the advantages of prepaid service over postpaid service? Do you think fixed prepaid service can replace fixed postpaid service?

2. What are the differences between fixed prepaid service and mobile prepaid service?

3. What are the four mobile prepaid service solutions? What are the advantages and disadvantages of these solutions?

4. Propose a solution so that, for a roaming mobile prepaid call origination, the trunk is not required to set up back to the home system of the prepaid customer. Can your solution apply to international roaming?

5. When a mobile user unsubscribes to the mobile service, the mobile identification number assigned to the user must be reclaimed. This reclaimed number must be kept unused for a period, in a process called *number aging*. Which service needs a longer aging period, prepaid or postpaid? Which country, the United States or Taiwan, needs a longer aging period?

6. In this chapter, it was stated that traffic congestion is not caused by the limited capacity of the service node in Taiwan. Why not? (Hint: Calling-party-pays billing is exercised in Taiwan.)

7. Show the call setup procedure where both the calling party and the called party are prepaid users and the called-party-pays policy is exercised.

8. In early 2000, U.S. cellular carriers are expected to invest billions of dollars to implement cellular billing and for customer care. Two of the most desirable attributes of the cellular billing systems are the flexibility of upgrade and ability to inform the billing experts quickly about the status of the system, to minimize any possible fraud and improve customer service. To speed up the billing information transmission, a cellular billing transmission standard called EIA/TIA IS-124 has been developed by working group 4 of TIA's TR 45.2 committee. IS-124 will allow real-time billing information exchange, which will help control fraud by reducing the lag time created by the use of overnighted tape messages. Version A of IS-124 also accommodates both U.S. AMPS and international GSM carriers, which is desirable for heterogeneous PCS system integration (described in Chapter 20) and third-generation core network interworking (described in Chapter 21). An important performance issue of cellular billing information transmission is the frequency of the billing information exchange. In the ideal case, records would be transmitted for every phone call to achieve the real-time operation. In this case, the billing mechanism is the same as the one used in the hot billing prepaid service. However, real-time transmission would significantly increase the cellular signaling traffic and seriously over-

load the signaling network of the PSTN. In order to achieve quick billing status report, a trade-off is therefore needed between the frequency of the billing information transmission and the signaling traffic. Design a heuristic algorithm to determine the frequency of the billing information transmission. (Hint: See the discussion in [Fan99b].)

General Packet Radio Service (GPRS)

In early 2000, only a small portion of GSM subscribers used data services, because existing GSM systems do not support easy access, high data rate, and attractive prices. GSM operators must offer better services to stimulate the demand. The solution is the *General Packet Radio Service* (GPRS). GPRS reuses the existing GSM infrastructure to provide end-to-end packet-switched services. GPRS standardization was initiated by ETSI/SMG in 1994. The main set of GPRS specifications was approved by SMG #25 in 1997, and was completed in 1999. GPRS products were developed in 1999, and service deployment has begun. The GPRS core network has also been developed for IS-136 TDMA systems, and is anticipated to evolve as the core network for the third-generation mobile systems as well.

To accommodate GPRS, new radio channels are defined. The allocation of these channels is flexible: One to eight time slots can be allocated to a user, or several active users can share a single time slot, where the uplink and the downlink are allocated separately. Radio resources can be shared dynamically between speech and data services as a function of traffic load and operator preference. Various radio channel coding schemes are specified to allow bit rates from 9 Kbps to more than 150 Kbps per user. GPRS fast reservation is designed to start packet transmission within 0.5 to 1 second. GPRS security functionality is equivalent to the existing

GSM security, where a ciphering algorithm is optimized for packet data transmission. By allowing information to be delivered more quickly and efficiently, GPRS is a relatively inexpensive mobile data service compared to Short Message Service (SMS) and Circuit-Switched Data.

This chapter provides a GPRS overview. We briefly describe the air interface, and discuss it for enhanced GPRS. We emphasize the individual protocols in the signaling plane, the industrial solutions of the GPRS network components, GPRS charging, and the development efforts from GSM to GPRS. We first describe the GPRS functional groups and architecture, then elaborate on GPRS nodes and the interfaces among these nodes. We also describe the GPRS solutions and work in progress by several GPRS vendors.

18.1 GPRS Functional Groups

The functional groupings (meta-functions) defined in GPRS include (1) network access, (2) packet routing and transfer, (3) mobility management, (4) logical link management, (5) radio resource management, and (6) network management.

GPRS network access supports the standard point-to-point data transfer and anonymous access (without authentication and ciphering). The functions include:

- Registration, which associates the Mobile Station (MS) identity with the packet data protocols.
- Authentication and authorization.
- Admission control, which determines the radio and network resources to be used for communication of an MS.
- Message screening, which filters out unsolicited messages.
- Packet terminal adaptation, which adapts data transmission across the GPRS network.
- Charging information collection for packet transmission in GPRS and external networks.

Packet routing and transfer functions route the data between an MS and the destination through the serving and *gateway GPRS Support Nodes* (GSNs). The functions include:

- Relay function that is used by the Base Station System (BSS) to forward packets between an MS and a serving GSN; it is also used by a serving GSN to forward packets between a BSS and a serving or gateway GSN.

- Routing, which determines the destinations of packets.

- Address translation and mapping that converts a GPRS network address to an external data network address and vice versa.

- Encapsulation and tunneling, which encapsulate packets at the source of a tunnel, deliver the packets through the tunnel and decapsulate them at the destination.

- Compression and ciphering.

- Domain name service functions, which resolve logical GSN names to their IP addresses.

Logical link management maintains the communication channel between an MS and the GSM network across the radio interface, which includes:

- Logical link establishment

- Logical link maintenance

- Logical link release

Radio resource management allocates and maintains radio communication paths, which include:

- Um management, which determines the amount of radio resources to be allocated for GPRS usage.

- Cell selection, which enables the MS to select the optimal cell for radio communication.

- Um-tranx, which provides packet data transfer capability, such as medium access control, packet multiplexing, packet discrimination, error detection and correction, and flow control across the radio interface between the MS and the BSS.

- Path management, which maintains the communication paths between the BSS and the serving GSNs.

Mobility management keeps track of the current location of an MS. Three different scenarios can exist when the MS enters a new cell and possibly a new routing area: cell update, routing area update, and combined routing area and location area update. Network management functions provide mechanisms to support OA&M functions related to GPRS.

18.2 GPRS Architecture

Figure 18.1 illustrates the GPRS network nodes and corresponding interfaces, although SMS-related components and the equipment identity register are not shown. In this architecture, MS, BSS, mobile switching center/visitor location register (MSC/VLR), and home location register (HLR) in the existing GSM network are modified. For example, the HLR is enhanced with GPRS subscriber information. Two new network nodes are introduced in GPRS. The *serving GPRS support node* (SGSN) is the GPRS equivalent to the MSC. The gateway GPRS support node (GGSN) provides interworking with external packet-switched networks, and is connected with SGSNs via an IP-based GPRS backbone network.

The MS and the BSS communicate via the Um interface. The BSS and the SGSN are connected by the Gb interface using frame relay. Within the same GPRS network, SGSNs/GGSNs are connected through the Gn Interface. When SGSN and GGSN are in different GPRS networks, they

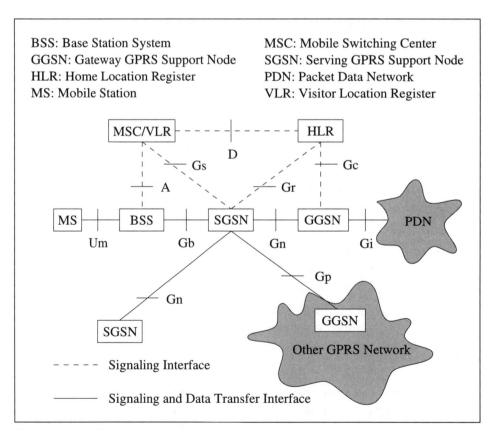

Figure 18.1 GPRS architecture.

are interconnected via the Gp interface. The GGSN connects to external networks through the Gi interface. The MSC/VLR communicates with the BSS using the existing GSM A interface, and with the SGSN using the Gs interface. The HLR connects to the SGSN via the Gr interface, and to the GGSN via the Gc interface. Both Gr and Gc follow the GSM Mobile Application Part (MAP) protocol defined in Chapter 10. The HLR and the VLR are connected through the existing GSM D interface. Interfaces A, Gs, Gr, Gc, and D are used for signaling, without involving user data transmission in GPRS. Note that the A interface is used for both signaling and voice transmission in GSM. Interfaces Um, Gb, Gn, Gp, and Gi are used for both signaling and transmission in GPRS.

The GPRS transmission plane is illustrated in Figure 18.2, which consists of a layered protocol structure for user information transfer and the associated control procedures (e.g., flow control, error detection, error

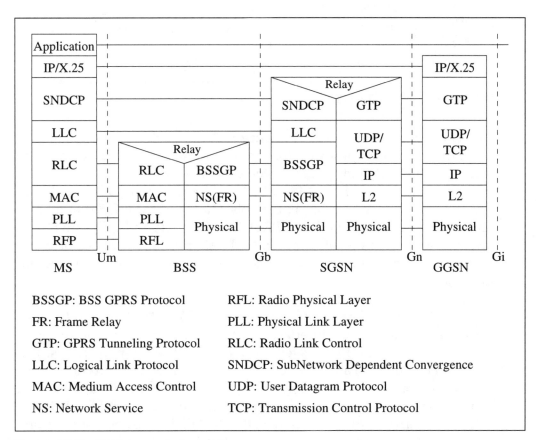

BSSGP: BSS GPRS Protocol   RFL: Radio Physical Layer

FR: Frame Relay   PLL: Physical Link Layer

GTP: GPRS Tunneling Protocol   RLC: Radio Link Control

LLC: Logical Link Protocol   SNDCP: SubNetwork Dependent Convergence

MAC: Medium Access Control   UDP: User Datagram Protocol

NS: Network Service   TCP: Transmission Control Protocol

Figure 18.2 GPRS transmission plane.

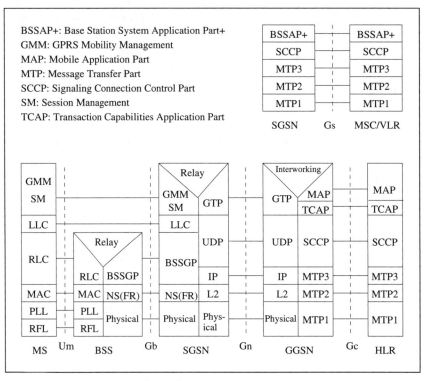

Figure 18.3 GPRS signaling plane.

correction, and error recovery). Figure 18.3 shows the GPRS signaling plane that consists of protocols for control and support of the transmission plane functions. Among these protocols, the GPRS-specific protocols include SNDCP, LLC, RLC, MAC, BSSGP, BSSAP+, and GTP. PLL, RFL, GMM/SM, and MAP are GSM protocols. (Note that GMM/SM and MAP are modified to accommodate GPRS). TCAP, SCCP, and MTP are SS7 layers. The other protocols are standard data protocols. Details of the layers of the transmission and the signaling planes will be elaborated on in Section 18.4.

The GPRS relay function in Figure 18.2 merits further discussion. In the BSS, this function relays *logical link control* (LLC) *packet data units* (PDUs) between the Um and Gb interfaces. In the SGSN, this function relays Packet Data Protocol (PDP) PDUs between the Gb and Gn interfaces. The Gb/Gn relay function adds sequence numbers to PDP PDUs received from the Subnetwork-Dependent Convergence Protocol (SNDCP) and from the Gi reference point, respectively. To transparently transport PDP PDUs between external networks and MSs, the PDP PDUs are encapsulated and decapsulated for routing, as described in Section 18.4.3.

Before we elaborate on GPRS mechanisms, we first introduce three GPRS terms: mobility management (MM) context, PDP context, and quality-of-service (QoS) profile. The MM context consists of the MM state and other MM-related information stored in MS and SGSN, as described in Sections 18.3.1 and 18.3.3. The MM states specify the MM activities of an MS. The state is IDLE if the MS is not attached to the GPRS mobility management. The state is STANDBY if the MS is attached to GPRS mobility management but has not obtained detailed location information. The state is READY if the location information for the MS has been identified on cell level. Note that a GPRS MS can be IMSI- and/or GPRS-attached. The IMSI attach is the same as that for a GSM MS. In GPRS attach procedure, both the MS and the SGSN are moved to the READY state; an MM context is created in each of MS and SGSN, and authentication/ciphering may be performed. At GPRS attach, a logical link is established between MS and SGSN.

The PDP contexts are stored in the MS, HLR, SGSN, and GGSN, as described in Sections 18.3.1, 18.3.3, and 18.3.4, which contain mapping and routing information for packet transmission between MS and GGSN. For each GPRS communication of an MS, a PDP context is created to characterize the session. After the PDP context activation, the MS is known to the GGSN, and communication to external networks is possible. An MS may have several activated PDP contexts if the terminal supports several IP addresses. When the MS is detached from GPRS, all PDP contexts are deactivated. A PDP context can be in one of the two PDP states: ACTIVE or INACTIVE. An MS in STANDBY or READY MM state may activate a PDP context, and moves its PDP state from INACTIVE to ACTIVE. The ACTIVE PDP context becomes INACTIVE when the PDP context is deactivated. A QoS profile is maintained in the PDP context to indicate radio and network resources required for data transmission. The QoS attributes include:

- *Precedence class* specifies three transmission priority levels. During congestion, the packets with lower priorities are discarded.

- *Delay class* specifies four delay levels. In 128-octet transfer, for example, the expected transfer speeds for delay classes 1–3 are less than 0.5 sec., 5 sec., and 50 sec., respectively. Delay class 4 supports best-effort transmission without specifying the transfer speed constraints.

- *Reliability class* defines residual error rates for data loss, out-of-sequence delivery, and corrupted data. There are five reliability classes. Reliability class 1 supports acknowledgment for GTP mode,

LLC frame mode, and RLC block mode, and the LLC data are protected. Reliability class 5 does not support acknowledgment, and the LLC data are not protected.

- *Peak throughput class* specifies the expected maximum data transmission rate. There are nine classes ranging from 8 Kbps to 2,048 Kbps.

- *Mean throughput class* specifies the average data transmission rate: There are 19 classes, ranging from the best-effort to 111 Kbps.

We elaborate on the usage of the MM/PDP contexts and the QoS profile in the subsequent sections.

18.3   GPRS Network Nodes

This section discusses the GPRS network nodes: MS, BSS, SGSN, GGSN, HLR, and MSC/VLR. We also describe the solutions for these nodes provisioned by equipment suppliers.

18.3.1   Mobile Station

A GPRS MS consists of a mobile terminal (MT) and terminal equipment (TE). An MT communicates with the BSS over the air. The MT is equipped with software for GPRS functionality in order to establish links to the SGSN. A TE can be a computer attached to the MT. The existing GSM MS does not support GPRS. For example, GPRS MS utilizes *automatic retransmission* (ARQ) at the data link layer to retransmit the error frames. In GSM, no retransmission is provided in a GSM voice channel. With multiple time slots, GPRS may provide high transmission rate. GSM offers only a single time slot for voice.

Three MS operation modes were introduced in the GPRS 07.60 specification. The Class A mode of operation allows simultaneous circuit-switched and packet-switched services. A duplexer is required to support this mode. The Class B mode of operation provides automatic choice of circuit-switched or packet-switched service, but only one at a time. A Class B MS involved in packet transfer can receive a page for circuit-switched activity, in which case, the MS suspends the data transfer for the duration of the circuit-switched connection and resumes the data transfer later, as explained in Section 18.4.4. The Class C mode of operation supports packet-switched data only. Neither the Class B nor the Class C mode requires a duplexer.

The MSs that access GPRS services may or may not contain GPRS-aware subscriber identity modules (SIMs). An MS maintains MM and PDP contexts to support GPRS mobility management. Some of the MM context fields stored in a GPRS-aware SIM are:

- International mobile subscriber identity (IMSI), which uniquely identifies the MS. IMSI is used as the key to search the databases in VLR, HLR, and GSN.

- *Packet temporary mobile subscriber identity* (P-TMSI), which is the GPRS equivalent of TMSI in GSM.

- Address of the routing area where the MS resides. A routing area is a subset of a location area defined in GSM.

- Current ciphering key, K_c, and its *ciphering key sequence number* (CKSN)

If the SIM is not GPRS-aware, these fields are stored in the mobile equipment, which equipment also stores several non-SIM-related fields, some of which are listed here:

- MM state (either IDLE, STANDBY, or READY, as described in Section 18.2).

- Identity of the cell where the MS resides.

- Ciphering algorithm defined in the GSM 01.61 specification.

- Radio access classmark for the radio capabilities (e.g., multiple time slot capability and power class) and SGSN classmark for network-related capabilities (e.g., ciphering capability).

For data-routing purposes, the MS maintains PDP contexts, including:

- PDP type (either X.25, PPP, or IP).

- PDP address (e.g., an X.121 address).

- PDP state (either ACTIVE or INACTIVE, as described in Section 18.2).

- Dynamic-Address-Allowed, which specifies whether the MS is allowed to use a dynamic address.

- Requested and negotiated QoS profiles, as described in Section 18.2.

GSM chip sets for GPRS MSs are available. For example, Siemens SMARTi (PMB6250) is a single-chip GSM multiband transceiver that supports multi-time-slot data, which can be used to implement a GPRS MS. Another example is Lucent's Sceptre 3 system-on-a-chip solution that enables full GPRS to 115.2 Kbps. By integrating digital signal processing, microprocessing, read-only memory, and random access memory on one chip, such technologies provide a flexible architecture for future MS design.

18.3.2   Base Station System

To accommodate GPRS, the base transceiver station (BTS) and the base station controller (BSC) in the BSS are modified, and a new component, the *packet control unit* (PCU) is introduced. The BTS is modified to support new GPRS channel coding schemes. The BSC forwards circuit-switched calls to the MSC, and packet-switched data (through the PCU) to the SGSN. A BSC can connect to only one SGSN. The Gb interface described in Section 18.4.2 is implemented to accommodate functions such as paging and mobility management for GPRS. The BSS should also manage GPRS-related radio resources, such as allocation of packet data traffic channels in cells.

As described in Section 18.4.1, the Um radio interface is modified to support GPRS features. To support GPRS traffic, the transmission capacity of the BSS is increased through a standard upgrade process.

The PCU can be viewed as equivalent to a *transcoder and rate adaptor unit* (TRAU) for the packet data services. The PCU is either colocated with the BTS or remotely located in the BSC or the SGSN. Most vendors follow the remote PCU option so that no hardware modifications to the BTS/BSC are required. In the remote option, the existing A-bis interface between the BTS and the BSC is reused, and the GPRS data/signaling messages are transferred in modified TRAU frames with a fixed length of 320 bits (20 ms). The PCU is responsible for the medium access control and radio link control layer functions, such as packet segmentation and reassembly, packet data traffic channel management (e.g., access control, scheduling, and ARQ), and radio channel management (e.g., power control, congestion control, and broadcast control information).

In the Nortel solution, the existing GSM BTS and second-generation BSC 12000 are reused, but with a software upgrade. The PCU and Gb functions are implemented in a PCUSN based on Nortel's GSM Passport Platform. The PCUSN concentration capability is up to 12 BSCs/cabinet. Similarly, in Alcatel's solution, both the BTS and BSC are reused with software upgrades. The PCU and Gb functions are implemented in the A935 MFS (multifunctional server) that can connect up to 22 BSSs and supports 480 activated GPRS radio channels per BSC. Ericsson's architecture assigns one PCU per BSC. A PCU can serve 512 BTSs and up to 4096 GPRS radio channels (1750 channels practically).

18.3.3 GPRS Support Node

Two kinds of GSNs are introduced in GPRS: a serving GSN (SGSN) and a gateway GSN (GGSN). The functionality of SGSN and GGSN can be combined in a physical node (e.g., Symmetry's UWS-GSN and Ericsson's Combined SGSN/GGSN) or distributed in separated nodes (e.g., Nortel, Motorola/Cisco, and Alcatel solutions). A GSN is typically implemented using a multiple processor system platform with hardware redundancy and robust software infrastructure that support uninterrupted operation. A vendor may develop its SGN product with various capacities. Ericsson, for example, has developed two GSN models. Model GSN-25 is a small-capacity GSN used to enable fast deployment of the GPRS service. With the same capability as GSN-25, Model GSN-100 provides larger capacity in terms of throughput and number of attached users.

18.3.3.1 Serving GPRS Support Node (SGSN)

The role of an SGSN is equivalent to that of the MSC/VLR in the current GSM network. Figure 18.4 (a) illustrates an SGSN product. SGSN connects

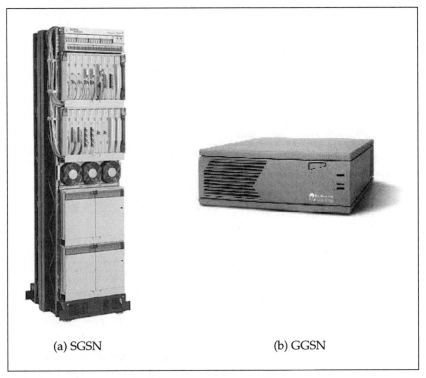

(a) SGSN   (b) GGSN

Figure 18.4 SGSN and GGSN (by coutresy of Nortel).

BSS to GSGN, which provides ciphering, mobility management (e.g., inter-SGSN routing area update and inter-PLMN roaming), charging, and statistics collection (i.e., support of billing records). To provide services to a GPRS MS, the SGSN establishes an MM context that contains mobility and security information for the MS. At PDP context activation, the SGSN establishes a PDP context that is used to route data between the MS and the GGSN. SGSN maintains MM/PDP context information when the MS is in one of the two MM states (STANDBY or READY). For an MS, the SGSN MM context includes:

- IMSI, P-TMSI, and mobile station ISDN number (MSISDN).
- MM state.
- Routing area identity and cell identity.
- Address of the VLR currently serving the MS.
- IP address of the new SGSN where the buffered packets should be forwarded.
- Authentication and ciphering parameters.
- Current ciphering key K_c and the selected ciphering algorithm.
- MS radio access capabilities and GPRS network access capabilities.
- MNRG (Mobile Station Not Reachable for GPRS flag) indicating whether activity from the MS should be reported to the HLR.
- NGAF (non-GPRS Alert flag) indicating whether activity from the MS should be reported to the VLR.
- PPF (Paging Proceed flag) indicating whether paging for GPRS and non-GPRS services can be initiated.

Each MM context associates with zero or more of the following PDP contexts (a partial list):

- PDP context identifier, PDP type, PDP address, and PDP state.
- Access point name to the external data network.
- Subscribed, requested, and negotiated QoS profiles.
- IP address of the GGSN currently used by the activated PDP context.
- Identifier of the charging records generated by SGSN and GGSN.

Most vendors developed SGSN based on existing multiple processor system products, where the control processors are configured with hot standby redundancy. Lucent's solution supports 40,000 attached users and 4,000 simultaneous active GPRS data sessions. For Nortel's Passport 8380G and Symmetry's UWS-GMS, the number of GPRS users that can attached to an SGSN is 50,000; the number of PDP context activation is 20,000; the number of SS7 links to VLR/HLR is 8; the number of E1 links for Gb interface is 10; and the throughput is 20 Mbps. In Alcatel's SGSN solution, the number of attached users is 52,000–96,000; the number of SS7 signaling links is 8; the number of E1 links to Gb interface is 16; and the throughput is 16–48 Mbps. It is clear that Alcatel's SGSN has a larger capacity than Nortel's or Symmetry's SGSNs. The reason is that, in Alcatel's solution, every GPRS network is supported by one SGSN; thus, a large-capacity SGSN is required.

18.3.3.2   Gateway GPRS Support Node (GGSN)

The GGSN is primarily provisioned by a router, which supports traditional gateway functionality such as publishing subscriber addresses, mapping addresses, routing and tunneling packets, screening messages, and counting packets. Figure 18.4(b) shows a GGSN product. A GGSN may contain DNS functions to map routing area identifiers with serving SGSNs and *Dynamic Host Configuration Protocol* (DHCP) functions to allocate dynamic IP addresses to MSs.

The GGSN maintains an activated PDP context for tunneling the packets of the attached MS to the corresponding SGSN. The information items include (a partial list):

- IMSI.
- PDP type and PDP address.
- Dynamic address indication.
- QoS profile negotiated.
- IP address of the SGSN currently serving this MS.
- Access point name of the external data network.
- Charging ID.
- MNRG flag, which indicates whether the MS is marked as not reachable for GPRS at the HLR.

Note that the GGSN does not need to record subscribed and requested QoS profiles. Both are maintained in the SGSN.

Most suppliers use existing router platforms to provide this function. For example, the Alcatel GGSN is developed based on the Cisco 7200 series router; Nokia's GGSN is based on its commercial IP routing platform; and Nortel's GGSN is based on a Bay Networks CES 4500. Existing

GGSN implementations typically support 5,000–48,000 simultaneous data tunnels, and 25,000–48,000 simultaneously attached data users. The switching capability is, for example, 20 Mbps in the Alcatel solution.

18.3.4 HLR and VLR

To accommodate GPRS subscription and routing information, new fields in the MS record are introduced in HLR; they are accessed by SGSN and GGSN using IMSI as the index key. These fields are used to map an MS to one or more GGSNs, update the SGSN of the MS at attach and detach, and store the fixed IP address and QoS profile for a transmission path. In the HLR, the GSN-related information includes (a partial list):

- IMSI and MSISDN.
- SS7 address of the SGSN, which serves the MS.
- IP address of the SGSN, which serves the MS.
- MS Purged for GPRS flag, which indicates whether the MM and PDP contexts of the MS are deleted from the SGSN.
- MNRG, which indicates whether the MS is not reachable for GPRS service.
- GGSN-list, which provides a GGSN IP address list to be contacted for MS activity when MNRG is set.

The PDP context-related information includes a PDP context identifier, PDP type, PDP address, QoS profile subscribed, and the access point to the external packet data network.

In MSC/VLR, a new field, SGSN number, is added to indicate the SGSN currently serving the MS. The MSC/VLR may contact SGSN to request location information or paging for voice calls. It also performs signaling coordination for Class B mobile through the Gs interface, and suspends/resumes GPRS activities through the A and Gb interfaces.

18.4 GPRS Interfaces

This section describes major GPRS interfaces, shown in Figure 18.1: Um, Gb, Gn, Gp, Gs, and Gi.

18.4.1 Um Interface

Um describes the radio interface between the MS and the BTS. GPRS radio technology is based on the GSM radio architecture, which introduces a new logical channel structure to control signaling and traffic flow over the Um radio interface. In this subsection, we elaborate on the Um channel structure, Um protocol layers, and the enhanced Um for GPRS.

18.4.1.1 Radio Channel Structure

The physical channel dedicated to packet data traffic is called a *packet data channel* (PDCH). Different packet data logical channels can occur on the same PDCH. The logical channels are described next.

GPRS utilizes *packet data traffic channel* (PDTCH) for data transfer. High spectral efficiency is achieved through time-slot sharing, whereby multiple users may share one PDTCH. Alternately, a user may simultaneously occupy multiple PDTCHs.

Several *packet common control channels* (PCCCHs) are introduced in GPRS. *Packet random access channel* (PRACH) is the only uplink PCCCH. It is sent from the MS to the BTS to initiate uplink transfer for data or signaling. The following downlink PCCCHs are sent from the BTS to the MS:

- **Packet paging channel.** Pages an MS for both circuit-switched and packet data services.

- **Packet access grant channel (PAGCH).** Used in the packet transfer establishment phase for resource assignment.

- **Packet notification channel.** Used to send a *point-to-multipoint multicast* (PTM-M) notification to a group of MSs prior to a PTM-M packet transfer.

- **Packet broadcast control channel (PBCCH).** Broadcasts system information specific for packet data. If PBCCH is not allocated, the packet data specific system information is broadcast on the existing GSM BCCH channel, described in Chapter 9, Section 9.1.4.

The following packet-dedicated control channels are defined in GPRS:

- **Packet associated control channel (PACCH).** Conveys signaling information, such as power control, resource assignment, and reassignment information. The PACCH shares resources via PDTCHs. An MS currently involved in packet transfer can be paged for circuit-switched services on PACCH.

- **Packet timing advance control channel in the uplink direction (PTCCH/U).** Used by an MS to transmit a random access burst. With this information, the BSS estimates timing advance. In the downlink, the BSS uses PTCCH/D to transmit timing advance information updates to several MSs.

GPRS common control signaling is conveyed on PCCCH. If the PCCCH is not allocated, the existing GSM CCCH described in Chapter 9, Section 9.1.4, is used. Two concepts are employed for GPRS channel management: *master-slave* and *capacity-on-demand*. In the master-slave concept, a master PDCH accommodates PCCCHs to carry all necessary control signaling for initiating packet transfer. Other PDCHs serve as slaves for user data transfer (PDTCH) and for dedicated signaling. In the capacity-on-demand concept, PDCHs are dynamically allocated based on actual amount of packet transfers. Also, the number of allocated PDCHs in a cell can be increased or decreased according to traffic changes. GPRS performs a fast release of the PDCH to share the pool of radio resources for both packet- and circuit-switched services.

We can use uplink packet transfer to illustrate how the logical channels described in this section are utilized. As shown in Figure 18.5, to initiate packet transfer, an MS makes a packet channel request via PRACH (message 1, Figure 18.5). This channel request procedure can be one-phase or two-phase. In one-phase access, the network assigns an uplink packet channel for a number of radio blocks to be transferred. The network informs the MS of this assignment through PAGCH (message 2). One or more PDCHs can be assigned based on the requested resources indicated in the PRACH. Alternatively, the MS may use RACH for a packet channel request. Since RACH has only one close value for GPRS messages, at most two PDCHs can be allocated. This information is delivered from the network to the MS using the AGCH.

If the network needs more information for resource reservation, it indicates the need for two-phase access in the PAGCH (message 2; the last message in phase 1). Specifically, the PAGCH allocates the uplink resources of PACCH (i.e., message 3) for MS to transmit the complete resource information. Then, by exchanging the uplink and downlink PACCHs (messages 3 and 4), the network obtains sufficient information for resource allocation.

The two-phase access can also be initiated by the MS when it is not satisfied with the assigned resources. If the MS does not receive the PACCH response from the network, it retries after a random back-off time. The packet resource assignment message specifies the start frame, slot assignment, and the assigned blocks per time slot for uplink transmission. The MS waits until the start frame arrives, then transmits radio blocks (e.g., messages 5, 6, and 7) according to the agreed block assignment. If the MS requires more radio resources, it can specify the request through

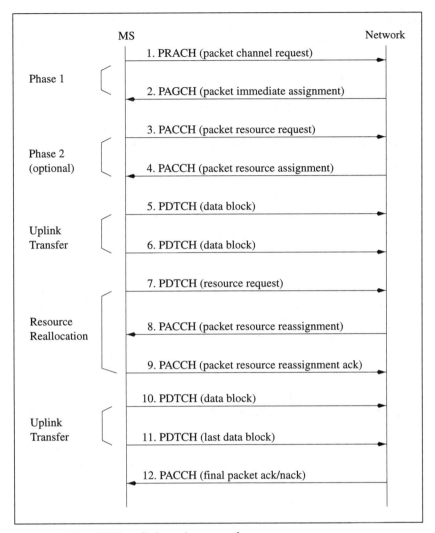

Figure 18.5   GPRS uplink packet transfer.

an assigned uplink block (message 7). The network and the MS then exchange the PACCHs (messages 8 and 9) to reallocate the resources for uplink transmission. When the MS completes the transmission, it indicates the last data block (message 11). The network then terminates the uplink transmission by returning the final packet acknowledgment (message 12).

In the preceding uplink transmission scenario, the allocated radio resources are fixed after assignment and reassignment. Alternatively, the resource can be allocated dynamically by "opening" and "closing" PDCHs for certain MSs. Furthermore, high-priority packets and pending control messages may temporarily interrupt a data transmission from a specific MS.

18.4.1.2 Um Protocol Layers

As shown in Figure 18.2, Um protocol layers include RF layer (RFL), physical link layer (PLL), and radio link control/medium access control (RLC/MAC). The physical RF layer performs modulation/demodulation received from or sent to the PLL. The PLL provides services for information transfer over a physical channel, including data unit framing, data coding, and the detection and correction of physical medium transmission errors.

The RLC/MAC layer provides services for information transfer over the GPRS physical layer. These functions include backward error correction procedures, enabled by the selective retransmission of erroneous blocks. RLC is responsible for block segmentation and reassembly, buffering, and retransmission with backward error correction. MAC is responsible for channel access (scheduling, queuing, contention resolution), PDCH multiplexing, and power control.

Four GPRS coding schemes—CS1, CS2, CS3, and CS4—are defined, whose characteristics are listed in Table 18.1. In a typical GPRS development, only CS1 and CS2 are implemented in the early stage. The table indicates that the GPRS channel coding schemes increase the data rate, but at the cost of decreasing protection (correction capability). The increased data rate adversely affects the link budget and, as a result, each cell's range. For GSM, the worst-case link budget is 142.5 dB, and the maximum cell range is 730 meters. On the other hand, the GPRS worst-case link budget is 128.5–135 dB; the maximum cell range is 290–450 meters.

18.4.1.3 Enhanced Data Rates for GSM Evolution

With GSM radio technology, GPRS provides only limited data capacity. To increase the GSM data rate, Enhanced Data Rates for GSM Evolution (EDGE) was introduced under the same GSM frame structure. EDGE

Table 18.1 Characteristics of the GPRS Coding Schemes

CODING SCHEME	CS1	CS2	CS3	CS4
User Data Rate	9.05 Kbps	13.4 Kbps	15.6 Kbps	21.4 Kbps
Correction Capability	Highest			None
Worst-Link Budget	135 dB	133 dB	131 dB	128.5 dB
Maximum Cell Range	450 m	390 m	350 m	290 m

standardization has been in progress, and the EDGE *link quality control* (LQC) scheme was agreed on during the first quarter of 1999. Based on EDGE, *enhanced GPRS* (EGPRS) provides user data rates two to three times higher than GPRS (up to 470 Kbps for indoor and 144 Kbps for outdoor), and its spectrum efficiency is two to six times higher than GPRS. These goals are achieved by utilizing 8-PSK modulation and adapting the user rate based on channel quality. To be compatible with the GMSK used in GSM, and DQPSK used in IS-136, EDGE accommodates both GMSK and 8-PSK. EDGE follows the same TDMA format, carrier spacing (200 KHz), symbol rate (271 Ksymb/s), burst format, and training sequences used in GSM. EGPRS also utilizes the same spectrum as GSM. Thus, EDGE can reuse GSM sites and frequency plan.

At the physical layer, blind detection of modulation is used to avoid signaling before changing modulation and parallel equalizations. In EDGE transmitter design, the *power amplifiers* (PAs) utilize a linear modulation that is more complex than the constant envelope modulation used in GSM. For the same PA, maximum average power for 8-PSK is lower than that for GMSK. The *peak-to-average ratio* (PAR) for 8-PSK is 3.2 dB while the PAR for GMSK is 0 dB. The design of an equalizer for an EDGE receiver is different from that in GSM. Basically, 8-PSK is more sensitive to interference than GMSK.

EDGE LQC combines link adaptation and incremental redundancy. Link adaptation selects *modulation and coding schemes* (MCSs) based on link-quality measurements. The link adaptation procedure is described in the following steps:

Step 1. The MS measures the downlink performance and reports the results to the BSS.

Step 2. The BSS measures the uplink performance, then chooses the up-link and downlink MCSs based on the collected measurements.

Step 3. The BSS sends an uplink MCS command to the MS.

Step 4. Based on the command, the MS selects an appropriate MCS for uplink transmission.

Incremental redundancy increases robustness for retransmission in EDGE. Specifically, the more often a data block is retransmitted, the more overhead (increments to acknowledgment and signaling) is added to the data block. Incremental redundancy relies little on measurements, which is mandatory for EDGE MSs.

To implement EDGE, the BTS in the existing GSM standard should be modified. Specifically, the transceiver units should be enhanced to accommodate a new power amplifier in the transmitter and a new equalizer in the receiver. Furthermore, the transmission capacity between BTS and BSC must be increased. EGPRS supports maximum bit rates up to 8×59.2 Kbps at the RLC/MAC layer. This high data rate can be achieved under good propagation conditions. Thus, EDGE and EGPRS are appropriate for indoor environments with pico and micro cells.

18.4.2 Gb Interface

The Gb interface connects the BSS and the SGSN, allowing many users to be multiplexed over the same physical resource. Unlike the GSM A interface where the resources of a circuit-switched connection are dedicated to a user throughout the whole session, the GPRS Gb interface only allocates resources to a user during the periods when data are actually delivered. As shown in Figure 18.2, the Gb interface protocol layers (from the highest to the lowest) include the LLC, the SNDCP, the base station system GPRS protocol (BSSGP), the network service (NS) Layer, link layer 2, and the physical layer. The Gb link layer 2 establishes frame relay virtual circuits between the SGSN and BSS. On these virtual circuits, the NS transports BSSGP packet data units (PDUs) between a BSS and an SGSN. On the BSS side, the Relay function is required to provide buffering and parameter mapping between the RLC/MAC (for the Um interface between the BSS and the MS) and the BSSGP (for the Gb interface between the BSS and the SGSN).

   LLC is a sublayer of layer 2. The purpose of LLC is to convey information between layer 3 entities in the MS and SGSN. LLC provides one or more logical link connections with sequence control (to maintain the sequential order of frames across a logical link connection), flow control, detection of transmission, format and operational errors on a logical link connection, and recovery from detected transmission, format, and operational errors. LLC maintains a ciphered data link between an MS and an SGSN, which is independent of the underlying radio interface protocols. This connection is maintained as the MS moves between cells served by the same SGSN. When the MS moves to a new SGSN, the existing connection is released, and a new logical connection is established with the new SGSN. The LLC layer supports several QoS delay classes with different transfer delay characteristics (described in Section 18.2). The LLC layer supports transmission with both acknowledged and unacknowledged modes.

   LLC provides service to the GPRS Mobility Management (GMM) protocol in the signaling plane (see Figure 18.3). GMM uses the services of the LLC layer to transfer messages between the MS and the SGSN.

GMM includes functions such as attach and authentication, and transport of session management messages for functions such as PDP context activation and deactivation.

In the transmission plane, shown in Figure 18.2, the SNDCP above the LLC performs multiplexing of data coming from the different sources to be sent across LLC. It also performs segmentation and reassembly and compression of redundant protocol information and user data. GPRS supports several network layer protocols to provide protocol transparency for the users of the service. It is intended that the introduction of new network layer protocols for transmission over GPRS will be possible without any changes to GPRS. SNDCP ensures that all functions related to transfer of network layer PDU are carried out in a transparent way by the GPRS network entities. Based on compression techniques, the SNDCP also provides functions that help to improve channel efficiency. The set of protocol entities above SNDCP consists of commonly used network protocols. They all use the same SNDCP entity, which then multiplexes the data coming from different sources to be sent using the service provided by the LLC layer.

18.4.2.1   Network Service

The NS layer delivers encapsulated packets between the SGSN and BSS that are connected directly by a frame relay link or indirectly through cascading links in a frame relay network. Each physical frame relay link supports one or more *network service virtual links* (NS-VLs). The NS-VLs are connected to construct an end-to-end virtual path between the BSS and SGSN. This path is called a *network service virtual connection* (NS-VC). The NS manages NS-VCs with operations such as:

- Blocking, when a NS-VC is not available.

- Unblocking, when a NS-VC becomes available again.

- Resetting, when, for example, a new NS-VC is set up.

- Testing, to check that an end-to-end communication exists between peer NS entities on a given NS-VC.

The NS also performs load sharing to distribute the packet traffic among the unblocked NS-VCs of the same BVC. The NS utilizes the UNITDATA service primitive to transfer packets, the CONGESTION service primitive to report congestion, and the STATUS primitive to inform the NS user of events such as a change in available transmission capabilities.

A group of NS-VCs supports a *BSSGP virtual connection* (BVC), used to transport packets between NS users. BVCs provide communication paths between BSSGP entities. Each BVC is used to transport BSSGP PDUs between peer point-to-point functional entities, peer point-to-multipoint functional entities, or peer-signaling functional entities. For every BVC, a QoS profile and the MS identification are used to create queues and contexts in both the SGSN and the BSS.

18.4.2.2   BSS GPRS Protocol

BSSGP provides the radio-related QoS and routing information required to transmit user data between a BSS and an SGSN. It also enables the SGSN and BSS to operate node management control functions. If an SGSN simultaneously communicates with multiple BSSs, there is one BSSGP protocol machine in the SGSN corresponding to each of the BSSs. Three service models are supported by BSSGP: BSSGP/RL, GMM, and NM.

■ The BSSGP service model in the SGSN controls the transfer of LLC frames across the Gb interface. The Relay (RL) service model in the BSS controls the transfer of LLC frames between the RLC/MAC function and BSSGP. Examples of the RL/BSSGP service primitives provided by the BSSGP are DL-UNITDATA and UL-UNITDATA. A UL-UNITDATA PDU is delivered from the BSS to the SGSN. A DL-UNITDATA PDU is delivered from the SGSN to the BSS. Besides the user information (an LLC packet), the PDU contains RLC/MAC-related information such as MS radio access capability, a QoS profile, and the PDU lifetime. If the PDU is queued in the BSS for a period longer than the PDU lifetime, it is discarded at the BSS. Based on the QoS profile, a layer 3 signaling PDU may be transmitted over the Um interface with higher protection than a data PDU. The PDU is either acknowledged, using RLC/MAC ARQ functionality, or unacknowledged, using RLC/MAC UNITDATA functionality.

■ The GPRS mobility management (GMM) service model performs mobility management functions between an SGSN and a BSS. Examples of the GMM service primitives provided by the BSSGP are PAGING, SUSPEND, and RESUME. The PAGING procedure is invoked by SGSN to inform the BSS of packet-switched (if initiated by the SGSN) or circuit-switched (if initiated by an MSC/VLR) transmissions. In this procedure, the SGSN will instruct the BSS to page one or more cells. To suspend a GPRS service, an MS initiates the SUSPEND procedure by requesting the BSS to send a SUSPEND

PDU to the SGSN. On the other hand, when an MS resumes its GPRS service, the BSS instructs the MS to update the routing area. Alternatively, the BSS may send a RESUME PDU to the SGSN to indicate that the MS should be resumed for GPRS service.

■ The network management (NM) service model handles functions related to the Gb interface and BSS/SGSN node management. Examples of the BSSGP-supported NM service primitives are FLOW-CONTROL-BVC and FLOW-CONTROL-MS, used to control the downlink loading of the BSS per BVC and per MS, respectively. No flow control is performed in the uplink direction because the packet-sending rate at the MS is anticipated to be lower than the packet-processing rate on the network side. There is a downlink buffer for each BVC. If a PDU in the downlink is not transferred to the MS before its lifetime expires, the PDU is deleted from the BVC downlink buffer; this action is reported to the SGSN. To control downlink transmission at the SGSN, a flow control message FLOW-CONTROL-BVC (FLOW-CONTROL-MS) with parameters such as the bucket size and the bucket leak rate for a given BVC (MS) are sent from the BSS to the SGSN.

18.4.3   Gn and Gp Interfaces

Both the Gn and Gp interfaces utilize the GPRS Tunneling Protocol (GTP). GTP tunnels user data and signaling messages between GSNs. In the Gn interface, the GSNs are within the same GPRS network, whereas Gp may involve GSNs from different GPRS networks. Basically, Gp is the same as Gn except that extra security functionality is required for internetwork communications over the Gp interface. The security functionality is based on mutual agreements between operators. With GTP, an SGSN may communicate with multiple GGSNs, and a GGSN may connect to many SGSNs. MS, BSS, MSC/VLR, and HLR are not aware of the existence of GTP.

In the transmission plane, shown in Figure 18.2, GTP is supported by the Transmission Control Protocol (TCP) for connection-oriented transmission, and is supported by the User Datagram Protocol (UDP) for connectionless transmission. GTP transmission uses a tunneling mechanism to carry user data packets. A tunnel is a two-way, point-to-point path. Tunneling transfers encapsulate data between GSNs from the point of encapsulation to the point of decapsulation. GTP implements out-of-band signaling so that the signaling path is logically separated from the data tunnels. In the signaling plane, GTP is supported by UDP, which enables the SGSN to provide GPRS network access for an MS.

More than one path may be established between two GSNs, either in the same network or in different networks, and a path may be used by one or more tunnels. A GTP tunnel is defined by the associated PDP contexts in two GSN nodes, and is identified with a tunnel ID. GTP performs (1) path management, (2) tunnel management, (3) location management, and (4) mobility management. In path management, the GSNs exchange the Echo_Request and Response message pair to quickly detect failures occurring in the path.

Location management is required if a GGSN does not support SS7 MAP for communication with an HLR. In this case, the interaction between the GGSN and the HLR is done indirectly through a specific GSN that performs GTP-MAP protocol conversion.

Tunnel management and mobility management are described in the following subsections.

18.4.3.1 GTP Tunnel Management

GTP tunnel management creates, updates, and deletes tunnels. Some of the tunnel management messages are described here.

To activate a PDP context for an MS, the Create_PDP_Context_Request and Response message pair is exchanged between SGSN and GGSN. The SGSN selects the Internet Protocol address of a GGSN from a list maintained in the Domain Name Service (DNS) server, and sends the Create_PDP_Context_Request message to that GGSN. If the GGSN does not respond, the SGSN continues to send the request message to the next GGSN in the DNS list until the request message is accepted or the DNS list is exhausted. Upon receipt of this message, the GGSN creates a PDP context entry for the MS, and generates a charging identification. The new entry allows the GGSN to route and charge packets between the SGSN and the external PDP network. Based on the capabilities and current load of the GGSN, the negotiated QoS may be more restricted than the requested QoS specified by SGSN. The GGSN returns a Create_PDP_Context_Response message to the SGSN. The message indicates whether TCP or UDP will be used to transport user data. Note that only one path is used between any given GSN pair to tunnel end-user traffic in both directions.

To update the routing area information or a PDP context, an SGSN sends the Update_PDP_Context_Request message to a GGSN. The message includes the new SGSN address, tunnel identification, and QoS negotiated. Upon receipt of this message, the GGSN may reject the update request if the QoS negotiated with the SGSN is not compatible (for example, the reliability class is insufficient to support the PDP type). The GGSN may also restrict the QoS negotiated based on its capabilities and the current load. If the GGSN returns a negative **Update_PDP_Context_Response** message, the SGSN deactivates the PDP context. GTP may also use this message pair to redistribute PDP contexts for load balancing.

To detach an MS or to deactivate a PDP context, an SGSN and a GGSN exchange the **Delete_PDP_Context_Request** and **Response** message pair. This action deactivates an activated PDP context. To activate a PDP context, the GGSN sends the **PDU_Notification_Request** message to the SGSN indicated by the HLR—that is, the SGSN serving the MS. When it receives this message, the SGSN requests that the MS activate the indicated PDP context, and replies with a **PDU_Notification_Response** message to the GGSN.

18.4.3.2 GTP Mobility Management

GTP mobility management supports functions such as GPRS attach, GPRS routing area update, and activation of PDP contexts.

When an MS moves from one SGSN to another SGSN, it sends P-TMSI to the new SGSN. The new SGSN then exchanges the **Identification_Request** and **Response** message pair with the old SGSN to obtain the IMSI of the MS. The IMSI is used to retrieve the MS record in the HLR. The **Identification_Request** and **Response** message pair is equivalent to the **MAP_SEND_IDENTIFICATION** message pair described in Chapter 11.

The **SGSN_Context_Request** message is sent from the new SGSN to the old SGSN to obtain the MM and all active PDP contexts of an MS. The message includes old routing area identification, the old P-TMSI, the new SGSN address, and so on. Upon receipt of the message, the old SGSN sends the requested contexts (MM context, PDP contexts, and LLC acknowledgment) to the new SGSN via the **SGSN_Context_Response** message.

After the new SGSN receives these contexts, it acknowledges the old SGSN by sending the **SGSN_Context_Acknowledge** message. This message implies that the new SGSN is ready to receive the data packets for the corresponding MS. Then the old SGSN starts to forward user data packets to the new SGSN.

18.4.4 Gs Interface

The Gs interface connects the databases in the MSC/VLR and the SGSN, which does not involve user data transmission. Base Station System

Application Part+ (BSSAP+) implements the functionality for the Gs interface. As shown in Figure 18.3, BSSAP+ utilizes SS7 Signaling Connection Control Part as the lower-layer protocol.

The BSSAP+ procedures coordinate the location information of MSs that are both IMSI- and GPRS-attached. It is also used to convey some GSM procedures via the SGSN. The paging, suspend, resume, and location update procedures are described here. Other Gs procedures can be found in GSM 09.18.

The paging procedure for MSC/VLR-based services allows the VLR to use GPRS to page a Class A or a Class B MS that is simultaneously IMSI- and GPRS-attached. By doing so, the system needs not repeat paging of an MS for both GSM and GPRS services, and the overall paging load on the radio interface is expected to be reduced. The VLR initiates this procedure by sending the **GPRS_PAGING** message to the SGSN. This message has a structure similar to the **PAGING** message delivered on the A interface. When the SGSN receives the **GPRS_PAGING** message, it checks to see if the MS is GPRS-attached and is known by the SGSN. If so, the SGSN sends the Gb **PAGING** message to the BSS, as described in Section 18.4.2. The SGSN then forwards the paging result back to the VLR. If the MS does not respond, the VLR or the BSS retransmits the paging message. The SGSN is not responsible for retransmission of the Gb **PAGING** message.

To perform circuit-switched activity for a Class B MS that is simultaneously IMSI- and GPRS-attached, the VLR uses the **SUSPEND** procedure to inform the SGSN to suspend the GPRS activities of the MS. When the MS sends the circuit-switched activity request to the VLR, the VLR waits for a period T6-1, then sends a **SUSPEND** message to the corresponding SGSN. Upon receipt of the **SUSPEND** message, the SGSN suspends the GPRS activity of the MS. If the MS sends a GPRS signaling message to the SGSN within a period T6-3, the SGSN accepts the message, and may inform the VLR of the situation. On the other hand, if the MS is unknown to the SGSN, the SGSN returns a **SUSPEND_FAILURE** message to the VLR. If the VLR does not receive a **SUSPEND_FAILURE** message within a period T6-2, then the suspend action is considered successful. Otherwise, the action fails.

Upon release of the circuit-switched activity for a Class B MS that is simultaneously IMSI- and-GPRS attached, the VLR sends a **RESUME** message to the SGSN to resume the GPRS activities for the MS. If the VLR does not receive a response message from the SGSN within a period T7, the VLR repeats sending the **RESUME** message up to N7 times. In the normal situation, the SGSN resumes the GPRS activities for the MS and returns a **RESUME_ACKNOWLEDGE** message to the VLR.

If a GPRS location update is initiated by an MS, the SGSN sends a **GPRS_LOCATION_UPDATING_Request** message to the VLR. The VLR checks to determine whether the IMSI is known. If not, the VLR retrieves the MM context of the MS from the HLR. If the SGSN does not hear from the VLR within a period T8-1, or if the VLR replies with a **GPRS_LOCATION_UPDATING_Reject** message, the SGSN informs the MS that the location update failed. If the update is successful, the VLR returns a **GPRS_LOCATION_UPDATING_Accept** message to the SGSN.

18.4.5 Gi Interface

GPRS interworks with the Public Switched Data Network (PSDN) and the Packet Data Network (PDN) through the Gi interface. In the Gi interface, GGSN serves as the access point of the GPRS network to the external data network. The interworking models to PSDN include X.25 and X.75; the interworking models to PDN include IP and Point-to-Point Protocol (PPP).

Both X.75 and X.25 are supported for GPRS interworking with PSDN. In these models, an MS is assigned an X.121 address, to be identified by PSDN. This X.121 address is either permanently allocated by the PSDN operator following the PSDN numbering plan, or dynamically assigned by the GPRS network at PDP context activation. In the latter case, the GPRS network maintains a free pool of X.121 addresses to be allocated to MSs.

GPRS interworks with intranets or the Internet based on the Internet Protocol (either IPv4 or IPv6). Viewing the GGSN as a normal IP router, the external IP network considers the GPRS network as just another IP network. The GPRS operator may maintain a firewall to restrict the usage of IP applications. In the firewall, GPRS may perform screening as specified by the operator or the subscriber. This feature is important to avoid unsolicited mobile-terminated connection (such as junk mail being sent to the MSs).

Either the external IP network or the GPRS network (specifically, the GGSN) manages a DNS. The IP address of an MS can be statically assigned, when the user signs up for services, or dynamically assigned at PDP context activation. If the IP address is dynamically allocated, the address assignment procedure is performed by the GGSN or an external DHCP server.

GPRS may transparently access the Internet and nontransparently access an intranet and ISP. In the transparent Internet access, the IP address of an MS is allocated from the GPRS operator's addressing space. This address is used for packet forwarding between the Internet and the GGSN and among the GGSNs. The MS need not send any authentication request at PDP context activation, and the GGSN need not be involved in user authentication and authorization. Domain name services are provided by the GPRS in this case.

In nontransparent access to an intranet or ISP, the IP address of an MS is allocated from the intranet/ISP address space where the address allocation server belongs to the intranet/ISP. At PDP context activation, the MS must be authenticated by the intranet/ISP using a security protocol agreed upon by the GPRS operator and the intranet/ISP. Domain name services are provided by the intranet/ISP.

GPRS may provide connection to the intranet/ISP through the transparent Internet access where a bearer service is provided to tunnel a private intranet using protocols such as IPsec. In this case, GPRS is involved in the security processes by using an IPsec security header or authentication header for user authentication and for the confidentiality of user data.

18.5   GPRS Procedures

This section describes GPRS attach/detach, PDP context manipulation, and RA/LA update, to illustrate how service primitives/messages in various GPRS interfaces interact with each other. The GPRS attach procedure establishes a logical link between the MS and the SGSN. The PDP context activation procedure allows data transmission between the MS and the external data network. The RA update procedure tracks the location of the MS and re-establishes the logical link between the MS and the SGSN.

18.5.1   GPRS Attach and Detach Procedures

This subsection describes attach and detach of PDP contexts. The message flow for the GPRS attach procedure is illustrated in steps 1.1–1.3 Figure 18.6.

> Step 1.1 (GMM/Um and Gb interfaces). The MS sends an **Attach Request** message to the SGSN. The generation of this message involves the GMM layer, described in Section 18.4.2. The message indicates whether GPRS attach or GPRS/IMSI attach will be performed.

> Step 1.2 (GTP mobility management/Gn interface). Assuming that after the last detach the MS moved from the old SGSN to the new SGSN, the new SGSN needs to obtain the IMSI of the MS from the old SGSN. The new SGSN sends an **Identification_**

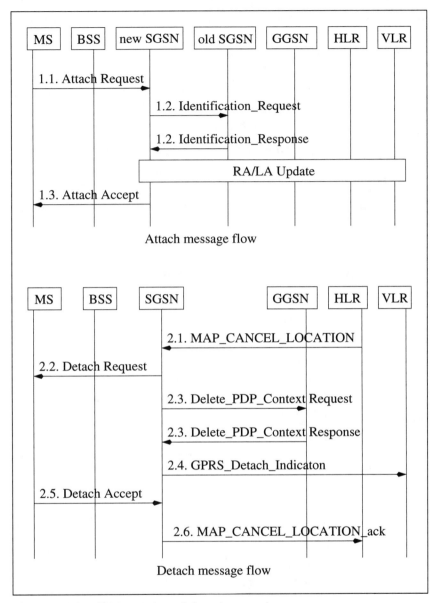

Figure 18.6 GPRS attach and detach procedures.

Request message that contains the old P-TMSI, as described in Section 18.4.3. The old SGSN uses the received P-TMSI to search for the IMSI of the MS. Then it returns the IMSI to the new SGSN by sending the **Identification_Response** message. On the other hand, if the IMSI search fails, the old SGSN responds with an appropriate error cause. In this case, the new SGSN will ask the MS to send its IMSI over the air interface. After the IMSI has been obtained, the SGSN may perform security procedures for MS authentication and ciphering.

For the first attach, or if the SGSN number has changed since GPRS detach, the RA (and possibly the LA) update is performed, as described in Section 18.5.3.

Step 1.3 (GMM/Um and Gb interfaces). The SGSN selects the radio priority for the short message service, and sends an **Attach Accept** message to the MS. If a new P-TMSI is allocated to the MS, the MS sends an acknowledgment to the corresponding VLR.

GPRS detach can be initiated by MS, SGSN, or HLR. Steps 2.1–2.6 in Figure 18.6 show the HLR-initiated detach procedure.

Step 2.1 (GSM MAP/Gr interface). Following the standard GSM MAP, the HLR sends the **MAP_CANCEL_LOCATION** message to the SGSN with cancellation type set to Subscription Withdrawn.

Steps 2.2 and 2.5 (GMM/Um and Gb interfaces). The SGSN sends the **Detach Request** message to the MS. The message includes the detach type parameter to indicate that the MS should not make a new attach and PDP context activation. At step 2.5, the MS returns **Detach Accept** and detaches itself from the network.

Note that detach type used depends on who initiates the detach procedure. In SGSN-initiated detach, the SGSN may request the MS to make a new attach. In MS-initiated detach, the detach type is specified by the MS to indicate whether the operation is for GPRS detach, IMSI detach, or combined GPRS and IMSI detach.

Step 2.3 (GTP tunnel management/Gn interface). As described in step 3.1 in Section 18.5.2, the SGSN and the GGSN exchange the **Delete_PDP_Context_Request** and **Response** message pair to deactivate the MS's PDP context in the GGSN.

Step 2.4 (BSSAP+ /Gs interface). If the MS was also IMSI-attached, the SGSN sends a **GPRS_Detach_Indication** message to the VLR. The VLR removes the association with the SGSN and handles paging and location update without going through the SGSN. (For example, the VLR will not send the **GPRS_Paging** message described in Section 18.4.4.)

Step 2.6 (GSM MAP/Gr Interface). After the MS detach operation is performed (at step 2.5), the SGSN sends the **MAP_CANCEL_LOCATION_ack** message to confirm the deletion of the MM and PDP contexts.

In both SGSN-initiated and MS-initiated detach procedures, the HLR is not involved. The message flow for the SGSN-initiated procedure is the same as that in Figure 18.6, except that steps 2.1 and 2.6 are removed. The MS-initated detach procedure is similar to that of the SGSN-initiated procedure, except that the **Detach Request** message is sent from the MS to the SGSN and the **Detach Accept** message is sent from the SGSN to the MS.

18.5.2 PDP Context Procedures

This subsection describes activation, modification, and deactivation of PDP contexts. The message flow for PDP context activation is illustrated in steps 1.1–1.3 of Figure 18.7.

Step 1.1 (GMM/Um and Gb interfaces). The MS sends an **Activate PDP Context Request** message to the SGSM, to indicate whether the MS will use a static or a dynamic PDP address. It also specifies the external data network to be connected and the desired QoS for the connection. After this message, security functions may be executed between the SGSN and the MS for authentication purpose. The SGSN checks the user subscription and QoS.

Step 1.2 (GTP tunnel management/Gn interface). The SGSN sends a **Create_PDP_Context_Request** message to GGSN, as described in Section 18.4.3. The activation creates a tunnel/logical link between a PDP context in the SGSN and a PDP context in the GGSN. The GGSN obtains the IP address from the external data network, and is forwarded to the MS. If the GGSN replies to the SGSN with a positive **Create_PDP_Context_Response** message, the SGSN activates the PDP context and is ready to forward packets between the MS and the GGSN.

Step 1.3 (GMM/Um and Gb interfaces). Based on the information received from the GGSN in step 1.2, the SGSN stores the GGSN address and the dynamic PDP address (if any) in the PDP context. The SGSN selects the radio priority based on the negotiated QoS, and returns an **Activate PDP Context Accept** message to the MS.

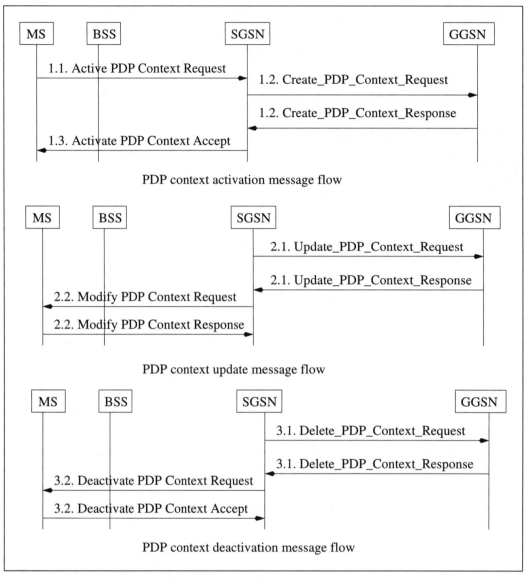

Figure 18.7 GPRS PDP context procedures.

After the PDP context activation, a connection between the MS and the external data network is established. The SGSN is ready to route and charge for packets delivered between the GGSN and the MS.

Steps 2.1 and 2.2 in Figure 18.7 show the message flow for PDP context update.

Step 2.1 (GTP tunnel management/Gn interface). As described in Section 18.4.3, the SGSN and the GGSN exchange the Update_PDP_Context_Request and Response message pair to update the PDP context.

Step 2.2 (GMM/Um and Gb interfaces). The SGSN and the MS exchange the Modify PDP Context Request and Accept message pair to update the PDP context at the MS. If the MS does not accept the new negotiated QoS, it deactivates the PDP context.

Steps 3.1 and 3.2 in Figure 18.7 show the message flow for PDP context deactivation initiated by the SGSN.

Step 3.1 (GTP tunnel management/Gn interface). As described in Section 18.4.3, the SGSN and the GGSN exchange the Delete_PDP_Context_Request and Response message pair to deactivate the PDP context. The GGSN removes the PDP context and reclaims dynamic PDP address (if any).

Step 3.2 (GMM/Um and Gb interfaces). The SGSN and the MS exchange the Deactivate PDP Context Request and Accept message pair. The MS removes the PDP context. Note that the SGSN may initiate this step immediately after the Delete_PDP_Context_Request is sent in step 3.1.

The GGSN or the MS can also initiate PDP context deactivation, but the message flows are different from that shown in Figure 18.7. In GGSN-initiated deactivation, the GGSN sends the Delete_PDP_Context_Request message to the SGSN. The SGSN then exchanges the Deactivate PDP Context message pair with the MS. Finally, the SGSN returns a Delete_PDP_Context_Response message to the GGSN.

In MS-initiated deactivation, the MS sends the Deactivate PDP Context Request message to the SGSN. The SGSN then exchanges the Delete_PDP_Context message pair with the GGSN. Finally, the SGSN returns the Deactivate PDP Context Accept message to the MS.

18.5.3 The Combined RA/LA Update Procedure

The combined RA/LA update procedure is illustrated in Figure 18.8 with the following steps:

Step 1 (GMM/Um and Gb interfaces). The MS sends a Routing Area Update Request to the SGSN. The message is generated from the GMM layer, described in Section 18.4.2, which specifies the

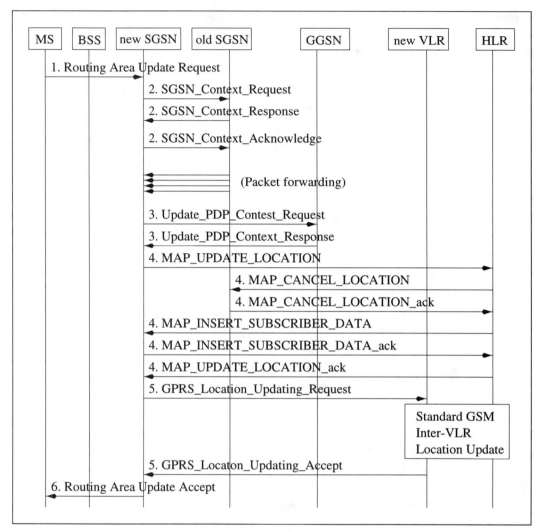

Figure 18.8 Combined RA/LA update message flow.

old RA identification, P-TMSI, and the update type (RA/LA update, in our example). Before forwarding this message to the SGSN, the BSS adds the global identity of the cell where the message was received.

Step 2 (GTP mobility management/Gn interface). As described in Section 18.4.3, the new SGSN obtains the MM and PDP contexts from the old SGSN by exchanging the **SGSN_Context_Request** and **Response** message pair. Security functions may be performed to support ciphering mode in the new connection. When the new SGSN is ready to receive data packets, it informs the old SGSN by sending the **SGSN_Context_Acknowledge** message. Then the old SGSN forwards the buffered data packets to the new SGSN. (Packet forwarding is performed if the packets sent from the network to the MS were being buffered in the old SGSN when the MS moved to the new SGSN.)

Step 3 (GTP tunnel management/Gn interface). Based on the description of Section 18.4.3, and step 2.1 in Section 18.5.2, the new SGSN exchanges the **Update_PDP_Context_Request** and **Response** message pair with all related GGSNs. The GGSNs update their PDP context fields.

Step 4 (GSM MAP/Gr interface). Following the standard GSM registration procedure described in Chapter 11, the new SGSN and the HLR exchange the **MAP_UPDATE_LOCATION** message and the acknowledgment to update the SGSN number maintained in the HLR. The HLR and the old SGSN exchange the **MAP_CANCEL_LOCATION** message and the acknowledgment to remove the MM and PDP contexts of the MS. The HLR and the new SGSN exchange the **MAP_INSERT_SUBSCRIBER_DATA** message and the acknowledgment to provide GPRS subscription data of the MS to the new SGSN. Based on the subscription data, the new SGSN determines whether the MS is allowed to receive service in the routing area. If not, the SGSN returns the **MAP_INSERT_SUBSCRIBER_DATA_ack** message with an error cause such as "GSN Area Restricted," and the update operation fails. On the other hand, if all checks are successful, the SGSN constructs an MM context for the MS.

Step 5 (BSSAP+ and GSM MAP/Gs and D interfaces). The update type is RA/LA in our example, so the procedures described in Section 18.4.4 are used to initiate LA update. From the new routing area identification, the new SGSN identifies the new

VLR through table lookup, and sends a **GPRS_Location_ Updating_Request** message to the VLR. This action is taken when the SGSN receives the first **MAP_INSERT_SUBSCRIBER_DATA** message. The new VLR updates the SGSN number for the MS. Then the VLR performs a standard GSM location update with HLR and the old VLR. After the LA location update, the new VLR acknowledges the new SGSN with the **GPRS_Location_Updating_Accept** message.

Step 6 (GMM/Um and Gb interfaces). The new SGSN sends the **Routing Area Update Accept** message to the MS to complete the RA/LA location update procedure. If the MS receives a new TMSI in this message, it sends an acknowledgment to the new VLR.

For a combined intra-SGSN and RA/LA update, the message flow is similar to that shown in Figure 18.8, except that steps 2 and 3 are not performed. In an intra-SGSN location update, no new SGSN is involved, and no packets need to be forwarded between SGSNs (eliminating step 2). Furthermore, there is no need to update the SGSN number in the HLR (eliminating step 3). For a pure RA update, which does not involve LA update, step 5 is eliminated.

18.6 GPRS Billing

In GSM, billing records are generated by MSCs. In GPRS, the charging information is collected by SGSNs and GGSNs. The SGSN collects charging information for radio resource usage by an MS. Depending on the agreement between the GPRS operator and the external network operator, a charge for the external packet network usage may be collected in the external network or in GGSNs of the GPRS network. If the visited GPRS network assigns a dynamic address to an MS, the charging of the GPRS and the external network is gathered and sent to the home GPRS network of that MS. Both SGSN and GGSN record the GPRS network resource usage. The SGSN collects the following charging information for an MS:

- Location information indicating whether the MS is in its home network or a visited network, the cell location, and so on.

- The amount of data transmitted through the radio interface for mobile-originating (MO) and mobile-terminating (MT) calls specified with QoS profiles and user protocols.

- The amount of time an MS occupies a PDP address.
- The amount of GPRS-related network resources and the GPRS network activity (e.g., mobility management) dedicated to the MS.

The GGSN collects the following charging information, together with the location information:

- The addresses of the destination and the source defined by the GPRS operator.
- The amount of data delivered between the MS and the external data network.
- The period that the MS has used the PDP addresses.

The data volume counted is at the SNDCP level in SGSN and at the GTP level in GGSN. Several types of call detail records (CDRs) are defined in GPRS. S-CDR is generated in the SGSN for the radio usage. G-CDR is generated by the GGSN for the external data network usage. M-CDR is generated by the SGSN for mobility management activity. Based on the preceding discussion, the SGSN generates the S-CDRs that contain at least the following fields: MO data volume, MT data volume, location information, SMS MO, SMS MT, associated QoS, and record duration. Similarly, the GGSN generates the G-CDRs with the following minimum set of fields: destination address, source address, data received, data sent, associated QoS, and record duration. Every CDR is associated with a subscriber's active PDP context. On the other hand, a PDP context may generate several S-CDRs and G-CDRs. A CDR is initiated based on PDP context activation, and is generated according to various criteria such as end-of-call, time-of-day accounting schedule, inter-SGSN routing area update, and so on. If an MS moves during a communication session, several CDRs may be generated from various GSNs and the external data networks. These CDRs are merged into one complete CDR by CDR matching. In the GSNs, the *charging gateway function* (CGF) is used to support charging information collection, immediate storage, and CDR transfer. CGF is either implmemented in a separate network node or is distributed among the GSNs.

GPRS operators collect and process the charging information in different ways. For GSM circuit-switched service, a user utilizes dedicated resources; in the GPRS packet-switched service, several users share the resources (especially if a PDP context activated for a long time involves only occasional packet transmissions). Thus, charging for packet-switched service is more difficult than for circuit-switched service. It is possible that the cost of measuring packets is greater than their values and that the existing

GSM billing systems may not be able to handle GPRS real-time CDR information. Therefore, a charging gateway is typically introduced to perform billing mediation based on information received from the SSGNs/GSGNs before the charging records are sent to the billing system.

A GPRS billing strategy can be: volume-oriented (per-kilobyte charge with uplink and downlink separated), transaction-oriented, content-based, flat-rate-oriented, or any combination of these. For example, a flat-rate charge can be exercised during off-peak times in conjunction with a volume-oriented charge during peak times. The charging rates can be further distinguished by the type and destination of the connection, duration of the connection, QoS, time of day, day of the week, or other criteria. GPRS may also provide reverse charging; however, reverse charging may not be applicable to certain external data network protocols. The charging methods of GPRS may follow the experiences from existing cellular digital packet data billing models. For example, AT&T PocketNet utilizes a combination of flat-rate and volume-oriented approach, wherein the charging for individuals is flat-rate-oriented while the charge for businesses is volume-oriented. BAM Cellscape exercises a transaction-oriented policy for services such as e-mail, and a flat-rate-oriented policy for PC-based Internet access.

Major GPRS infrastructure vendors support charging functions as part of their GPRS solutions. In Nortel's solution, the CDRs are generated based on GGSN Radius BSAC (Bay Secure Access Control) accounting and SGSN MDP (Magellan Data Provider) mechanisms. The S-CDR and G-CDR contents are based on ETSI GSM 12.15 standard, and the CDRs are collected in the SGSN and/or GGSN. The charging information is then forwarded to the billing gateway that provides enhanced features such as flexible CDR filtering and formatting to generate billing records for the subscribers. Initially, prepaid service is provisioned using a hot billing (CDR-based) approach (see Chapter 17). Ericsson's *centralized billing gateway* (BGw) provides enhanced CGF for merging and filtering CDRs. The advanced processing option of BGw R7.0 provides features such as CDR matching, rating, and a database interface. With the rating feature, the BGw uses the CDR price tag to, for example, translate volume-based data into time-based data that can be handled by the billing scheme. The database feature securely stores partial results so that CDR matching can be performed at the end of a communication session. Alcatel's charging gateway utilizes the A1338 CDR collector. Based on GTP protocol over TCP/IP, the A1338 provides reliable real-time collection of M-CDR, S-CDR, and G-CDR. The processing rate is 300 CDRs per second. The charging gateway performs functions such as aggregation of intermediate S-CDR and G-CDR, CDR storage, backup/restore, and postprocessing.

18.7 Evolving from GSM to GPRS

By reusing the GSM infrastructure, most GPRS implementation costs in existing GSM nodes are software-related. As illustrated in Table 18.2, the major hardware impact on the GSM network is limited to the addition of a PCU-model to the BSC, and the introduction of two new node types, SGSN and GGSN. A GPRS software upgrade can be performed efficiently. In many vendor solutions, GPRS software can be remotely downloaded to BTSs, so that no site visits are needed. In the MS development, a major challenge is to resolve the power consumption issue. To support data-related features (e.g., multiple time-slot transmission), a GPRS MS consumes much more power than a standard GSM MS.

A desirable characteristic of the GPRS protocols is that each layer can be reused to support features in different GPRS nodes. The GPRS stack is designed so that multiple copies of every layer can be distributed across multiple processors. Thus, it can smoothly scale network capacity to handle large volumes of data. For example, the same SNDCP code can support both SGSN and MS. In other words, the SGSN code can be reused in the MS. GPRS protocol products can be implemented in general computer languages. For example, Trillium delivers its GPRS protocol software in standard C programming language. Lucent/Optimary GmbH provides GPRS protocol stack customization with a man-machine interface that is designed to be both modular and portable.

Table 18.2 GSM Network Elements Impact by GPRS

ELEMENT	SOFTWARE	HARDWARE
MS	Upgrade required	Upgrade required
BTS	Upgrade required	No change
BSC	Upgrade required	PCU interface
TRAU	No change	No change
MSC/VLR	Upgrade required	No change
HLR	Upgrade required	No change
SGSN	New	New
GGSN	New	New

GPRS is typically deployed in two phases. Phase 1 implements basic GPRS features, which include:

- Standard packet services delivery; that is, point-to-point packet bearer service
- Support for CS-1 and CS-2 channel coding schemes
- GPRS internal network interfaces such as Gn, Gb, Gp, and Gs
- Flexible radio resource allocation; that is, multiple users per time slot and multiple time slots per user
- Support for Classes B and C MSs
- GPRS charging; for example, packet-based billing and QoS-based billing
- GSM-based services, such as SMS over GPRS
- IP and X.25 interfaces to packet data network
- Static and dynamic IP address allocation
- Anonymous access
- Security; that is, authentication and ciphering

In phase 1 development, most vendors cover parts or all of these features with some variations. For example, Nortel's phase 1 development also considers advanced virtual private network features. Alcatel's phase 1 deployment covers the entire network with a limited investment, such as BSS software update, a single A935 MFS per MSC site, and one SGSN and one GGSN for the entire network. In Ericsson's phase 1 development, the applications are based on IP, X.25, and SMS.

GPRS phase 2 development includes the following features:

- Enhanced QoS support in GPRS
- Unstructured octet stream GPRS PDP type
- Access to ISPs and intranets
- GPRS prepaid
- GPRS advice of charge
- Group call
- Point to multipoint services

In Nortel's phase 2 development, the capacities of SGSN and GGSN are significantly increased. Inter-SGSN routing area update is implemented, and inter-GPRS network roaming is supported. In Ericsson's phase 2 development, the enhanced applications include PTM services, multicast, and group call. In Alcatel's phase 2 development, 935 MFS are smoothly upgraded; the SGSN and GGSN capacities are increased; and security is enhanced.

18.8 Summary

This chapter provided an overview of GPRS. We described the GPRS architecture and the related interfaces. Based on our discussion, the benefits of GPRS include efficient radio usage, fast setup/access time, and high bandwidth based on multiple time slots. GPRS reuses the GSM infrastructure so that both circuit-switched and packet-switched services coexist under one subscription. GPRS also provides a smooth path to evolve from GSM to the third-generation mobile network. Specifically, a third-generation network can continue to utilize the GPRS IP backbone network. However, GPRS has its limitations. For example, based on existing GSM technology, radio resources for GPRS in a cell are limited, and the GPRS data rate is probably too low for many data applications. This problem can be resolved by introducing the EDGE or the third-generation radio technologies described in Chapter 21.

Although GPRS is an emerging technology driven by the equipment suppliers instead of the push from the customers, it has generated strong interest among service providers. Due to the explosive growth of Internet applications, it is believed that data access is an important trend for mobile services. An obvious advantage of GPRS is that no dial-up modem connection is required to access data. After PDP context activation, the MS becomes an "always-on" device that facilitates instant connections. This feature is required for mobile computing, whereby information should be sent or received immediately as the need arises. Several potential GPRS applications have been identified:

- *Vertical applications for specific data communication requirements of companies.* Since a mobile phone can be an always-on device, a GPRS MS can always be connected to deliver information. Examples include traffic management (e.g., fleet management, vehicle tracking, vehicle control, and guidance) and monitoring automation (e.g., telemetry and security).

- *Horizontal applications for individual users.* In these types of applications, the mobile phone is a media device enabling moving users to receive services such as entertainment (e.g., games and music), location information (e.g., restaurants, cinema, hotels, and parking), and so on.

GPRS also allows commerce transactions when the customers are in motion. Examples include online banking transactions, stock transactions, gambling, ticketing (e.g., for cinema, airlines, and trains), online shopping, and so on. The high immediacy feature of GPRS is essential for commerce transactions, where it is unacceptable to keep a customer waiting.

For a moving user, GPRS is ideal for immediate handling of functions such as quick access to PIM information, e-mail, or note-taking, thereby eliminating the need to access the desktop or laptop's full-featured applications and accompanying broad range of peripherals and services.

For an in-depth reading of GPRS specification documents, the reader is recommended to start with the general descriptions in [ETS98h, ETS98f] and continue on to specific topics such as Um in [ETS97g, ETS97d, ETS97e, ETS97c, ETS98g], Gb in [ETS97b, ETS98b, ETS98c], Gs in [ETS97f], Gn/Gp in [ETS98i], Gi in [ETS98e], ciphering in [ETS97c], and charging in [ETS98d]. GPRS deployment for IS-136 is described in [Fac99]. Also, the vendor view of GPRS can be found on several Web sites [Sym, Tri99, Nok00, Sie, Alc, Eri99]. For the GPRS suppliers' market share, the reader is referred to [Mob00].

18.9   Review Questions

1. Describe the GPRS architecture and protocols. How many of them already exist in GSM?

2. To accommodate GPRS, what modifications are made to BSS?

3. Compare the remote PCU and the local PCU approaches. The PCU products described in this chapter are all remote PCU. In which situation would you consider deploying local PCU?

4. Which part of the GPRS interface should be modified if ATM replaces frame relay?

5. Compare the channel request procedure in GPRS with that in GSM.

6. What is EDGE? Is it appropriate to use EDGE in large cells? Some operators are very interested in developing EDGE, while others look for third-generation technologies. Compare these deployment strategies.

7. Explain why PDP context fields stored in MS, HLR, GGSN, and SGSN are different, and why PDP context is not stored in the VLR.

8. Why does GSM utilize GPRS to carry out location update for circuit-switched services?

9. Describe IMSI attach and GPRS attach. Why does GSM/GPRS need attach procedures? New attach may be requested in SGSN-initiated GPRS detach but not in HLR-initiated detach. Why?

10. In terms of the number of data links that can be established, what is the difference between a GPRS data connection from an MS to the external data networks and a dial-up connection to the data network?

11. In Alcatel's GPRS solution, every GPRS network is supported by one SGSN and GGSN. In Nortel's solution, several SGSNs and GGSNs are used to support one GPRS network. Compare these two approaches.

12. In the Gb interface, which procedures are specific for a Class B MS?

13. Describe the relationship of the Gb paging/suspend/resume procedures and the Gs paging/suspend/resume procedures.

14. Draw the message flow for the SGSN-initiated and MS-initiated PDP context deactivation procedures.

15. At step 1 of the GPRS location update procedure in Section 18.5.3, why does BSS need to send cell identity to the SGSN? Is this required in the GSM location update procedure? Why or why not?

16. Draw the message flows for intra-SGSN RA/LA update and inter-SGSN RA update.

17. Compare GPRS with CDPD, described in Chapter 8. What are the fundamental differences between the two services and what are the design guidelines shared by them?

18. How do you implement prepaid service in GPRS? Can standard prepaid approaches described in Chapter 17 be used for GPRS prepaid?

Wireless Application Protocol (WAP)

In a mobile network, wireless data are delivered with several constraints. In order to be portable, size and weight establish limits for wireless handheld devices, which results in a restricted user interface (small displays and keypads), less powerful CPU, and reduced memory capacity. Also, compared with its wireline counterpart, the wireless network has limited bandwidth, longer latency, and a lower degree of reliability. These limitations should be carefully addressed so that the wireless handheld devices can access Internet applications that are typically designed for desktop computers.

In June 1997, Ericsson, Motorola, Nokia, and Phone.com founded the Wireless Application Protocol (WAP) Forum. The WAP Forum has drafted a set of global wireless protocol specifications for many wireless networks, which has been offered to various industry groups and standards bodies. Most handset manufacturers have committed to WAP-enabled devices, and many mobile operators have joined the WAP Forum. WAP has attracted significant attention for the following reason: Until early 2000, wireless data services have not been as successful as mobile network operators expected. By providing a better environment in which to integrate the Internet, WAP is anticipated to significantly improve the wireless data market.

To converge wireless data and the Internet, WAP integrates a lightweight Web browser into handheld devices with limited computing and memory capacities. The wireless application protocols implemented in both the WAP gateway and the WAP handsets enable a mobile user to access Internet Web applications through a client/server model. Furthermore, WAP allows developers to utilize existing tools to generate Web applications for mobile users.

This chapter introduces the WAP model, the WAP protocol stack, and WAP mechanisms such as user agent profile and caching. Then we show how WAP can be implemented on various wireless bearer services. Finally, we describe several tools that can be used to develop WAP applications and the Mobile Station Application Execution Environment (MExE), which integrates WAP into third-generation mobile systems.

19.1 WAP Model

Figure 19.1 illustrates an example of WAP network architecture. Here, a WAP handset (a handheld device) communicates with the origin server (see (1) in Figure 19.1) through the mobile network. The origin server is a standard Hypertext Transfer Protocol (HTTP)/Web server, which can be developed by using tools such as Perl and Cold Fusion. On the origin server, a given resource (e.g., content to be viewed by the users) resides in or is to be created. (Note: A resource is a network data object or service that can be identified by an Internet-standard Uniform Resource Locator (URL). Resources may be available in representations such as multiple languages, data formats, sizes, and resolutions.)

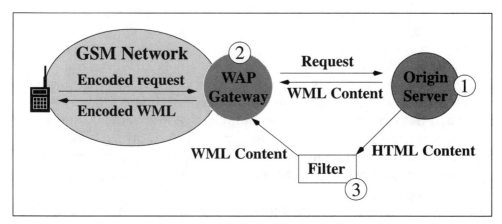

Figure 19.1 A WAP network configuration.

The contents received by the WAP handset are encoded in the compact binary format of *Wireless Markup Language* (WML) so that they can be efficiently delivered in the bandwidth-limited mobile network. The WAP Gateway, located between the Internet and the mobile network ((2) in Figure 19.1), receives the WAP request from the handset, decodes the request from binary format into text format, and forwards it to the origin server. The origin server parses the received WAP request and determines what to retrieve. If the URL specifies a static file, the origin server retrieves the file and returns the file to the WAP Gateway via HTTP. If the URL specifies a CGI application, the origin server launches the application. If the origin server provides the WML contents, it returns the WML deck (to be elaborated upon later) with the retrieved result to the WAP Gateway. The origin server may only provide HTML contents and thus cannot understand WML, in which case, the HTTP response of the origin server is first sent to an HTML filter ((3) in Figure 19.1). This HTML filter is typically built into the WAP Gateway, which translates the HTML text into WML format. The WAP Gateway verifies the HTTP header and the WML content sent from the origin server, and encodes them into WML bytecodes. The result is then sent to the WAP handset.

WAP provides end-to-end security if the WAP handset and the origin server communicate directly using WAP protocols. WAP utilizes a *micro browser* that optimizes the Web browser for the wireless environment. Specifically, the micro browser is a lightweight client that can be accommodated by a handheld device with limited memory capacity. A micro browser allows the WAP handset to browse contents in standard data formats. To support this model, Internet URLs are used to identify WAP content on origin servers. WAP content is given a specific type that is consistent with Internet *content typing*, and the WAP micro browser processes the content based on its type. The *content formats* can be display markup (WML), calendar information, electronic business card objects, images, and scripting languages such as WMLScript.

WML is an XML language designed to be suitable for use in handheld mobile devices. WML is a page description language that describes the WAP content presented in the WAP handset, the input options available in the handset, and the response of the user agent. Note that a user agent is a device or software that interprets content (e.g., WML), which also acts on behalf of the user with the applications. The agent can be a textual browser, voice browser, a search engine, and so on.

WML documents are divided into a set of *cards*, each representing one unit of interaction between the user and the user agent. A user can navigate among cards from WML documents. The user reviews the card's contents, optionally enters requested information and makes choices, then moves on to another card. Instructions embedded within cards may invoke services on origin servers as needed by the particular interaction. Several cards are grouped into a *deck*, the basic WML unit that the origin server can send to a user agent.

WMLScript is a lightweight procedural scripting language. It enhances the standard browsing and presentation facilities of WML with behavioral capabilities, supports more advanced user-interface behavior, and adds intelligence to the WAP handset. It also provides a convenient mechanism to access the WAP handset and its peripherals, and reduces the need for round-trips to the origin server.

WAP defines a user-interface model for handheld devices. As a mouse is used in a desktop, the up/down scroll keys are used in a WAP handset to navigate cards. *Soft keys* are used to perform context-specific functions and menu option selection. For a device with a large screen, the micro browser provides additional features for content display. An example of a WAP phone is the Nokia 7110. This phone is equipped with a large display (high-contrast graphical display of size 96 × 65 pixels), micro browser, NaviTM roller, predictive text input, calendar, Chinese interface, and phone book. Weighing 141 grams, the Nokia 7110 is a GSM 900/1800 dual-band handset that supports data rates up to 14.4 Kbps. The Ericsson R320 is another GSM 900/1800 dual-band WAP phone with built-in data capabilities, voice memo, full graphics display, and a complete Chinese interface. As a third example, the Ericsson Mobile Companion MC 218 is a WAP handheld device with a keyboard; it includes PDA features such as a calendar and contact manager. It is equipped with fax capability for image sending/receiving.

19.2 WAP Gateway

The WAP Gateway utilizes Web proxy technology to provide efficient wireless access to the Internet. A proxy plays the roles of both server and client, making requests on behalf of the client. Because the WAP handset (a client) cannot directly communicate with the origin server (a Web server), the WAP Gateway serves as a proxy to handle the requests from the WAP handset, and passes the requests to the origin servers. On the Internet side, the WAP Gateway translates requests from the WAP protocol stack to the Internet protocol stack (HTTP and TCP/IP). On the wireless network side, the encoder/decoder in the WAP Gateway performs WML text and bytecode conversion to reduce the information transmitted over the wireless networks.

The WAP Gateway typically supports the DNS service to resolve the domain names used in URLs. It also provides quick response to the WAP handsets by aggregating data from different origin servers, and by caching frequently used information (see Section 19.4.2). Though the WAP specifications do not specify mechanisms for charging or subscription management, the WAP architecture suggests that appropriate charging information can be collected in the WAP Gateway, where the WAP security protocol can be used to authenticate the subscriber.

Although it is not defined in the WAP specifications, WAP Gateway may use the *distillation* technique to perform on-demand transformation, which effectively reduces the wireless traffic. Distillation is highly lossy, real-time, datatype-specific compression that preserves most of the semantic content of a document. It scales down a color image by reducing the number of colors and, thus, the size of the representation, or reduces the frame size, frame rate, and resolution of video to create a reduced-quality representation. The distilled representation allows the user to quickly retrieve a simplified version of an object. If more information of the object is required, *refinement* is used to fetch extra information to enhance the distilled object. Although on-demand transformation increases the latency at the proxy, studies indicate that this technique significantly reduces end-to-end latency with better output for the clients. By installing dynamic adaptation mechanisms in the WAP Gateway, wireless handheld devices can leverage a powerful infrastructure to achieve capabilities they could not achieve on their own.

The WAP Gateway is a middleware product available on the market. The Motorola WAP Gateway and the Ericsson WAP Gateway are based on the Windows NT platform. APiON and CMG developed their WAP Gateways on the Unix platform. Nokia's WAP Gateways are developed in both Unix and Windows NT. Nokia offers a free download of its WAP Gateway beta product from its Web site, www.forum.nokia.com.

19.3   WAP Protocols

WAP specifications define a set of lightweight protocols, designed to operate over a variety of wireless bearer services. These services can be IP-based (e.g., GPRS, described in Chapter 18, and CDPD, described in Chapter 8) or non-IP-based (e.g., SMS, described in Chapter 12, and USSD, in Section 9.5). It is clear that the wireless bearers have very different

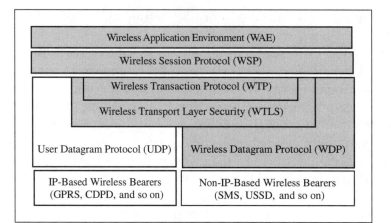

Figure 19.2 WAP protocol stack.

QoS (quality of service) characteristics. The WAP protocols compensate for or tolerate these varying QoS requirements. Details of the wireless bearer support for WAP are given in Section 19.5. The WAP protocol stack illustrated in Figure 19.2 is described in the sections that follow:

19.3.1 Wireless Datagram Protocol (WDP)

The WDP defines the WAP transport layer. WDP offers a consistent service to the upper-layer protocols of WAP. With WDP, the higher WAP layers can function independently of the underlying wireless network. Because different functions are provided by the bearers, different bearer adaptations are required so that WDP can operate over those bearers to maintain the same WDP service and service primitives to the higher WAP layers. For IP-based wireless bearer networks, the User Datagram Protocol (UDP), defined in RFC 768, is adopted as the WDP protocol definition, and no bearer adaptation is required. UDP provides port-based addressing. IP, defined in RFC 791, provides segmentation and reassembly required by the WAP connectionless datagram service. For a non-IP-based bearer, adaptation is required, as described in Section 19.5. Note that the need for bearer adaptation decreases with the efficiency of the bearer.

19.3.2 Wireless Transport Layer Security (WTLS)

WTLS defines the WAP security layer, which optimizes the industry-standard Transport Layer Security (TLS) protocol so that it can be used in narrowband communication channels. WTLS supports unchanged and uncorrupted data integrity delivery with encryption, and performs authentication and denial-of-service protection. The WTLS features can be enabled or disabled by the applications.

19.3.3 Wireless Transaction Protocol (WTP)

WTP defines the WAP transaction layer. WTP provides functions similar to TCP, except that WTP has reduced the amount of information needed for each transaction. In other words, WTP is "lighter" than TCP, which saves processing and memory costs in a WAP handset.

WTP is message-oriented. The basic unit of interchange is an entire message instead of a stream of bytes. WTP supports three types of transaction: unreliable one-way requests, reliable one-way requests, and reliable two-way, request-reply transactions. To provide reliability, WTP uses unique transaction identifiers, acknowledgments, duplicate removal, and retransmissions. A WTP user can confirm each received message to enhance reliability.

19.3.4 Wireless Session Protocol (WSP)

WSP defines the WAP session layer, which is optimized for low-bandwidth bearer networks with relatively long latency. WSP supports content exchange for client/server applications by establishing a session from client to server and releasing that session in an orderly manner. The life cycle of a WSP session is not tied to the underlying transport. When a session is idle, WSP may suspend the session to release network resources and to save power consumption of the WAP handset.

A session may be resumed at a different bearer network. A lightweight reestablishment protocol allows the session to be resumed without the heavy overhead required when establishing a new session. Two session service types are defined in WSP: a connection-oriented service that operates above WTP and a connectionless service that operates above WDP or WTP.

The current version of WSP is suitable for browsing applications, in which the WAP Gateway makes the connection between WSP clients and standard HTTP servers. WSP supports HTTP functionality and semantics with compact encoding for air-link transmission, a common facility for reliable and unreliable data push, and protocol feature negotiation.

19.3.5 Wireless Application Environment (WAE)

WAE defines the WAP application layer, which provides an environment for mobile operators and content providers to efficiently build applications on top of different wireless platforms. WAE defines a set of content formats, including images, phone book records, and calendar information. It also defines a micro browser for WML, WMLScript, and wireless telephony applications. As mentioned before, WML is designed for small-screen displays, and does not assume that the user has a mouse for user input. Since WML is specified as an eXtensible Markup Language (XML) document type, WML applications can be easily developed using existing XML authoring tools.

WAE also supports User Agent Profile (UAProf) and push technologies. With UAProf, a WAP handset can describe its capability to application servers or other network entities so that the servers/network entities can generate contents based on the handset's capability. This feature allows the applications to exploit the maximum potential of WAP handsets. (We elaborate on UAProf in Section 19.4.1.)

With the push mechanism, a trusted application server can send information directly to the application environment for processing. Push allows applications to alert the user when time-sensitive information changes. Applications generating events, such as telephony applications and emergency services, can benefit from using push technology. Another advantage of push is in multicasting. If the same information will be requested by several users, the network can save network resources by broadcasting the data once to all users instead of sending one copy to each of them. To fully utilize this mechanism, users are allowed to register their interests (e.g., when and how often a data object should be pushed) to the server. The server then pushes the data objects based on the users' interests.

19.3.6 Remark for WAP Protocol Layers

Every layer of the WAP stack provides a well-defined interface to support external applications. For example, WAE user agents are built on top of WAE; applications over transactions are built on top of WTP; and applications over datagram transport are built on top of WDP. Products of WAP protocols are available in the market. Nokia, for example, has WAP protocols and development tools implemented using ANSI C with a small memory footprint.

As this discussion clarifies, WAP protocols are designed to reduce the amount of information delivered over the limited-bandwidth wireless network. Unlike TCP, which is tuned to perform well in traditional networks, where packet losses are almost always due to congestion, WAP also considers lossy links of wireless networks due to bit errors and handoffs. As reported in the WAP white paper, a stock quote query example indicates that WAP uses 50 percent fewer packets than HTTP/TCP/IP to deliver the same information.

19.4   WAP UAProf and Caching

This section uses user agent profile and caching as examples to show WAP mechanisms tailored for wireless networks.

19.4.1   User Agent Profile

Existing markup language contents are designed for PCs with large displays and large memory capacities. Under the existing Internet technologies, WAP handsets may not be able to store and display the received contents. To resolve this issue, WAP specifies the User Agent Profile (UAProf), also known as Capability and Preference Information (CPI), that allows content generation to be tailored based on the WAP handset's capabilities. The CPI consists of information gathered from the device hardware, active user agent software, and user preferences, which may include:

- Hardware characteristics, such as screen size, color capabilities, image capabilities, and manufacturer.

- Software characteristics, including operating system vendor and version, support for MExE (to be described in Section 19.7), and a list of audio and video encoders.

- Application/user preferences, such as browser manufacturer and version, markup languages and versions supported, and scripting languages supported.

- WAP characteristics, including WMLScript libraries, WAP version, and WML deck size.

- Network characteristics, such as device location, and bearer characteristics (e.g., latency and reliability).

CPI is likely to be preinstalled directly on the device. This information is initially conveyed when a WSP session is established with the WAP Gateway. The WAP handset then assumes that the WAP Gateway caches the CPI and will apply it to all requests initiated during the lifetime of the WSP session.

19.4.2 Caching Model

The WAP user agent caching model tailors the HTTP caching model to support WAP handsets with limited functions. For cached resources that will not be changed during user retrievals, the resources can be efficiently accessed by the WAP handsets without revalidation. A time-sensitive cached resource is set to "must-revalidate." If this cached resource is stale when the user tries to go back in the history, the user agent revalidates this cached source. In general, navigation and processing within a single cached resource does not require revalidation, except for the first fetch. Examples include function calls within a single WMLScript compilation unit and intradeck navigation within a single WML deck.

The HTTP caching model is sensitive to time synchronization. Since WAP follows this model, a reliable time-of-day clock should be maintained in the WAP Gateway. If a WAP user agent does not have access to a time-of-day clock, it should exchange the time-of-day request and response message with the WAP Gateway and synchronize with the clock value returned from the WAP Gateway.

Another important issue for caching is security. The private information in the user agent cache is protected from unintended or malicious access. WAP Gateways implementing a caching function must obey all security-related considerations defined in HTTP.

Several studies indicate that the hit rate of caching can be more than 50 percent, which significantly reduces the utilized network resources. Complementary techniques, such as push, described in Section 19.3.5, and *prefetching*, can be used to speed up Web access. Prefetching is based on the fact that after retrieving a page from the origin server, the WAP user may spend some time viewing the page. During this period, the WAP handset, as well as the air link of the wireless network, are idle, providing time that can be used to prefetch the next page so that when the user proceeds to retrieve the information, the page is available immediately. In this way, transmission delay can be reduced. However, if the prefetched data is not used by the user, the network resources used by prefetching are wasted. Furthermore, it is difficult to charge the user if the operator does not know whether the prefetched data are actually used.

19.5 Wireless Bearers for WAP

The WAP protocol stack is built on top of wireless bearer services. For IP-based bearers such as GPRS, standard UDP is used to support the WAP stack. Figure 19.3 illustrates the protocol stack for implementing WAP over GPRS. Since no GPRS bearer adaptation is required to support WAP, it is relatively easy to implement WAP features in GPRS handsets. It is clear that WAP can be accommodated in GPRS by including the standard WAP layers (WAE, WSP, and WTP) in the GPRS MS. Similarly, GSM circuit-switched data service, IS-136 circuit-switched/packet-switched data, CDPD, IS-95 data service, Japan PDC, and PHS data services can support WAP without bearer adaptation.

For non-IP-based bearers, bearer adaptation is required to support WDP. Basically, the adaptation should provide: (1) destination port, (2) source port, and (3) packet segmentation and reassembly.

Non-IP-based bearers for WAP include GSM SMS, GSM USSD, ReFlex, and IS-637 SMS. We use GSM USSD as an example to show how bearer adaptation is achieved. The reader is referred to Section 9.5 for USSD details. USSD provides a two-way alternate interactive service that allows only one end node (MS or the network) to transmit at a time. This mechanism does not support full-duplex datagram service as required by WAP.

As illustrated in Figure 19.4, a new protocol layer called USSD Dialog Control Protocol (UDCP) has been developed to support full-duplex

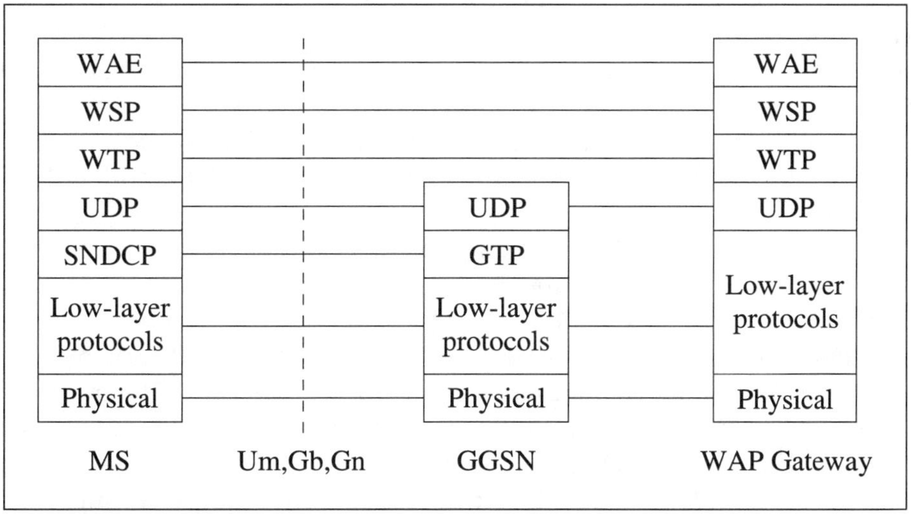

Figure 19.3 WAP protocol stack over GPRS.

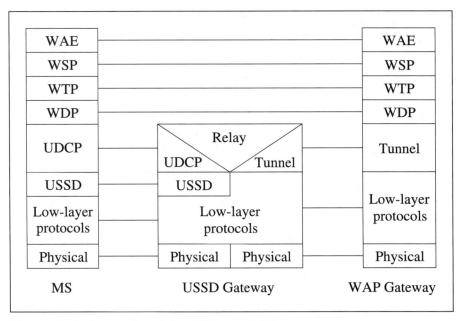

Figure 19.4   Protocol stack for WAP over USSD.

service from the USSD two-way alternate dialog. UDCP resides at the MS and USSD Gateway. It includes the IP addresses of the source and destination (i.e., the WAP handset and the WAP Gateway) in the string to be delivered by the USSD. USSD typically establishes and terminates a dialogue between each data transmission. The UDCP maintains a USSD dialogue connection as long as there is data to be sent. It also reestablishes the dialogue after failure.

To implement UDCP, a USSD string consists of the message text and the SMS User Data Header (UDH), defined in GSM 03.40. The UDH consists of one or more *information elements* (IEs). The standard ETSI *port number IE*, *fragmentation IE*, and an IE containing the UDCP header are included in the UDH.

The UDCP user (i.e., WDP) sends data by issuing the UDCP-Data request primitive. The user data consists of the port number IE, the fragmentation IE, and the WDP user data. When it is the remote entity's turn to send, the local UDCP user is allowed to initiate UDCP-Data request primitives. Since the USSD dialogue is half-duplex, data must be buffered until the local UDCP provider gets its turn to send. If the data cannot be delivered within one USSD operation, the More-To-Send flag is set. This triggers the remote UDCP provider to return an operation enabling the local UDCP provider to send the remaining data.

When a USSD string is received, the UDCP provider locates the UDCP IE in the UDH and extracts the data portion. The data portion of the UDCP IE contains the UDCP packet data unit, which is then forwarded to the UDCP user (i.e., WDP). If segmentation and reassembly are necessary, the fragmentation IE is included in the UDH.

19.6   WAP Developer Toolkits

WAP developer toolkits assist developers to compose and test WAP application software that will run on origin servers. The toolkits can also be used for WAP application demonstrations. They provide convenient environments in which developers can write, test, and debug applications; on, for example, a PC-based simulator. Several WAP development tools are available. Ericsson's WapIDE (Integrated Developer's Environment) SDK (Software Developers Kit) is an integrated development environment for creating WAP services. It consists of three main components: a WAP browser, an application designer, and a server toolset. It can be used to design applications for Ericsson WAP handsets such as the R320, R380, and PDA such as MC218. The Ericsson WapIDE is free for download from the Web site www.ericsson.com/wap/developer/. The Motorola SDK includes a development environment for both WAP and VoxML applications. This SDK is available at www.motorola.com/MIMS/MSPG/mix/mix.html.

Phone.Com UP.SDK is another free WAP application development toolkit that can be downloaded from www.phone.com/developers/. UP.SDK enables Web developers to quickly and easily create HTML and WML information services and applications. The SDK includes UP.Simulator that simulates the behavior of an UP.Browser-enabled device. The simulator runs on either Windows 95 or Windows NT.

The Nokia WAP SDK software provides development tools similar to the Ericsson and Phone.Com products. The free Nokia WAP Toolkit is available from the Nokia Wireless Data Forum at www.forum.nokia.com. The Nokia SDK includes WML and WMLScript encoders, a WAP simulation client with a mobile phone user interface, and WAP application debugging support. The simulation client includes a WML browser (WMLScript interpreter and WMLScript libraries), WML and WMLScript editors, and debugging views. This simulator gives a real-time content depiction on a WAP-enabled handset.

Each of the WAP development tools described in this section provides a simulator. The simulator can run applications in local mode, which simulates a WAP handset, GSM network, and WAP Gateway, as shown

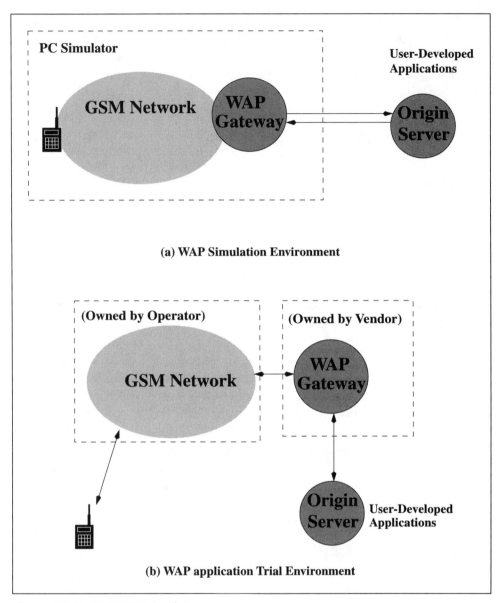

Figure 19.5 WAP SDK simulator.

in Figure 19.5(a). Furthermore, these vendors also provide free access of their WAP Gateways, so that WAP application developers are able to test a complete set of WAP-enabled services and APIs. As shown in Figure 19.5(b), a developer can create a new application and actually test it with a WAP handset (by connecting the origin server of the new application to the vendor-supported free WAP Gateway). Note that the whole application development process involves neither the GSM operator nor the vendor who offers free WAP Gateway access.

19.7 Mobile Station Application Execution Environment

The Mobile Station Application Execution Environment (MExE) is specified in the third-generation system UMTS to provide a standard execution environment for an MS to access Internet and intranet services. Like WAP, the MExE upper-layer protocols are independent of the type of underlying wireless network, although its transport layer may be adapted to support the specific features of the wireless bearers.

The concept of an MExE classmark is introduced to classify the MS capabilities (processing, memory, display, and interactive capabilities) in receiving MExE services. It is clear that the usage of MExE classmark is very different from the existing MS classmark described in Chapter 9, Section 9.1.1.

- *MExE classmark 1 is based on WAP.* A classmark 1 MS and the MExE Service Environment (MSE) interact via WSP.

- *MExE classmark 2 is based on PersonalJava.* It provides a run-time system to support more powerful applications and more flexible man-machine interfaces. MExE classmark 2 requires more processing, storage, display, and network resources. It also supports MExE classmark 1 applications through a WAP micro browser. A classmark 2 MS interacts with the MSE through HTTP or HTTP-derived protocols.

Based on the classmark, MExE allows the MS to negotiate its supported capabilities (specified in UAProf, described in Section 19.4.1) with an MExE service provider (i.e., WAP Gateway) at the first contact. After this *capability negotiation*, the MS and the MSE may perform *content negotiation* to select the best representation of an entity (e.g., service or image) when there are multiple representations of the entity available in the MSE.

Java's MExE MS (i.e., classmark 2 MS) supports the features specified in PersonalJava. The PersonalJava APIs provide a standard execution environment from which to access the user interface via the java.awt, and to allow Internet/intranet connections via the java.net package. The Java MExE MS also supports the JavaPhone APIs that extend the PersonalJava

APIs to provide telephony functionality (i.e, wireless profile), including application installation and power management.

The mandated services and applications for Java MExE include WAP browser support, described in the previous sections, and network protocol support for HTTP, HTTPS, and mailto.

The WAP Forum has a formal liaison with ETSI/MExE to cross-reference the WAP specification for defining a compliance profile in GSM and UMTS.

19.8 Summary

Based on [WAP99c], [WAP98a], and [WAP99a], this chapter provided an overview of the Wireless Application Protocol (WAP). WAP development is considered important in the wireless industry because of its attempt to develop an open standard for wireless protocols, which is independent of vendor and air interface. Furthermore, by including WAP in the MExE specification, WAP can smoothly evolve for third-generation mobile networks. The WAP specification is open to the public (see www.wapforum.org/). Specifications for WDP, WTLS, WTP, WSP, and WAE are given in [WAP99e, WAP99h, WAP99g, WAP99f], and [WAP99d]. Detailed implementation for UAProf, caching, and UDCP are described in [WAP98b] and [WAP99b], respectively. Several techniques for mobile access to Web resources are provided in the October 1998 special issue of *IEEE Personal Communications Magazine*. MExE is specified in [ETS00]. Documents for PersonalJava to support MExE can be accessed from the Web site http://java.sun.com/products/personaljava/. Further reading for WAP can be found in [WAP99i, Man00].

19.9 Review Questions

1. What are the design guidelines for WAP? What are the disadvantages of implementing TCP/IP directly over the mobile network?

2. Describe the WAP protocol stack. In which situation is WTP not used?

3. Describe distillation. Which layer of WAP implements this mechanism?

4. What is a user agent profile? What happens if a user agent profile is not used in WAP? How can distillation and a user agent profile be used together?

5. Describe the caching mechanism. What are the important issues in designing the WAP caching model? What are the differences between the HTTP caching model and the WAP caching model?

6. Compare caching, pushing, and prefetching. For example, what is the impact of these mechanisms on billing?

7. What are the extra overheads incurred in UDCP for the USSD bearer adaptation of WDP? Does UDCP actually allow WAP to provide duplex datagram service?

8. Describe the implementation of SMS bearer adaptation for WDP. Is it easier to adapt SMS for WDP or to adapt USSD?

9. Visit the Web sites of Ericsson, Nokia, and Phone.Com SDKs. Compare their tools. Try to implement a stock quote service using any of these SDKs.

10. Describe GSM classmark, GPRS classmark, and MExE classmark.

11. What is capability negotiation? What is content negotiation?

12. Some people [Her98] argue that WAP is not useful because content providers must provide simplified WAP compatible information, and end users must accept simplified alphanumeric content. They conclude that WAP will not achieve long-term success. Do you agree or disagree? Why?

Heterogeneous PCS

Recently, the integration of different PCS systems has been proposed, particularly the integration of cellular and low-tier PCS systems to realize the advantages of the individual systems. J. Rizzo and N. Sollenberger proposed approaches that focus on the "different radio technology, different network technology" integration; the integrated system is referred to as a *multitier system*. W. C. Y. Lee described approaches that focus on the "different radio technology, same network technology" integration; this system is referred to as *multiservices, multisystems broadband radio*. In this chapter, we generalize the concept of PCS system integration, and refer to the integrated system as *heterogeneous PCS* (HPCS). Our discussion focuses on integrating existing systems. The HPCS concept is also used in the new-generation mobile network (see Chapter 21), especially for core network integration.

This chapter first describes the types of PCS system integration, then moves on to the implementation issues for integrating the systems.

20.1   Types of PCS System Integration

In HPCS, if the service areas of the individual PCS systems do not overlap, the major advantage of integrating these systems is to extend the coverage of the service area. If the service areas of the individual PCS systems do overlap, the systems typically operate in different frequency bands, and the major advantage of integration is to increase the capacity or the number of communication circuits in the same area. Furthermore, depending on the technologies—that is, cellular or low-tier PCS of the individual systems—other benefits may be offered by HPCS. Consider the integration of a cellular system and a low-tier PCS system as an example. From the viewpoint of the cellular system, the quality of circuits is improved, and from the viewpoint of the low-tier PCS, higher user mobility is supported. Table 20.1 lists the possible combinations of cellular and low-tier PCS technologies.

A basic requirement of HPCS is *downward-compatibility*. That is, following integration the HPCS users will receive services from multiple PCS systems. At the same time, the original users of the individual PCS systems will still receive services from their systems without being affected by HPCS. Depending on the network and the radio technologies, three types of integration are being considered:

Table 20.1   Integration of Cellular and Low-Tier PCS Technologies

TECHNOLOGY	ADVANTAGES	EXAMPLES
Cellular/Cellular (Overlapping)	Increasing capacity	PCS1900/GSM-900
Cellular/Low-tier PCS Low-tier PCS/Low-tier PCS (Overlapping)	Increasing capacity Improving circuit quality Increasing the user mobility	DECT/GSM-900, PACS/AMPS, unlicensed PHS, and licensed PACS
Cellular/Cellular Cellular/Low-tier PCS Low-tier PCS/Low-tier PCS (Nonoverlapping)	Extending Coverage	All examples listed above and IS-136/AMPS, IS-95/AMPS, IS-95/AMPS, and unlicensed PHS and licensed PACS

20.1.1 Similar Radio Technologies, Same Network Technology (SRSN)

In the SRSN integration, the individual systems use the same network management (for roaming and call control) technology and the same radio technology, though the radio systems operate either at different power levels or at different frequency bands, as detailed here:

SRSN with different power levels. The cell sizes of a cellular system are large, and the cells are typically referred to as *macrocells*. Using the same air interface and the network management procedures as those for the macrocell system, the concept of *microcells* introduces low-complexity base stations that have low-power consumption and small coverage areas. In some sense, the microcell technology evolves along the direction of low-tier PCS technologies. Microcell layout improves frequency reuse, and the microcells typically overlap with macrocells to increase the capacity of HPCS. The microcells must "borrow" some radio channels from the (nonoverlapping) neighboring macrocells, thereby slightly reducing the performance of these cells.

SRSN with different frequency bands. The same radio technology may be implemented in different frequency bands. Integration of these SRSN systems results in a *multiband* system. An example is a dual-band GSM network where an integrated network consists of GSM at 900 MHz and a *digital cellular system* (DCS) at 1.8 GHz. (In 1997, DCS1800 was renamed GSM1800.) Since these systems use different frequency bands, the overlapping areas do not cause interference problems. Thus, HPCSs such as GSM-900/DCS-1800 may effectively increase the capacity of PCS. Most of the recent GSM MSs are able to switch between GSM and DCS. In 2000, the largest GSM/DCS dual-band system was developed by FarEastone in Taiwan.

20.1.2 Different Radio Technologies, Same Network Technology (DRSN)

Examples of DRSN are IS-136/AMPS and IS-95/AMPS. The radio systems of IS-136, based on TDMA technology, or IS-95, based on CDMA technology are different from that of AMPS (based on FDMA technology). All of these PCS systems share the same network protocol, namely IS-41. The purpose of the IS-136/AMPS and IS-95/AMPS integration is to serve as a graceful way to gradually replace the old AMPS technology with the new IS-136 or IS-95 technologies. The IS-136 technology, which is compatible with AMPS, is operational in most of the cellular markets in the United States. IS-95 systems have been deployed in many places such as Los Angeles, California, and South Korea.

20.1.3 Different Radio Technologies, Different Network Technologies (DRDN)

DRDN typically integrates cellular systems (high-tier) with low-tier PCS systems in the hope of maintaining the advantages of both technologies. In DRDN, the low-tier has priority for call delivery over the high-tier because the low-tier has the advantages of lower call delivery cost and better circuit quality compared to the high-tier. Examples of DRDN include AMPS-PACS and GSM-PACS, developed in Telcordia. Another example is the DECT and GSM interworking that provides DECT with roaming capability using the GSM MAP protocol. Note that DECT does not has its own core network protocol.

20.2 Tier Handoff

The type of integration has a significant effect upon the implementation of HPCS. One of the issues is *tier handoff*, or handoff between different systems. In a PCS system, when an MS moves from one cell to another during a conversation, the radio link between the MS and the new cell must be established, and the radio link between the MS and the old cell must be removed. The FDMA and TDMA PCS systems employ a *hard handoff* approach, whereby a MS talks to only one base station at a time, as described in Chapter 3, Section 3.2.

In an IS-95 CDMA system, the entire spectrum is used by each base station. During the handoff procedure, the MS commences communication with a new base station without interrupting communication with the old base station. As described in Chapter 4, Section 4.3, in this *soft handoff*, an identical frequency is assigned between the old base station and the new station, which provides different-site selection diversity to enhance the signal.

HPCS also needs to handle *tier handoff*, when an MS switches from one tier to another during the conversation. If the systems do not overlap, tier handoff does not occur, and tier handoff is not an issue. For the microcell/macrocell architecture in SRSN, both macrocell and microcell systems follow the same air interface and network signaling protocol.

Thus, tier handoff is exactly the same as the normal handoff in a single system.

For SRSN with different frequency bands, the integrated systems are the same, except for the frequency bands at which the systems operate. Thus, we anticipate that tier handoff is not as simple as that for the microcell/macrocell architecture, but is not difficult to implement. FarEastone reported that 8 percent of handoffs are tier handoffs in its dual-band network.

For DRSN, it is clear that modifications are required to perform tier handoff. Soft handoff in IS-95 is clearly not compatible with the hard handoff in AMPS. Also, the MAHO/TDMA handoff in IS-136 is not compatible with the MCHO/FDMA handoff in AMPS. When an IS-95 or an IS-136 traffic channel is switched to an AMPS traffic channel, a modified MCHO/FDMA handoff is executed. In the current IS-95 implementation, it is possible to perform handoff from IS-95 to AMPS, but not the reverse direction.

For DRDN, especially when the subband spacing of channels is different for the involved PCSs, tier handoff is almost impossible. First, the integrated systems may use different handoff approaches. For example, AMPS follows NCHO and PACS follows MCHO. Similarly, GSM follows MAHO and DECT follows MCHO. To perform tier handoff just like a normal handoff, the handoff procedures for both integrated systems must be significantly modified. Even if the handoff approaches are similar for the integrated systems, such as the combining of AMPS and CT2+, where both systems use NCHO, the implementations are typically very different. (Note: The original CT2 specification did not include handoff features.)

The best option is probably to have the DRDN network automatically redial and reconnect the call during tier handoff. For example, when an MS intends to move from the low tier to high tier during the conversation, the DRDN disconnects the call at the low tier following the low-tier call termination procedure, then reconnects the call at the high tier, following the high-tier call setup procedure. It is not clear if the time required for tier handoff is justified, or that users would find it acceptable.

20.3 Registration for SRSN/DRSN

Another important HPCS implementation issue is *roaming management*. Three aspects—registration, call delivery, and MS identity—of HPCS roaming management are discussed in this and subsequent sections.

In HPCS, particularly DRDN, the network may need to identify the individual PCS, in addition to knowing the VLR address within the system. For SRSN and DRSN, there is no need to identify the individual system, and a standard mobility management procedure such as IS-41 can be used for HPCS without any modifications:

- For SRSN, the heterogeneous base stations operating at different power levels or different frequency bands may connect to the same MSCs following the same network signaling protocol. Thus, from the viewpoint of the MSCs, these base stations can be treated in the same way; that is, the heterogeneous BSs can be controlled by the same VLR.

- For DRSN, it is more likely that the heterogeneous base stations are grouped into different VLRs. Since the structures of the VLRs and the HLRs are the same for the individual systems, the HLRs can be merged into one HLR, and the VLRs from different systems can talk to the single HLR using a standard mobility management protocol. If the MS is in an area where more than one individual system is available, then either the MS or the network may select the active tier. If the network is responsible for the tier selection, then modifications to the registration procedure, which are similar to but simpler than those for DRDN, are required. DRDN registration is described in the next section.

20.4 DRDN Registration

For DRDN, different systems use different registration and authentication procedures, and the information stored in mobility databases such as VLR and HLR is different. Thus, modifications to the registration protocols are required to accommodate DRDN. For example, besides VLR and HLR, an *access manager* (AM) is introduced to PACS, and an *alert ID* for paging is stored in VLR/AM, which is not found in AMPS. For a PACS/AMPS integration, network protocols also must be modified. For a PACS, DECT, or CT2 system that connects to a wireless PBX within a building, MS reregistration may be required to determine whether an MS is still in the system. Reregistration is not required in AMPS or some implementations of GSM. Other GSM implementations use reregistration for fault-tolerance purposes, as described in Chapter 11, Section 11.3.

To minimize the cost of DRDN roaming management integration, the *multitier HLR* (MHLR) approach has been proposed to integrate the HLRs

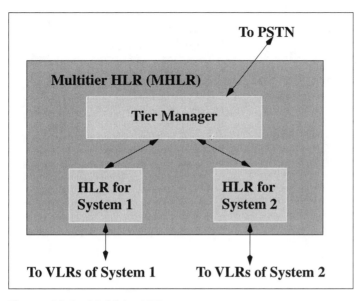

Figure 20.1 Multitier HLR.

of the individual systems. It may be difficult to merge the HLRs of DRDN into a single HLR because the formats and the operations of the HLRs are different. A good alternative is to build a *tier manager* that communicates with the different HLRs, as shown in Figure 20.1.

With the MHLR, two registration strategies have been proposed for DRDN. For demonstration purposes, we consider a two-tier DRDN system that consists of a low-tier PCS such as PACS, and a high-tier PCS system such as AMPS.

20.4.1 Single Registration (SR)

The MS is allowed to register with the MHLR on only one tier at any given time. In a two-tier system, if the low tier is available, the user always receives the services from the low tier. Since access to the low tier has the advantages of low cost and high circuit quality, the MS is instructed to register to the low tier when the low tier is available. Otherwise, the user registers to the high tier. Figure 20.2 illustrates how SR works. This figure offers a logical view of the MHLR, where the high-tier and the low-tier HLRs are merged into one HLR. H1 in the figure represents a high-tier VLR, and L1 and L2 represent low-tier VLRs. Since a VLR-controlled area of the high tier is much larger than that of the low tier, it is reasonable to assume that L1 and L2 are covered by H1.

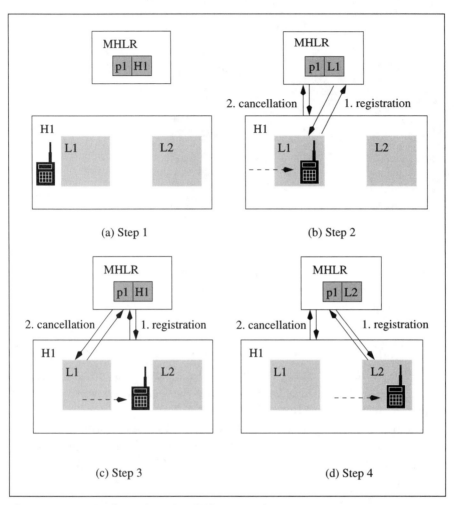

Figure 20.2 Single registration (SR) protocol.

The MS p_1 moves from H1 to L1 in Figure 20.2(b), from L1 to H1 in Figure 20.2(c), then from H1 to L2 in Figure 20.2(d). The SR protocol is built on a standard registration protocol such as IS-41. Thus, when p_1 moves from one tier to another, a registration operation is performed at the new tier, and a deregistration (cancellation) operation is performed at the old tier, as shown in Figures 20.2(b), (c), and (d).

20.4.2 Multiple Registration (MR)

The MS is allowed to register with the MHLR on multiple tiers simultaneously at any given time. In MR, the individual tiers perform their own

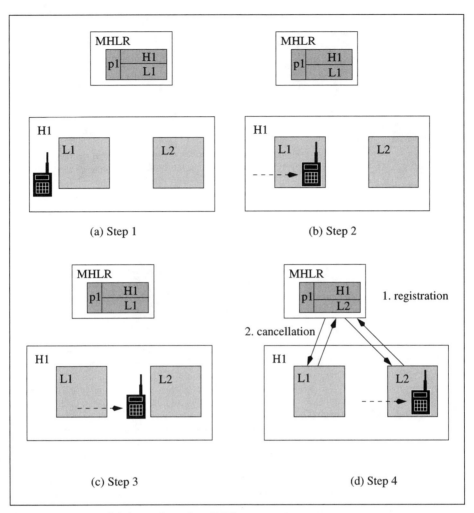

Figure 20.3 Multiple registration (MR) protocol.

roaming management as if they are not integrated. The tier manager of the MHLR keeps track of the currently, or most recently, visited high-tier and low-tier VLRs of an MS. Figure 20.3 illustrates how MR works.

To illustrate, assume that the MS has last visited L1. At step 1 in Figure 20.3(a), p_1 is in H1 and the most recently visited low-tier VLR is L1. Thus, at step 2 in Figure 20.3(b), when p_1 moves back to L1, no registration operation is performed. Similarly, no action is taken at step 3 in Figure 20.3(c), and the registration operation is performed at step 4 in Figure 20.3(d), if the currently visited low-tier VLR L2 is different from the latest visited VLR L1. Figures 20.2 and 20.3 indicate that MR generates less registration traffic than SR does.

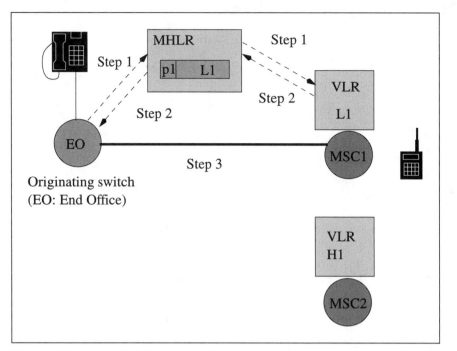

Figure 20.4 SR call-delivery procedure.

20.5 Call Delivery

For the HPCSs that use SR, the call-delivery procedure follows a standard mobility management protocol, such as IS-41, illustrated in Figure 20.4. Suppose that a wireline user dials the *mobile identification number* (MIN) of the MS p_1. The call is set up using the following steps:

Step 1. The originating switch queries the MHLR to find the location of p_1. Based on the location record, the MHLR queries the VLR for routing information.

Step 2. The VLR returns the routable address of the MSC where p_1 is located back to the originating switch via the MHLR.

Step 3. The originating switch sets up the trunk to the MSC, based on the routable address. The MS p_1 is paged, and the conversation starts.

For the HPCSs that use MR, the MHLR does not know the current tier where p_1 resides. Thus, the network selects a tier for call delivery based on some heuristics. If the first try selects the wrong tier, the network

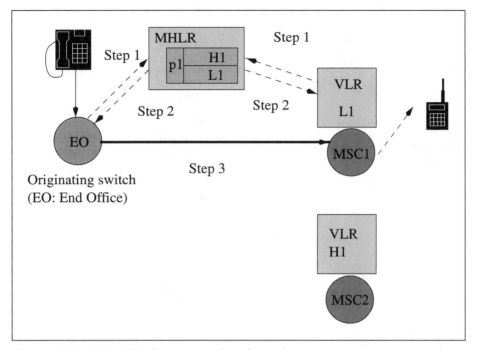

Figure 20.5   MR call-delivery procedure (part 1).

tries another tier. The call-delivery procedure is illustrated in Figures 20.5 and 20.6.

In Figure 20.5, steps 1–3 of MR are the same as those of SR, except that MHLR needs to select a tier at step 1. After the trunk is set up at step 3, the network may realize that the MS is not in the selected tier. If so, the setup trunk must be released, as shown in step 4 of Figure 20.6; the same call-delivery procedure for the other tier is performed in steps 5–7 of Figure 20.6. It is clear that if the MHLR selects the wrong tier, the penalty is very high. To reduce the penalty, the MS may be paged at step 1 of the call-delivery procedure when the VLR is queried. If the MS is not found, the MHLR tries the other tier before it returns the routable address to the originating switch (see steps 3 and 4 in Figure 20.7). Note that PACS is the only PCS system that pages the MS at the VLR query step in the call-delivery procedure. For other PCS systems, to page the MS before the routable address is returned, the call delivery procedure must be modified. To increase the probability that MR succeeds at the first try, some heuristics can be considered. For example, we can keep the timestamp of every registration in the MHLR. For a call delivery, the MHLR may first select the tier with the latest registration for call setup.

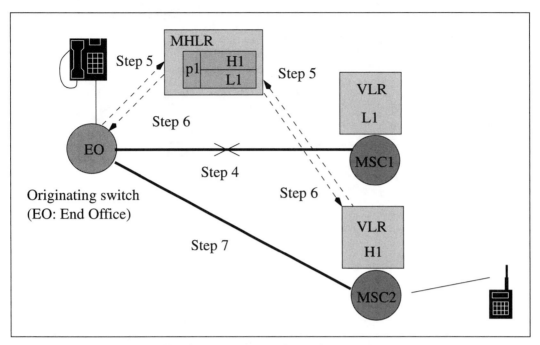

Figure 20.6   MR call-delivery procedure (part 2).

20.6   User Identities and HPCS MSs

An HPCS user may have a single identity or multiple identities. To accommodate multiple user identities, different identification numbers should map to the same HLR record. The mapping can be implemented with the concept of the MHLR. That is, the mapping function is performed at the tier manager, and the individual HLRs do not need to be modified.

For microcell/macrocell SRSN, the user has only one identity and one MS. For DRSN and DRDN, an HPCS user may carry multiple MSs or a multimode MS. A PCS user may already own MSs for different PCS services. If the user would like to order the HPCS that integrates the already-subscribed PCS services, it is probably more economical to keep the original multiple MSs. There are two other reasons that multiple MSs are used in HPCS:

- An HPCS may consist of more than two PCS systems, and the service provider may offer any arbitrary combination of these PCS systems upon request by a user. In this case, it may not be cost effective to manufacture multimode MSs for all possible combinations, especially since a user may drop and/or add PCS systems.

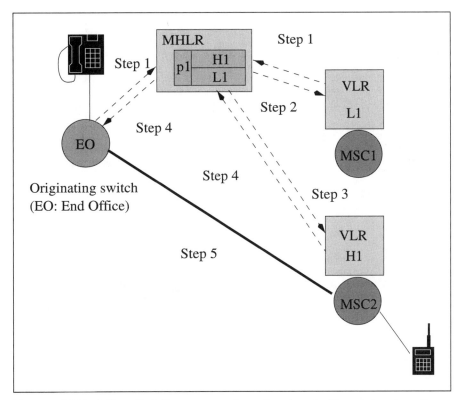

Figure 20.7 MR call-delivery procedure (paging before returning the routable address).

- An HPCS may include special purpose PCS systems. For example, a wireless LAN-based PCS system in a building may offer a high transmission rate for video or mobile computing services. A high bit rate video phone for the system is useless when the user leaves the building, and it may not be appropriate to integrate a "heavy" video phone with a light MS used for other PCS systems.

If multiple MSs are used, typically it is the user's responsibility to select the tier by turning on the MS of the active tier and turning off the MSs of the idle tiers. If the network is responsible for tier selection, MR is probably a more adequate choice than SR.

In terms of roaming management, it makes sense to develop multimode MSs for HPCS. IS-136/AMPS and IS-95/AMPS dual-mode MSs are required in the IS-136 and IS-95 specifications. DECT and GSM dual-mode MSs have been developed for in-building and out-of-building usage, respectively. A switching mechanism may be provided in the multimode

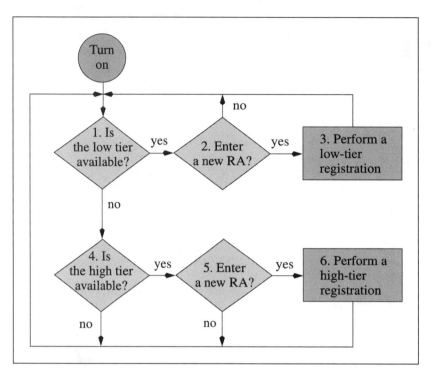

Figure 20.8   SR mobile station.

MS for the user to manually select the tier, or the MS may be intelligent enough to implement SR or MR. Figure 20.8 shows the flowchart of an SR MS, where the MS stays in the low tier if the low tier is available. If the low tier is not available but the high tier is, the MS stays in the high tier until the low tier is available again.

Figure 20.9 illustrates the flowchart for an MR MS, where the MS monitors both the low tier and the high tier at the same time. Note that the flowcharts for both SR and MR are very similar, which implies that it is easy to implement the two registration approaches in one MS by adding only a few lines of code to the microkernel of the MS.

20.7   Summary

Based on the article published in [Lin96b], this chapter described heterogeneous PCS systems and their evolution into HPCS. HPCS development has been motivated by business needs. One telephony industry trend is

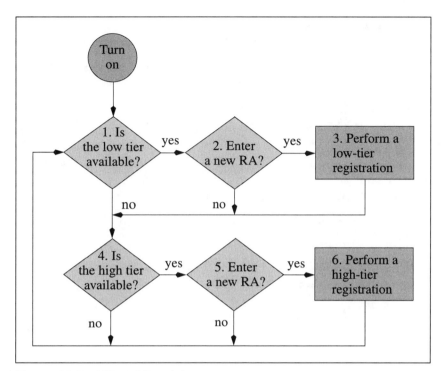

Figure 20.9 MR mobile station.

wireless business consolidations to create stronger regional/national market coverage. Examples include AT&T's acquisition of McCaw's cellular operations; cellular operations merging of Bell Atlantic and NYNEX; and the merging of Vodafone and AirTouch in the late 1990s. After consolidations, the PCS operating companies will own PCS systems of the same or different cellular/low-tier PCS technologies, which will be either overlapping or disjoint. Integrating different PCS systems to provide universal PCS service to the users will be necessary. One of the most important technical issues is to minimize the extra signaling traffic generated by the need for tier management.

Performance modeling of HPCS is still at its early stage. And a major business issue is to integrate PCS systems owned by different service providers. There is no conclusion regarding billing platform for tier switching. We anticipate that exciting HPCS stories will continue to emerge in the following years. Further reading on DRDN and DRSN can be found in [Riz95] and [Lee96], respectively. DECT with roaming capability using the GSM MAP protocol is described in [ETS96a]. The multitier HRL approach is analyzed in [Lin96c].

20.8   Review Questions

1. Describe SRSN and DRSN. Give examples for these types of mobile systems.

2. Suppose that a GSM operator owns two licenses, one at 900 MHz and the other at 1.8 GHz. The operator may deploy two independent GSM900 and DCS1800 GSM networks or a dual-band GSM network. What are the advantages of the dual-band network over the two single-band networks in terms of call origination, call termination, and handoff? (Hint: See [Lin00b, Lai99b].)

3. Is it easy to implement tier handoff for DRDN? Why or why not?

4. What is the major difference between the SR and the MR schemes?

5. What has to be done in an MR MHLR solution to make the call-delivery procedure possible?

6. Who selects the tier if the user has multiple MSs?

7. What is the difference between an MR- and an SR-capable mobile station?

8. Implement an adaptive mechanism that dynamically switches between MR and SR based on call/movement behavior of an MS.

9. Consider a multitier PCS system architecture that integrates three individual tiers: a high-tier system, a licensed low tier, and an unlicensed low tier. A single multitier HLR (MHLR) is used. Design a registration protocol where the MS is allowed to register to the MHLR on only one tier at any given time. Also, propose an intelligent algorithm for the MS to determine whether to perform registration in various situations to reduce the registration traffic. (Hint: See the algorithms in [Lin96c, Par97].)

10. The Interworking Location Register (ILR), developed by Ericsson, supports intersystem roaming between PCS 1900 and an AMPS network. The ILR consists of an AMPS HLR and a PCS 1900 HLR. Based on this configuration, design the AMPS/GSM 1900 roaming capability.

CHAPTER

21

Third-Generation
Mobile Services

International Mobile Telecommunications 2000 (IMT-2000), a representative name for *third-generation* (3G) mobile communication systems, aims to provide an effective solution for the next-generation mobile services. Progressing from the previous two generations, the technologies for 3G mobile systems have been significantly improved in terms of system capacity, voice quality, and ease of use. A short historical review of mobile communication evolution reveals that the first generation system, AMPS, described in Chapter 1, Section 1.2.1, realized cellular concepts, including frequency reuse and handoffs. AMPS is an analog cellular phone service that allows users to make voice calls within one country. AMPS has been improved to provide roaming between the US and other countries in late 1990. GSM (Chapter 9), IS-136, and IS-95 (Chapter 1, Section 1.2), on the other hand, comprises second-generation (2G) systems, which provide significant functional enhancements such as voice coding, digital modulation, forward error correction, and channel equalization. These systems provide digital mobile phone services that substantially strengthen fax, data, and messaging capabilities, and that allow users to roam in many countries.

3G systems are expected to offer better system capacity and higher data transmission speed to support wireless Internet access and wireless multimedia services (including audio, video, and images). To bridge

2G technologies to 3G technologies, EDGE and GPRS (Chapter 18) were introduced; they are typically referred to as 2.5G technologies. The initiation of 3G came from manufacturers, not operators. Work on 3G started around 1992, when ITU formed Task Group (TG) 8/1 working on FPLMTS which was later renamed IMT-2000 in 1996 or 1997. Work in TG 8/1 was accelerated in 1994, which involved government agents, manufacturers, and operators around the world. In 1996, NTT and Ericsson initiated 3G development. In 1997, the U.S. Telecommunications Industry Association (TIA) chose the CDMA technology for 3G. In 1998, ETSI also selected the CDMA technology for 3G. In the same year, Wideband CDMA (W-CDMA), cdma2000, and 3G time division duplexing (TDD) were developed by the Universal Mobile Telecommunications System (UMTS), TIA 45.5, and China/Europe, respectively. The 3G technology supports 144 Kbps bandwidth, with high-speed movement (e.g., in vehicles), 384 Kbps with pedestrian (e.g., on campus), and 2 Mbps for stationary (e.g., in buildings). The services will include high-quality voice, Internet/intranet access, and multimedia.

21.1 Paradigm Shifts in Third-Generation Systems

The progressive trend in the convergence of personal computing, networking, and wireless technologies will change the way we live forever. Wireless data transmission via mobile systems offers tremendous opportunities for technologists and entrepreneurs to provide their services at the right place and the right time. For wireline telecommunication in the United States, data traffic already exceeds voice traffic. It is anticipated that the same trend will be observed in mobile telecommunications. Based on the preceding discussion, the concepts of third-generation systems introduce two paradigm shifts:

- *The shift from voice-centric traffic to data-centric traffic demands a packet-based infrastructure instead of the traditional circuit-based infrastructure.* This new mobile core network architecture implies that cost of communications becomes distance-insensitive. Technical challenges for this paradigm shift include maintaining quality of services and improving protocols to support streaming traffic such as voice and video. To satisfy this paradigm shift, the GPRS network architecture, described in Chapter 18, was introduced to bridge 2G systems to 3G systems.

Furthermore, because the benefits of a single, worldwide, homogeneous, ubiquitous communications network outweigh all the challenges ahead, the trend is unstoppable. IS-41 and GSM MAP eventually will be merged to support worldwide roaming. It is also essential to strengthen mobile IP to support mobility functions such as seamless handoff.

■ *Data applications continue to evolve.* As a result, advanced application protocols and human interfaces become very crucial in practical applications. End users will demand the same capabilities whether from wireless or wireline services. The challenges of this paradigm shift are that the wireless network is bandwidth-constrained when compared to its wireline counterpart, and portable terminals are usually limited by practical size, weight, power consumption, and display constraints. To address this paradigm shift, the Wireless Application Protocol (WAP) and MExE, described in Chapter 19, proposes several technologies to support wireless data applications.

3G wireless communication requires a very broadband spectrum and fast data rate to support high-quality Internet access and multimedia services. Bandwidth, however, is always limited. Table 21.1 lists the existing spectrums used by the 2G systems and the new spectrum allocated for 3G. According to the table, only 25 percent (155 MHz out of 628 MHz) of the spectrum is newly created for terrestrial 3G usage. Since the 2G systems will eventually be upgraded into 3G, the 2G spectrums will be reused for 3G. Thus, the utilization of spectrum in different bands for 3G is essential. Furthermore, to use the resources more efficiently, better channel and source-coding techniques, such as space-time coding and grammar-

Table 21.1 Terrestrial Spectrum Allocation for 2G and 3G Systems

SPECTRUM	BANDWIDTH	SYSTEMS
800 MHz	50 MHz	AMPS, IS-95, IS-136
900 MHz	50 MHz	GSM-900
1500 MHz	48 MHz	Japan PDC
1700 MHz	60 MHz	Korean PCS
1800 MHz	150 MHz	GSM-1800
1900 MHz	120 MHz	PCS
2100 MHz	155 MHz	3G

based lossless data compression, are being developed for MPEG-4, with toll-quality voice at a data rate much lower than 8 Kbps.

To accommodate flexible 3G applications that are compatible with the existing Internet applications, significant efforts have been devoted to enhance portable handset capabilities, including the WAP with micro browser, and new man-machine interfaces, such as voice recognition.

21.2 W-CDMA and cdma2000

The CDMA-based 3G standards selected from numerous proposals to ITU have become the major stream for IMT 2000. In particular, W-CDMA and cdma2000 are two major proposals for third-generation systems. Even though both systems are CDMA-based, many distinguishing features can be identified, as listed in Table 21.2. For one, W-CDMA uses dedicated time division multiplexing (TDM) pilot signal, whereby channel estimation information is collected from another signal stream. This approach reduces the overall pilot power. In contrast, cdma2000 uses common code division multiplexing (CDM) pilot, whereby channel estimation information can be collected with the signal stream. W-CDMA does not need base station timing synchronization, whereas base station timing synchronization in cdma2000 can provide decreased latency and a reduced chance of dropping calls during soft handoff.

Since both W-CDMA and cdma2000 have been simultaneously adapted for the 3G standard, harmonization of these two systems becomes necessary to make IMT-2000 deployment successful. Two crucial events have significantly enhanced harmonization of W-CDMA and cdma2000. The first is Ericsson's acquisition of Qualcomm's infrastructure division, which resolved contention of intellectual property rights (IPR) between the two companies. The second event is the adoption of Operators Harmonization

Table 21.2 Comparison of W-CDMA and cdma2000

TECHNOLOGY	W-CDMA	CDMA2000
Chip Rate	4.096 MCps	3.6864 MCps
Forward Link Pilot Structure	Dedicated Pilot with TDM	Common Pilot with CDM
Base Station Timing Synchronization	Asynchronous	Synchronous
Forward Link Modes		A multicarrier mode capable of overlay onto IS-95 carriers

Group (OHG) recommendations by all major players. OHG has drawn its harmonization framework heavily from W-CDMA and cdma2000. The goals are:

- To provide the foundation for accelerated growth in the 3G millennium.

- To create a single integrated 3G CDMA specification and process from the separate W-CDMA and cdma2000 proposals being developed by Third-Generation Partnership Project (3GPP) and 3GPP2.

OHG's efforts have resulted in:

- A direct spread mode with 3.84 mega chip rate (MCps) for new frequency bands, and a multicarrier mode with 3.6864 MCps for operation overlaid to IS-95 signals.

- A CDM pilot added to the direct spread mode.

- A harmonized solution for SCDMA (a TDD mode third-generation system proposed by China).

The manufacturing community has agreed to cross-license intellectual property on fair, reasonable, and nondiscriminatory terms for 3G development. However, due to political reasons, the two chip rates and two synchronous and asynchronous systems (as listed in Table 21.3) are likely to coexist. Furthermore, the equipment suppliers have their own concerns on current markets and wireless technologies. Thus, it is likely that 3G harmonization cannot be achieved at the physical layer. Instead, more efforts will be spent on interoperability of higher layer protocols for W-CDMA and cdma2000, which results in higher costs with degraded performance.

The activities of the 3G development so far have focused on physical and MAC layers. From 13 ITU CDMA submissions, three radio modules (modes) were selected for 3G CDMA radio access:

Table 21.3 Harmonization Agreement of the 3G CDMA Modes

MODE	FDD (DS)	FDD (MC)	TDD
Chip Rate	3.84 MCps	3.6864 MCps	3.84 MCps
Common Pilot	CDM	CDM	To Be Determined
Dedicated Pilot	TDM	CDM	To Be Determined
Base Station Synchronization	Asynchronous/ Synchronous	Synchronous as cdma2000	To Be Determined

- Direct sequencing (DS) frequency division duplex (FDD) mode 1
- Multicarrier (MC) FDD mode 2
- Time division duplex (TDD) mode

The characteristics of the three modes are listed in Table 21.3. The DS mode will be based on the W-CDMA proposal, and the MC mode will be based on the cdma2000 proposal. The TDD mode is an unpaired band solution to better facilitate indoor cordless communications; it has been intensively studied in China. This mode provides asymmetric data services and is a potential low-cost solution. Note that two TDMA modes have also been selected as the 3G radio access: UWC-136 single-carrier (SC) and DECT frequency time (FT).

21.3 Improvements on Core Network

Harmonization for higher 3G layer protocols are still in progress. OHG has identified ANSI-41 (IS-41) (described in Chapter 5), GSM MAP, described in Chapters 11–14), and IP-based networks as three major modules of core networks for the 3G systems. Thus, 3G internetwork roaming will be an important task in 3G harmonization. All five radio access modes, described in the previous section, should fully support ANSI 41 and GSM MAP. An operator may select one or more radio modules together with one or more core network modules to implement a 3G system under the regulatory requirements.

Furthermore, network-related procedures are optimized to reduce the signaling traffic. We give an example in this section. To reduce the international roaming signaling traffic, 3GPP 23.119 specification proposed an approach to limit the signaling traffic between the visited mobile system and the home mobile system. This approach introduces a *gateway location register* (GLR) between the VLR/SGSN and the HLR. From the viewpoint of the VLR/SGSN at the visited network, the GLR is treated as the roaming user's HLR located at the home network. From the viewpoint of the HLR at the home network, the GLR acts as the VLR/SGSN at the visited network. (Note: to simplify our discussion, we ignore GPRS—i.e., the involvement of SGSN—from now on. A question in Section 21.10 will ask the reader to reproduce the GPRS procedures in Chapter 18, Section 18.5 with the involvement of GLR.)

The HLR and the GLR communicate through the D interface, shown in Chapter 10, Figure 10.1, where the GLR serves as the VLR. The VLR and the GLR also communicate through the D interface, but now the GLR is serving as the HLR. After the first registration, all subsequent registration operations in a visited network are performed locally between the VLRs and the GLR; the "remote" HLR is not involved. The GLR is physically located in the visited network and interacts with all VLRs in the visited network.

When a user roams to a visited network, the first registration is performed following the steps illustrated in Figure 21.1 and described here:

Step 1. When the VLR receives the registration request form the MS, it identifies the subscriber as a roamer and sends a **MAP_UPDATE_LOCATION** message to the GLR. The GLR does not find the profile of the user, and determines that the user is registering in this network for the first time. The GLR stores the VLR number and serving MSC number, and sends a **MAP_UPDATE_LOCATION** message to the HLR. In this message, the GLR address is used as the VLR number.

Step 2. The HLR performs the standard registration operation by treating the GLR as if it were the VLR.

Step 3. The HLR cancels the MS record at the old VLR (not shown in this figure) and sends the **MAP_INSERT_SUBSCRIBER_DATA** message to the GLR.

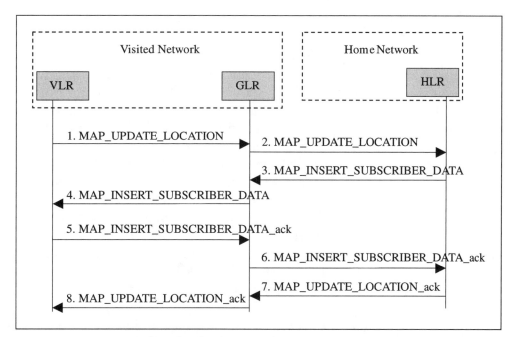

Figure 21.1 Message flow for the first registration with GLR.

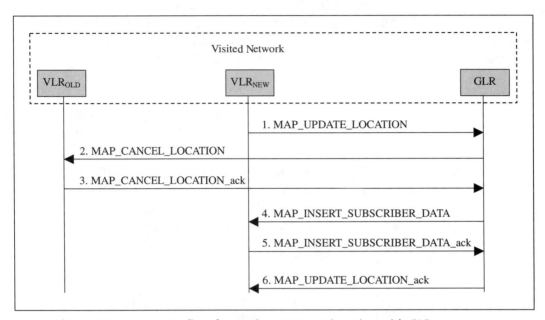

Figure 21.2 Message flow for a subsequent registration with GLR.

Step 4. The GLR stores the subscriber's information in the message and forwards the **MAP_INSERT_SUBSCRIBER_DATA** message to the VLR.

Steps 5–8. These steps acknowledge the messages in steps 1–4.

After the first registration, subsequent registrations are performed between the GLR and the VLRs, as shown in Figure 21.2. The procedure follows the standard GSM registration, but with the GLR serving as the HLR; that is, the GLR supplies the user profile of the MS to the new VLR and cancels the MS record from the old VLR.

When the roamer moves to another network (either the home network or a new visited network), the old visited network will remove the user record at the GLR. The procedure is illustrated in Figure 21.3. We assume that the user moves from the visited network back to the home network. The message flow in Figure 21.3 follows standard GSM registration/cancellation procedures, except that the HLR sends the **MAP_CANCEL_LOCATION** message to the GLR instead of the old VLR. The GLR transports the cancellation to the old VLR and deletes the MS record in the GLR.

For a mobile termination call, the procedure is similar to the one described in Chapter 11, Section 11.1.2, with the following exception:

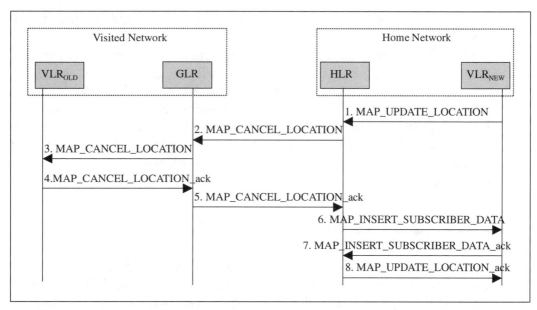

Figure 21.3 Message flow for the location cancellation with GLR.

In Figure 21.4, the HLR queries the location of the MS by sending the **MAP_PROVIDE_ROAMING_NUMBER** message to the GLR, and the GLR transports this message to the VLR. The VLR returns the MSRN, which is forwarded by the GLR to the HLR. Then the HLR continues the standard

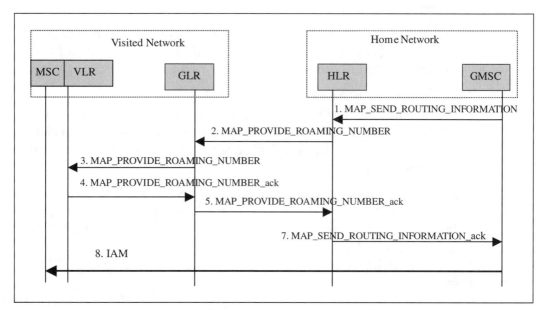

Figure 21.4 Message flow for mobile termination call with GLR.

GSM call termination procedure by sending the ISUP IAM message to set up the call.

Compared to the standard GSM procedure, the first registration with a GLR exchanges extra local messages, but reduces international signaling messages exchanged in each of the subsequent registrations. Mobile call termination using the GLR require additional local message exchanges. Call origination at the visited network is not affected by the presence of a GLR. It is clear that the GLR approach effectively reduces the signaling cost when the home network and the visited network are located in different countries.

21.4   Quality of Service in 3G

From the viewpoint of end users, QoS should be provided on an end-to-end basis. QoS attributes should be general but simple, and their number should be small. From the viewpoint of the network, QoS will be defined with a set of parameters. The 3G QoS control mechanism should (1) efficiently utilize resources based on the ability to dynamically change QoS parameters during a communication session, (2) interwork with current QoS schemes, and (3) present end-to-end QoS to the users with appropriate mapping. The end-to-end service on the application level uses the bearer services of the underlying networks, partitioned into three segments:

- The local bearer service provides a connection between terminal equipment (TE) and a mobile terminal (MT). A TE can be a PC or PDA connected to the 3G network through an MT.

- The 3G bearer service provides 3G QoS.

- An external bearer service provides the connection to the other party in the call. This bearer may utilize several network services (e.g., another 3G bearer service) connecting to the other party of the communication session.

The 3G bearer service consists of two parts. Over the radio interface, the *radio access bearer service* provides confidential transport of signaling and user data for moving users over the radio interface (between the MT and the core network). The *core network bearer service* utilizes a 3G backbone network service that covers layer 1 and layer 2 functionality (e.g., ATM or IP-based).

The *QoS classes* defined for mobile networks are very different from fixed networks due to the restrictions and limitations of the air interface. Based on delay sensitivity, four QoS classes have been defined for 3G (specifically, UMTS) traffic: conversational, streaming, interactive, and background. Conversational class is defined for the most delay-sensitive applications (traditional voice calls and VoIP), and the transfer delay is strictly limited. Streaming class is defined for one-way real time video/audio (e.g., video-on-demand). Both conversational and streaming classes will need better channel coding and retransmission to reduce the error rate in order to meet the required QoS.

Interactive and background classes are defined for delay-insensitive services. The interactive class is used for applications such as Telnet, interactive e-mail, and Web browsing. The background class is defined for activities such as FTP or the background downloading of e-mails. Among the traffic classes just listed, the conversational class is most delay-sensitive, and the background class is the most delay-insensitive.

In addition to the traffic classes, several QoS parameters have been defined in 3G TR 23.907, including maximum, minimum, and guaranteed bit rates; delivery order, maximum packet size, reliability, and so on. A major challenge for defining 3G QoS is compatibility among the QoS parameters defined for existing mobile networks (such as GPRS QoS described in Chapter 18) and the fixed network (such as the Internet). The QoS mapping for circuit-switched services between a 3G network and a 2G network (such as GSM) is easy. In 2G circuit-switched services, only channel type and bandwidth (number of utilized time slots) can vary. For handoff between 3G and 2G networks, only reliability, delay, and bandwidth are meaningful parameters.

As described in Chapter 18, many QoS parameters are defined in GPRS, requiring more complex mapping rules between a 3G network and a GPRS network. Consider Web browsing as an example. This 3G interactive-class application does not need to set the mean throughput class in GPRS. This application meets the GPRS reliability classes 1 and 2 for error-sensitive nonreal-time traffic that cannot cope with data loss or can only tolerate infrequent data loss. Furthermore, the application is mapped to GPRS delay classes 2–4 (i.e., from best-effort delivery to five-second mean transfer delay for 128 octets). For background download of files, the 3G QoS is mapped to GPRS reliability class 2 (unacknowledged GTP mode) and GPRS delay class 4 (best-effort).

For Internet applications, the 3G QoS should be mapped to Internet QoS definitions, and attributes for integrated services (IntServ) and differentiated services (DiffServ). The QoS parameters of these two Internet service types are controlled by the applications (i.e., the TE). These application-specific IP QoS parameters are mapped into packet QoS by a

3G gateway node at the border of the 3G core network. RSVP support of IntServ requires flow establishment and aggregation in the 3G packet core network. For DiffServ, 3G network QoS management inserts QoS profiles into packets.

21.5   Wireless Operating System for 3G Handset

Handset technologies play an important role in 3G service provisioning. Mobile operators cannot launch services without appropriate handset support. The number of 2G handsets has already exceeded the number of PCs. As cellular telephones become less expensive, they will continue to penetrate the consumer market very quickly and deeply. This trend will continue in 3G mobile communication only when the cost of handsets can remain reasonably low in spite of advances in technology.

In 2G circuit-switched mobile communications, the major service is voice, whereas 3G packet-switched mobile communication supports wideband, IP, and multimedia-based (or data-oriented) communication. It is expected that 3G handsets will be equipped with complicated functions and features to accommodate complex information access. Our experience with mobile service operation, however, indicates that most subscribers are not experts and are not willing to make the effort to understand complicated handset operations. As a result, a user-friendly customized handset design is essential.

In general, a 3G handset integrates the functions of both a 2G handset and a personal data assistant (PDA). To support such wireless multimedia devices, a sophisticated wireless operating system (OS) tailored for handset use is required. Since handsets are limited by their size, weight, and power consumption, the wireless OS should satisfy the following requirements:

- Unlike laptop computers that need several minutes to start up and access applications, the wireless OS for handsets should provide immediate access to applications.

- The wireless OS should be modular so that handsets for different purposes need to use only subsets of modules and can remove the unused modules, reducing the amount of software resident in the handsets.

- The wireless OS should support low-powered CPUs so that the battery life of the handset can be extended.

■ The 3G handset will be switched on and off. Thus, the wireless OS should be protected in a read-only-memory chip, which implies that the size of the OS will be very limited.

21.5.1 Wireless OS Examples

At least three major wireless OSs are available in the market:

Windows Consumer Electronics (WinCE) OS. Developed by Microsoft and carefully designed as a subset of the Windows NT OS system. WinCE satisfies the wireless OS requirements just described.

Casio and Siemens joined to develop the next-generation WinCE-enabled smart phones. They will have a 65K color screen and wireless Internet and multimedia capabilities, including video and quality digital audio.

EPOC OS. Developed by Psion for its communicator, organizer, and subnotebook products. Symbian, (a company formed by Nokia, Ericsson, and Motorola), uses EPOC as the wireless OS platform for next-generation handsets.

An example of an EPOC-enabled handset is Ercisson's R380, a fully featured smart phone for dual-band operation in a GSM network. It combines the function of a traditional mobile phone with those of a high-quality PDA. Among its features are support of a WAP browser, e-mail, a contact manager (phone numbers/e-mail/address book, etc.), handwriting recognition, and voice recognition for dialing/answering. The R380 is equipped with an IrDA port through which a PC can make a wireless connection.

PalmOS. Developed by 3Com's Palm Computing organizers, and aggressively designed to support wireless applications.

QUALCOMM has developed a PalmOS-enabled CDMA smart phone called PdQ. PdQ allows users to make calls, track appointments, catalog contact data, send/receive e-mails, and surf the Internet. Sony has licensed PalmOS to produce the next version of PalmOS for a wider range of devices, including smart phones.

It is unlikely that a single wireless OS standard will exist in the near future. Most handset manufacturers utilize multiple standards with interoperability among the various wireless operating systems.

Platforms such as WAP will be used to develop new applications for handsets. Robust voice and handwriting recognition technologies should be developed to support user interfaces for these services. Information

426 **Wireless and Mobile Network Architectures**

retrieval via handsets is expected to become much simpler through the optimization of those technologies. A key guideline is that the designs should follow user customs and habits. Furthermore, 3G handset development should be evaluated using criteria such as content retrieval capability, portability (weight, size, battery life), cost, performance, and the usefulness of the device when it is offline.

21.5.2 EPOC

We use EPOC as an example to illustrate the functionality of a wireless OS for devices such as smartphones and communicators. EPOC provides communication to the outside world through serial and sockets, dial-up, TCP/IP, and PC connect. The EPOC core consists of the following components: base, engine support, graphics, a system interface, and a graphical user interface (GUI), as described here:

Base component. Consists of a portable runtime system, kernel, file server, user library, and file server APIs; and delivers tools. EPOC's runtime system consists of E32 (kernel executive and server) with a kernel API for device drivers and F32 (bootstrap loader, file services, file system API, and ROM testing command shell). To install EPOC on a target device requires implementing a ROM that runs E32, F32, and the text shell.

The kernel executive is a privileged library with functions invoked by threads. It does not involve resource allocation. The kernel server is the highest-priority thread, handling requests with kernel-side resource allocation.

Engine support component. Provides APIs for data manipulation, an application architecture (for identifying programs to open data such as a file, an attachment, an embedded object, and so on), resource files and utilities, the standard C library, and text tools.

Graphics component. Provides a high-level GUI framework including drawing and user interaction, fonts, printing, views, and text entry.

Several wireless OS features distinguish EPOC from a traditional OS. For example, the EPOC kernel is lightweight in the sense that it requires only a small amount of code to run in privileged mode. The kernel supports preemptive multitasking, enabling context switching between threads to be done quickly. Also, EPOC R5 supports fixed processes that can be swapped much more quickly than nonfixed user processes. Finally, a power model is used by the kernel and device drivers to turn off devices and power sources when they are not active.

21.6   Third-Generation Systems and Field Trials

This section describe several 3G systems and field trials conducted by service provider and equipment vendors.

21.6.1   DoCoMo W-CDMA Field Trial

NTT DoCoMo has promoted W-CDMA experiments since 1996. The trial architecture is shown in Figure 21.5, which consists of mobile stations (MSs), a base transceiver station (BTS), and base station control equipment (MCC-SIM).

21.6.1.1   DoCoMo W-CDMA Mobile Station

Several MS types are specified in DoCoMo W-CDMA experiments. The Function Test Mobile Station is used for measurement and testing. It allows easy change of internal MS parameters and provides measured data (e.g., bit error rate, reception level, interference level, and delay

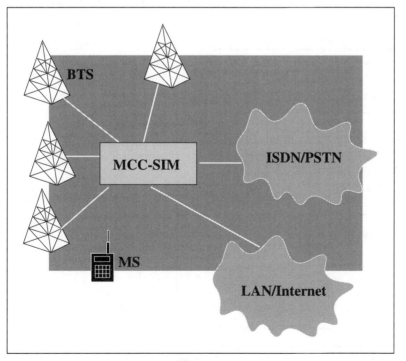

Figure 21.5   DoCoMo W-CDMA trial system.

Table 21.4 DoCoMo Experimental W-CDMA Mobile Stations

MODEL	FUNCTION TEST MS	SMALL TERMINAL 1	SMALL TERMINAL 2
Weight	10 Kg	2.5 Kg	130g
Max. TX Power	4.8W	0.8W	0.3W
Data Bit Rates	64–384 Kbps	64 Kbps	Voice Only

profile) to the data connection equipment. Small Mobile Terminal 1 supports data communications for indoor and outdoor experiments. Small Mobile Terminal 2 support speech communication. Some characteristics of these MSs are listed in Table 21.4. Several application-experiment terminal types are also specified, including visual phone, MPEG-4 video phone, mobile multimedia communicator, and mobile video Web phone. The W-CDMA MS hardware consists of four parts, as illustrated in Figure 21.6:

- High-gain and high-efficiency antenna.

- Radio transceiver with high-quality linear amplifier, high adjacent channel selectivity reception, and low-power consumption.

- Baseband signal processing with high integration and low power consumption.

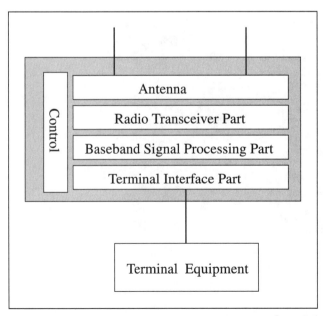

Figure 21.6 DoCoMo W-CDMA mobile station configuration.

■ Terminal interface part, which supports ISDN and Ethernet interfaces (possibly through infrared or bluetooth).

■ Control part, which performs traditional MS functions as well as multicall control and diversity (soft) handoff control.

The experimental MS uses a real-time OS called μI-TRON3 to control layer 2 and layer 3 tasks, as well as terminal interface. The MS also includes a user identification module (UIM) that has similar functionality to the GSM SIM.

21.6.1.2   Base Station Equipment

As shown in Figure 21.7, the base station equipment consists of a BTS and Mobile Communications Control Center-Simulator (MCC-SIM). The base station hardware was developed by Ericsson, Fujitsu, Lucent, NEC, and Matsushita, and supports the user plane and layer 1 of the control plane. A general-purpose operating system called VxWorks runs on this hardware platform. Through common system calls, an application program (AP) has been developed for layer 2 and layer 3 of the control plane. The BTS consists of modulation and demodulation equipment (MDE) and an

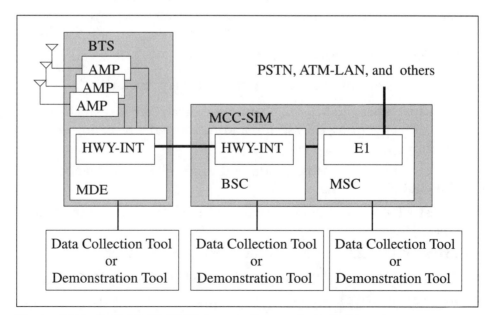

Figure 21.7 DoCoMo W-CDMA base station equipment.

amplifier (AMP). The MDE is responsible for radio signaling processing; an AMP provides transmission/reception amplification. Each sector has an AMP, and all AMPs connect to one MDE. The MCC-SIM consists of base station controller (BSC) and mobile switching center (MSC). The BSC is responsible for radio circuit control and *diversity connection*. Diversity refers to simultaneous connection between one MS and multiple BTSs (up to three). It is indicated that 50 percent of the calls should be supported by two-BTS diversity, and 5 percent of calls by three-BTS diversity. The BSC is responsible for selecting and combining uplink signals from multiple BTSs. Path selection/combination is required when an MS connects to multiple BTSs. The BTS and the MSC is connected by a 1.544 Mbps or 6.321 Mbps ATM transmission line through the A-bis interface. ATM AAL-2 is used for low-speed communication such as voice. AAL-5 is used for high-speed packet service. The highway interface (HWY-INT) of a BSC supports up to seven BTS connections. The MSC provides switching control, error control, and interfaces to analog telephone, an ISDN device, ATM-LAN, and PSTN. The packet processing rate of the MSC is about 10 Mbps. The E1 interface supports termination for voice, N-ISDN, and packet. Synchronization among nodes (i.e., BTS, BSC, and MSC) allows up to 5 ms error. Every node can connect to either a data collection tool or a demonstration tool. The data collection tool measures bit error rate and frame error rate characteristics, delay profiles, and data storage function. The demonstration tool provides display for transmission quality and the status of various controls. Both tools support real-time display.

21.6.1.3 Experiment Testing Items

The testing items of DoCoMo W-CDMA experiments include:

- To test whether the MS can acquire the perch (broadcast) channel code of neighboring cell/sector, and measure the receiving signal instantly.
- To test whether the MS can add and drop cells/sectors smoothly without interruption.
- To test ATM transmission efficiency for integration of various traffic types.
- To test sector and base station equipment configuration.
- To test layers 2 and 3 control signal protocol of air interface.
- To verify the RAKE combining function of the MS when signals from multiple paths are received.

- To investigate radio transmission characteristics of various data types.
- To verify the system capacity for subscribers.

The applications considered in the experiments included 8 Kbps high-quality voice, 384 Kbps–2Mbps packet transmission, ISDN unrestricted digital data, and so on. Testing for MS merits further discussion. The experiments conduct general test items and W-CDMA-specific items:

General MS test items. On the transmission side, the test items include transmission frequency, maximum transmission power, adjacent channel leakage power, modulation accuracy, transmission inter-modulation, and so on. These items are measured by a modulation analyzer with receiver function of 4.096 MHz bandwidth. On the reception side, the test items include reception sensitivity, adjacent channel selectivity, reception intermodulation sensitivity, and so on.

W-CDMA-specific test items. The code domain power measurement charts separate channel power. The fast-closed loop transmission power control test sends layer 1 signal at the downlink to control the transmission power. Then a spectrum analyzer measures this control characteristic.

Note that the chip rate of the DoCoMo W-CDMA system is 4.096 MCps. As described in Section 21.2, this chip rate is no longer consistent with the FDD(DS) chip rate harmonized by OHG.

21.6.2 Lucent cdma2000 System

In the 3G road map of Lucent, the IS95A system has evolved into IS95B, cdma2000 3G-1X, and then cdma2000 3G-3X. IS95B provides 20 percent capacity increase over IS95A by handoff improvement. In the Lucent cdma2000 3G-1X implementation, new software has been installed. Furthermore, the 3G-1X CDMA channel unit (CCU-1X) has been installed to handle both IS-95 cdmaOne and 3G-1X traffic simultaneously. CCU-1X can be mixed with the existing cdmaOne CCU-20 cards. Both cdmaOne and 3G-1X can coexist on the same carriers and sectors; there is no need to change footprint, real estate, power, or antenna. Compared with IS-95A, cdma2000 3G-1X has doubled voice capacity, improved error correction and power control, lengthened mobile battery life, and provided faster pilot search. cdma2000 3G-3X significantly improves packet data transmission. It provides advanced MAC, multimedia QoS, and simultaneous voice and data. Some characteristics of 3G-1X and 3G-3X are listed in

Table 21.5 Characteristics of cdma2000 3G-1X and 3G-3X

MODEL	3G-1X	3G-3X
Carrier Bandwidth	1.25 MHz	3.75 MHz
Ubiquitous Data Rate	144 Kbps	384 Kbps
Peak Data Rate	307.2 Kbps	1.0368 Mbps

Table 21.5; Figure 21.8 illustrates the Lucent cdma2000 architecture. In this architecture, these three Flexent base station (BS) models have been developed:

- The Flexent microcell is a compact and lightweight BS with flexible installation, such as pole mount and wall mount. It operates at 10W at 800 MHz and 8W at 1.9 GHz, and is aimed for in-building services, RF hole filling, and hot spots. The Flexent microcell is compatible with existing networks, and supports one carrier for IS-95A, IS-95B (up to 40 channel elements), or 3G-1X (up to 128 channel elements).

- The Flexent CDMA module cell upgrades the Flexent microcell by accommodating next-generation CDMA radio components. With up

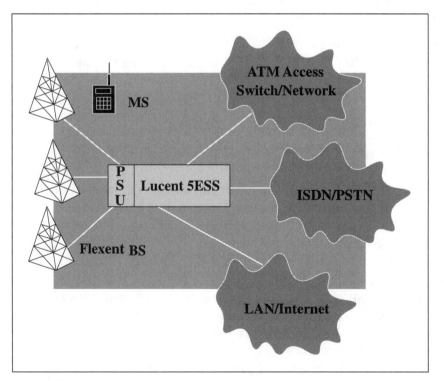

Figure 21.8 Lucent cdma2000 architecture.

to 16W–20W power consumption, it supports three IS-95A or 3G-1X carriers per sector. Every CCU-20 channel card supports up to 40 logical channel elements per carrier per sector for cdmaOne (IS-95). Every CCU-1X channel card supports up to 128 logical channel elements per carrier per sector for 3G-1X. The Flexent module cell can also accommodate 3G-3X radio when it is available.

■ Flexent CDMA MicroMini 5100 BS supports up to two carriers/three sectors, which operates at 16W for both 800 MHz and 1.9 GHz. The baseband unit (BBU) is separated from the radio frequency unit (RFU). One BBU can support three RFUs and up to six CCUs.

The 5ESS packet switch unit (PSU) connects to BS through frame relay. With wireless data IWF, the 5ESS PSU connects to dual LAN to provide Internet access.

21.7 Other Trial Systems

This subsection describes three 3G trial systems developed by Nortel, Ericsson, and Motorola. Figure 21.9 illustrates the Nortel W-CDMA trial system. This system operates at 1920–1940 MHz (uplink) and 2110–2130

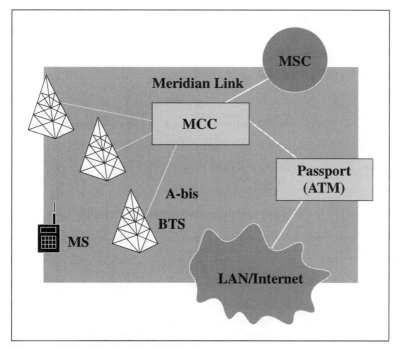

Figure 21.9 Nortel W-CDMA trial system.

MHz (downlink). The base transceiver station (BTS) consists of six power amplifiers. The power of every sector in the BTS is 20W. A sector is allocated one or two 5 MHz carriers. The mobile communication control center (MCC) consists of a *radio network controller* (RNC) and an ATM switch. The RNC can connect up to three BTSs over the A-bis interface. The MCC ATM switch supports ISDN and OC-3 interfaces. The trial system connects to a Nortel GSM network and PSTN through a Meridian CTI link (ISDN interface to MSC). The MCC connects to the IP network through an ATM backbone. The MSs used in this system were developed by Panasonic. The terminals can support an 8.8 Kbps voice handset, a 64 Kbps PCMCIA card, or a video phone. The services supported by this system include 8.8 Kbps voice, 64 Kbps circuit-switched data, and 384 Kbps packet-switched data. Figure 21.10 illustrates Nortel W-CDMA voice communication terminal prototype. Figure 21.11 illustrates Nortel W-CDMA card type terminal prototype. Figure 21.12 illustrates the Ericsson W-CDMA trial system, which operates in the same frequency bands as the Nortel system. The system consists of three BTSs and one RNC and MSC running on W-CDMA operations system (WOS). Every BTS can support up to six sectors, where every sector is allocated one or two 5 MHz carriers.

Figure 21.10 Nortel W-CDMA voice communication terminal prototype (by courtesy of Nortel).

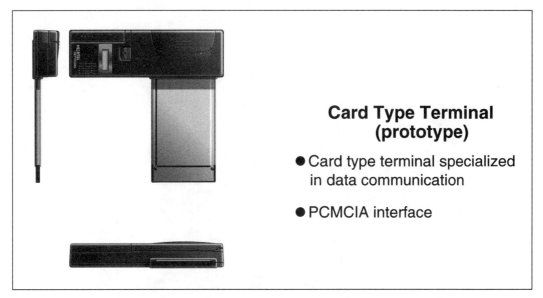

Figure 21.11 Nortel W-CDMA card type terminal prototype (by courtesy of Nortel).

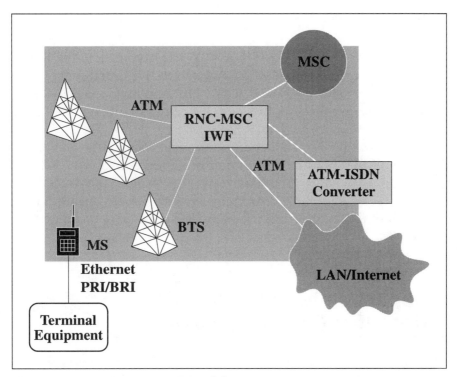

Figure 21.12 Ericsson W-CDMA trial system.

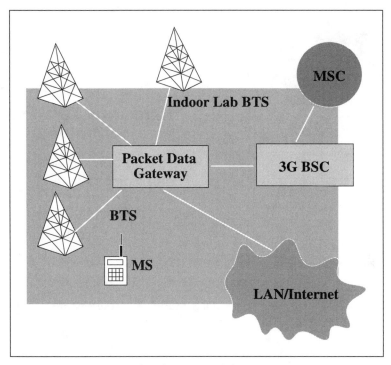

Figure 21.13 Motorola cdma2000 trial system.

The output RF power of each sector is 20W. A BTS connects to the RNC using the pre-Iub interface. The RNC connects to the MSC using the pre-Iu interface. Data are transferred among BTS, RNC, and MSC via ATM. The services include 8 Kbps voice; 64, 128, and 384 Kbps circuit-switched data; and 472 Kbps packet-switched data.

Figure 21.13 shows the Morotola cdma2000 trial system. The Motorola system consists of three outdoor BTSs and one indoor BTS. The BTSs are connected to a packet data gateway (PDG) through ATM AAL2 and AAL5 interfaces. The PDG communicates with the BSC using ATM AAL5. Through Ethernet, the PDG connects to IP network experiments of IP-based services.

21.8   Impact on Manufacture and Operator Technologies

This section describes the impact of third-generation mobile services on the manufacture and operator technologies.

21.8.1   Impact on Infrastructure Technologies

Due to the concerns about current markets, the strength of certain technologies and competition strategies, compromises have been made among the infrastructure vendors for 3G development. The arguments for W-CDMA and cdma2000, described in Section 21.2, provide a good example.

In building the 3G packet-switching infrastructure, quality of service (QoS) for data transmission is one of the most important issues. This is particularly true for applications such as wireless voice over IP (VoIP), described in Chapter 16. In the 2G circuit-switched infrastructure, QoS can be assured because a call is typically assigned a fixed amount of resources throughout the communication session. In packet-switching, on the other hand, reliable connections with large bandwidth, minimized RF bit error rate, dynamic channel allocation, and smooth handoffs are desirable. Dynamic resource allocation is required to assure different data rates for different applications with required QoS. Fast data session setup and release are necessary to allow users to retrieve and send data conveniently. The 3G QoS issues were discussed in Section 21.4.

To effectively utilize the radio channels in 3G, it is desirable to develop a vocoder with a low bit rate (for capacity) but with high performance (for voice quality). Advanced data compression techniques for lossy compression (for video, image, graphical, and audio objects) and lossless compression (for text and binary objects) are also essential. Since 3G air interface has significant improvement in bandwidth, reliable packet routing and low cost backbone (namely fiber) equipment is needed to handle the massive amount of data.

A knowledge-based 3G core network should be developed to utilize transfer techniques such as compression, caching, and prefetching. For example, servers in the network will cache and supply local content. "Data warehouses" in 3G core network enable corporate customers to query databases without investing in additional servers of their own. This inclusion makes the network intelligent. Furthermore, the network solution should provide a service platform capable of quickly deploying new services for end users (enterprise). The solutions include WAP and MExE, described in Chapter 19. To support global roaming, 2G mobility management should be optimized, as described in Section 21.3.

21.8.2   Impact on Mobile Operators

3G is an emerging technology driven by the equipment suppliers, instead of by the push from customers. This increases the risk faced by mobile operators. The operators want the best technologies with low cost, low risk, and high performance. However, there is no assurance of 3G infrastructure cost from manufacturers, and no guarantee of 3G satisfaction from users. To quote William C. Y. Lee, "The operators have no choice but to take it."

A great challenge of 3G development for the operators is to select technical parameters so that their 2G systems can evolve toward 3G services to the greatest extent possible. For example, to evolve cdmaOne networks into 3G, the operators should consider whether cdma2000 3G-1X should be deployed today; they need to evaluate whether cdma2000 will be a technical winner for 3G; they need to forecast whether the Asia-Pacific market will be a large one for cdmaOne in the near future; finally, they must estimate the transition cost to cdma2000.

To evolve IS-136 and GSM networks into 3G, the operators should: consider whether GPRS or EDGE will be the right interim step toward 3G; evaluate whether W-CDMA will be a low-risk system once fully developed; estimate the cost to transition from GSM to W-CDMA; and evaluate whether to consider cdma2000.

As we have emphasized several times, the key feature of 3G is its capability to deliver broadband and multimedia services, in addition to the 2G services such as voice, messaging, and low-speed data. In 2G, limited revenue streams are possible because mobile service providers are the only business players, and so can be "isolated" from the outside world. On the other hand, even though delivery of voice-based information remains the major business in the initial stage, data transmission support for Internet and multimedia applications involving content providers is essential to 3G network operation. Multiple revenue streams will emerge because mobile networks will open to content providers. Service cost will experience revolutionary change from the conventional 2G charge on voice delivery. This aspect was already partially addressed from the technical viewpoint when we discussed the GPRS charging model in Chapter 18, Section 18.6. From a business perspective, by integrating contents into wireless services, many players will share the revenue from individual calls and operations. The traditional voice-orientated billing process has left network operators with inflexible billing and an inadequate customer support infrastructure. Typical metered-billing systems will become inapplicable. A University of California at Berkeley study concluded that people would pay to avoid metered billing for data services. Thus, a billing model for customers must be flexible. For example, we expect that corporate customers will accept complex billing for lower costs, while individual customers will require simple and predictable billing.

Costs must be reduced if data transmission is to attract customers to wireless multimedia services that involve large-volume data transmission. The consumers are demanding fair price for fair values based on their experience with existing wireline Internet services. For voice delivery, charges for wireless service have been significantly reduced to be competitive to wireline service. Customers may expect the same business model for wireless data; thus, reduced profit margins are necessary, and network operators must seek operation efficiency to be competitive. For example, network operators will be less motivated to provide subsidies to PDA-based 3G handsets. Driven by the need to reduce costs, the process of subsidy elimination is already taking place in the United States.

21.9 Summary

This chapter described the development of the third-generation (3G) mobile network. The 3GPP activities for W-CDMA and the 3GPP2 activities for cdma2000 are based on the keynote speeches by William C. Y. Lee [Lee99b] and L.-N. Lee [Lee99a]. The specification of the gateway location register is given in [3GP99a]. The QoS for 3G (specifically UMTS) is defined in [3GP99b]. Details of wireless OS products are described in [Mob00] and [Her98]. Details of EPOC can be found in [Sym99]. The NTT DoCoMo W-CDMA field trial documents can be found in [DoC98]. The progress of 3G trial systems can be obtained from the Web sites of individual vendors. The Berkeley survey on data service can be found in [Wig98]. All Third-Generation Partnership Project activities and documents are available from the Web sites www.3GPP.org and www.3GPP2.org.

A small group of people have already started working on fourth-generation (4G) systems. Though their objectives have yet to be defined, unlike the 3G vendor-driven approach, most operators feel that the development of 4G systems should be public-interest driven. That is, the operators will listen to users and instruct the vendors to develop systems that fit customers' needs.

21.10 Review Questions

1. Compare W-CDMA and cdma2000 in terms of the pilot signal structure and base station synchronization.

2. Reimplement the GPRS procedures described in Chapter 18, Section 18.5, with the involvement of GLR.

3. Design an architecture and location update procedure that integrates IS-41 and GSM MAP.

4. In what situation will GSM operators use GLR in their networks?

5. What kind of information should be stored in the GLR? Are the fault-tolerance procedures described in Chapter 11 affected when GLR is introduced?

6. Show how to map the QoS parameters from 3G to GPRS for VoIP, as described in Chapter 16.

7. Suppose that an AMPS operator would like to migrate its network to 3G directly. Which technology should be chosen? W-CDMA, cdma2000, or some third alternative?

8. What are the criteria for evaluating 3G handset design?

9. Most 3G system trials consider three BTSs. Is three the right number of BTSs for the trials?

10. What are the differences between the W-CDMA trial systems by Nortel and Ericsson?

Paging Systems

Traditional paging is a one-way, personal wireless alerting/messaging system. The first paging system was developed by Charles F. Neergard, a radio engineer who, while hospitalized, could not tolerate the constant, loud-volume paging of doctors in the hospital. In recent years, paging service has become popular. The largest paging industry today is in the Asia-Pacific region. Information delivered in a paging system can be one of the following four types:

Alert tone. The receiver is a *tone pager* with a dedicated telephone number. When the number is dialed, the pager is triggered. The advantage of tone paging is that it utilizes a small amount of air time to generate tone-type messages. However, there are only a limited number (typically four) of alert tones that can be used to identify the callers. While it is technically feasible to generate many different tones, most users cannot remember a large number of distinct tones.

Voice message. In some tone paging systems, a voice message may be transmitted after the beep. The receiver is a *voice pager* that can receive up to several minutes of voice messages. However, speech consumes large quantities of air time, and may not be cost-effective for some public paging systems. Some voice paging systems utilize the spare capacity of existing cellular networks for the nonreal-time (offline) transmission. In this offline transmission, messages are typically delivered within minutes.

Digit string. The receiver is a *numeric pager*. The pager has a small LCD screen to display the digit string. Typically, the string is the telephone number of the caller. The string can also be a coded message. This coded message is generated by the paging center from the request of the caller, and the message is decoded by a codebook built into the pager. This type of paging is efficient in air-time usage, much like tone paging. Numeric paging was introduced in the early 1980s, and was the most popular form of paging in the mid-1990s. Eventually, numeric paging will be replaced by alphanumeric paging to be described next.

Text strings. The receiver is an *alphanumeric pager*, which has a fairly large screen to display several text strings. Alphanumeric paging was introduced in the late 1980s. Since the caller needs special input devices or a special input procedure with a regular phone set, alphanumeric paging was not as popular as numeric paging in the mid-1990s. Recently, paging service providers began to offer various input methods (such as PDA, operator attendant, and e-mail input) to eliminate the need for special input devices. Consequently, alphanumeric paging is becoming more popular than numeric paging.

Depending on the paging system, the paging process itself can be manual or automatic. In a manual paging system, the caller sends a message to the paging operator via a telephone call. The operator then delivers the message to the pager through the paging network. In Taiwan, many paging companies utilize manual systems to deliver texts to alphanumeric pagers. In an automatic paging system, a paging terminal automatically processes incoming requests and delivers the messages to the pagers. This chapter focuses on automatic paging.

22.1 Paging Network Architecture

Figure 22.1 illustrates an example of the paging network architecture. The network consists of six basic elements.

User terminal equipment (input device). The caller sends messages using terminal equipment—a telephone handset, a computer with modem, or specific input device. The alert tone and the numeric messages are typically generated from telephone handsets and are delivered through the PSTN; the alphanumeric messages are generated

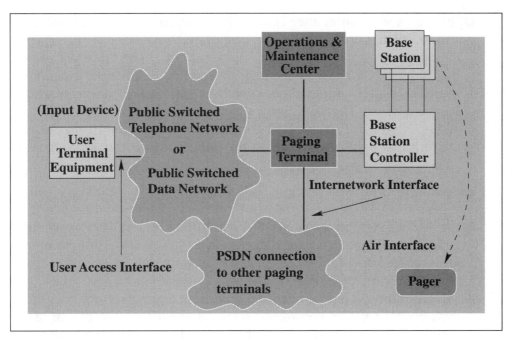

Figure 22.1 Example of the paging network architecture.

by computers or telephone handsets through the operator of a paging terminal, and are delivered to the paging network through the PSDN.

Paging terminal. Through the user access interface, the messages are sent to the paging terminal. A high-capacity paging terminal is capable of supporting more than 1 million pagers, and is typically connected to a central office of the PSTN through T1 or E1 trunks. A high-capacity paging terminal can support in excess of 1900 input lines. It may also connect to other paging terminals, with the interconnected paging terminals communicating via an internetwork interface. The paging terminal maintains a customer database that contains information (such as pager number, pager code, and types of message) necessary to alert the individual pager and the information for billing. Based on the destination pager's record in the customer database, the paging terminal may deliver the message to its base station controllers or forward the message to other paging terminals. A voice message can be converted into text for an alphanumeric pager. The paging terminal may store the message in a mailbox with the capacity for several hundred hours of voice storage.

The paging terminal can be maintained (e.g., to remove or install cards) locally or remotely when the system is in operation.

Operation and maintenance center. The operation, administration, and maintenance functions of a paging network are conducted by the operations and maintenance center (OMC). The OMC accesses the customer database of the paging terminal to add new customer records, delete terminated customer records, collect billing information, and so on. The OMC may also page the customers through the paging terminal. Typical OMC commands include read (from the paging terminal database), write (to the paging terminal database), and alert (a specific pager).

Base station controller. A base station consumes high power when transmitting a paging signal, and is in low-power mode when it is idle. The services of an alerted pager may be limited to specific geographical areas smaller than the areas covered by the paging terminal. A base station controller links the paging terminal to the base stations by powering up the base stations.

If the radio channel is shared by different paging service providers, then the base station controllers must be coordinated so that at most one paging signal is transmitted in the air at a time. In *simulcast paging*, the paging signal is sent to multiple paging transmitters simultaneously. In *transmitter sequencing*, the paging signal is sent to multiple paging transmitters sequentially. Although transmitter sequencing does not use air time efficiently (more time is required to communicate with a pager), it may be required when simulcasting from two transmitters creates a region where the pager cannot receive reliable data from either transmitter.

Base station. Base stations can be designed for two-way voice, although most of them are for one-way paging. Three transmission technologies are available to deliver the messages from the paging terminal to the base stations: leased telephone lines, PSDN (X.25), or satellite-based networks. Satellite communications technology is typically used between the paging terminal and dispersed base stations, but not between the base stations and the pagers.

Base stations broadcast the message to the pager over radio links. The radio path between a base station and its pagers can be dedicated paging channels, FM radio, or subcarriers of TV stations. In the last case, a signal is superimposed on the normal TV or radio channel, which does not interfere with the normal TV broadcast. The signal is extracted by the pager to obtain the paging message.

Base stations have high transmitter power of hundred watts to kilowatts in order to penetrate walls of buildings, and high antennas for large coverage areas. Strong one-way radio transmission allows low-complexity, low-power-consumption paging receivers.

In simulcasting, the messages from the paging terminal may arrive at the base stations asynchronously because the distances from the paging terminal to the base stations may not be the same. Different time lag values or *audio equalizers* are used at the base stations to synchronize message reception.

Pager. A pager consists of four basic components: a receiver, a decoder, control logic, and a display, as illustrated in Figure 22.2. The receiver is tuned to the same RF frequency as the base station to receive and demodulate the paging signals. The decoder decodes the binary information, identifies the code for the pager and rejects messages for other pagers. A pager may share the same code with other pagers for group paging, or it may be assigned multiple page codes (typically up to four) for different paging functions. The control logic provides service features and operation functions, such as *duplicate message* detection (to ensure that the repeated messages are not stored in memory), *message locking* (to ensure that the selected messages are not overwritten), *message freeze* (to keep the current message on the screen for reading), multiple *alerting modes* (such as audible tone, visual flashing, or silent vibrating), and so on.

A pager is typically powered by a single battery. Battery-saving techniques are used to conserve power by periodically switching the pager into a low-power mode. When the pager is off, stored messages are retained in nonvolatile memory.

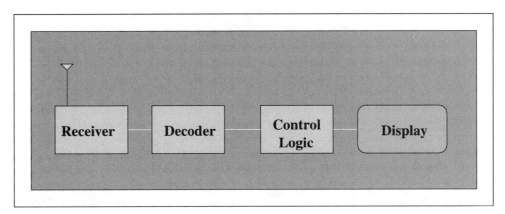

Figure 22.2   Pager architecture.

22.2   User Access Interface

The caller sends the paging request to the paging terminal through a user access interface. Protocols for this interface include analog trunk protocols and digital protocols. We describe two digital protocols, Telocator Alphanumeric Input Protocol (TAP) and Telocator Message Entry Protocol (TME), for alphanumeric paging.

22.2.1   Telocator Alphanumeric Input Protocol (TAP)

In TAP, the caller prepares the pages to be sent in advance, reducing air time consumed by online text creation. To send the message, the input device dials the paging terminal's number. After the line is connected, the caller (input device) and the paging terminal exchange messages, as described here (the characters between the symbols "<" and ">" are ASCII control codes):

Msg1 (caller→paging terminal). The input device sends a carriage return:

$$\text{Msg1} =''< CR >''$$

and repeats the message at a two-second interval until the paging terminal replies. If the paging terminal does not reply after three repetitions, the paging request fails.

Msg2 (paging terminal→caller). Within one second of receipt of Msg1, the paging terminal requests the input device to provide the pager ID by sending the sequence:

$$\text{Msg2} =''ID =< CR >< LF >''$$

where $< LF >$ is the line-feed symbol.

Msg3 (caller→paging terminal). In response, the input device sends a string:

$$\text{Msg3} =''< ESC >< SST >< PPPPP >''$$

to the paging terminal. The escape character, $< ESC >$, indicates that the paging information will be sent in automatic dump mode. In the substring, $< SST >$, the first two alphanumeric characters, "SS", represent the type of service. For example, the combination "SS = PG" means that the information will be sent as a pair of two fields, where field 1 contains the pager ID and field 2 contains the message. The last character, "T", represents the type of input devices. For example, IXO or PETs devices are in the category "$T = 1$". The (optional) six digits "$< PPPPP >$" comprise the password of the input device, which may be interpreted as a caller ID or a system entry key.

Msg4 (paging terminal→caller). When the paging terminal receives Msg3, one of the following three actions occurs:

- If the request is accepted, an acknowledgment is sent to the input device:

$$\text{Msg4} =" < CR >< ACK >< CR >"$$

- If the format of Msg3 is not correct, the paging terminal will request retransmission by sending a negative acknowledgment message:

$$\text{Msg4} =" < CR >< NAK >< CR >"$$

- If the paging terminal is not available to handle the paging request, the request is rejected by a forced disconnect message:

$$\text{Msg4} =" < CR >< ESC >< EOT >< CR >"$$

where $< EOT >$ is the end-of-transmission symbol.

Msg5 (paging terminal→caller). If Msg4 is a positive acknowledgment, the paging terminal will prepare for message input and, when it is ready, will send a go-ahead sequence to the input device:

$$\text{Msg5} =" < CR > [p < CR >"$$

Msg6 (caller→paging terminal). The input device starts to send the paging information to the paging terminal. The information is partitioned into data blocks of 256 bytes. Every block consists of three control characters, a message text of length up to 250 characters, and a three-character checksum. For illustration, we assume that the service type is "PG1" and the paging information is partitioned into two data blocks; that is, two transmissions are required to deliver the message text. Then the first block is delivered in the following format:

$$\text{Msg6} =" < STX > Pager\_ID < CR > Text < CR > Cksum < ETB >"$$

where the control character $< STX >$ represents the start transmission symbol, and the control character $< ETB >$ is used as a block terminator if the transaction is continued into the next block. *Pager_ID* is a string of ASCII digits to identify the destination pager, *Text* is a part of the paging message, and *Cksum* is the three-character checksum.

Msg7 (paging terminal→caller). After receiving Msg6, one of the following actions is taken:

- If the transmission is correct, a positive acknowledgment is sent back to the input device:

$$\text{Msg7} =" < Message\_Sequence >< CR >< ACK >< CR >"$$

- If a transmission or checksum error occurs, the following negative acknowledgment is sent to request the input device to resend Msg6:

$$\text{Msg7} =" < Message\_Sequence >< CR >< NAK >< CR >"$$

Note that *Message_Sequence* is optional. In some systems, this field may be included only in the last response message (i.e., Msg10) before disconnection.

Msg8 (caller→paging terminal). If the input device sends the last block, the message is of the form:

$$\text{Msg8} =" < STX > Pager\_ID < CR > Text < CR > Cksum < EXT >"$$

where $< EXT >$ indicates that Msg8 is delivering the last piece of the paging information.

Msg9 (paging terminal→caller). When the paging terminal receives Msg8, one of three situations may occur. The first two situations are the same as those of Msg7. The last situation occurs when the transmission violates a system rule; for example, the destination pager cannot be paged. Then Msg8 is abandoned using the following replied message:

$$\text{Msg9} =" < Message\_Sequence >< CR >< RS >< CR >"$$

The abandoned reason is given in *Message_Sequence*.

Msg 10 (caller→paging terminal). If Msg9 is of type "$< ACK >$" or "$< RS >$", the input device completes the transmission by sending:

$$Msg10 =" < EOT > < CR >"$$

Msg11 (paging terminal→caller). The paging terminal breaks the connection by sending:

$$Msg11 =" < Message\_Sequence > < CR > < ESC > < EOT > < CR >"$$

where *Message_Sequence* reports the degree of acceptability of the information received on this service.

After the paging terminal sends a message, a timer of at least four seconds is set (for Msg2, the timer is eight seconds). Similarly, a timer of at least 10 seconds is set for the input device after it sends a message. The connection is terminated after any timer expiration.

22.2.2 Telocator Message Entry Protocol (TME)

TME is the data input protocol of the Telocator Data Protocol (TDP), which is considered a successor to the TAP protocol. TME relaxes the 7-bit, even-parity TAP coding format, and allows unrestricted 8-bit data transfer. It also relaxes the TAP conventional short ASCII text messages by provisioning for long messages of text or binary data (e.g., e-mail with attached files, spreadsheets, and database information). TME extends the TAP one-way paging to two-way communications. It also provides new service features such as *priority paging* (to indicate that a request is a priority or emergency page to be sent immediately), *deferred paging* (to send a page at a particular time of day), *periodic paging* (to send a page periodically until a cancel message is received), *message forwarding*, and *message deletion* (e.g., to cancel periodic paging).

TME follows the OSI model, except that the presentation and session layers are not required. TCP/IP provides the recommended lower layer (the network layer and below) protocols for TME, although other protocols such as X.25 can also be used to support the TME application layer. When the input device requests connection to the paging terminal in the TCP/IP solution, it addresses TCP port number 4076. This is automatically done by the socket interface port number to uniquely identify itself as the client application.

The TME application layer is specified by the Remote Operations Service Element (ROSE). All TME operations are defined using the ASN.1 notation and Packed Encoding Rules. There are ten basic TME operations, three of which are described here:

- The `login` operation establishes a session connection between the input device and the paging terminal. This operation takes the caller password as an optional argument. This password is required when operations such as `deleteOp` for deleting a paging request or `dir` for listing the messages (which have been sent to or from the subscriber's account) currently in the system are to be performed in the session.

- The `send` operation sends a message from the input device to the paging terminal. The message consists of an envelope and the message content to be delivered. The paging terminal forwards only the message content to the destination pager. The data can be transparent, tone-only, numeric, alphanumeric or 8-bit Wireless Message Format (WMF) data.

- The `logout` operation terminates a communication session. This operation may be issued by the request of the input device or the system operator, or as a result of the expiration of the inactivity timer or the session timer. The session can also be terminated if situations such as security violation or resource shortage occur.

22.3   Intersystem Interface

To extend paging service coverage, paging terminals can be connected to form paging terminal networks. To receive *intersystem paging* services, the pager must keep the paging terminal updated about its location. This information specifies the group of paging terminals to receive the paging requests and is stored in the customer database of the paging terminal. Several proprietary protocols, such as Glenayre Data Link Module (DLM) protocol and Spectrum Data Link Handler (DLH) protocol, have been developed for paging terminal networks. However, two paging terminals using different protocols cannot talk to each other, so network paging gateways are needed to perform protocol conversions. Worldwide, several hundred gateways are used to connect the paging terminal networks.

An industry standard protocol called Telocator Network Paging Protocol (TNPP) has been developed for paging terminal connections. TNPP is a point-to-point communication protocol that can be built on top of TCP/IP networks. To move paging request data from the source to the destination in a TNPP network, a routing algorithm is required, although routing of paging requests is not covered in the TNPP specifications. The DLH network is based on the same point-to-point philosophy. In contrast, the DLM network uses a token-passing protocol, whereby every paging terminal is connected to a DLM, and a token is passed around the DLMs. Only the DLM that grasps the token can transmit the paging request data; all the other DLMs listen, and the destination DLMs read the data from the network and pass the data to their paging terminals.

A TNPP packet has a 4-byte source address and a 4-byte destination address. It uses a 2-byte sequence number to distinguish the new and the retransmitted packets. A 2-byte *inertia counter* is used to limit the number of nodes visited by the packet so that the packet will not travel in the network forever.

Like TAP, TNPP is an ASCII-oriented protocol. After a packet delivery, the destination node may reply with one of the four characters to the source node:

- "$< ACK >$": The delivery is successful.
- "$< NAK >$": An error occurs; the packet must be resent.
- "$< CN >$": The destination address is invalid; the packet is cancelled.
- "$< RS >$": The destination node cannot process the packet.

Both the source and the destination nodes can send packets to each other at the same time.

TNPP can be used for satellite communications between the paging terminals. In this application, however, the destination paging terminal cannot acknowledge the receipt of information in TNPP satellite communications. To provide reliable satellite transmission, a retransmission technique is used to transmit multiple copies of the message to the destination.

22.4 Air Interface

Several signaling formats have been used in the paging air interface. The Post Office Code Standardization Advisory Group (POCSAG) was initiated by the British post office during 1970. Many paging systems are based on this protocol. In early 1990, several high-speed protocols became available, including European Radio Message System (ERMES), approved by ETSI; FLEX, developed by Motorola; and Advanced Paging Operations Code (APOC), developed by Philips Telecom. We describe POCSAG and ERMES in this section.

22.4.1   POCSAG

POCSAG was designed as a one-frequency, one-operator paging network that cannot be extended for multinetwork operation. The POCSAG coding format can accommodate 2 million pagers. The original format was specified to operate at 512 bps. Without modifying the coding format, POCSAG can be operated at 1200 bps, and up to 2400 bps for some applications. As illustrated in Figure 22.3, the POCSAG coding format consists of a 576-bit preamble and one or more 544-bit batches. The preamble is a string of an alternating "1010..." pattern used to identify the POCSAG signal. The decoder of the pager utilizes the preamble to synchronize with the data stream.

Each 544-bit batch consists of one 32-bit frame-synchronization codeword and eight 64-bit frames. The frame-synchronization codeword has a unique bit pattern used to identify the beginning of a batch. Every frame consists of two 32-bit codewords. A codeword can be an address, a message, or an idle pattern. As shown in Figure 22.3, an *address codeword*

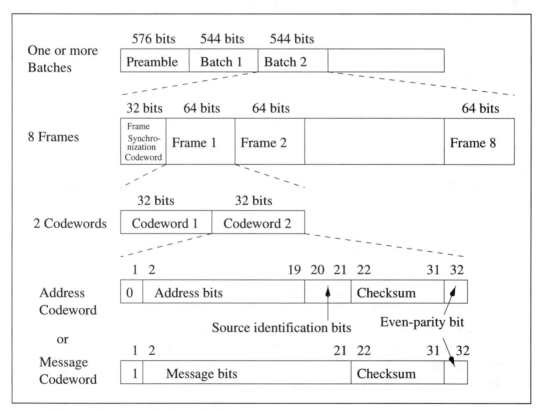

Figure 22.3 POCSAG coding format.

consists of five fields. The first field is a bit 0. The second field is an 18-bit address. The third field is a 2-bit source identifier used to identify four different paging sources. The fourth field is a 10-bit error detection and correction code, which can be used to correct single bit errors and detect multiple bit errors. The last field is an even-parity bit. The structure of a *message codeword* is similar to the address codeword except that the code-word begins with 1 and bits 2–21 are occupied by the message text. An *idle codeword* is a unique bit pattern. An address codeword is always followed by zero or more message codewords. If the second half of a frame is empty, it will be padded with the idle codeword to ensure that every frame has 64 bits.

A pager can be paged only during one of the eight frames (the 3-bit pattern of the frame is stored in the pager). Thus, the receiver of the pager can be turned off during the other seven frames to reduce power consumption. POCSAG is efficient for large-volume data transmission. For small-volume data transmission, air time may be wasted because many frames will be inserted with idle codewords.

22.4.2 ERMES

ERMES is an open system developed by consensus with operators and manufactures. It is an International Telecommunications Union (ITU)-recommended paging code standard. The ERMES air interface I1 operates with 16 frequencies in the radio band—169.4125–169.8125 MHz. It uses a 4PAM (four-level pulse amplitude modulated) FM modulation scheme. In this scheme, four frequencies are used to represent the binary codes 00, 01, 10, and 11. At any moment, only one of the four frequencies is used to transmit the signal, and 2-bit information is delivered at the moment. By using a forward-error correction technique, the effective transmission rate is 3750 bps. ERMES has improved the paging capacity over POCSAG by a factor of 4 (in terms of the number of users per Hz). Every ERMES pager is identified by a 35-bit *radio identity code*. Thus, the address space is large enough to accommodate hundreds of millions of pagers.

ERMES partitions every hour into 60 *cycles*, as shown in Figure 22.4. Every cycle is partitioned into five subsequences, and every subsequence is partitioned into 16 batches. Battery-saving mode is implemented such that a pager is programmed to be paged on specific subsequences or cycles. Like POCSAG, information in a batch is partitioned into codewords. Every nine codewords are grouped into a *codeblock*. Instead of transmitting the codewords sequentially, the codewords in a codeblock are interleaved; that is, the previous bits of all the nine codewords are transmitted before

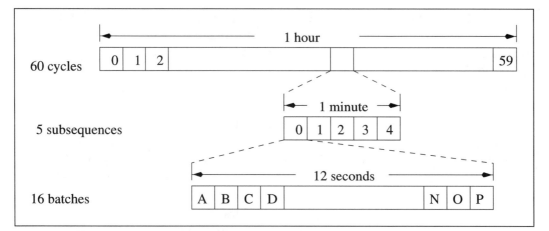

Figure 22.4 ERMES frame structure.

the next bits are transmitted. Due to the bursty error nature of radio transmission, codeword interleaving is likely to spread only 1- or 2-bit errors to each of several codewords, which can be easily fixed by the error-correction mechanism.

22.5 Summary

The materials in this chapter are excerpted from the article published in [Lin97e]. History of paging systems and details of various paging types and paging architectures can be found in [Ros95, Dzi95a, Hon93]. The satellite communications technology used between the paging terminal and the dispersed base stations is described in [Mil96]. Technologies for the radio path between a base station and the pagers are elaborated in [Pae93]. Details of TAP and TDP can be found in [Gle91] and [PCI95a], respectively. In TDP, the TME application layer is specified by the Remote Operations Service Element (ROSE) [ITU94b, ITU94c]. All TME operations are defined using the ASN.1 notation and Packed Encoding Rules [ITU94a]. Standards and specifications for TNPP are given in [PCI95b, Mos95, Dye96]. High-speed protocols such as ERMES and FLEX are discussed in [Lax96] and [Hon93], respectively.

Traditional paging systems do not provide confirmation that the correct messages have been delivered to the pager. A potential solution to this problem is the two-way paging system. These systems can be implemented using cellular phone network facilities, such as the short message service of the GSM protocol described in Chapter 12. Several vendors have developed two-way paging solutions: For example, Motorola's 2-Way Word Messaging, which can be found at the Web site: http://commerce.motorola.com/consumer/QWhtml/pager_cat.html. With two-way paging, the billing structure can be significantly changed [Com95]. A traditional paging carrier charges pager wearers on a monthly (flat-rate) basis. With paging confirmation, message sender satisfaction can be significantly improved, and it is possible to implement calling-party-pays (CPP) billing program.

Paging is a typical example of computer telephony integration. Several software packages are already available to bridge the Internet to paging networks. Computers with Web or e-mail applications can be used as the input devices to send messages to the pagers. If the pagers are replaced by sophisticated PDAs or portable notebooks, and if the paging networks are equipped with two-way communications capability, the resulting architecture becomes a platform for mobile computing. That said, because mobile service and mobile handsets are now inexpensive, the paging market has been significantly affected. Most paging services are designed for niche markets segregated from the mobile services.

22.6 Review Questions

1. Describe four types of pagers. What kinds of information can be delivered by different types of pagers?

2. Describe the architecture of the paging system. What is the function of the paging terminal in a typical paging network architecture? What are paging terminal networks and TNPP?

3. In TAP, why is the timeout period at the input device longer than that at the paging terminal?

4. Compare TAP with TME. What functionality should be added to support two-way paging for these two user access interfaces?

5. How does a pager achieve power saving? Compare it with power saving in GSM and CDPD.

6. What are simulcast paging and transmitter sequencing?

7. Describe an architecture to integrate paging system and the Internet.

8. Some paging service providers in Taiwan offer a "call after paging" service that allows call connection after paging. With this service, the calling party dials the pager number of the called party. When the called party receives the paging message, he or she finds a phone and dials a specific number. Then the calling party and the

called party are connected for phone conversation. Describe how this service can be implemented.

9. Based on the POCSAG coding format, explain why POCSAG can accommodate 2 million users. Compare POCSAG with ERMES. What are the benefits of ERMES? When is the usage of POCSAG more efficient than that of ERMES?

10. Can we use satellite communication technique for transmission between a paging BS and a pager?

11. How do you modify a one-way paging system into a two-way paging system?

12. Short message service, described in Chapter 12, is available in mobile phone services. Will paging be totally replaced by short messaging?

13. What are the differences between the voice mailbox of mobile services and a voice pager?

14. To eliminate the need to type a paging message, a manual paging system allows the caller to describe the paging message through a phone call. The attendant then inputs the message and sends it to the destination. From the customer's view, what are the advantages and disadvantages of this service?

Wireless Local Loop

Wireless local loop provides two-way communication services to stationary or near-stationary users within a small service area. This technology is intended to replace the wireline local loop. In telephony, *loop* is defined as the circuit connecting a subscriber's telephone set with the line-terminating equipment at a central office. The trunks start from the central office in the loop, and are broken down into several smaller bundles of circuits after some distance from the central office. These circuits are eventually separated into "drops" for individual subscribers. The cost of the loop tends to be dominated by these drops on the end-user side, which is typically referred to as the expensive "last mile." This is particularly true for rural areas. The central office switch is typically the first point-of-traffic concentration in the PSTN, especially for older installations where, on the line side of a switch, all facilities from the line-interface card to the end-user equipment are dedicated to a single telephone number. Newer installations connect residential neighborhoods or business campuses to the central office and use statistical multiplexers to concentrate traffic. However, the last few hundred yards of wiring from a residence to the statistical multiplexer—the local loop—is always dedicated. Wireless local loop offers at least two advantages over wireline local loop: ease of installation and deployment (installation of expensive copper cables can be avoided) and concentration of resources.

Telecommunication operators are looking for wireless technology to replace part of the hard-wired infrastructure. Wireless local loop (WLL) technology is under consideration because radio systems can be rapidly developed, easily extended, and are distance-insensitive (up to a given threshold). WLL eliminates the wires, poles, and ducts essential for a wireline network; in other words, the WLL approach significantly speeds the installation process. WLL systems find applications in competitive telecommunications markets, in developing telecommunications markets, and in rural and remote markets that would not be economically served by conventional wireline access technologies. The issue of security must be also considered. Currently, deployed WLL systems are based on a wide range of radio technologies, including satellite technology, cellular technology, and microcellular technology.

23.1   Wireless Local Loop Architecture

A simplified version of the TR-45 architectural reference model for WLL is shown in Figure 23.1. This architecture consists of three major components: the wireless access network unit (WANU), the wireless access subscriber unit (WASU), and the switching function (SF).

Wireless access network unit (WANU). Consists of several base station transceivers or radio ports (RP), a radio port control unit (RPCU), an access manager (AM), and a home location register (HLR), as required. WANU should provide for authentication and air interface privacy, radio resource management, over-the-air registration of subscriber units, and so on. It may also be required to provide

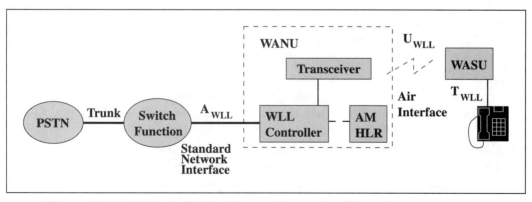

Figure 23.1   TR-45 wireless local loop reference model.

operation and maintenance (OAM), routing, billing, and switching functions, as appropriate or necessary. The WANU also provides protocol conversion and transcoding of voice and data. To support voice-band data and Group 3 Facsimile, an interworking function (IWF) may also be required.

The TR-45 reference model combines the RP and the RPCU into a single functional network element, the WANU. In practice, these devices may not be colocated.

Wireless access subscriber unit (WASU). Provides an air interface, U_{WLL}, toward the network, and a "traditional" interface, T_{WLL}, toward the subscriber. This interface includes protocol conversion and transcoding, authentication functions, OAM, and signaling functions. The power supply is provided locally. A modem function may also be required to support voice-band data so that analog signals such as data and fax can be transported over the air digitally and reconstructed by the IWF in the network. The U_{WLL} interface can use proprietary protocols or standard air interfaces for PCS systems such as AMPS, GSM, DECT, IS-136, or PACS. The T_{WLL} interface can be RJ-11, RJ-45, and so on. An O_{WLL} interface is defined to provide the OAM interface to the WLL system.

Switching function (SF). Associated with a switch that can be a digital switch with or without Advanced Intelligent Network (AIN) capability, an ISDN switch, or a mobile switching center (MSC). The transmission backhaul between WANU and SF can be leased line, cable, or microwave. Compared with the leased line and cable approaches, microwave has the advantages of speed and flexibility in deployment, and does not need to consider right-of-way when crossing third-party property. On the other hand, the deployment of microwave transmission has to consider frequency availability, tower height restrictions, and the limitations of antenna size. Furthermore, the installation should consider future obstructions that may impinge the radio path, such as new buildings, tree growth, and so on.

The A_{WLL} interface between the WANU and the SF can be ISDN-BRI or one of the following standards:

- IS-634, an extension to the GSM A-interface specification to accommodate for other air interfaces such as PACS, IS-95, and IS-136, includes support for mobile-controlled handoff, soft handoff, and IS-41C authentication and privacy protocols.

- IS-653, an ISDN-based A-interface for 1800 MHz personal communications switching centers (PCSC), supports PACS, J-STD-014, TIA IS-661 (a composite CDMA/TDMA air interface compatibility standard for personal communications in 1.8–2.2 GHz for licensed and unlicensed applications or omnipoint), J-STD-009, -10, -11 IS-136, J-STD-007 GSM, J-STD-008 IS-95, J-STD-015, and W-CDMA air interface compatibility standard for 1.85–1.99 GHz PCS applications.

- Bellcore (changed to Telcordia in 1998) GR-303, a multi-T1 interface to a digital switch, supports POTS, ISDN, and special lines, such as coin-operated phones, and so on.

- ITU v5.1 and v5.2 are international equivalents to GR-303.

The interface between the radio system network elements and the non-AIN digital switch can be via GR303 interface with robbed-bit signaling, which allows WLL to interface with any end-office digital switch. The WLL services are transparent to the switch. The switch sees a logical line appearance, that is, a line per subscriber with no concentration at the A_{WLL} interface in the TR-45 reference model.

The radio system supports both fixed and mobile subscribers; however, mobility is limited to the areas served by a single WLL controller. Wide area roaming is not supported. The AM handles authentication and privacy. The maximum data rate supported on the A_{WLL} interface is 56 Kbps; thus, 64 Kbps clear channel data cannot be supported. Mobility management signaling between RPCU and AM/HLR may use any available transport, such as TCP/IP or native X.25.

Alternatively, the services and features can be supported by the HLR or an AIN service control point (SCP). The architecture shown in Figure 23.2

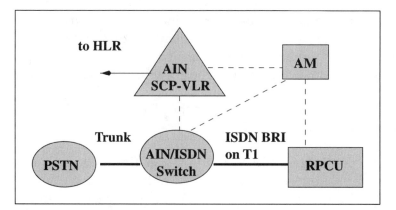

Figure 23.2 WLL system with features derived from the HLR.

takes advantage of the existing AIN capabilities of the switch. The subscriber databases reside in the HLR. Features (such as wide area roaming)
supported by the system are not the same as the features supported by the
switch. The WLL controller uses existing call control and mobility management protocols. Mobility management protocol between the access
manager and the VLR may use ISDN noncall-associated signaling (NCAS;
see Chapter 7), SS7 Transactions Capabilities Application Part (TCAP; see
Chapter 5, Section 5.1), or other transport options. Mobility management
protocol between the WLL controller and the AM may use any available
transport options.

As mentioned earlier, in order for the air interface to pass voice-band
data and Group 3 Facsimile, a network data IWF is usually required.
Figure 23.3 gives a general view of the network architecture to support
interworking of these wireless and wireline data services. One approach
is to use X.25 protocols on ISDN B or D channels for the intermediate
network and to assume that the remote network is the PSTN. The radio
access system refers to the radio devices and the (nonswitched) wireline
backhaul necessary to connect the radio ports or base stations to their
controllers. The controllers are connected via an intermediate network to
the data IWFs. The IWF converts the digital data on the air interface to
a form suitable for transmission in the other networks. This may include
rate adaptation and the termination of specialized error- and flow-control
radio link protocol. The IWF must also be on a network through which
the desired data application (represented as a "host") is reachable. The
wireline network on which the IWF and host reside is called the *remote
network*.

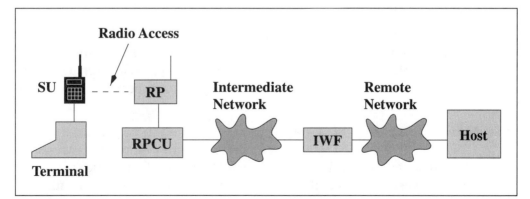

Figure 23.3 Generalized network architecture for wireless-to-wireline data interworking.

23.2   Deployment Issues

To compete with other local loop technologies, WLL should provide sufficient coverage and capacity, high circuit quality, and efficient data services. Furthermore, the WLL cost should be competitive with its wireline counterpart. Several issues are considered in WLL development:

Spectrum. Efficient spectrum management is the key to the success of WLL. The implementation of WLL should be flexible enough to accommodate different frequency bands, as well as non-continuous bands.

A WLL can be implemented in the *licensed bands*. Only a few interfering systems can operate at the same licensed band in the same region, so WLL is expected to be high-frequency-efficient with static service quality. The disadvantage is that the access to licensed bands requires government permission, incurring an additional fee. An alternative is the *unlicensed band* where any device can operate without government permission, provided that it conforms to specified requirements, such as maximum and average power ratings. However, interference from other devices may affect the quality of WLL.

To avoid "spectrum jam" with other PCS services, one may consider *broadband WLL* at 28 GHz, a frequency that is relatively uncontested and easy to license in most countries. The higher the frequency, the greater the requirement for a *line-of-sight* (LOS) radio path, due to higher path losses. This can be mitigated to some extent by higher antenna gains, but this requires that directional antennas be aimed at each other. Also, propagation loss caused by the flora is much more severe at higher frequencies as are rain fades.

Service quality. Customers expect WLL to offer the same quality as its wireline counterpart. The quality requirements include *link quality* (toll voice and data transmission quality), *reliability*, and *fraud immunity*. Compared with the wireline system, these requirements are more difficult to achieve for WLL.

Network planning. WLL penetration is required to be greater than 90 percent. To achieve this goal, efficient network planning is essential. The installation of a WLL is different from that of a mobile system. A mobile system should allow moving users to access services within its service area. On the other hand, WLL assumes that the customers are not moving. Thus, based on the customer population density at fixed locations, the installation of WLL increases the importance of tasks such as adjusting the antenna height and placing subscriber units.

Economics. The major cost of WLL is electronics, whereas the cost in wireline is in physical aspects (including rights-of-way) and installation. The trend indicates that electronics will become cheaper, while labor and installation will become more expensive. Thus, WLL is often, if not always, competitive.

23.3 TR-45 Service Description

The TIA ad hoc group specified standards for WLL in TR-45, including the interface between the radio equipment and the local switching system, the interface to the operations system, and the radio air interface between the subscriber unit and the network radio port. The group also defined a set of standard services, custom calling features, and custom local area signaling service (CLASS) features for a WLL system. Desirable custom calling features include: call waiting, call-forward/busy, call-forward/default, call-forward/no answer, call-forward/unconditional, and three-way calling. In addition to these important features, TR-45 has identified several optional features, including speed dialing, added directory number with distinctive ringing, and businesslike services such as multiline custom calling features. Desirable CLASS features include: customer-originated trace, automatic recall, automatic callback, calling number delivery, and voice mail.

The WLL radio should support Centrex business services, including:

- *Call coverage features*: hunt groups, call forward, voice mail service, and attendant service

- *Call handling features*: call transfer, conference calling, and call park

- *Convenience features*: speed calling, automatic dial, ring again, busy override, and calling-line ID

Centrex dialing plans, end-user management, line restrictions, authorization codes, virtual access to private networks, station message detail recording, and direct inward dialing should also be supported. In addition, WLL systems should provide trunk circuits to support interfaces required for private branch exchanges (PBXs). Key telephone system lines, coin, credit card, and debit card telephones are applications that should be supported by the WLL technology. Since user information is transmitted over the air, communications privacy should be provided.

TR-45 cites V.22 (1200 bps), V.22 bis, V.27 (4800 bps), V.29 (9600 bps) and Group 3 Facsimile as required voice-band data rates to be supported by the WLL technology. User data rates over 9.6 Kbps are considered optional by TR-45 because higher data rates are difficult for the TIA cellular air interface standards, and it is not the intent of the ad hoc WLL group to preclude non-TIA standards. From a service provider perspective, 28.8 Kbps voice-band data and ISDN BRI data are desirable WLL services. Additional WLL services include two-way short message service, D channel packet service, Ethernet interface, dialed 64-Kbps data port, X.25, two-line service, virtual second line, and power-on registration of subscriber units.

23.4   Wireless Local Loop Technologies

WLL systems can be based on one of the following four technologies: satellite, cellular, low-tier PCS/microcellular, and fixed wireless access.

23.4.1   Satellite-Based Systems

These systems provide telephony services for rural communities and isolated areas such as islands. Satellite systems are designed for a Gaussian or Rician channel with a K factor greater than 7 dB, which can either be designed specifically for WLL applications or be piggybacked onto mobile satellite systems as an adjunct service.

Of these, the former offers quality and grade of service associated with wireline access, but it may be expensive. The latter promises to be less costly but, due to bandwidth restrictions, may not offer the quality and grade of service associated with POTS. An example of a satellite-based technology specifically designed for WLL is the Hughes Network Systems (HNS) Telephony Earth Station (TES) technology. This technology can make use of virtually any geostationary earth orbit (GEO) satellite on the C-band or Ku-band. Satellite technology has been used to provide telephony to remote areas of the world for many years. Such systems provide alternatives to terrestrial telephony systems, where land lines are not cost-effective or where an emergency backup is required.

Many satellite systems are proposed to offer mobile satellite services, including the Inmarsat International Circular Orbit (ICO) system, Iridium, Globalstar, Odyssey, American Mobile Satellite Corporation (AMSC), Asia Cellular Satellite (ACeS), and Thuraya mobile satellite system. These systems are specialized to support low-cost mobile terminals primarily for low-bit-rate voice-data applications. Fixed applications are a possible secondary use, along with mobile applications. There is a great deal of difference between these systems, especially as pertains to the orbit and the resultant propagation delay. The number of satellites and the propagation delay pose very different constraints on system design, so that there is no true representative system. For example GEO satellite systems are not required to support handoff even for most mobile applications. Mid-earth orbit (MEO) and low earth orbit (LEO) satellite systems require handoff capability for all fixed and mobile applications because the satellites are in motion relative to the earth's surface even when the terrestrial terminal is fixed. This can be problematic if the handoff needs to be supported in the wireline switch. MSCs support sophisticated mobility functions such as link handoff. MSCs, however, do not typically support ordinary switching functions such as hunt groups, which are highly desirable in a WLL system.

23.4.2 Cellular-Based Systems

These systems provide high-power, wide-range, median subscriber density, and median circuit-quality WLL services. Cellular-based WLL technologies are primarily used to expand basic telephony services. They typically operate in the mobile frequency bands at 800–900 MHz, 1.8–1.9 GHz, and sometimes at 450 MHz or 1.5 GHz.

This approach offers both mobility and fixed wireless access via the same platform as cellular. For relatively sparsely populated rural and even urban settings, WLL technologies based on existing cellular systems can be economical as well as rapidly deployable. TIA group TR-45 is considering IS-136 (U.S. digital TDMA), IS-95 (U.S. digital CDMA) and PCS-1900 (GSM)-based systems for WLL. These systems are all optimized for cellular telephony, that is, for a Rayleigh fading channel with millisecond fade durations and with 5 to 10 msec of delay spread. They include sophisticated facilities/services and, therefore, overhead bandwidth, capabilities not necessarily required for WLL applications. The resultant limited user bandwidth represents a fundamental limitation of such systems for WLL. However, the resultant coverage areas of the base stations are more than a compensatory trade-off, especially to meet voice and low-bandwidth data needs.

As mentioned, cellular systems are optimized for high-tier coverage. Support for mobiles traveling in excess of 100 mph and cell sizes up to 10 miles in radius are necessary (although we do not recommend talking on a mobile phone while driving at 100 mph). To achieve these goals requires extensive signal processing, which translates into high delay and high overhead and may lead to low user bandwidth. These systems are not well suited to deployment indoors and in picocells. Additional complexity of the air interface with the same low-user bandwidth is necessary. As an example, GSM uses high-overhead forward-error correction (FEC) with high-delay (100 to 600 msec) intraburst interleaving and equalization to correct for high fade rates. Block coding is also employed. The result is low user bandwidths, typically limited to 9.6 Kbps data rates. In developing countries, such data capability limitations can be more than adequately compensated for by the large coverage areas and consequent rapid deployment.

23.4.3   Low-Tier PCS or Microcellular-Based Systems

These systems provide low-power, narrow-range, high subscriber density, and high circuit-quality WLL services. These technologies are considered to facilitate rapid market entry and to expand the capacity of the existing infrastructure. They typically operate in the 800 MHz, 1.5 GHz, 1.8 GHz, and 1.9 GHz frequency bands.

Compared with the cellular-based WLL, more base stations are required in low-tier PCS-based WLL to cover the same service area. Service providers may consider low-tier WLL technologies when an existing infrastructure is in place to support backhaul from many base stations to the switch or when wireline-like services and quality are essential. Low-tier systems such as PACS and PHS are designed to operate in a Rayleigh fading environment, and can tolerate intermediate delay spreads of up to 500 nsec. The basic user channel is typically 32 Kbps, with aggregation possible for much higher user bandwidths. The ANSI standard PACS system was designed specifically to support WLL, in addition to supporting limited mobility, up to 40 mph. Low-tier PCS and high-tier cellular air interfaces intended for WLL can be connected to conventional switches and do not require an MSC. Overlapping coverage areas and support of limited handoff between neighboring base stations or radio ports are desirable in WLL systems as they improve the ability to perform maintenance, increase the robustness of the system, improve blocking statistics, and provide for alternative access during exceptional propagation activity. Such limited handoff can easily be supported by a radio port or base station controller, and need not have any impact on the switch. Low-tier technologies, such as DECT, have been studied for their potential use for WLL. In general, such technologies were designed for an indoor Rayleigh channel with delay spreads less than 100 nsec and picocellular coverage areas. Repeaters are used to compensate for small coverage areas, but this technique cuts into the overall capacity of the system. The narrow range, however, limits the delay spread impairment.

23.4.4   Fixed Wireless Access (FWA) Systems

FWAs are proprietary radio systems designed specifically for fixed wireless applications, which may or may not be extensible to PCS. The primary disadvantage of the cellular approach is its limitation on toll-quality voice and signaling transparency. The primary disadvantage of low-tier PCS and microcellular approaches is their narrow radio coverage range. Nonstandard fixed wireless access technology can address these issues and become more efficient. Such systems include the Interdigital TDMA system, Okidata, a proprietary TR-45 interim standard from the JTC, and Interdigital broadband CDMA technology. The FWA systems for zonal areas are designed to cover the local telephone area directly from PSTN switches. Systems for rural areas provide connection at the remote ends of rural links to the end users. These systems usually replace part of the loop distribution and part of a very long drop.

23.5   Examples of WLL Products

In this section, several WLL systems are described to illustrate the WLL technologies, including HNS Quantum System, Lucent Wireless Subscriber System, HNS E-TDMA System, PACS WLL System, and QUALCOMM QCTel System.

23.5.1   HNS Terminal Earth Station Quantum System

The HNS terminal earth station (TES) product is used in the Intelsat network to provide remote access telephone service. There are approximately 100 TES networks worldwide, in addition to the Intelsat network, and more than 10,000 remote site stations. The TES system is a satellite-based voice and data communications network. The network is configured with mesh connectivity between multiple earth stations. TES provides call-by-call demand-assigned multiple access (DAMA) circuits and preassigned circuits, via single-hop, single-channel-per-carrier (SCPC) communications paths between earth stations. It supports both public and private networks, and is capable of operating with any telephony interface from individual subscribers to toll switches and major gateways. The air interface employs quadrature phase-shift keying (QPSK) or binary phase shift keying (BPSK) modulation, depending upon the user information and coding rates. FEC is provided at Rate 1/2 or Rate 3/4. Scrambling is used to spread the transmitted energy across the satellite channel bandwidth. Differential coding resolves phase ambiguity in the demodulated signals. Voice is coded using 32 Kbps adaptive differential pulse code modulation (ADPCM), defined in ITU-T G.721, or 16 Kbps low-delay-code-excited linear predictive (LD-CELP), defined in ITU-T G.728.

The TES network elements can be mapped into the TR-45 functional architecture model, shown in Figure 23.1. The network architecture for TES is shown in Figure 23.4, and is described as follows:

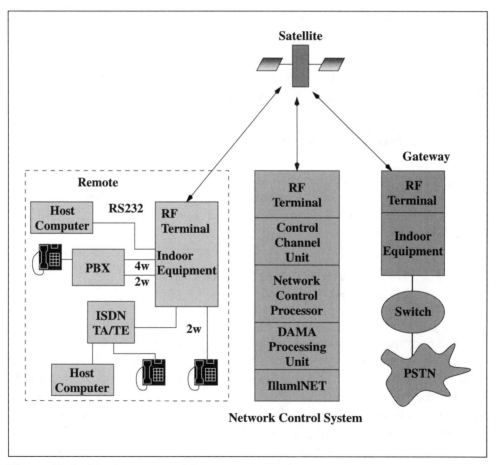

Figure 23.4 TES Quantum architecture.

- An outdoor RF terminal and antenna plus indoor IF and baseband equipment perform the WASU functions. Several standard TES subscriber unit models are available. High-power amplifier (HPA) power options include 5, 10, and 20 watts for C-band, and 2, 5, 8, and 16 watts for Ku-band. A reflector antenna (typically 1.8 meters to 3.8 meters in diameter) is required. TES remote terminals communicate with each other and the network control system (NCS) using single-channel-per-carrier access to virtually any Ku- or C-band satellite.

- The TES terrestrial interfaces toward the user include four-wire and two-wire ear and mouth (E&M) or single-frequency (SF) in-band signaling, RS-232, RS-449, and V.35 data interfaces. As can be seen in Figure 23.4, single-line versions for two-wire, RS-232, and ISDN interfaces are provided. In addition, multiline access to a PBX can also be supported. The TES ISDN earth station provides 56 Kbps pulse-code-modulated (PCM) voice.

- The WANU equipment logically includes the satellite, terminal equipment, and the NCS. Voice calls and asynchronous data calls can be made on demand under the control of the centralized DAMA processing equipment of the NCS. Satellite channels for user information are allocated only for the duration of these connections.

TES supports telephony, synchronous and asynchronous data, facsimile, ISDN BRI data, and E1 and T1 tracking between remote terminals anywhere in the system. Voice and data traffic are transferred directly between remote terminals, not via the NCS, to minimize the delay of using a single satellite hop. Features and services are based on the remote PBX rather than on the centralized PSTN interface such as an E1 or T1 trunk.

23.5.2   Lucent Wireless Subscriber System

Lucent's Wireless Subscriber System (WSS) is a cellular-based WLL. This system typically supports 800–5000 subscribers per switch-controlled area, and the capacity can be enhanced with a more powerful processor. The system architecture illustrated in Figure 23.5 is described as follows:

- The subscriber unit is AMPS-compatible, and communicates with the base station using the EIA/TIA-553 air interface that follows FDMA/FDD at the 824–849 MHz and 869–894 MHz frequency bands.

- The base station is a standard Lucent AUTOPLEX System 1000 Series 1 Cell Site. The coverage area of a base station ranges from 12 Km to

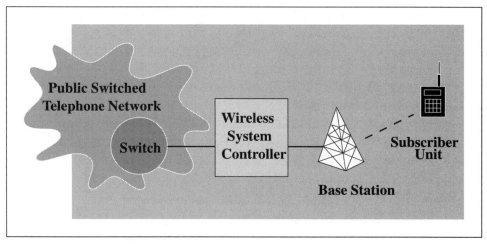

Figure 23.5 Lucent Wireless Subscriber System architecture.

40 Km. The capacity of a base station can be up to 96 channels. The base station contacts with the subscriber unit by the air interface and connects to the wireless system controller (WSC) via a T1 line (with the basic 24-channel 1.544 Mbps pulse-code modulation system).

- The WSC connects to a switch (central office) in the PSTN using either analog trunks or T1/E1 digital multiplexed trunks. Call control is done by R1 or R2 in-band signaling. OAM signaling is done via SS7 or X.25. During call setup, the WSC validates the subscriber unit using its electronic serial number.

Other cellular-based WLL systems include Alcatel A9500 (based on GSM/ETACS), Hughes GMH 2000 E-TDMA (to be described in the next subsection), and Siemens (based on GSM and GSM 1800).

23.5.3 HNS E-TDMA

E-TDMA, developed by HNS, is an extension to the IS-136 TDMA standard that supports cellular-based WLL with increased capacity and improved network performance while maintaining the large coverage area typical of cellular standards. E-TDMA has the following features:

- E-TDMA offers a choice of subscriber unit platforms, including *single-subscriber unit* (SSU) and *multiple-subscriber unit* (MSU). The system is capable of supporting up to 96 lines, depending on the subscriber traffic load and MSU provisioning. SSU supports high-capacity digital voice, fax, and data transparently. It uses a standard

RJ-11 interface and enables multiple terminal connections as simple extensions on a single access unit or per directory number. SSUs are appropriate for locations with low population densities, such as residences and small businesses. MSU provides access to the WLL system in areas of high population densities, such as hotels and apartment buildings. MSU and radio resources are allocated on a call-by-call basis that reduces the required hardware. Operations and maintenance of both SSUs and MSUs are supported by a remote terminal diagnostic protocol to assess performance and respond to end-user issues. Over-the-air activation is also supported to improve system installation. The system can download software to subscriber units to take full advantage of remote system upgrade.

- The E-TDMA base station provides an improved control channel to dynamically assign channels and time slots to active speakers. By automatically accounting for unexpected or changing interference conditions, adaptive or dynamic channel assignment can increase the capacity of a cellular radio technology over centrally engineered, fixed, and static assignment. A 5 Kbps voice coder is also used, which, by itself, more than doubles the capacity over IS-136. The implementation of discontinuous transmission (DTX), along with digital speech interpolation (DSI), means that both the base station and the subscriber station transmit only when speech is present (about 40 percent of the time); thus, the radio resource is effectively shared among the users. Because of these design elements, E-TDMA has a capacity advantage of between 7 to 17 over the benchmark AMPS system, depending on the per-base-station channel pool size and other factors.

E-TDMA supports a wide variety of country-variant signaling. Tones and line-signaling variations are software programmable, and in a number of cases settable via system parameters. Both 16 KHz metering and polarity reversal signaling mechanisms for pulse signaling can be supported, if they are generated and supported by the switching system. Thus, E-TDMA can interface to a wide variety of metering and public payphone equipment. HNS-configured E-TDMA can interface to a mobile switching center when both mobile and WLL applications need to be supported. HNS E-TDMA can also interface to a class 5 end-office switch when both WLL and wireline POTS with full-feature transparency need to be supported. Depending on the subtending switching equipment, E-TDMA is capable of supporting virtually all vertical features and CLASS features recommended by TR-45, including call waiting, call forwarding, and conference calling. Currently, E-TDMA systems for WLL applications are installed in nine countries with a potential aggregate capacity of up to 1 million subscriber units.

23.5.4 PACS WLL System

The ANSI standard Personal Access Communications System (PACS) WLL System is a low-tier PCS-based WLL. The low-power PCS technology supports high circuit quality (32 Kbps voice coding) and low-latency data with high user bandwidths. The system architecture is illustrated in Figure 23.6.

Low-tier technologies for PCS typically rely on antenna diversity of one form or another, to accommodate slow to moderate fades. Strategies include TDD diversity, preselection diversity, and switched antenna diversity. No equalization or FEC is required; therefore, the full bandwidth of the channel is available for user information. PACS is designed to cover a broad range of venues not optimally served by typical cellular systems, including high-density WLL. PACS has features that set it apart from other PCS and cellular standards. For example, PACS supports both public and private key authentication and privacy. It operates in both FDD and TDD modes and can interoperate across a wide variety of public and private networks in both licensed and unlicensed spectrums. It has a rich suite of packet and circuit data protocols and spans a wide range of venues from large outdoor microcells to indoor picocells.

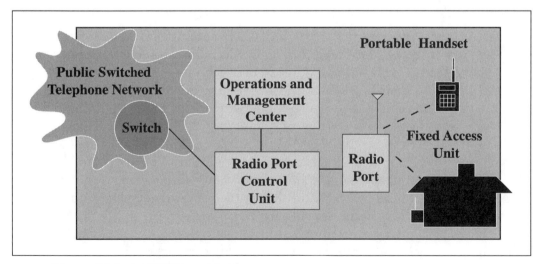

Figure 23.6 PACS/WLL architecture.

The PACS WLL System has these features:

- There are two types of user terminals in PACS/WLL: *portable handset* (subscriber unit) and *fixed-access unit*. The fixed-access units convert the radio signal to an RJ-11 interface signal to the customer premises equipment. The user terminal communicates with the radio port following the JTC/PACS air interface, that is, TDM/TDMA in the 1850–1910 MHz and the 1930–1990 MHz frequency bands. The maximum transmitter power is 200 mW, and the average power is 25 mW. No echo canceller is required. The capacity of a handset is a single line.

- The radio port (RP), which supports eight radio channels, corresponds to WANU transceiver units in the TR-45 architecture. The coverage area of an RP is 0.5–2 Km for the portable handsets and more than 2 Km for the fixed-access units. The RP connects to the radio port control unit (RPCU) by E1, T1, HDSL, or DSL technologies. The maximum transmitter power is less than 10W. Using HDSL, the RPs can be powered by the RPCU out to 1.2 Kft at 130 volts.

- The radio port control unit (RPCU) provides management and control functions between the RP and the PSTN. Several RPCUs are connected to a switch by one or more ISDN BRIs. The RPCU connects to the operations and maintenance center (OMC) by X.25. The RPCU performs call-control functions and user authentication/encryption functions, and reports monitoring results to the OMC.

Other low-tier PCS-based WLL systems include DECT-based systems such as Alcatel A4220, Motorola DRA 1900, Siemens DECTlink, Lucent SWING, Ericsson DRA 1200, and CT2-based systems such as Orbitel Linktel, Dassault Easynet, and Nortel Proximity 'L'.

23.5.5 QUALCOMM QCTel

The QUALCOMM QCTel WLL system is a fixed wireless access WLL. A basic six-sector QCTel system may support 24,000 subscribers. The QCTel technology supports 8 Kbps voice and up to 7.2 Kbps data rate. QCTel supports limited mobility, and the subscriber unit can be a portable handset. The system architecture is shown in Figure 23.7 and is described as follows:

- The handset communicates with the base station transceiver using CDMA/FDD at the 800 MHz, 900 MHz, and 1.8–2.2 GHz frequency bands. The handset supports multiple lines. The transmission power is controlled with the maximal value of 2W.

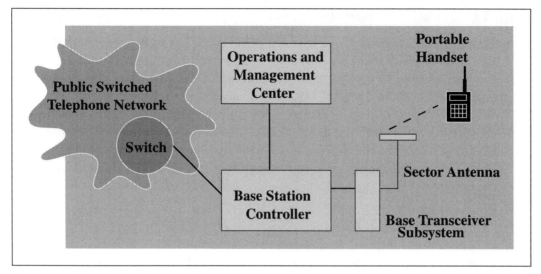

Figure 23.7   QUALCOMM QCTel architecture.

- The base transceiver station (BTS) communicates with the handset using the IS-95 air interface. The maximum transmission power is 50W. The cell range is 25 Km. Up to 45 voice channels can be handled by a BTS. Up to 20 BTSs may be colocated with the base station controller (BSC) at the central office, or 30 BTSs may be connected to a BSC using T1/E1 technology per area (up to three areas).

- The base station controller (BSC), placed in the central office, connects to a switch in the PSTN using T1, E1, T3, or E3 digital multiplexed trunks. Call control is achieved by R2 in-band signaling, and the OMC signaling is done via SS7 or X.25.

Other fixed wireless access WLL systems for zonal areas include CDMA-based systems such as the DSC Airspan, Granger CD2000, and Siemens CDMAlink; and TDMA-based systems such as Jenoptic FAS and Nortel Proximity 'l' (TDMA).

Systems for rural areas include the Alcatel 9800 (TDM), and TDMA-based systems such as SR Telecom SR500 and TRT/Phillips IRT.

23.6   WLL OAM Management Functions

In this section, we focus on a product called WLL-OAM to describe the WLL OAM management functions. Written in 35,000 lines of C++ code, WLL-OAM provides the OAM services necessary to control and monitor

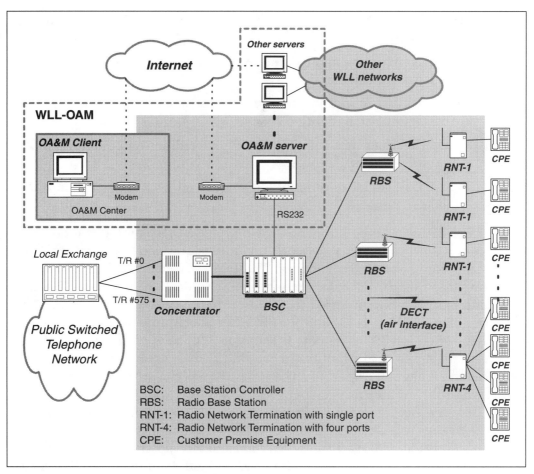

Figure 23.8 DECT WLL system and its OAM.

the equipment in a DECT WLL system, whose architecture is illustrated in Figure 23.8. The network elements managed by WLL-OAM are:

- WANU, including the base station controller (BSC) and radio base station (RBS)

- WASU, called the *radio network termination* (RNT)

- Customer premise equipment (CPE; e.g., a telephone set) connected to the RNT

Every network element is assigned an ID used to access the corresponding object in WLL-OAM. Five OAM management function types are provided in WLL-OAM:

Type 1: Network configuration functions. Report the configuration information of the WLL.

Type 2: Network element status functions. Monitor the status of the WLL network elements.

Type 3: Failure detection functions. Detect the errors/failures occurring in the WLL network elements.

Type 4: Testing functions. Test the functionalities and qualities of the network elements.

Type 5: Call statistics functions. Provide call performance data from the WLL network.

For BSCs, the type 1 function *system configuration* provides topology information for the WLL network, including equipped RBSs and registered RNTs connected in the network. The type 2 function *BSC information* provides the BSC ID, date/time, bootstrap indication, and so on. The date and time of a BSC are used to synchronize the time-related information between the WLL-OAM and the BSC. The bootstrap indication records the time when the BSC is rebooted. The type 3 function *board failure detection* reports circuit board failures in the BSC. When WLL-OAM detects a failure, it alerts the operator. The type 4 function *loopback test* verifies the availability of transmission between WLL-OAM and the BSC.

For the RBS, no type 1 function is defined. The type 2 function *RBS information* includes the RBS ID, channel assignment, and so on. The type 3 functions include *power failure detection* and *RBS failure detection*. The type 4 function *RBS loopback test* verifies the availability of the transmission link between the RBS and the BSC.

For RNT, the type 1 functions *registration* and *deregistration* allow an RNT to attach and detach the WLL system. The registration function authenticates an RNT, and the deregistration function cancels authority of an RNT. The type 2 functions include *RNT information* and *CPE presence detection*. The RNT information includes the RNT ID, attached CPE ID, registration status, DECT identities, password, and so on. CPE presence detection helps the operator to determine whether an unreachable calling service is caused by the customer. Type 3 functions include *power failure detection* and *low-battery voltage detection* allowing WLL-OAM to detect power failure and abnormality of backup battery. The type 4 functions include *ring/ring trip test*, *tone generation test*, and *RNT loopback test*. The ring/ring trip test instructs the RNT to ring the CPE. This test verifies the availability of transmission between the BSC and the CPE. The tone generation test instructs the RNT to generate a tone to the CPE. The tone

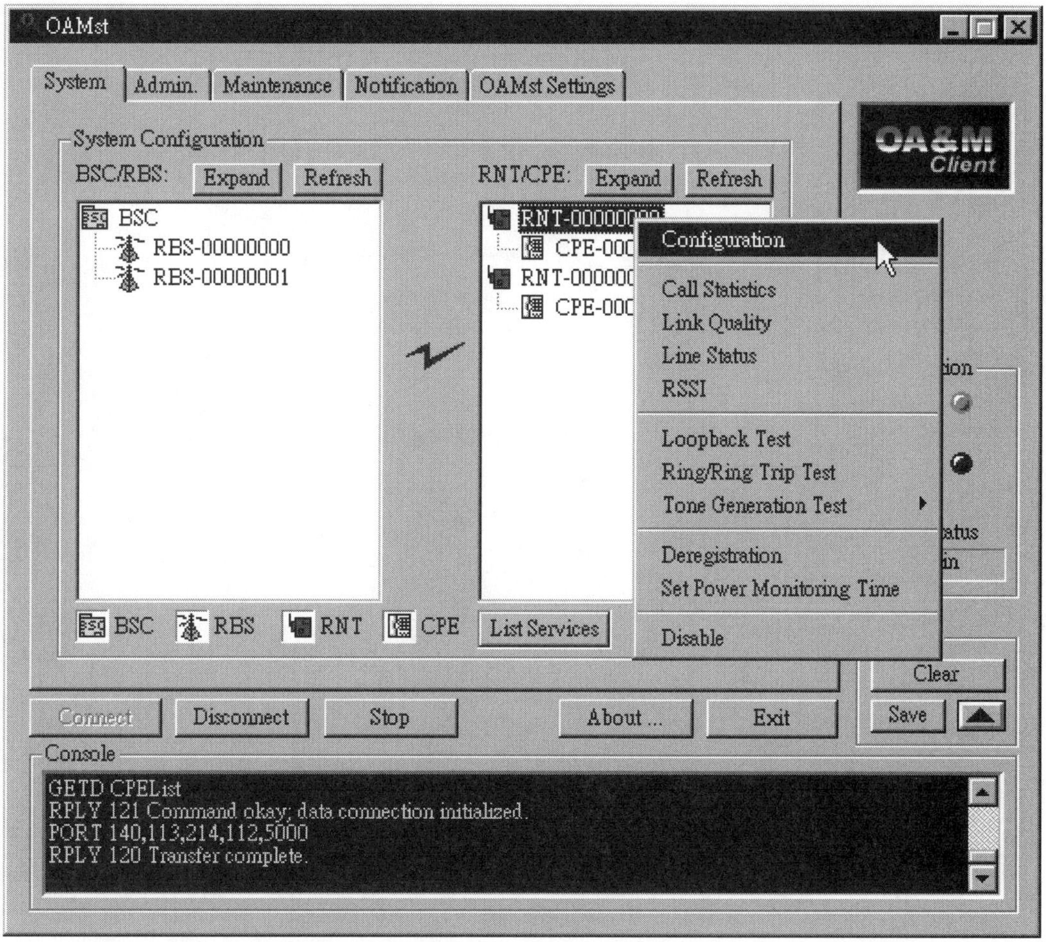

Figure 23.9   Main dialogue page of WLL-OAM.

patterns include *dial tone, busy tone, ring tone,* and so on. This test helps the operator to verify the tone-generation functions on the RNT. The loopback test verifies the availability of transmission between the RNT and the BSC. The type 5 functions perform *statistics of call attempts, RSSI measurement,* and *frame error rate (FER) detection.* The call statistics include the number of successful call attempts, the number of dropped call attempts, and the number of blocked call attempts. The operator uses this information to reallocate wired and wireless resources in network planning. The RSSI indicates radio signal strength received by the RNT during a conversation. The FER value is measured to evaluate the radio link quality during a conversation.

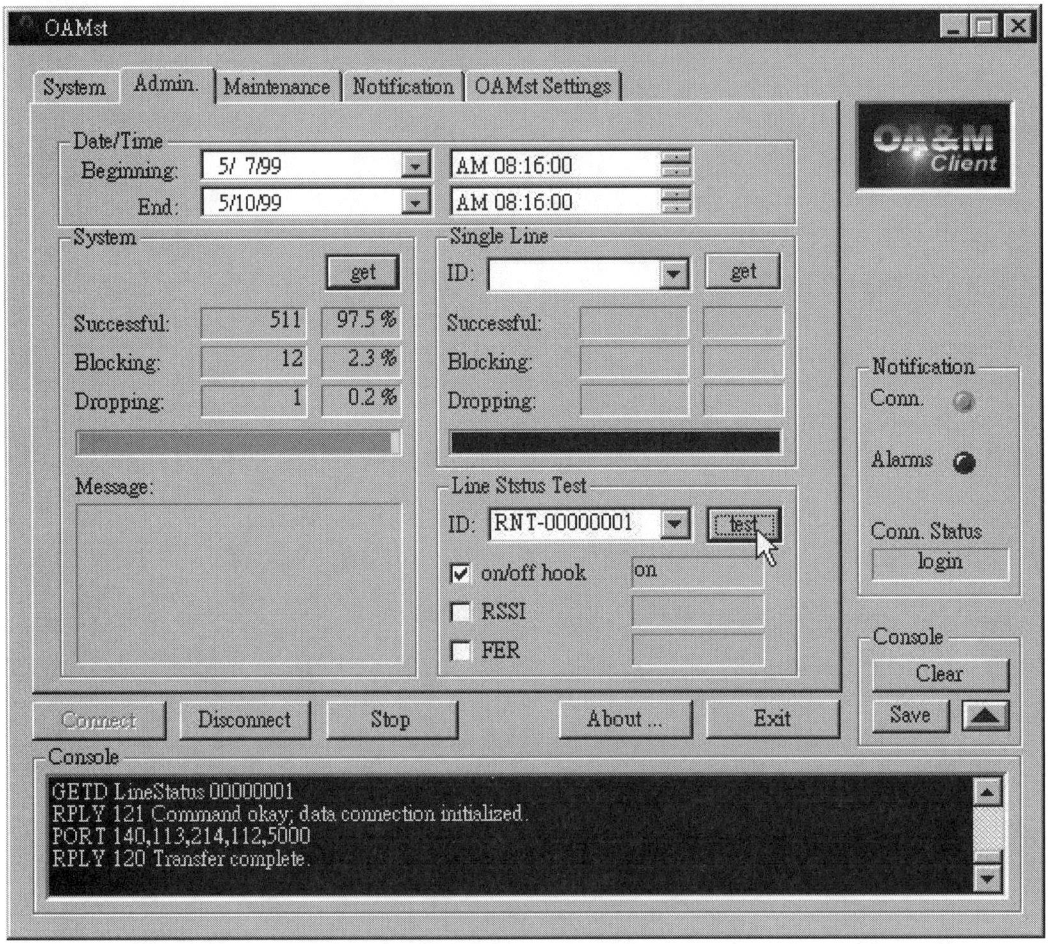

Figure 23.10   Administration page of WLL-OAM.

WLL-OAM provides a friendly graphical user interface for the operator to access OAM management functions. Figure 23.9 shows the main page of WLL-OAM, which illustrates the network elements connected to the WLL. Figure 23.10 shows an administration page that allows the operator to perform actions on a particular line connected to a telephone set.

23.7   Summary

The information in this chapter is based on the article published in [Lin97h]. Wireless local loop (WLL) provides two-way calling services to stationary, or "fixed," users, and is intended to replace its wireline counterpart. To compete with other local loop technologies, WLL should provide sufficient coverage and capacity and high circuit quality, and offer efficient data services [Lev96]. The TIA ad hoc group in TR-45.1 specified standards for WLL [TIA96]. It also defined a set of standard services, custom calling features, and CLASS features [Bel93a] for a WLL system. Furthermore, WLL may support limited mobility management by using any available transport options [Var97]. In order for the WLL air interface to pass voice-band data and Group 3 Facsimile, a network data IWF is usually required [Har94a, Bel94e].

Microwave backhaul [Lit96] should be seriously considered to reduce the transmission cost. For densely populated urban environments, low-tier PCS-based WLL technologies support higher user bandwidths, and can offer features and quality more commonly associated with conventional wireline access.

Currently deployed WLL systems are based on a wide range of radio technologies [Noe97, Cou96], including satellite [Hug96], cellular [Sch96], microcellular [Zan97, Noe96b], and fixed wireless access. The main advantages of cellular-based WLL systems over low-tier PCS-based WLL systems include coverage, speed of deployment, and spectrum efficiency. The fundamental disadvantage is its small user bandwidth. This trade-off implies a market for both system types, and the choice depends on which feature is more critical.

Currently, there are several hundred wireless WLL systems (either trials or commercial systems). Northern Business Information expects that an average of 6 million WLL lines will be added annually. Most WLL lines will be deployed in the Asia-Pacific region, Latin America, and Eastern Europe. As analyzed in [Dzi95b] WLL is often, if not always, competitive.

23.8 Review Questions

1. What is the most important reason to use WLL instead of its wireline counterpart?

2. What are the main modules specified in the TR-45 Wireless Local Loop Reference Model?

3. What are the main deployment issues to deal with in WLL? Point out which of these issues do not exist in wireline local loop.

4. Describe four major technologies for WLL systems. What are the advantages and disadvantages of these approaches?

5. Compare GEO, MEO, and LEO. Which of these technologies for WLL need to implement handoff?

6. Iridium implements switches within satellites so that calls are routed among the satellites before they reach the destination earth stations. What are the advantages and disadvantages of this architecture?

7. Can we develop a WLL system by modifying a cellular system? If so, what are the advantages and the disadvantages of this approach?

8. In your opinion, what are the benefits of using IS-95 CDMA technology for WLL? Do you need to implement sensitive power control and soft handoff mechanisms?

9. Design a system that accommodates both public mobile services and WLL. What are the major performance considerations in your design?

10. To support fax and payphone services, which capabilities should be built in WLL?

11. In WLL OAM, detecting the presence of a phone set connected to the WASU is not trivial. Describe how this feature can be implemented.

Wireless Enterprise Networks

Modern corporations consider information and information exchange as important assets that underlie the operation of an enterprise. To create a companywide information utility—that is, an *enterprise network*, it is necessary to provide communications at the corporate and the departmental levels. As wireless technology advances, wireless products are gradually being integrated with enterprise networking to provide employee mobility, or the so-called cordless terminal mobility, both within the company and via a bridge to the outside world. This chapter explains how wireless communication affects enterprise telephony, and although we focus on telephony, the discussion can be generalized to accommodate the corporate data aspects of enterprise networking. (Several proposed IP-based enterprise wireless networks were elaborated in Chapter 16.)

24.1 Enterprise Telephony

Due to large volumes of telephony traffic in business environments, it is desirable to control the escalating costs associated with the telecommunications services of a company. In office buildings, a typical communication solution is the private branch exchange (PBX) system, a switch that con-

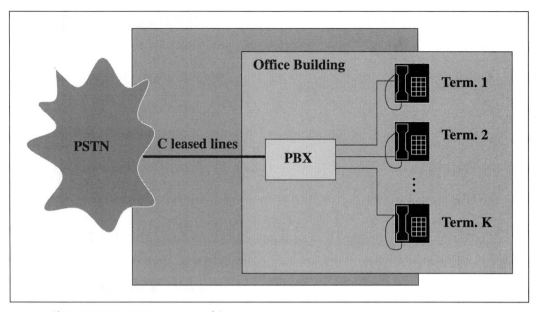

Figure 24.1   PBX system architecture.

nects the telephone links from an office building to the PSTN. Figure 24.1 illustrates a PBX system where the number, K, of the internal telephone lines is larger than the number, C, of the external leased lines. A computer-controlled PBX is illustrated in Figure 24.2, where a call-control switching card is installed in the personal computer. This card controls several telephone line/trunk interfaces in the peripheral module, the box on the left of the monitor in Figure 24.2.

For a large corporation with multiple locations, it is desirable to reduce the long-distance calling expenses among the different company locations. The solution is found in private lines or *virtual networks* (VNs) that provide hard-wire connections among corporate locations. These lines are leased and are therefore billed to the company on a flat, monthly basis. Figure 24.3 illustrates an example of a virtual network where solid lines represent connections among switches of the PSTN, and dashed lines represent parts of the capacity of the solid connections used in the virtual network to connect locations A, B, and C of a company. In the past, such solutions were adequate for a static business setup; however, changes in the business environment are transforming people's mode of operation and work habits. Many corporate employees spend time away from their assigned wired phones but are still in their offices or at other locations of the company. Companies are becoming aware of the opportunities that

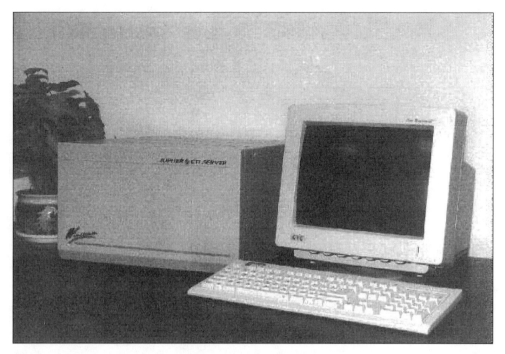

Figure 24.2   PBX system (courtesy of WinComm Corp.).

mobility offers: to increase productivity, provide better customer service, and to lead to future cost savings. Thus, companies are increasingly adding mobility solutions—that is, enterprise wireless telephony—to their existing networks and continuously integrating them as seamlessly as possible.

Unlike its public cellular counterpart, enterprise wireless telephony is free of air-time charges. This emerging wireless solution is particularly attractive to manufacturing, health care, hospitality, transportation, and utility companies. For example, with wireless technology, technicians can be quickly contacted and dispatched to fix a broken machine, thereby saving money by reducing downtime; doctors and nurses can be reached easily by colleagues and patients in a hospital. For general business, enterprise wireless telephony frees employees from being tied to their telephones, thus improving the efficiency of their operations.

However, there are significant problems that require solutions to support an enterprise wireless network:

■ *High maintenance cost for dedicated equipment, backup facilities, and mobility management, and vulnerability to facility outages.* The public

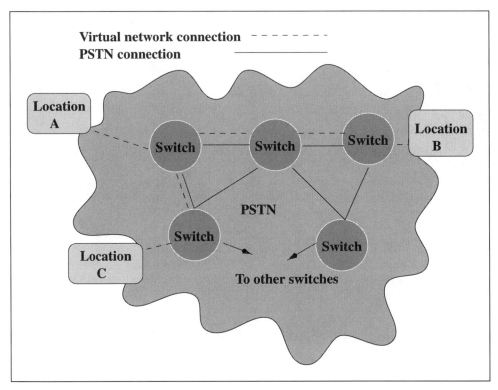

Figure 24.3 Virtual network architecture.

telecommunication system experience indicates that wireless systems are more expensive to maintain than their wired counterparts, and are more vulnerable to facility outages. The same situation is expected for enterprise networking. In addition to the hardware reliability solutions, significant efforts have been invested in providing reliability to network management for public wireless systems, particularly for mobility management. To date, it is not clear whether the enterprise wireless network can borrow this solution from its public counterpart.

■ *Constant need for reengineering due to growth or downsizing.* To expand a business, it is necessary to constantly adapt the wireless network to end-user requirements that are critical to an employee's business missions. Though many new wireless products have been developed recently, they must be carefully evaluated before implementing an enterprise network solution. Networks may be planned or reengineered at the enterprise level, encompassing the entire organization to support an integrated information environment. At the office level, planning should fit the specific needs of the department under the enterprise network platform. In other words, for the office, evolving the network tends to be more near-term application-oriented, while at the enterprise level, the development should focus more on the long-term application-independent technology. It is important to assure that selections of current and near-term technologies will facilitate transition to the long-term targets.

These issues are similar to those encountered in wired networks, but the solutions have to be tailored to suit the wireless nature. For enterprise wireless, these issues are still open, and will be the subject of major research directions for academic study as well as industry development.

24.2   Enterprise Location System

A location system tracks the location of a person or equipment in an office building. The basic functions of the system provide one-way communications from the user/equipment to the system. The system can also be extended to two-way communications. An example of two-way location system is the Olivetti & Oracle Research Limited (ORL) infrared network. (Note, in January 1999, ORL was acquired by the AT&T Laboratories, and was renamed as AT&T Laboratories Cambridge.)

In a location system, several sensors are placed in the office building and are connected to a wired network, as shown Figure 24.4. Employees or equipment are located by wearing *location badges*, which are the size of a credit card. This badge periodically transmits a message to the sensor in the room. Based on the location message, the system updates or reconfirms the location of the badge.

By integrating the location system with distributed databases, an enterprise network may offer communication services to a user who does not carry any communication equipment except for the location badge. Consider a network that connects communication and computing facilities in an office building. Through location badges, every user in the building can be tracked instantly. Suppose that employee A of the system visits the office of employee B. When someone attempts to communicate with employee A, the system locates A at B's office. If A is not carrying any communication equipment, the system may direct the "call" to available communication equipment at B's office. For example, B's telephone set will ring if the communication request to A is a phone call. This service also utilizes intelligent call forwarding, so if the caller is sending e-mail to A, the message will appear on B's computer with appropriate protection;

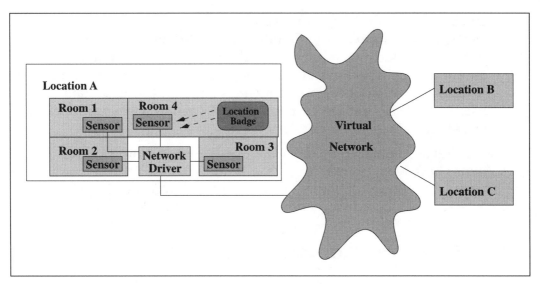

Figure 24.4   The location system.

or the message may be forwarded to B's fax machine if no computer is available.

A major performance issue of the location system is the determination of the frequency, or how often, that a badge transmits location or registration messages. If the messages are sent very frequently, then the badge may consume too much power. On the other hand, if the messages are sent too infrequently, the system may not accurately locate the position of the user, and calls to the user may be lost. Therefore, in this subsection, we consider both fixed registration intervals and exponential registration intervals. Fixed registration intervals seem to be a natural choice. That said, with exponential registration intervals, repeated collisions (two badges may send signals to a sensor at the same time, which results in lost messages) can be reduced in the same way as the exponential backup retry strategy used in a slotted Aloha network. (The impact of registration frequency on message collisions with other badges in the same coverage area is beyond the scope of this book.) In terms of implementation cost, the complexities of generating fixed intervals and exponential intervals are basically the same. Thus, it is important to investigate the lost-call performance of the two schemes. We propose analytic and simulation models to investigate the location system. From our performance models, the following observations were made:

- Location systems with exponential registration intervals have the same lost-call probability as those with fixed intervals. Thus, with equal lost-call probability and reduced likelihood of collision, exponential registration intervals are a good choice for the location system in terms of reducing repeated collisions.

- The lost-call probability p_l increases linearly in proportion to the call arrival rate and the registration interval. Table 24.1 lists p_l for various exponential registration intervals and exponential location residence times with the mean of two hours. The table indicates that, for example, if the average time for a user to stay in a location is two hours, and the call arrival rate is one call per hour, then by increasing the registration interval from 5 seconds to 20 seconds, the lost-call probability increases from 0.14 percent to 0.55 percent.

- By decreasing the registration frequency (and thus saving the badge power), the location system may still maintain low lost-call probability. Table 24.1 indicates that if the average time for a user to stay in a location is two hours, and the call arrival rate is one call per hour, then by increasing the registration interval from 5 seconds to 20 seconds (and thus reducing transmit power by 75 percent), the lost-call probability can still be maintained below 0.6 percent.

Another interesting phenomenon is that if the user movement pattern is more irregular, the potential of losing a call becomes smaller.

Based on the concept of location system, many interesting projects are in progress. Two location-based projects called *sentient computing* and *active bats* are being conducted at the AT&T Laboratories at Cambridge, UK. In sentient computing, computers utilize a location system to gain a detailed sense of the real world in order to create advanced context-aware applications. For example, videophones can be made to follow conference participants around a room by automatically selecting the relevant camera for the best view. The bat project allows small, low-power ultrasonic tags carried on a person or fixed to objects to be located within 10 cm in

Table 24.1   Probability p_l of Losing a Call after a Move*

REGISTRATION FREQUENCY	CALL ARRIVAL RATE		
	1 PER 2 HR.	1 PER HR.	1.5 PER HR.
1 per 20 sec.	0.276243%	0.550964%	0.824176%
1 per 10 sec.	0.138504%	0.276625%	0.414365%
1 per 5 sec.	0.0693481%	0.1386%	0.207756%

*One move per two hours

three dimensions. According to Andy Hopper at Cambridge University, "With active bat, it is possible to determine the spatial relationships of people, displays, telephones, keyboards, and so on, and configure them automatically to create a truely active office environment." Details of active badges and sentient computing can be found in www.uk.research.att.com.

24.3   Bluetooth

The efforts to develop an integrated voice/data home wireless network started in 1998, when two working groups began establishing industry standards in this area: the Home RF Working Group (HRFWG) and the Bluetooth Special Interest Group (SIG). Bluetooth technology was a spin-off of an internal Ericsson project on wireless connectivity. Understanding that it would be the best way to make the technology successful, Ericsson made Bluetooth available to the rest of the industry. Consequently, along with Nokia, IBM, Intel, and Tobisha, Ericsson founded Bluetooth. In addition to these two groups, a company named Home Wireless Network (HWN) debuted proprietary home wireless products in January 1999. HWN, with Lucent as its major investor, is targeting home and small businesses, offering integrated voice and data products.

As data and voice merge in the everyday lives of people, an integrated cordless system based on the Bluetooth technology should facilitate access to voice and data. It should also stir the growth of cordless phones, and expand to small office applications. Bluetooth operates in the 2.4–2.483 GHz ISM band. It utilizes fast-frequency hopping with spread-spectrum techniques, whereby packets are delivered in specified time slots at up to 723.2 Kbps. Bluetooth units (such as mobile handsets, PCs, PDAs, printers, and so on) can be connected through the Bluetooth radio link to form a piconet in the office environment.

Figure 24.5 illustrates the Bluetooth protocol stack. A host controller interface is defined, which provides higher-layer protocols and a command interface to control the baseband and link manager, and to access hardware status and control registers. The Bluetooth protocols are described as follows.

24.3.1   Bluetooth Core Protocols

These include Bluetooth RF, baseband, Link Manager Protocol (LMP), Logical Link and Control Adaptation Protocol (L2CAP) and Service

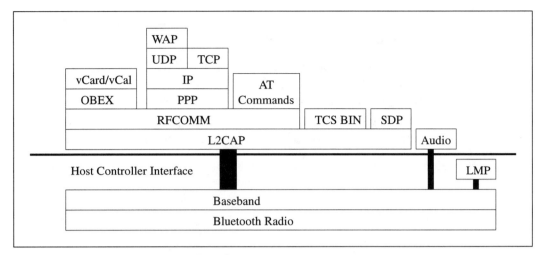

Figure 24.5 Bluetooth protocol stack.

Discovery Protocol (SDP). The physical links can be *synchronous connection-oriented* (SCO) or *asynchronous connectionless* (ACL). Both SCO and ACL can be encrypted, and are supported with FEC and CRC error correction. The SCO packets are used to deliver both audio and data while the ACL packets are used for data only.

The baseband enables the physical RF link between Bluetooth units. Inquiry and paging procedures are used to synchronize the hopping frequency and clock of Bluetooth units. The LMP performs authentication and encryption, and negotiates baseband packet sizes to set up the connection between Bluetooth units. During the connection, LMP monitors the states of a Bluetooth unit and controls the unit's power modes as well as duty cycles.

In parallel with LMP, L2CAP adapts upper-layer protocols by providing connection and connectionless data services. L2CAP performs multiplexing, segmentation, reassembly, and group abstractions. In Bluetooth Specification 1.0, L2CAP supports only ACL.

SDP is used to query device information and service characteristics before the link among Bluetooth units is established.

24.3.2   Other Bluetooth Protocols

These include:

Bluetooth Cable Replacement Protocol. A *serial cable emulation protocol* called RFCOMM. RFCOMM emulates RS-232 control and data signals over the Bluetooth baseband. RFCOMM provides serial line transport capabilities for upper-level protocols.

Telephony Control Protocols. Include Telephony Control Protocol-Binary (TCS-BIN) and AT-commands. TCS-BIN is used to define mobility management and video/data call control. Bluetooth AT-commands are based on ITU-T Recommendation V.250, GSM 07.07 (see Chapter 12, Section 12.5) and the commands used for fax services.

Adopted Protocols. Divided into two stacks:

- *Point-to-Point Protocol (PPP).* Used to support WAP (through UDP) and TCP. Details of WAP were given in Chapter 19.

- *Object Exchange Protocol (OBEX).* A session protocol, which provides the same basic functionality as HTTP, but in a lightweight manner. vCard and vCalendar are content formats transferred by OBEX in Bluetooth. vCard defines the format for electronic business cards. vCalendar defines personal calendar entries and scheduling information.

24.3.3   Bluetooth Usage Models

Bluetooth supports several usage models, each of which utilizes a profile to define the protocols that support it. The list of usage models includes:

File transfer supported by OBEX and SDP. Used, for example, to exchange electronic business cards.

Internet bridge supported by AT-commands, PPP, and SDP. Provides, for example, a wireless Internet connection to a PC.

LAN access supported by IP and SDP. Provides wireless LAN access.

Synchronization supported by OBEX (through Ir Mobile Communications) and SDP. Provides personal information management (PIM) synchronization between two Bluetooth units (e.g., PDAs); the synchronized information includes phone book, calendar, message, and similar services.

Three-in-One Phone, supported by TCS-BIN, SDP, and audio. Allows a handset to function like a cordless phone, a walkie-talkie, or a cellular phone.

24.4   Enterprise PCS: Office Level

Enterprise personal communications services (PCS) network provides two-way communications for employees at different locations of a company. At the office level, where only one office building is considered, a PBX system may integrate with wireless technology to support users with mobility at the workplace. Figure 24.6 illustrates a wireless PBX (WPBX) architecture, where the PBX is connected to k base stations (BSs) instead of wireline telephones. BS i is equipped with c_i radio channels; that is, at most c_i handsets can simultaneously connect to the PBX through BS i. The PBX is connected to the PSTN with C telephone lines. For example, in commercial WPBX systems using CT2 technology, with $c_i \le 8$, and systems using DECT technology, with $c_i \le 12$, the coverage area of a BS is typically less than 100–200m in diameter. WPBX call origination and call delivery are similar to that for a wireline PBX system:

Call origination. When a handset dials a phone number, the number is received by the base station through the radio signal. After the call request is forwarded to the WPBX, the call setup process is the same as that for a wireline phone connected to the PBX.

Call delivery. When a remote party calls a handset, the PSTN sets up the trunk from the switch of the calling party to the WPBX. The WPBX

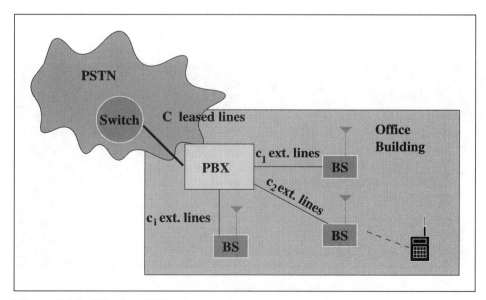

Figure 24.6   Wireless PBX system.

sends the dialed number to all base stations to page the handset. When the handset responds, the communication path is set up to the handset through the corresponding base station.

24.4.1   Local Area Wireless: An Example of WPBX

At the office level, the WPBX solution should offer the same service features as its wireline counterpart. That is, services such as call holding, call transferring, conference call, speed dialing, programmable phone book, displaying/clearing messages or the calling number from someone within the building, are features that should be provided. Call accounting, system management, remote maintenance, and interfaces to networks of other locations of the company are also very important.

An example of WPBX systems is the Local Area Wireless (LAW) system developed by TECOM. The PBX of the LAW system is shown on the left in Figure 24.7. This PBX is digital equipment that supports complete switching functions, operator and voice message services, and group and emergency calls. The PBX connects to several personal computers through RS232 ports. These computers provide operations, administration, and maintenance (OA&M) functions. The PBX connects to the PSTN by E1 or T1 trunks. The base station of the LAW system is shown on the right in Figure 24.7. The interface between the base station and the PBX is based on ISDN. The maximum number of base stations connected to a PBX is five. The maximum distance between a base station and the PBX is 600m

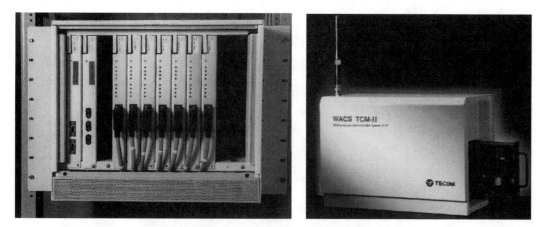

Figure 24.7   LAW PBX (left) and LAW Base Station (right; both courtesy of TECOM).

(which is also bounded by ISDN specifications). A base station supports 5–20 radio channels using TDMA technology. The radio coverage of a base station ranges from 200m to 500m. A handset of the LAW system looks like a typical mobile handset.

The LAW system supports more than 40 office functions, such as speed dialing, redialing, letter input, billing display, incoming call record, and so on.

24.4.2   Capacity Planning for WPBX

In WPBX capacity planning, the number, C, of the external lines and the number, c_i, of the radio channels for BS i (see Figure 24.6) should be carefully selected. The goal is to minimize the blocking probability of a call while maximizing the usage of the external lines, thus minimizing cost. We have constructed an analytic model to study how the allocation of C and c_i affects call blocking. By simplifying the analytic model, we demonstrate the results for a WPBX system with two base stations. Figure 24.8(a) depicts the blocking probabilities as a function of C. In this figure, $c_1 = c_2 = 12$, and $12 \leq C \leq 23$. Let the expected call holding time be $1/\mu$ minutes, and the call arrival rates to the two BSs be λ_1 and λ_2, respectively. For simplicity, let $\lambda_1 = \lambda_2 = \lambda$. We consider call arrival rate $\lambda = 4\mu$, 4.5μ, and 5μ, respectively. (That is, if the mean call holding time is 1 minute, the call arrival rates to a cell is 4 calls per minute, 4.5 calls per minute, and 5 calls per minute.) It is intuitive that when C is small, increasing C significantly decreases the blocking probability. On the other hand, when C is large, increasing C has only a minor effect on the blocking probability. Thus, there exists a *threshold point* C^* beyond which increasing C does not significantly improve performance. The figure indicates that $C^* = 18, 19$, and 20 for $\lambda = 4\mu$, 4.5μ, and 5μ, respectively.

Figure 24.8(b) provides insight to determine whether C or c_i should be increased for a fixed quantity of traffic. In this figure, $\lambda = 5\mu$; and for each N, the plus sign (+) represents the blocking probability where $C = N$, and $c_1 = c_2 = 12$. We use this setup as the base case to compare with the next three scenarios. The asterisk (*) represents the blocking probability for the case where $C = N + 1$ and $c_1 = c_2 = 12$. The $\diamond$ symbol represents the blocking probability for the case where $C = N + 2$ and $c_1 = c_2 = 12$. The $\circ$ symbol represents the blocking probability for the case where $C = N$ and $c_1 = c_2 = 13$. The figure indicates that to reduce the blocking probabilities when C is small (e.g., $C < 19$), it is more effective to increase C than to increase both c_1 and c_2. On the other hand, the result reverses when $C \geq 19$.

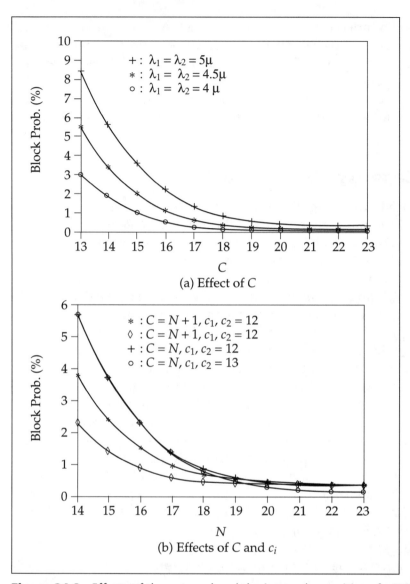

Figure 24.8   Effects of the external and the internal capacities of a WPBX.

Figure 24.8(b) also indicates that when $C > 20$ (see the $+$ curve), increasing C (see the $*/\diamond$ curves) does not improve the performance, as already indicated in the previous discussion. For $C < 17$, increasing c_1 and c_2 does not improve the performance (see the $+$ and the $\circ$ curves).

This simple example indicates that changing C and c_i may have very different impacts on the blocking probability of the WPBX system.

24.5   Enterprise PCS: Enterprise Level

At the enterprise level, where the whole enterprise network is considered, mobility management should be added to the network so that an employee can be reached at any company location using a single phone number. To support mobility among different sites of the company, the enterprise virtual network should provide data capability to transfer signaling messages for mobility management. For example, signaling information can be delivered through the Internet or an intranet. Furthermore, if the handset is allowed to switch to public PCS services when an employee moves out of corporate areas, mobility management functions should be integrated with public PCS networks.

When planning an enterprise PCS network, one should consider scalability to meet expanding needs for the current PCS network before investing in a completely new system. At the office level, the size of a WPBX system can be made scalable by enabling the addition of more base stations and handsets as the organization grows. Furthermore, the system should be able to cope with future data, messaging, and multimedia demands. At the enterprise level, the system should be able to deliver high-traffic density and free roaming as new locations are included.

An enterprise PCS system may use a single database for mobility management, as illustrated in Figure 24.9. In this figure, the WPBXs are connected by internal circuits or the virtual network. Only one WPBX is connected to the PSTN, designated as location A in Figure 24.9. A *location register* (LR) is colocated with the WPBX connected to the PSTN. When an employee moves from location B to location C, it sends a registration message to the LR through the WPBX at location C, and the message path is $a \rightarrow b \rightarrow c \rightarrow d$, as shown in Figure 24.9. When someone outside the company calls the employee, the call is sent to the WPBX at location A. The LR is queried to find the location of the employee via the message path $e \rightarrow d$. When the WPBX receives the routing information, it routes the call to the WPBX at location C, and the employee's handset is paged. The call setup path is $e \rightarrow c \rightarrow b \rightarrow a$.

An alternative mobility management architecture is illustrated in Figure 24.10. This architecture follows the two-level database approach for public PCS, described in Chapter 2, Section 2.2. The differences between architecture 1 and architecture 2 are:

- The WPBX in every location is connected to the PSTN.

- Every WPBX is connected to a visitor location register (VLR).

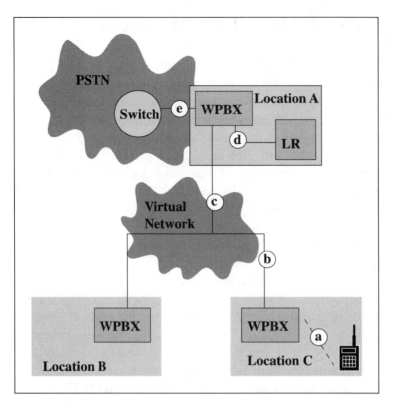

Figure 24.9 Wireless enterprise mobility management architecture 1.

In architecture 2, a home location register (HLR) is logically separated from all locations of the company. All the WPBXs are connected by means of a virtual network. When a handset moves into a location, the VLR of the location first records the presence of the handset, then sends a registration message to the HLR, which updates the current location of the handset. To deliver a call from the PSTN to the handset, the caller may dial to any of the WPBXs. The most likely WPBX is the local one. The VLR of the called party's last location is queried to see whether the called party is in the location. If so, the call is connected locally. If not, the HLR is queried to provide the routing information, and the call path is set up to the WPBX where the handset resides.

Note that there are several variations to architecture 2. For example, the VLRs may be removed, and the registration procedure will be similar to that of architecture 1. The advantage of architecture 2 is that a call from the PSTN can be connected to an arbitrary WPBX; and if the called handset is in the same WPBX, there is no need to query the remote HLR through

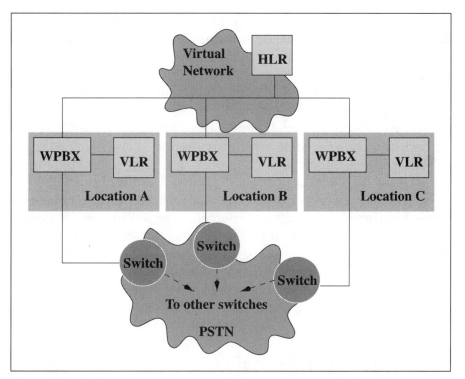

Figure 24.10 Wireless enterprise mobility management architecture 2.

the virtual network. On the other hand, architecture 1 may be attractive if the locations of a company are less spread out and maintaining VLR databases is the dominant cost. The preceding argument is especially true when remote query operations are expensive for companies with distant locations. To conclude, selection of the wireless enterprise mobility management architecture is a trade-off between remote query costs and database maintenance costs.

24.6 Summary

Based on the article published in [Chl98a], this chapter discussed the wireless segment for enterprise networks. We introduced the location system and the PCS system for the enterprise environment. For the location system, we explained how badge registration frequency affects tracking performance. An example of two-way location system, Olivetti Research Limited (ORL) infrared network, is described in [Har94b].

Analytic and simulation models are proposed in [Lin98a] to investigate lost-call performance of the location systems. The impact of registration frequency on message collisions with other badges in the same coverage area is detailed in [Har94b].

We described the enterprise PCS at two levels: office and corporate. At the office level, resource planning for wireless PBX is important. Allocation issues of external leased lines and internal extension lines were discussed. Analytic and simulation models are constructed in [Lai98, Lai99a] to study WPBX resource allocation. A complete description for PBX can be found in [Lin97b]. Campbell [Cam95] provides an introduction to in-building wireless phone systems. Issues for wired enterprise networks are discussed in [Bro92]. Piconet in offices can be built through Bluetooth. Details of Bluetooth can be found in [Met99] and the references therein. At the corporate level, mobility management was discussed, generally enough to accommodate various types of virtual networks, to establish the design and the implementation guidelines for the enterprise wireless system.

24.7   Review Questions

1. In the one-way enterprise location system, how can you evaluate the impact of repeated collision? How many calls will be lost due to repeated collision?

2. Design a performance model to investigate a two-way enterprise location system. What are the input parameters and output measures? (Hint: See the modeling approach in [Lin98a].) Can a two-way location system be a better solution for repeated collision than the one-way system?

3. In an enterprise location system, we observed that when the user movement pattern is more irregular, the potential of losing a call becomes smaller. Can you explain this phenomenon?

4. In WPBX, the number, C, of lines between the PBX and the PSTN is smaller than the sum of the radio channels in all BSs. On the other hand, in a public mobile system, the number of links between an MSC and other switches is larger than the number of radio channels connected to the MSC. Why?

5. What does it mean that the number, C, of external lines at a WPBX has a threshold, C^*, for efficiency? Implement a performance model to

investigate the WPBX that allows handoff during phone conversation. Does the threshold, C^*, exist for various user mobility? (Hint: See the model in [Lai99a].)

6. Why are mobility management procedures (such as registration and location tracking) unnecessary at the office level of a wireless enterprise network?

7. How do companies usually connect their offices for telephony communication?

8. What is a "cheap" solution to transfer signaling information between offices?

9. Consider a wireless enterprise telephony system where the WPBXs in the various corporate buildings are connected with unreliable microwave links. Since the links may be disconnected, location update procedure may be incorrectly exercised, which results in misrouted calls. Design a location update algorithm that eventually corrects the location information after a failure link is recovered. Evaluate your algorithm in terms of misrouting call probabilities. (Hint: See [Lin98b].)

References

[3GP99a]   3rd Generation Partnership Project (3GPP), Technical Specification Group Core Network. "Gateway Location Register (GLR)—Stage2." Technical Report 3G TS 23.119 version 1.0.0, 3GPP, 1999.

[3GP99b]   ——— Technical Specification Group Services and System Aspects QoS Concept. Technical Report 3G TR 23.907, version 1.2.0, 3GPP, 1999.

[Aky95]   Akyildiz, I.F., and Ho, J.S.M. "Dynamic Mobile User Location Update for Wireless PCS Networks," *ACM-Baltzer Journal of Wireless Networks*, 1(1): 187–196, 1995.

[Aky96]   Akyildiz, I.F., Ho, S.M., and Lin, Y.-B. "Movement-Based Location Update and Selective Paging for PCS Networks," *IEEE/ACM Transactions on Networking*, 4(4): 629–638, August 1996.

[Alc]   Alcatel. www.alcatel.com/telecom/rcd/netsol/operator/mobile/gprs.

[Ame97]   American's Network. "We don't want any." *American's Networks*, October, 1 1997.

[ANS89]   ANSI/EIA/TIA. Mobile Station-Land Station Compatibility Specification. Technical Report 553, EIA/TIA, 1989.

[ANS92a]   American National Standard for Telecommunications (ANSI)— Signaling System Number 7: Integrated Services Digital Network (ISDN) User Part, Issue 2, Rev. 2. Technical Report ANSI T1.113, ANSI, 1992.

[ANS92b]   ———— Message Transfer Part (MTP), Issue 2, Rev. 2. Technical Report ANSI T1.111, ANSI, 1992.

[ANS92c]   ———— Signaling Connection Control Part (SCCP), Issue 2, Rev. 2. Technical Report ANSI T1.112, ANSI, 1992.

[ANS92d]   ———— Transaction Capabilities Application Part (TCAP), Issue 2, Rev. 2. Technical Report ANSI T1.114, ANSI, 1992.

[Ans96]   Anschutz, T.A. "A Historial Perspective of CSTA," *IEEE Communications Magazine*, pp. 30–35, April 1996.

[Ara98]   Arango, M., Dugan, A., Elliott, I., Huitema, C., and Pickett, S. Media Gateway Control Protocol (MGCP). Technical Report draft-huitema-MGCP-v0r1.txt, Internet Engineering Task Force, 1998.

[ATT87]   AT&T. *5ESS Switch Information Guide*. AT&T Network Systems, 1987.

[Att98]   Attenborough, N., Sandbach, J., Sadat, U., Siolis, G., Cartwright, M., and Dunkley, S. "Feasibility Study and Cost Benefit Analysis of Number Portability for Mobile Services in Hong Kong." Technical Report, National Economic Research Associates, February 1998.

[Bel91]   Bellcore. Bell Communications Research Specification of Signaling System Number 7, Issue 2. Technical Report TR-NWT-000246, Bellcore, 1991.

[Bel93a]   ———— "A Guide to New Technologies and Services." Technical Report SR-BDS-000828, Bellcore, 1993.

[Bel93b]   ———— Common Channel Signaling Network Interface Specification Supporting Network Interconnection, Message Transfer Part, and Integrated Services Digital Network User Part, Issue 2. Technical Report TR-TSV-000905, Bellcore, 1993.

[Bel93c]   ———— Compatibility Information for Interconnection of a Wireless Services Provider and a Local Exchange Carrier Network, Issue 2. Technical Report TR-NPL-000145, Bellcore, 1993.

[Bel93d]   ———— PCS Access Services Interface Specification in Support of PCS Routing Service, PCS Home Database Service, and PCS IS-41 Message Transport Service, Issue 1. Technical Report TA-TSV-001411, Bellcore, 1993.

[Bel94a]   ———— CCS Network Interface Specification Supporting Wireless Services Providers, Issue 1. Technical Report GR-1434-CORE, Bellcore, 1994.

[Bel94b]   ———— Generic Criteria for Version 0.1 Wireless Access Communications Systems (WACS) and Supplement. Technical Report TR-INS-001313, Issue 1, Bellcore, 1994.

[Bel94c]   ———— LSSGR: Common Channel Signaling Section 6.5. Technical Report GR-606-CORE, Bellcore, 1994.

[Bel94d]   ———— Switching and Signaling Generic Requirements for Network Access Services to PCS Providers. Technical Report GR-2801-CORE, Bellcore, 1994.

[Bel94e]   ———— WACS Protocols Supporting Wireless Data Services. Technical Report GR-2850-CORE, Issue 1, Bellcore, 1994.

[Ber88]   Bernhardt, R.C. "An Improved Algorithm for Portable Radio Access," *IEEE VTC*, pp. 163–169, 1988.

[Ber89a]   ———— "Performance Aspects of Two-Way Transmission in Portable Radio Systems," *IEEE Vehicular Technology Conference*, 1989.

[Ber89b]   ———— "User Access in Portable Radio Systems in a Co-channel Interference Environment," *IEEE J. Select. Areas Commun.*, 7(1): 49–58, 1989.

[Ber91]   ———— "Time-Slot Management in Digital Portable Radio Systems," *IEEE Transactions on Vehicular Technology*, 40(1): 261–272, 1991.

[Bou93]   Bout, Sparreboom, Brouwer, and Prasad. A Mathematical Model for Dynamic Channel Selection in Conformity with the Digital European Cordless Telecommunications Standard. Proc. IEEE Personal Indoor and Mobile Radio Conference, September 1993.

[Bro92]   Brosemer, J.J., and Enright, D.J. "Virtual Networks: Past, Present, and Future." *IEEE Communications Magazine*, 30(3): 80–85, March 1992.

[Bud95]   Budka, K. Cellular Digital Packet Data: Channel Availability. Proc. IEEE Personal Indoor and Mobile Radio Conference, 1995.

[Cam95]   Campbell, R. "In-Building Wireless Phone Systems," *Wireless for the Corporate User*, 1995.

[CCI91]   CCITT. Numbering Plan for the ISDN Era. Technical Report Recommendation E.164 (COM II-45-E), ITU-T, 1991.

[CDP95]   CDPD Forum. Cellular Digital Packet Data System Specification: Release 1.1. Technical report, CDPD Forum, Inc., January 1995.

[Cha98]   Chang, M.-F., Lin, Y.-B., and Su, S.-C. "Improving Fault Tolerance of GSM Network," *IEEE Network*, 1(12): 58–63, 1998.

[Che99]   Chetham, A. "The Numbers Games—GSM in Hong Kong," *Mobile Communications Asia*, pp. 6–8, February 1999.

[Chl96]   Chlamtac, I., Farago, A., Henk, T., and Gordos, G. Optimizing Bandwidth Allocation in Cellular Networks. IEEE Global Telecommunications Conference, GLOBECOM'96, London, England, November 1996.

[Chl98a]   Chlamtac, I., Khasnabish, B., and Lin, Y.-B. "The Wireless Segment for Enterprise Networking," *IEEE Network*, 12(4): 50–55, 1998.

[Chl98b]   Chlamtac, I., Lin, Y.-B., and Redi, J. "When Mobility Meets Computation," *Encyclopedia of Microcomputers* (James G. Williams, Ed.), p. 22, 1998.

[Chl99a]   Chlamtac, I., Fang, Y., and Zeng, H. Call-Blocking Analysis for PCS Networks under General Cell Residence Time. IEEE WCNC, New Orleans, September 1999.

[Chl99b]   Chlamtac, I., Liu, T., and Carruthers, J. Location Management for Efficient Bandwidth Allocation and Call Admission Control. IEEE WCNC, New Orleans, September 1999.

[Chu91]   Chuang, J.C.-I. "Autonomous Adaptive Frequency Assignment of TDMA Portable Radio Systems," *IEEE Transactions on Vehicular Technology*, 40(3): 627–635, August 1991.

[Chu92]   ―――― Performance Issues and Algorithms for Dynamic Channel Assignment. IEEE GLOBECOM '92, 1992. Orlando, FL, December 6–9.

[Chu98]   Chuang, Y.-M., Lee, T.-Y., and Lin, Y.-B. "Trading CDPD Availability and Voice-Blocking Probability in Cellular Networks," *IEEE Network*, 2(12): 48–54, 1998.

[Cla68]   Clarke, R.H. "A Statistical Model of Mobile-Radio Reception," *Bell System Technical Journal*, p. 47, 1968.

[Com95]   Communications International. "Two-Way Pager Wager," *Communications International*, 1995.

[Coo94]   Cook, C.I. "Development of Air Interface Standards for PCS," *IEEE Personal Communications Magazine*, 1(4): 30–34, 1994.

[Cou96]   Couesnongle, M. "Communications International," *Telecommunications*, pp. 14–18, 1996.

[Cox95]   Cox, D.C. "Wireless Personal Communications: What Is It?" *IEEE Personal Communications Magazine*, pp. 20–35, April 1995.

[Cro96]   Cronin, P. "An Introduction to TSAPI and Network Telephony," *IEEE Communications Magazine*, pp. 48–54, April 1996.

[D'H96]   D'Hooge, H. "The Communicating PC," *IEEE Communications Magazine*, pp. 36–42, April 1996.

[DoC98]   DoCoMo. Special Issue on W-CDMA System Experiment (1). *NTT DoCoMo Technical Journal*, 16(3), 1998.

[Dye96]   Dye, B. "Real-Time Strategies Announces a New Path to Paging Networks." www.rts-inc.com/rts/press/043096.htm, April 1996.

[Dzi95a]   Dziatkiewicz, M. "Voice Paging Service Niche," *America's Network*, 99(19): 30–32, June 1995.

[Dzi95b]   ―――― "Wireless Local Loops," *America's Network*, 99(21): 46–75, November 1 1995.

[EIA91a]   EIA/TIA. Cellular Radio-Telecommunications Intersystem Operations: Automatic Roaming. Technical Report IS-41.3-B, EIA/TIA, 1991.

[EIA91b]   ―――― Data Communications. Technical Report IS-41.5-B, EIA/TIA, 1991.

[EIA91c]   ―――― Intersystem Handoff. Technical Report IS-41.2-B, EIA/TIA, 1991.

[EIA91d]   ―――― Operations, Administration, and Maintenance. Technical Report IS-41.4-B, EIA/TIA, 1991.

[EIA92]   ―――― Cellular System Dual-Mode Mobile Station—Base Station Compatibility Standard. Technical Report IS-54, EIA/TIA, 1992.

[EIA93a]   ―――― Cellular Radio-Telecommunications A_i–D_i Interfaces Standard. Technical Report IS-93, EIA/TIA, 1993.

[EIA93b]   EIA/TIA. Cellular Radio-Telecommunications Intersystem Operations: Authentication, Signaling Message, Encryption and Voice
Privacy. Technical Report TSB-51, EIA/TIA, 1993.

[EIA93c]   —— Mobile Station-Base Station Compatibility Standard for Dual-
mode Wideband Spread-Spectrum Cellular System. Technical Report
IS-95, EIA/TIA, 1993.

[EIA94]   —— 800 MHz TDMA Cellular Radio Interface—Mobile Station–
Base Station Compatibility—Digital Control Channel. Technical
Report IS-136, EIA/TIA, 1994.

[EIA95]   —— Cellular Intersystem Operations (Rev. C). Technical Report
IS-41, EIA/TIA, 1995.

[Eri99]   Ericsson. GPRS—Always Connected, Always On-Line. Private Com-
muniations. Viewgraph: ERA/LKG/T-99: 0023 Rev. A, 1999.

[ETS91a]   ETSI. Common Air Interface Specification to Be Used for the Interworking between Cordless Telephone Apparatus in the Frequency
Band 864.1 MHz, Including Public Access Services, I-ETS 300 131:
1990, June 1991.

[ETS91b]   —— Digital European Cordless Telecommunications Services and
Facilities Requirements Specification. Technical Report ETSI DI/RES
3002, European Telecommunications Standards Institute, 1991.

[ETS92a]   —— Integrated Services Digital Network (ISDN): Closed User
Group (CUG) Supplementary Service Digital Subscriber Signalling
System No. 1 (DSS1) Protocol. Technical Report ETS 300 138, ETSI,
1992.

[ETS92b]   —— Supplementary Service Description. Technical Report ETS 300
138, ETSI, 1992.

[ETS92c]   ETSI/TC. Detailed Signalling Interworking within the PLMN and
with the PSTN/ISDN. Technical Report Recommendation GSM 09.09,
ETSI, 1992.

[ETS93a]   —— Technical Report Recommendation GSM 03.47, ETSI, 1993.

[ETS93b]   —— European Digital Cellular Telecommunications System
(Phase 2); Common Aspects of PLMN Network Management. Technical Report Recommendation GSM 12.01, ETSI, 1993.

[ETS93c]   Ibid.

[ETS93d]   ETSI/TC. European Digital Cellular Telecommunications System
(Phase 2); Network Management Procedures and Messages on the
A-bis Interface. Technical Report Recommendation GSM 12.21, ETSI,
1993.

[ETS93e]   —— Objectives and Structure of GSM PLMN Management. Technical Report Recommendation GSM 12.00, ETSI, 1993.

[ETS93f]   —— Performance Management and Measurements for a GSM
PLMN. Technical Report Recommendation GSM 12.04, ETSI, 1993.

[ETS93g]   —— Subscriber, Mobile Equipment, and Service Data Administration. Technical Report Recommendation GSM 12.02, ETSI, 1993.

[ETS93h]   ETSI/TC. Location Registration Procedures. Technical Report Recommendation GSM 03.12, ETSI, 1993.

[ETS93i]   ——— Mobile Radio Interface Layer 3 Specification. Technical Report Recommendation GSM 04.08, ETSI, 1993.

[ETS93j]   ——— Numbering, Addressing, and Identification. Technical Report Recommendation GSM 03.03, ETSI, 1993.

[ETS93k]   ——— Organization of Subscriber Data. Technical Report Recommendation GSM 03.08, ETSI, 1993.

[ETS93l]   ——— Restoration Procedures, Version 4.2.0. Technical Report Recommendation GSM 03.07, ETSI, 1993.

[ETS93m]   ——— Technical Realization of the Short Message Service Point-to-Point, Version 4.6.0. Technical Report Recommendation GSM 03.40, ETSI, 1993.

[ETS94a]   ——— European Digital Cellular Telecommunications System (Phase 2); Network Configuration Management. Technical Report Recommendation GSM 12.06, ETSI, 1994.

[ETS94b]   ——— Security Management. Technical Report Recommendation GSM 12.03, ETSI, 1994.

[ETS94c]   ——— Subscriber Related Call and Event Data. Technical Report Recommendation GSM 12.05, ETSI, 1994.

[ETS94d]   ——— General Requirements on Interworking between the PLMN and the ISDN or PSTN, Version 4.6.0. Technical Report Recommendation GSM 09.07, ETSI, 1994.

[ETS94e]   ——— Interworking between the PLMN and the CSPDN, Version 4.0.2. Technical Report Recommendation GSM 09.04, ETSI, 1994.

[ETS94f]   ——— Mobile Application Part (MAP) Specification, Version 4.8.0. Technical Report Recommendation GSM 09.02, ETSI, 1994.

[ETS94g]   ——— Mobile Radio Interface Signaling Layer 3 (Phase 2), Version: 4.2.0. Technical Report Recommendation GSM 04.07, ETSI, 1994.

[ETS94h]   ——— Point-to-Point (PP) Short Message Service (SMS) Support on Mobile Radio Interface, Version 4.5.0. Technical Report Recommendation GSM 04.11, ETSI, 1994.

[ETS96a]   ——— DECT/GSM Interworking Profile; General Description of Service Requirements, Functional Capabilities, and Information Flows. Technical Report DE/RES-03048, ETSI, 1996.

[ETS96b]   ——— Unstructured Supplementary Service Data (USSD), Stage 2. Technical Report Recommendation GSM 03.90, Version 5.0.0, ETSI, 1996.

[ETS97a]   ——— Alphabets and Language-Specific Information. Technical Specification. Technical Report Recommendation GSM GSM 03.38, Version 5.6.0 (Phase 2+), ETSI, 1997.

[ETS97b]   ——— European Digital Cellular Telecommunications System (Phase 2+); GPRS Base Station System (BSS)—Serving GPRS Support Node (SGSN) Interface; Gb Interface, Layer 1. Technical Report Recommendation GSM 08.14, Version 6.0.0, ETSI, 1997.

[ETS97c] —— GPRS Ciphering Algorithm Requirements. Technical Report Recommendation GSM 01.61, Version 6.0.1, ETSI, 1997.

[ETS97d] —— GPRS Mobile Station—Serving GPRS Support Node (MS-SGSN) Logical Link Control (LLC) Layer Specification. Technical Report Recommendation GSM 04.64, Version 6.3.0, ETSI, 1997.

[ETS97e] —— Serving GPRS Support Node (SGSN) Subnetwork-Dependent Convergence Protocol (SNDCP). Technical Report Recommendation GSM 04.65, Version 6.2.1, ETSI, 1997.

[ETS97f] —— Visitors Location Register (VLR) Gs Interface, Layer 3 Specification. Technical Report Recommendation GSM 09.18 Version 1.2.0, ETSI, 1997.

[ETS97g] —— European Digital Cellular Telecommunications System (Phase 2+); Overall Description of the GPRS Radio Interface, Stage 2. Technical Report Recommendation GSM 03.64, Version 7.0.0, ETSI, 1997.

[ETS97h] —— Specification of the SIM Application Toolkit for the Subscriber Identity Module—Mobile Equipment (SIM-ME) Interface. Technical Report Recommendation GSM 11.14, Version 6.3.0, ETSI, 1997.

[ETS97i] —— Unstructured Supplementary Service Data (USSD), Stage 1. Technical Report Recommendation GSM 02.90, Version 5.1.0, ETSI, 1997.

[ETS97j] —— Stage 3. Technical Report Recommendation GSM 04.90, Version 5.0.1, ETSI, 1997.

[ETS97k] —— Use of Data Terminal Equipment—Data Circuit-Terminating; Equipment (DTE-DCE) Interface for Short Message Service (SMS) and Cell Broadcast Service (CBS). Technical Report Recommendation GSM 07.05, Version 5.3.0, ETSI, 1997.

[ETS98a] —— Telecommunications and Internet Protocol Harmonization Over Networks (TIPHON): Description of Technical Issues. Technical Report TR 101 300, Version 1.1.5, ETSI, 1998.

[ETS98b] —— European Digital Cellular Telecommunications System (Phase 2+); GPRS Base Station System (BSS)—Serving GPRS Support Node (SGSN) Interface-Network Service. Technical Report Recommendation GSM 08.16, Version 7.1.0, ETSI, 1998.

[ETS98c] —— Serving GPRS Support Node (SGSN) BSS GPRS Protocol (BSSGP). Technical Report Recommendation GSM 08.18 Version 7.0.0, ETSI, 1998.

[ETS98d] —— European Digital Cellular Telecommunications System (Phase 2+); GPRS Charging. Technical Report Recommendation GSM 12.15, ETSI, 1998.

[ETS98e] —— GPRS Interworking between the Public Land Mobile Network (PLMN) Supporting GPRS and Packet Data Networks (PDN).

Technical Report Recommendation GSM 09.61, Version 7.1.0, ETSI, 1998.

[ETS98f]   ——— GPRS Service Description, Stage 1. Technical Report Recommendation GSM 02.60, Version 7.0.0, ETSI, 1998.

[ETS98g]   ——— Mobile Station (MS) Supporting GPRS. Technical Report Recommendation GSM 07.60, Version 7.0.0, ETSI, 1998.

[ETS98h]   ——— GPRS Service Description Stage 2. Technical Report Recommendation GSM GSM 03.60, Version 7.0.0 (Phase 2+), ETSI, 1998.

[ETS98i]   ——— GPRS Tunneling Protocol (GTP) across the Gn and Gp Interface. Technical Report Recommendation GSM GSM 09.60, Version 7.0.0 (Phase 2+), ETSI, 1998.

[ETS99]   ——— ETSI Guide Intelligent Network (IN); Number Portability Task Force (NPTF); IN and Intelligence Support for Service Provider Number Portability. Technical Report Recommendation EG 201 367, Version 1.1.1, ETSI, 1999.

[ETS00]   ——— UMTS Mobile Station Application Execution Environment (MExE); Functional Description; Stage 2. Technical Report Recommendation 3G TS 23.057, Version 3.0.0, ETSI, 2000.

[Fac99]   Faccin, S., Hsu, L., Koodli, R., Le, K., and Purnadi, R. "GPRS and IS-136 Integration for Flexible Network and Services Evolution," *IEEE Personal Communications*, 6(3): 48–54, 1999.

[Fan99a]   Fang, Y., and Chlamtac, I. "Teletraffic Analysis and Mobility Modeling for PCS Networks," *IEEE Transactions on Communications*, 47(7): 1062–1072, July 1999.

[Fan99b]   Fang, Y., Chlamtac, I., and Lin, Y.-B. "Billing Strategies and Performance Analysis for PCS Networks," *IEEE Transactions on Vehicular Technology*, 48(2): 638–651, 1999.

[Fan00a]   Fang, Michael Y., Chlamtac, I., and Fei, H. "Analytical Results for Optimal Choice of Location Update Interval for Mobility Database Failure Restoration in PCS networks," *IEEE Transactions on Parallel and Distributed Systems*, 2000.

[Fan00b]   ——— "Failure Recovery of HLR Mobility Databases and Parameter Optimization for PCS Networks," *Journal on Parallel and Distributed Computing*, 60: 431–450, 2000.

[FCC96]   FCC Memorandum Opinion and Order. Telephone Number Portability. Technical Report CC Docket No. 95–116, RM 8535, FCC, 1996.

[Fle96]   Flegg, R. "Computer Telephony Architecture: MVIP, H-MVIP, and SCbus," *IEEE Communications Magazine*, pp. 60–64, April 1996.

[Fos93]   Foschini, G.J., Gopinath, B., and Miljanic, Z. "Channel Cost of Mobility," *IEEE Transactions on Vehicular Technology*, 42(4): 414–424, November 1993.

[Gan72]   Gans, M.J. "A Power-Spectral Theory of Propagation in the Mobile-Radio Environment," *IEEE Transactions on Vehicular Technology*, VT-21(1): 27–37, 1972.

[Gar97]   Garg, V.K., Smolik, K.F., and Wilkes, J.E. *Applications of CDMA in Wireless/Personal Communications*. Upper Saddle River, NJ: Prentice-Hall, 1997.

[Gle91]   Glenarye Electronics. IXO TAP Protocol. Technical Report GLP-3000-180, Glenarye Electronics, 1991. See also: ftp://mirror.lcs.mit.edu/telecom-archives/technical/ixo.tap.protocol.

[Gra98]   Granberg, O. "GSM on the Net," *Ericsson Review*, (4): 184–191, 1998.

[Gud90]   Gudmundson, B., and Grimlund, O. Handoff in Microcellular Based Personal Telephone Systems. WINLAB Workshop, 1990.

[Gud91]   ——— "Analysis of Handover Algorithms," *IEEE VTC*, 1991.

[Haa98]   Haas, Z., and Lin, Y.-B. "On Optimizing the Location Update Costs in the Presence of Database Failures," *ACM/Baltzer Wireless Networks Journal*, 4(5): 419–426, 1998.

[Har94a]   Harasty, D. et al. "Architecture Alternatives for Wireless Data Services: Interworking with Voiceband Modem," *IEEE NPC'94*, pp. 16–18, 1994.

[Har94b]   Harter, A. and Hopper, A. "A Distributed Location System for the Active Office," *IEEE Network Magazine*, pp. 62–70, January 1994.

[Hat80]   Hata, M., and Nagatsu, T. "Mobile Location Using Signal Strength Measurements in a Cellular System," *IEEE Transactions on Vehicular Technology*, VT-29(2): 245–251, 1980.

[Hau94]   Haug, T. "Overview of GSM: Philosophy and Results," *International Journal of Wireless Information Networks*, 1(1): 7–16, 1994.

[Her98]   Herschel, Shosteck. The Strategic Implications of Computing and the Internet on Wireless: The Competitive Blur through 2008. Technical Report, Herschel Shosteck Associates, Ltd., 1998.

[Hew95]   Hewlett-Packard. HP E4250A AccessSS7 System. Technical Report 5964-0307E, Hewlett Packard, 1995.

[Hol92]   Holtzman, J.M. Adaptive Measurement Intervals for Handoffs. Technical Report WINLAB-TR-26, WINLAB, Rutgers University, 1992.

[Hon86]   Hong, D., and Rappaport, S.S. Traffic Model and Performance Analysis for Cellular Mobile Radio Telephone Systems with Prioritized and Nonprotection Handoff Procedure. *IEEE Transactions on Vehicular Technology*, VT-35(3): 77–92, August 1986.

[Hon93]   Hon, A.S. An Introduction to Paging—What It Is and How It Works, www.mot.com/MIMS/MSPG/Special/explain_paging/ptoc.html, 1993.

[Hor98]   Horrocks, J., and Rogerson, D. *Implementing Number Portability*. Ovum, Ltd., 1998.

[Hug96]   Hughes Network Systems. TES Quantum. Technical Report 1022896-0001, Rev. B, Hughes Network Systems, 1996.

[INF98]   INFOCOMM. Intelligent Prepaid System (IPS) Functional Description. Technical Report PDIPS-00-00001-FD, INFOCOMM, 1998.

[INP97]   INPW. Generic Switching and Signaling Requirements for Number Portability, Issue 1.05. Technical Report, Illnois Number Portability Workshop, 1997.

[ITU88]   ITU-T. Charging and Accounting in the International Land Mobile Telephone Service Provided via Cellular Radio Systems. Technical Report Recommendation D.93, ITU-T, 1988.

[ITU92a]   ——— Information Technology—Open Systems Interconnection-Systems Management: Summarization Function. Technical Report Recommendation X.738, ITU-T, 1992.

[ITU92b]   ——— TMN Management Services: Generic Network Information Model. Technical Report Recommendation M.3100, ITU-T, 1992.

[ITU93a]   ——— Location Register Restoration Procedures. Technical Report Recommendation Q.1004, ITU-T, 1993.

[ITU93b]   ——— Log Control Function. Technical Report Recommendation X.735, ITU-T, 1993.

[ITU93c]   ——— Operations and Quality of Service Universal Personal Telecommunication (UPT). Technical Report, ITU-T, 1993.

[ITU94a]   ——— ASN.1 Encoding Rules, Packed Encoding Rules (PER). Technical Report X.691 ITU-T, 1994.

[ITU94b]   ——— Remote Operations: Concepts, Model, and Notation. Technical Report X.880 ITU-T, 1994.

[ITU94c]   ——— Remote Operations: OSI Realization—Remote Operation Service Element (ROSE), Protocol Specification. Technical Report X.882 ITU-T, 1994.

[ITU96a]   ——— Event Report Management Function. Technical Report Recommendation X.734, ITU-T, 1996.

[ITU96b]   ——— TMN Management Services: Overview. Technical Report Recommendation M.3200, ITU-T, 1996.

[ITU98]   ——— Call Signalling Protocols and Media Stream Packetization for Packet-Based Multimedia Communication Systems. Technical Report H.225 ITU-T, Version 3, 1998.

[ITU99]   ——— Packet-Based Multimedia Communications Systems. Technical Report H.323 ITU-T, Version 3, 1999.

[Jai94a]   Jain, N., and Basu, K. Queueing Model of CDPD Implementation on American Cellular Systems. ITC Mini Seminar: Mobility and Intelligent Networks, 1994.

[Jai94b]   Jain, R., Lin, Y.-B., Lo, C.N., and Mohan, S. "A Caching Strategy to Reduce Network Impacts of PCS," *IEEE Journal on Selected Areas in Communications*, 12(8): 1434–1445, 1994.

[Jai95]   Jain, R. and Lin, Y.-B. "Performance Modeling of an Auxiliary User Location Strategy in a PCS Network," *ACM-Baltzer Wireless Networks*, 1(2): 197–210, 1995.

[Jen97]   Jeng, J.-Y., Lin, C.-W., and Lin, Y.-B. "Dynamic Resource Scheduling for GSM Data Services," *IEICE Transactions on Communications*, 80-B(2): 296–300, 1997.

[Jen97c]   Jeng, J.-J.-Y., Lin, Y.-B., and Chen, W. "Dynamic Resource Assignment Strategies for PCS Data Services," *Information Sciences: An International Journal*, (109): 211–225, 1998.

[Jen98b]   Jeng, J.-Y., Lin, C.-W., and Lin, Y.-B. "Flexible Resource Allocation Scheme for GSM Data Services," *IEICE Transactions on Communications*, 81-B(10): 1797–1802, 1998.

[JTC95]   Joint Technology Committee (JTC). Personal Access Communications System Air Interface Standard. Technical Report JTC(AIR)/95.06.08-SP-3418, T1/TIA Joint Technical Committee, 1995.

[Kan88]   Kanai and Furuya. "A Handoff Control Process and Microcellular Systems." *IEEE Vehicular Technology Conference*, 1988.

[Kob94]   Kobayashi, T. Development of Personal Handy-Phone System. *International Telecommunication Symposium '94*, 1994.

[Lai98]   Lai, W.R., and Lin, Y.-B. Resource Planning for Wireless PBX Systems. *International Journal of Wireless Information Networks*, 5(4): 249–256, 1998.

[Lai99a]   ——— "Effects of Cell Residence Times on Wireless PBX Systems," *ACM/Baltzer Wireless Networks*, 5: 479–488, 1999.

[Lai99b]   Lai, W.-R., Lin, Y.-B., and Rao, C.-H. Modeling and Analysis of Dual-Band GSM. *KICS/IEEE/IEICE Journal of Communications and Networks*, 1(3): 158–165, 1999.

[Lax96]   Lax, A. The European Radio Message System, http://194.2.180.16/home.htm, 1996.

[Lee99a]   Lee, L.-N. Third-Generation Wireless Communications and Beyond, *Keynote Speech, 2nd ACM Modeling, Analysis, and Simulation of Wireless and Mobile Systems*, Seattle, 1999.

[Lee95]   Lee, W.C.Y. *Mobile Cellular Telecommunications Systems*. New York: McGraw-Hill, 1995.

[Lee96]   ——— Will Wireless Communications Come to an End? *Keynote Speech, Proc. 2nd Intl. Mobile Computing Conf.*, 1996.

[Lee98]   ——— *Mobile Communications Engineering*, 2nd ed. New York: McGraw-Hill, 1998.

[Lee99b]   ——— IMT-2000 (G3G) Strategy and Key Technical Issues. The Next-Generation Wireless Communications Conference, FarEastone, Taiwan, 1999.

[Lev96]   Levin, M., Epstein, B., Gil, A., and Maityahu, I. "WLL Network Deployment: An Operator's Perspective," *Telecommunications*, pp. 65–73, 1996.

[Lin94a]   Lin, Y.-B. "Determining the User Locations for Personal Communications Networks," *IEEE Transactions on Vehicular Technology*, 43(3): 466–473, 1994.

[Lin94b]   Lin, Y.-B., and Noerpel, A. "Implicit Deregistration in a PCS Network," *IEEE Transactions on Vehicular Technology*, 43(4): 1006–1010, 1994.

[Lin94c]   Lin, Y.-B., Mohan, S., and Noerpel, A. "Channel Assignment Strategies for Handoff and Initial Access for a PCS Network," *IEEE Personal Communications Magazine*, 1(3): 47–56, 1994.

[Lin94d]   ——— "Queueing Priority Channel Assignment Strategies for Handoff and Initial Access for a PCS Network," *IEEE Transactions on Vehicular Technology*, 43(3): 704–712, 1994.

[Lin94e]   Lin, Y.-B., Noerpel, A., and Harasty, D. A Nonblocking Channel Assignment Strategy for Handoffs." Proc. IEEE ICUPC, 1994.

[Lin95a]   Lin, Y.-B., "Failure Restoration of Mobility Databases for Personal Communication Networks," *ACM-Baltzer Journal of Wireless Networks*, 1: 365–372, 1995.

[Lin95b]   Lin, Y.-B., and DeVries S.K. "PCS Network Signaling Using SS7," *IEEE Personal Communications Magazine*, pp. 44–55, June 1995.

[Lin96a]   Lin, Y.-B. "Modelling of Anchor Radio System Handoff," *International Journal of Wireless Information Networks*, 3(3): 139–145, 1996.

[Lin96b]   Lin, Y.-B. and Chlamtac, I. "Heterogeneous Personal Communications Services: Integration of PCS Systems," *IEEE Communications Magazine*, 34(9): 106–113, 1996.

[Lin96c]   Lin, Y.-B., Chang, L.F., Noerpel, A.R., and Park, K. "Performance Modeling of Multitier PCS System," *International Journal of Wireless Information Networks*, 3(2): 67–78, 1996.

[Lin96d]   Lin, Y.-B., Noerpel, A., and Harasty, D. "The Subrating Channel Assignment Strategy for PCS Handoffs." *IEEE Transactions on Vehicular Technology*, 45(1): 122–130, February 1996.

[Lin96e]   Lin, Y. B. "Mobility Management for Cellular Telephony Networks, *IEEE Parallel and Distributed Technology*, 4(4):65–73, 1996.

[Lin97a]   ——— "Impact of PCS Handoff Response Time," *IEEE Communications Letters*, 1(6): 160–162, 1997.

[Lin97b]   ——— *Telephone Network and PBX Software*, Weikeg Publisher, Taipei, Taiwan, 2000.

[Lin97c]   ——— "OA&M for GSM Network," *IEEE Network Magazine*, 11(2): 46–51, March 1997.

[Lin97d]   ——— "PACS Network Signaling Using AIN/ISDN," *IEEE Personal Communications Magazine*, 4(3): 33–39, 1997.

[Lin97e]   ——— "Paging Systems: Network Architectures and Interfaces," *IEEE Network Magazine*, 11(4): 56–61, July/August 1997.

[Lin97f]   ——— "Performance Modeling for Mobile Telephone Networks," *IEEE Network Magazine*, 11(6): 63–68, November/December 1997.

[Lin97g]   ——— "Reducing Location Update Cost in a PCS Network," *IEEE/ACM Transactions on Networking*, 5(1): 25–33 , 1997.

[Lin97h]   ——— "Wireless Local Loop," *IEEE Potentials*, 16(3): 8–10, August/September 1997.

[Lin97i]   Lin, Y.-B. et al. Adaptive Scheme for PCS Authentication. USA Patent, Number 5606596, 1997.

[Lin97j]   Lin, Y.-B., Mohan, S., Sollenberg, N., and Sherry, H. "An Improved Adaptive Algorithm for Reducing PCS Network Authentication Traffic," *IEEE Transactions on Vehicular Technology*, 46(3): 588–596, 1997.

[Lin98a]   Lin, Y.-B., and Lin, P. "Performance Modeling of Location Tracking Systems," *ACM Mobile Computing and Communications Review*, 2(3): 24–27, 1998.

[Lin98b]   Lin, Y.-B., S.-C. S. Chen, and C.-S. Yang. "Mobility Management for Wireless Systems with Unreliable Backhaul Links," *IEEE Communications Letters*, 2(5): 122–124, 1998.

[Lin98c]   Lin, Y.-B., and Tsai, W.-N. "Location Tracking with Distributed HLRs and Pointer Forwarding," *IEEE Transactions on Vehicular Technology*, 47(1): 58–64, 1998.

[Lin99a]   Lin, P., Lin, Y.-B., and Jeng, J.-Y. "Improving GSM Call Completion by Call Reestablishment." *IEEE Journal on Selected Areas in Communications*, 1999.

[Lin99b]   Lin, Y.-B. "PBX-Based Mobility Manager for Wireless Local Loop," To appear in *International Journal of Communication Systems*, 2000.

[Lin99c]   Lin, Y.-B., and Chuang, Y.-M. "Modeling Sleep Mode for Cellular Digital Packet Data," *IEEE Communications Letters*, 3(3): 63–65, 1999.

[Lin99d]   Lin, Y.-B., and Pang, A.-C. "Comparing Soft and Hard Handoffs," *IEEE Transactions on Vehicular Technology*, 1999.

[Lin99e]   Lin, Y.-B., and Rao, C.-H. "Number Portability for Telecommunication Networks," *IEEE Network*, 13(1): 56–62, 1999.

[Lin00a]   Lin, Y.-B. Overflow Control for Cellular Mobility Database," *IEEE Transactions on Vehicular Technology*, 49(2): 520–530, 2000.

[Lin00b]   Lin, Y.-B., Lai, W.R., and Chen, R.J. "Performance Analysis for Dual-Band PCS Networks," *IEEE Transactions on Computers*, 49(2): 148–159, 2000.

[Lit96]   Little, S. "Going Wireless on the Transmission Side," *Telecom Asia*, 7(9): 30–40, October 1996.

[Liu98]   Liu, T., Bahl, P., and Chlamtac, I. "Mobility Modeling, Location Tracking, and Trajectory Prediction in Wireless ATM Networks," *IEEE Journal on Selected Areas in Communications*, 16(6): 922–936, 1998.

[Luc97]   Lucent Technologies. 5ESS-2000 System Function Manual, Software Release 8.1. Technical Report, Lucent Technologies, 1997.

[Lyc91]   Lycksell, E. GSM System Overview. Technical Report, Swedish Telecommunications Administration, 1991.

[Man00]   Mann, S. *Programming Applications with the Wireless Application Protocol: The Complete Developer's Guide*. New York: John Wiley & Sons, 2000.

[Mas94]   Mason, C. "CDPD: The Promises and the Challenges," *Wireless*, 3(6), November/December 1994.

[Met99]   Mettalle, R. Bluetooth Protocol Architecture, Version 1.0. Nokia, 1999.

[Mic96]   Microsoft. *Win32 SDK: Win32 Telephony (TAPI)-MSDN Library*. Microsoft, 1996.

[Mil96]   Miller, P. "Advancing the Art of Wireless and Paging Networks," *Wireless—2nd Annual Buyer's Guide*, p. 20, 1996.

[Mob00]   Mobile Lifestreams Limited, www.mobileGPRS.com, 2000.

[Mod90]   Modarressi, A.R., and Skoog, R.A. "Signaling System No. 7: A Tutorial," *IEEE Communications Magazine*, July 1990.

[Moh94]   Mohan, S., and Jain, R. Two User Location Strategies for Personal Communications Services (PCS). *IEEE Personal Communications Magazine*, 1(1): 42–50, 1994.

[Mos95]   Moskowitz, J. Paging Protocols, at www.rts-inc.com/rts/protocol.htm, 1995.

[Mou92]   Mouly, M., and Pautet, M.-B. *The GSM System for Mobile Communications*. M. Mouly, 49 rue Louise Bruneau, Palaiseau, France, 1992.

[Mur91]   Murase, S., and Green. "Handover Criterion for Macro- and Microcellular Systems," IEEE VTC, 1991.

[Nan95]   Nanda, S., Chawla, K. and Budka, K. CDPD over Shared AMPS Channels: Interference Analysis, Proc. IEEE Personal Indoor and Mobile Radio Conference, 1995.

[NAN98]   North American Numbering Council (NANC). Local Number Portability Administration Working Group Report on Wireless Wineline Integration. Technical Report, North American Numbering Council, May 1998.

[Noe95]   Noerpel, A.R., Chang, L.F., and Lin, Y.-B. PACS Contention Algorithm for Initial Access and Handoff. *Fifth WINLAB Workshop*, pp. 217–226, 1995.

[Noe96a] ——— "Performance Modeling of Polling De-registration for Unlicensed PCS," *IEEE Journal on Selected Areas in Communications*, 14(4), 1996.

[Noe96b] Noerpel, A.R., Lin, Y.-B., and Sherry, H. "PACS: Personal Access Communications System," *IEEE Personal Communications Magazine*, pp. 32–43, June 1996.

[Noe97]   Noerpel, A.R. WLL: Wireless Local Loop—Alternative Technologies." IEEE PIMRC, Helsinki, Finland, 1997.

[Nok00]   Nokia. www.nokia.com/networks/17/gprs/gprs1.html, 2000.

[Nov96]   Novell Inc. and AT&T Corp. Netware Telephony Service (Telephony Service Application Programming Interface), Release 2.21. Novell Inc. and AT&T Corp., 1996.

[Oft97a] Oftel. Number Portability Costs and Charges. Technical Report, Office of Telecommunications, January 1997.

[Oft97b]   ――― Number Portability in the Mobile Telephony Market. Technical Report, Office of Telecommunications, July 1997.

[One98]   Oneglia F. (contact person). Editor's Proposal for the Recommendation Q.N.P. Technical Report TD 35 Rev 3, ITU-T, 1998.

[Pad95]   Padgett, J.E., Gunther, C.G., and Hattori, T. "Overview of Wireless Personal Communications," *IEEE Communications Magazine*, pp. 28–41, January 1995.

[Pae93]   Paetsch, M, *Mobile Communications in the United States and Europe*. Norwood MA: Artech House, 1993.

[Par97]   Park, K.I., and Lin, Y.-B. "Registration Methods for Multitier Personal Communications Services," *IEEE Transactions on Vehicular Technology*, 46(3): 597–602, 1997.

[Paw94]   Pawlowski, C., and McConnell, P. "CDPD Air Interface Basics," *Telephony*, December 5, 1994.

[PCI95a]   Personal Communications Industry Association (PCIA). Telocator Data Protocol. Technical Report, www.mot.com/MIMS/MSPG/pcia_protocols/tdp, Personal Communications Industry Association, July 1995.

[PCI95b]   ――― Telocator Network Paging Protocol Version 3.7. Technical Report, www.mot.com/MIMS/MSPG/pcia_protocols/tnpp, Personal Communications Industry Association, July 1995.

[Per98]   Perkins, C. E. *Mobile IP: Design Principles and Practices*. Reading, MA: Addison-Wesley, 1998.

[Por93]   Porter, P., Harasty, D., Beller, B., Noerpel, A.R., and Varma, V. "The Terminal Registration/Deregistration Protocol for Personal Communication Systems," *Wireless '93 Conference on Wireless Communications*, July 1993.

[Qui93]   Quick, R.F., Jr. An Overview of the Cellular Digital Packet Data (CDPD) System." *Proc. IEEE Personal Indoor and Mobile Radio Conference*, 1993.

[Rad92]   Radio Advisory Board of Canada. CT2Plus Class 2: Specification for the Canadian Common Air Interface for Digital Cordless Telephony, Including Public Access Services, Annex 1 to radio Standards Specification 130, 1992.

[Ram94]   Ramsdale, P.A. "Personal Communications in the UK—Implementation of PCN using DCS 1800," *International Journal of Wireless Information Networks*, 1(1): 29–36, 1994.

[Rao00]   Rao, H. C.-H., Lin, Y.-B., and Chou, S.-L. "iGSM: VoIP Service for Mobile Networks," *IEEE Communications Magazine*, 4(38): 62–69, 2000.

[Riz95]   Rizzo, J.F., and Sollenberger, N. "Multitier Wireless Access," *IEEE Personal Communications Magazine*, 2(3): 18–31, 1995.

[Ros95]   Rose, D. A Very Brief History of Paging, http://exmachina.com/histpage.shtml, 1995.

[Sam93]   Sampath and Holtzman. Estimation of Maximum Doppler Frequency for Handoff Decisions. IEEE VTC, 1993.

[Sam94]   —— Adaptive Handoffs through Estimation of Fading Parameters. IEEE ICC, 1994.

[Sch96]   Schulz, R.C. *Wireless Technology and PCS Applications*. GLA International, 1996.

[Sie]   Siemens. www.siemens.de/ic/networks/gg/ca/n3-p31-2.pdf.

[Sla98]   Slavick, F. "Counting Down Prepaid Services," *Billing World*, pp. 44–50, September 1998.

[Sre96b]   Sreetharan, M., and Kumar, R. *Cellular Digital Packet Data*. Norwood, MA: Artech House, 1996.

[Ste90]   Steedman, R. "The Common Air Interface MPT 1375," *Cordless Telecommuinications in Europe*, Tuttlebee, W.H.W. ed. Springer Verlag, 1990.

[Stu96]   Stuber, G.L. *Principles of Mobile Communication*. Norwell, MA: Kluwer, 1996.

[Sul96]   Sulkin, A. "PBX Market Perks Up," *Business Communications Review*, 26(1): 40–43, January 1996.

[Sur95]   Surace, K.J. A Comparision of CDPD and Circuit-Switched Data," Wireless Newsgroup (comp.std.wireless), March 1995.

[Sym]   Symmetry Communications Systems. www.symmetrycomm.com.

[Sym99]   Symbian. EPOC Overview: Summary. Technical Report Revision 1.0(007), Symbian, 1999.

[Tay97]   Taylor, M.S., Waung, W., and Banan, M. *Internetwork Mobility: The CDPD Approach*, Upper Saddle River, NJ: Prentice-Hall, 1997.

[Tek91]   Tekinary, S. and Jabbari, B. "Handover Policies and Channel Assignment Strategies in Mobile Cellular Networks." *IEEE Communications Magazine*, 29(11): 42–47, 1991.

[Tek92]   —— "A Measurement-Based Prioritization Scheme for Handovers in Cellular and Microcellular Networks." *IEEE Journal on Selected Areas in Communications*, pp. 1343–1350, October 1992.

[TEL95]   TELEFOCUS. "Industry Wrestles with Number Portability," *Telephony*, 228(10), March 6, 1995.

[TIA96]   Telecommunications Institute of America (TIA). Ad Hoc Wireless Local Loop. Technical Report TR45, Telecommunications Institute of America, 1996.

[Tot95]   Toth, V.J. "Preparing for a New Universe of Toll-Free Numbers," *Business Communications Review*, 25(21): 22–24, November 1995.

[Tow95]   Towle, T.T. "TMN as Applied to the GSM Network," *IEEE Communications Magazine*, pp. 68–73, March 1995.

[Tri99]   Trillium Digital Systems. GPRS White Paper, at www.trillium.com, 1999.

[Tsa99]   Tsai, W.-N., and Lin, Y.-B. "A Performance Study of CDPD," to appear in *Information Sciences: An International Journal*, 119(1-2):41–56, 1999.

[Tut97]   Tuttlebee, W. (ed)," *Cordless Telecommunications Worldwide*. Springer Verlag, 1997.

[Var97]   Varma, V., and Panday, V. Functional Architecture for PACS Wireless Local Loop System. ATIS, PACS Providers Forum, T1P1.3/96–246R1, January 27, 1997.

[Vij93]   Vijayan, R., and Holtzman, J.M. "A Model for Analyzing Handoff Algorithms," *IEEE Transactions on Vehicular Technology*, 42(3):351–356, 1993.

[WAP98a]   WAP Forum. Wireless Application Protocol Architecture Specification. Technical Report, WAP Forum, 1998.

[WAP98b]   ——— Wireless Application Protocol Cache Model Specification. Technical Report, WAP Forum, 1998.

[WAP99a]   ——— Wireless Application Protocol White Paper. Technical Report, WAP Forum, 1999.

[WAP99b]   ——— Wireless Application Protocol over GSM Unstructured Supplentary Service Data. Technical Report, WAP Forum, 1999.

[WAP99c]   ——— Wireless Application Protocol V1.1 to V1.2. Technical Report, WAP Forum, 1999.

[WAP99d]   ——— Wireless Application Protocol Wireless Application Environment Overview, Version 16, June 1999. Technical Report, WAP Forum, 1999.

[WAP99e]   ——— Wireless Application Protocol Wireless Datagram Protocol Specification, Version 14, May 1999. Technical Report, WAP Forum, 1999.

[WAP99f]   ——— Wireless Application Protocol Wireless Session Protocol Specification, Version 28, May 1999. Technical Report, WAP Forum, 1999.

[WAP99g]   ——— Wireless Application Protocol Wireless Transaction Protocol Specification, Version 11, June 1999. Technical Report, WAP Forum, 1999.

[WAP99h]   ——— Wireless Application Protocol Wireless Transport Protocol Specification, Version 11, February 1999. Technical Report, WAP Forum, 1999.

[WAP99i]   WAP Forum Ltd. *Official Wireless Application Protocol: The Complete Standard with Searchable CD-ROM*. WAP Forum, Ltd. 1999.

[Wig98]   Wiggins, R. "Will You Pay for Bandwidth? The Berkeley INDEX Experiment," *Internet Buzz*, 1(27), 1998. See also www.webreference.com/outlook/column27/.

[Yac93]   Yacoub, M.D. *Foundations of Mobile Radio Engineering*. CRC Press, 1993.

[Yan99]   Yang, W.-Z., Chang, M.-F., and Lin, Y.-B. "Priority Call Service for PCS Networks," *SCS Transactions Special Issue on Wireless Networks*, 3(16): 102–122, 1999.

[Yoo93]   Yoon, C.H., and Un, K. "Performance of Personal Portable Radio Telephone Systems with and without Guard Channels," *IEEE Journal on Selected Areas in Communications*, 11(6): 911–917, August 1993.

[Yu 99]   Yu, H.-C., Lin, Y.-B., Chen, K.C., Liu, C.J., Liu, K.C., and Hsu, J.S. A Study of Number Portability in Taiwan. Technical Report, National Chiao Tung University, April 1999.

[Zan97]   Zanichelli, M. "Cordless in the Local Loop," in *Cordless Telecommunications Worldwide*, Walter Tuttlebee, ed. London: Springer, 1997.

[Zen99]   Zeng, H., and Chlamtac, I. Handoff Traffic Distribution in Cellular Networks. IEEE WCNC, New Orleans, September 1999.

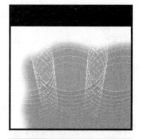

Index